THE
ANXIETIES
OF
AFFLUENCE

THE ANXIETIES OF AFFLUENCE

CRITIQUES OF AMERICAN
CONSUMER CULTURE,
1939–1979

Daniel Horowitz

University of Massachusetts Press

AMHERST AND BOSTON

LC 2003016300
ISBN 1-55849-432-4
Designed by Jack Harrison
Set in Adobe Garamond with Smaragd display by
Binghamton Valley Composition
Printed and bound by The Maple-Vail Book Manufacturing Group

Library of Congress Cataloging-in-Publication Data
Horowitz, Daniel, 1938–
The anxieties of affluence : critiques of American consumer culture,
1939–1979 / Daniel Horowitz.
p. cm.
Includes bibliographical references and index.
ISBN 1-55849-432-4 (Cloth : alk. paper)
1. Consumption (Economics)—United States—Psychological aspects.
2. Consumption (Economics)—Moral and ethical aspects—United States.
3. Intellectuals—United States—Attitudes. 4. Acquisitiveness—Moral and ethical aspects.
5. Affluent consumers—United States—Psychology.
6. Consumption (Economics)—United States—Public opinion.
7. Wealth—United States—Public opinion. 8. Public opinion—United States.
I. Title.
HC110.C6 H577 2004
339.4'7'097309045—dc22
2003016300

British Library Cataloguing in Publication data are available.

To Helen

Bramo avere mille vite,
per consacrarle a te.

Bramo avere mille cori,
per consacrarli a te.

Ma in questo che ti dono,
più ch'in mille, vi sono amor, costanza e fe.

How I yearn to have a thousand lives,
To dedicate them all to you.

How I yearn to have a thousand hearts,
To dedicate them all to you.

But in this one that I give you,
More than in a thousand, there are
Love, constancy, and faith.

GEORGE FRIDERIC HANDEL, *Ariodante*

Contents

Tables

THE
ANXIETIES
OF
AFFLUENCE

Introduction

Why does affluence cause so much anxiety? This book examines how American writers worried about affluence from the end of the Great Depression of the 1930s through the late 1970s, from a time when prosperity seemed uncertain to one when it expanded into a mass expectation and then to the point where millions of people took it for granted. It begins as wartime conditions were forcing the nation to consider the relationship between consumer spending, democracy, and the struggle against fascism. It ends with the energy crisis that sparked a discussion about an era of diminished expectations. Focusing on major books, as well as on the contexts in which they appeared, this study illuminates how key twentieth-century thinkers came to terms with consumer culture. The emphasis is on the persistent but shifting tension between a commitment to self-restraint and the achievement of satisfaction through commercial goods and experiences. Affluence raised troubling issues of individual authenticity and social equality even as it promised the achievement of personal satisfaction in ways that strengthened the link between democracy and capitalism. It prompted questions about the political implications of defining American superiority in the language of consumer acquisition.

Challenges posed by the growth of consumer culture after the late 1930s compelled the attention of many of America's most influential writers. They struggled with problems that connected affluence with a series of larger issues: the spread of mass culture; the meaning of the cold war; the implications for politics of a world that seemed increasingly privatized and controlled. They also pondered the challenges that the spread of wealth posed to national

1

character, to the environment, and to people who did not share in the nation's bounty. Throughout the six decades under consideration here, authors struggled to find meaning in a society suffused with affluence and consumer culture, terms used interchangeably in this book. If they were not always successful in resolving thorny issues, they nonetheless help us understand the importance of using critical intelligence to identify values that survive in a world where commercial goods and experiences are everywhere to see and to be concerned about. Watching them grapple with these dilemmas illuminates the struggle to find ways of guiding people through a world saturated by commercial goods and experiences.[1]

Five major themes animate this work. First, I explore the persistence of highly charged, moralistic attitudes to consumer culture and then sketch the emergence of a post-moralist outlook beginning in the 1970s. Second, I show how certain writers, out of a desire to reject or reformulate Marxism, embraced psychology as an explanation for and a solution to social problems. Third, I focus on the factors that determined the power of books in this era to set the terms of public discussion. Related to this is a fourth issue, the role of intellectuals in shaping social movements, public conversations, and policy considerations. Fifth, this book charts the hegemony of the cold war consensus in the 1950s and shows how, beginning in the 1960s, new events and ideas challenged its legitimacy. Also deserving of attention are the influence of émigré intellectuals on American cultural criticism, the relationship of academic debates to national discussions, the emergence of women and African Americans as writers and as subjects of concern, and the globalization of the understanding of affluence.

The relationship between morality and affluence, the book's first major theme, brackets this study and reminds us of the persistent hope among intellectuals that Americans would curtail their spending habits and turn to loftier goals. From early in the nation's history, writers worried about the moral implications of consumers' self-indulgence and the consequences of changing patterns of comfort and luxury. Opposed to excessive commercialism and what they saw as the corruptions of luxury, they proposed instead varying combinations of genuine work, self-control, democracy, public welfare, high culture, meaningful recreation, and authentic selfhood. During the nineteenth and early twentieth centuries, social critics articulated what I call traditional or conservative moralism. Those who expressed this deeply embedded sentiment focused their anxieties on workers and immigrants, especially their consumption of alcohol and their participation in expressive ethnic traditions that stood in opposition to the "proper" behavior of bourgeois Americans. Around World War I there emerged the new or modern moralists (for whom we can use the colloquial word "puritans"), who were concerned about the effect of commercialized mass consumption on the entire society, but especially the middle class. Conformity, self-indulgence, and passivity were the problem, higher and more authentic pursuits or folk culture their alternatives. In using the loaded term "moralist," I do not mean to tar it with a skeptic's brush. We all do and should make moral judgments. Yet some moralism I find problematic because it seems to rest more on self-righteous judgments of people who are simply struggling to make ends meet than on an engagement with the moral implications of social conditions and analysis. For example, the writings of Christopher Lasch appear to me filled with patronizing arrogance; Ralph Nader's approach often contains an unexamined and condescending puritanism. Other versions are more attractive: I appreciate the way Michael Harrington, Rachel Carson, Betty Friedan, and Martin Luther King Jr. used the new moralism to ground a critique that proved so effective in building social movements. As a third stage in the history of moral responses to affluence, in the 1970s there emerged a post-moralist vision among feminists, anthropologists, and cultural critics who countered those who stressed the power of capitalism to mold consumers, and emphasized instead the liberatory and democratic possibilities of consumer culture.

Although the new or modern moralism remained powerful among many commentators discussed in this book, not everything stayed the same. The goods and services on which Americans spent their money were among the most important forces in making writers, over time, more sharply critical of consumer culture. My discussion begins with Lewis Mumford's assertion of modern moralism and then examines challenges to that position offered on the eve of World War II. We see opposition to puritanism in the *Ladies' Home Journal* study *How America Lives* (1941) and in the writings of the market researcher Ernest Dichter and consumer surveyor George Katona in the years surrounding the war. In the 1950s, a moralist vision that scolded suburbanites was at its height. Some writers in the 1950s and early 1960s—David M. Potter, John Kenneth Galbraith, Vance Packard, and Betty Friedan—embraced and tried to reformulate that outlook. Others, especially Oscar Lewis, used the study of a passionate folk society to critique it. Then there were those who politicized ethical outrage: Rachel Carson, Michael Harrington, Paul Goodman tentatively; and then Ralph Nader, Martin Luther King Jr., and Paul Ehrlich forcefully. Finally, the energy crisis of the 1970s reinvigorated a moralist vision. Later on there emerged alternative possibilities—including the post-moralism so evident toward the end of the century.[2]

A second major theme is how Marxist social analysis gave way to psychological explorations, in the process diminishing attention to social and structural circumstances. The attraction Marxism had for intellectuals in the

1930s and 1940s is a crucial part of this story. The seedbed of American social thought for the following two decades was the engagement with Marxism and labor unions in the 1940s, especially for the native-born figures considered here. In the ensuing years they rejected, qualified, or reformulated their ideology, and in that process psychology, especially a psychology of self-realization, played a critical role. In this story, Abraham H. Maslow was a key, albeit unwitting, figure: he was the brother-in-law of Lewis; Katona used his work to prove his case for the importance of aspiring consumers; Friedan transformed his ideas to suit feminist purposes; and President Jimmy Carter's adviser Pat Caddell turned to him to bolster the argument that there was something more rewarding to life than materialistic satisfactions. For some, such as Lasch, vacuous personal fulfillment was a foil. For others, such as Dichter, it was a positive good used to critique puritanism and sanction spending. For people such as Packard and Friedan, it provided a way of undergirding a critical stance in an atmosphere in which Marxism was politically suspect. For still others, such as King, a religiously based interpretation of self-love shaped a radical critique of excessive materialism. Psychology had so much traction precisely because it was possible to rely on it for such varying purposes. It provided an alternative to the pleasures of affluence, and commentators used it in diverse and conflicting ways.[3]

The story of how pathbreaking best-selling books set the terms of public discussion is the narrative's third theme. Popular books spoke to audiences in ways that established the terms of debates, generated social momentum, and helped define oppositional identities. Writings on affluence, addressed to specialized audiences by Dichter and Katona in the immediate postwar period, emerged as best-sellers in the late 1950s, with David Riesman's *The Lonely Crowd: A Study of the Changing American Character* (1950) and Potter's *People of Plenty: Economic Abundance and the American Character* (1954) paving the way for Galbraith's *The Affluent Society* (1958) and Packard's *The Hidden Persuaders* (1957), *The Status Seekers* (1959), and *The Waste Makers* (1960). For a decade beginning in the late 1950s, best-selling or at least widely read books by authors on the left had real influence. Particularly significant for our purposes, these books served as jeremiads warning their readers of their profligate ways. Along the way we see the role of magazine editors, literary agents, and the rise of television in the development of these books. Some of the books—Friedan's *Feminine Mystique* (1963) and Harrington's *The Other America* (1962)—happened to appear at a moment when America was on the verge of discovering women's oppression and poverty. Yet this was also a critical period in the history of the American left, a time when the book-buying public was ready to listen to critiques of the society. With the publication of Lasch's *Culture of Narcissism* in 1979, a book whose author was reformulating a radical tradition in what many considered a politically ambiguous manner, the tradition of left-leaning jeremiads may have reached a dead end. After the 1970s, changes in the publishing industry and in the nature of the social sciences, as well as the rightward shift in American politics, dramatically transformed the landscape for popular books on affluence. As the epilogue makes clear, by the late 1990s, self-help books teaching Americans everything from how to lead a simple life to how to become millionaires commanded immense audiences and helped transform their authors into merchandisable commodities. These books in turn overshadowed influential reassertions of the new moralism. They also made it harder to see the emergence of post-moralism.

Closely linked to the impact of influential books is the role intellectuals played in shaping social movements, public discussions, and policy, the fourth theme that weaves throughout this book. During World War II, not only Mumford but also Galbraith at the Office of Price Administration (OPA) and Friedan as editor of the Smith College student newspaper hoped that by chastising consumption they would animate American politics and force consumers to reconsider their profligate ways. Characteristically, the work of Dichter, Katona, and Potter, though not without powerful ideological messages, abjured overt political positions. In contrast, works by Friedan, Harrington, and Carson in the early 1960s played key roles in sparking social movements. That tradition reached a critical turning point with the publication in 1965 of Nader's *Unsafe at Any Speed: The Designed-In Dangers of the American Automobile*, a book whose author used the notoriety of a best-seller to launch and then sustain a social movement. Over time, writers of popular books, no longer having to disguise their politics, were able to engage more openly in political discourse. This enabled their books to be read as politically inspiring by audiences already engaged but now looking for analysis to undergird their activism. By the late 1960s, books tended to follow consumer activism or to work hand in hand with it rather than initiate it.

Another important element of the story is the link between books and the trajectories of their authors' lives. I begin with Mumford's inevitably dashed hopes during World War II that he might help persuade the public to use the wartime circumstances to cure their excessive penchant for consumption. I then turn to Dichter and Katona, two writers whose words had immense impact on their respective fields of advertising and public policy, and who hoped to reach a wider public audience. In contrast, other writers I consider here had a generalized impact on the reading public but usually failed to capitalize on that impact in the more elusive arena of public policy. In this story there are all sorts of complications. Some authors, such as Potter, struggled with the conflicting roles of specialized academic and public intellectual.

Packard eschewed any ambition larger than influence and sales as he wrote books that enabled him to sustain a career as a writer. Almost alone among those discussed, he both kept his distance from his own notoriety and relished his financial success. Friedan used the popular impact of a book to launch a feminist movement over which she soon lost control. Galbraith had success in the mid-1940s as an OPA administrator who implemented policies that encapsulated his moral response to consumption. In the late 1950s his book had immense general impact but little success in promoting his specific agenda. A number of writers—Friedan, Harrington, Ehrlich—hid their radicalism, which soon after publication they revealed in more forthright political action.

In the 1960s we come to a shift in the relationship between authors and politics. Carson, Harrington, Goodman, and Lewis struggled to have an impact, but a variety of circumstances made that goal elusive. Carson's and Lewis's lives were cut short by early deaths. Carson's book launched a social movement that she did not live to see. During her lifetime, however, the residue of cold war fears made it difficult for her to speak her mind fully. In *Children of Sánchez* (1961), Lewis also could not speak his mind frankly. As a consequence, he articulated a concept—the culture of poverty—that had an impact opposite to what he intended, for he could not clarify his meaning until it was too late. Goodman and Harrington reshaped the Old Left into a new set of ideas well suited to the early 1960s. Harrington sustained an impact through his writing even though his socialism ended his immediate and dramatically direct involvement in the formulation of the war on poverty. In addition, as a new generation on the left emerged after the early 1960s, Harrington found himself a rebel without an appreciative audience among the young. With *Growing Up Absurd: Problems of Youth in the Organized System* (1960), Goodman helped create the New Left, and his writings continued to influence the movement after he and members of the younger generation had parted ways.

The late 1960s mark a critical turning point in the relation between books and social movements, between writers and public action. Nader's book enabled him to develop the leadership style and infrastructure necessary to sustain a social movement. With King, a social movement preceded his book, albeit a movement that relied considerably on sermons preached in black churches. Then in 1967 he wrote *Where Do We Go from Here: Chaos or Community?*, which he hoped would give new energy to a social movement he had helped create but control of which was slipping from his grasp. At times the emergence of the civil rights movement from its grass roots made books seem irrelevant or tardy. With the environmental movement, which drew its strength from those in the middle class and above, it was books (like

Ehrlich's *Population Bomb* of 1968) rather than sermons that played vitally important roles. Shifts in the relationship between social movements and the printed word resulted in both the fragmentation of intellectuals as a group and developing uncertainties surrounding the roles they could fulfill.

Three of the books I discuss helped create the climate of opinion in the energy crisis of the late 1970s: Daniel Bell's *Cultural Contradictions of Capitalism* (1976), Robert N. Bellah's *Broken Covenant* (1975), and Christopher Lasch's *Culture of Narcissism* (1979). In preparation for his "malaise" speech of July 15, 1979, Jimmy Carter met with these men, three of the nation's leading intellectuals. The president's engagement with their books fully illustrates the complex ironies of the involvement of intellectuals in politics and of politicians with intellectuals. Bell had no illusions about balancing participation and observation. Lasch, after having denounced intellectuals for their flirtation with politicians, now found himself meeting in the White House with an appreciative president. Bellah was at first hopeful but then frustrated in his effort to get an attentive president to follow his advice. Although Carter engaged the ideas of the nation's leading intellectuals perhaps more than any other president since the Founding Fathers, he did so largely to salvage his political fate.

Finally, this is the story of the rise and fall of the cold war consensus. The book explores what kinds of criticism the cold war made possible, how that consensus was shaken in the 1970s when affluence seemed spent, and more generally what transpired when the consensus became delegitimated. It charts the shift from the celebration of democratic affluence as a basis for American superiority to less confident understandings of the impact of global markets on national life. From the late 1940s through the mid-1960s, businesspeople, politicians, the mass media, and many leading intellectuals trumpeted the benefits of the American way of life. They celebrated democratic capitalism, which, in contrast to Soviet totalitarianism, had produced ever-growing prosperity and in turn provided the foundation for an egalitarian and harmonious society. They saw workers increasingly entering the middle class, expert managers replacing wealthy and avaricious capitalists, immigrants assimilating, and poverty disappearing. Social divisions seemed to diminish dramatically, especially since race was off their radar screen. Dispassionate experts, and the New Deal welfare state, now in stasis, were well on the way to solving social problems. With God on the nation's side, the American dream was triumphing over the Soviet nightmare. What worried observers about affluence was the debased tastes of most Americans, reduced to the lowest common denominator and undercutting the influence and resilience of high culture.

The book opens on a nation recovering from the Great Depression even as it struggled with issues raised by World War II. The depression had challenged capitalism, including its ability to sustain a high and growing standard of living. During the war, Mumford, *How America Lives*, and the OPA all reflected some aspect of the battle to strengthen democracy and capitalism, and within that context to think through the role of consumer culture in a postwar world. Ultimately the task, reflected so well in the writings and work of Katona and Dichter, was to link democracy, capitalism, and consumption into a compelling triad, with restraint thrown to the winds. The rest of this book deals with the story of how writers after the mid-1950s wrestled with the legacy of consensus. From a Burkean perspective, Potter explored the way affluence undermined the social order of a people of plenty in a work that most readers took to be more appreciative of what it analyzed than it actually was. The story continues by showing how the consensus was robbed of legitimacy beginning in the 1960s. Yet it also suggests that in some quarters, challenges to consensus never took hold. Galbraith, Packard, and Friedan began the critique from within when they embraced key elements of the consensus and then reformulated that tradition. Goodman, Harrington, Lewis, and Carson broke with the cold war assumption that the psychic struggles of suburbanites were what most compelled attention and articulated new ways of attacking affluence. Nader, King, and Ehrlich launched attacks on the core of the consensus, both in their writings and through their activism. Bell and Bellah grew up in the orbit of the Old Left. Later, along with Lasch (from a liberal background), they worked, not always with success, to think through alternatives to cold war liberalism. For them, the connection between capitalism, democracy, and consumer culture had become the problem. In the pessimistic 1970s, they struggled valiantly, if not always successfully, to fashion an alternative. In the end, the effort was more one of critique than of creation. The bewildering alternatives available by century's end underscored how the cold war consensus had provided an anchor that, whatever its considerable faults, was an anchor nonetheless.

Writers who grappled with the subject of affluence in the postwar world did so at a time of unprecedented economic growth. To be sure, the road to increasing personal and national wealth was not smooth. Wars, recessions, an energy crisis, and threats to the environment served as reminders that change and progress were not the same. Not everyone partook equally of the consumer cornucopia. Millions of Native Americans, African Americans, Latinos, poor whites, and the working poor did not share fully in affluence. Nonetheless, the period from 1939 to century's end saw a series of fundamental transformations in how Americans lived. In 1958 dollars, the per capita share of the GNP in 1939 stood at $1,598, $3,555 in 1970, and almost

$7,000 in 2000. Statistics, however, only begin to tell the story. In 1939, most homes in the United States did not have central heating, and a substantial percentage did not have running water, to say nothing of television sets or several cars. The typical suburban home of the immediate postwar period contained less than 1,000 square feet; nearly 20 percent of the new homes constructed at century's end were at least three times that size. In 2000, 18 percent of all households possessed three or more vehicles. In 1939, a small number of passengers flew commercially, in propeller-driven planes that had to stop on cross-country trips. At century's end, every day Americans boarded jet planes in the United States to fly nonstop to Tokyo, the leading city in a nation with which we were at war fifty-five years before. Even in the early 1960s, to make a trans-Atlantic telephone call it was necessary to have a reservation. In the year 2000, it was possible to communicate, immediately and inexpensively, with virtually any part of the world by phone or e-mail. Consequently when intellectuals were responding to affluence in the years since the beginning of World War II, they were aiming at a moving target.

I have focused on writers whose books were especially timely, influential, and symptomatic of larger issues. I use the term "intellectual" rather generously, to include not only skeptical observers but also activists, a president, and several writers who were more celebratory than critical. The juxtaposition in this book of canonical authors (Daniel Bell and Lewis Mumford, for example) with non-canonical ones (Ernest Dichter, Betty Friedan, Ralph Nader) enlarges our understanding of postwar intellectual history. The people I have selected demonstrate considerable continuities with issues on which others have focused, such as the meaning of culture, the importance of authenticity, and the process of coming to terms with Marxism. Yet making abundance and consumer culture central and providing unexpected juxtapositions of figures enriches our sense of the chronology whereby ideas developed and our understanding of the relationship between ideas, major events, and social movements. In important ways, this approach makes postwar thought more complicated, multivocal, and multilayered.[4]

The writers under consideration lived within a world of common experiences and ideas. However much the conditions of their personal lives differed, they were all aware of the transformation of the nation from the straitened conditions of the depression to the often exuberant prosperity of the 1950s and 1960s. Epochal events of the 1930s—the economic collapse of Western economies and the rise of totalitarianism in Germany—shaped the generation that came of political and intellectual age in that decade and in the 1940s. The disillusionment many of them experienced with socialism, Marxism, communism, and the labor movement at various points in the 1930s and 1940s caused them to rethink their commitments, and even to find non-

Marxist means of bolstering an adversarial stance. As the postwar period proceeded, a host of events shaped their consciousness: not only the prosperity and apparent conformity of the 1950s but also the emergence of the civil rights movement in the same decade and then later the insurgent politics of the 1960s, the war in Vietnam, Watergate, and the energy crisis.

Moreover, they inhabited a defined intellectual universe. Their politics diverged, often dramatically, but they all had to come to terms with how the cold war consensus, as a counter to Soviet totalitarianism, emphasized the beneficence of democratic capitalism and the widespread affluence of an expanding middle class. Though the writers under consideration here were not close friends, and indeed few if any of them knew the others personally, they read and often reviewed one another's books. More important, they inhabited a world of shared ideas and books. Many kept in mind the two classics of 1950s social criticism—David Riesman's *Lonely Crowd* and William H. Whyte's *Organization Man* (1956). Riesman's surprise best-seller, written by a lawyer turned public intellectual and academic, intensified interest in understanding the American national character, in figuring out where to locate autonomy in an affluent middle-class world, and in replacing economic determinism with explanations that focused on culture and personality. Whyte, a writer for *Fortune*, invoked many of the same issues, reinforced the problematic emphasis on middle-class suburbanites, and underscored what it meant to write a serious book that reached an eager audience of book buyers.

Most of the writers analyzed here had to come to terms with the contribution of members of the Frankfurt Institute for Social Research, especially after the early 1960s, when its impact took hold on native-born authors. The Frankfurt school, as it is called, opened in the German city in 1923 and counted among its members Theodor Adorno, Hannah Arendt, Max Horkheimer, Leo Lowenthal, Walter Benjamin, and Herbert Marcuse. In Germany and then as émigrés in the United States, members of the Frankfurt school, unlike more orthodox Marxists, offered a rich and powerful neo-Marxist analysis of middle-class life and mass culture. They insisted on the connection between economic and social forces on the one hand and acts of creativity on the other. For them, culture, whether high or mass, was the product of generalized social relations. Unlike more orthodox Marxists, they believed that the exercise of power involved more than the one-to-one ideological consequences of class interests or more generally the impact of economic forces on other realms of existence. In modern society what they called the culture industry had succeeded in shaping taste, especially since intermediary institutions such as the family had weakened. Yet members of the Frankfurt school also held out the possibility that culture—that created by the exceptional composer as well as that performed in a circus—had a critical function in holding up an alternative version of reality. Artistic creativity was thus the origin of protest, and under social conditions different from those of modern capitalism might provide the basis for an improved way of life. If some, like Adorno, emphasized the oppressive nature of the capitalist system, others, like Benjamin, stressed the possibility of liberation. They imagined what they called an affirmative culture which increased human happiness by unifying production and consumption.

In the meantime, in Germany in the 1920s and 1930s as well as in the United States during the war and then the postwar period, powerful forces of the dominant society, especially the culture industry, made alternative social possibilities increasingly impossible to imagine let alone realize. Modern capitalism and authoritarian politics turned democratic popular culture into mass culture, a process that involved the fetishizing of commodities. It ripped objects from their condition of human production and turned them instead into possessions from which alienated humans took false comfort. As Martin Jay has written, "The culture industry administered a nonspontaneous, reified, phony culture rather than the real thing. The old distinction between high culture and low culture all but vanished in the 'stylized barbarism' of mass culture." As Jay has noted, members of the Frankfurt school concluded that "the culture industry enslaved men in far more subtle and effective ways than the crude methods of domination" of earlier times, producing resigned, conforming subjects. All this made for a dismal prospect, with popular culture offering fading opportunities for resistance.[5]

Conformity and resignation without the possibility of any alternative—this was the prospect that New York intellectuals articulated beginning in the late 1940s as they looked out across the landscape of affluence. Writers among them such as Dwight Macdonald and Lionel Trilling dominated much of American intellectual life until the 1970s and stood as gatekeepers for almost any serious public discussion about consumer culture. This was especially true in the 1950s. This group, initially on the anti-Stalinist left, recoiled from a society embracing a crass commercial culture which they believed threatened the high culture embodied in great works of art. What horrified them was the way a corrupted mass culture reigned, absorbing and then debasing creativity, for example, by reproducing Piet Mondrian's paintings on beach towels and by obliterating the folk culture which had provided so much comfort to intellectuals during the depression. The result, which they saw all around them in 1950s America, was modern capitalism absorbing and commodifying the critical functions of culture, producing a debased, trivialized, heterogeneous society, visible most clearly in the affluent middle-class suburbs. A powerful "masscult" had captured an easily manipulated middle class and offered a watered-down "midcult" that was destroying the avant-garde.[6]

This book begins with the story of how the Great Depression, the rise of totalitarianism in Europe, and World War II established the connection between the defense of democratic capitalism and the promise of the postwar expansion of affluence. The depression left millions of Americans with a wide range of unsatisfied desires and many influential intellectuals with a sense that the economic system had failed. Social critics found alternatives to American capitalism and bourgeois life in socialism and communism, as well as in the folkways of ordinary Americans. The specter of European totalitarianism affected people in different ways; some saw similarities between Nazism and communism, while others differentiated between the two. There was, however, no minimizing the long-term impact of European events on American views of consumption and mass culture. Especially as they sought to comprehend the rise of National Socialism in Germany, American observers began to realize the implications of their interpretations of changes in the American standard of living. A new appreciation of democracy went hand in hand with profound concern about mass culture. World War II intensified the search for a connection between democracy and consumption. Rationing, taxation, material shortages, and patriotism underscored the importance of a chastened standard of living. Yet wartime prosperity—advanced by the creation of millions of jobs and by tremendous military expenditures—ended the depression and started millions of Americans on the road to a more comfortable way of life.

Wartime household budget studies and discussions about spending reflect the improvement in the standard of living of millions of American families. They also show how social scientists, policy makers, and journalists recognized the importance of prudence and self-restraint among consumers. *How America Lives* (1941), a *Ladies' Home Journal* study of the way sixteen American families spent their lives and their money, revealed a wide range of living patterns. It also evidenced an interest in demonstrating how the democratic nature of American life would prevent the emergence of totalitarianism on these shores. As the war approached, some American intellectuals, especially on the left, including non-Marxist interventionists such as Lewis Mumford, hoped that U.S. entry into the conflict would persuade or force American citizens to live less materialistic lives. By the time the war ended in 1945, Mumford had realized, in ways that were simultaneously political and private, what later generations of writers would learn, often reluctantly: that the growth of affluence defied calls for chastened consumption.

In chapter 2, I consider the golden age of modern capitalism in the United States, an extraordinary quarter-century following the end of World War II. This was an exceptional time when the flowering of national affluence prompted awe and anxiety at home and abroad. I focus on two émigrés—

Ernest Dichter and George Katona—who, beginning in the mid-1940s, celebrated American consumers as the force that provided the economy and society with prosperity and stability. They wrote during the years following the end of World War II, when the celebration of America's achievement as an affluent society was at its height. Recovery from the depression and the war itself—a period when circumstances had required American households to restrain their purchasing—spread the benefits of national wealth throughout much of the nation. Tens of millions of American families moved into new suburban houses, bought television sets for the first time, traded in old automobiles in order to enjoy new styles and features, ate meals at nationally franchised restaurants, and took longer vacations farther away from home. Although many writers responded with horror to these changes, Dichter and Katona, émigrés who had fled the advance of Hitler across Europe in the 1930s, believed that a consumption economy would prevent the United States from experiencing the totalitarianism, inflation, and social disruption that had devastated Europe during the interwar period.

Ernest Dichter, an émigré psychologist and influential market researcher, captured the optimism about the new consumer culture that suffused the writings of many observers immediately after the war. In hundreds of studies he carried out for corporations beginning in the late 1930s, and in a series of postwar books, he offered a vision of a world filled with consumable goods which, as symbols of creative self-expression, would help defeat communism abroad and sustain an American middle class. His was a decidedly anti-puritanical vision, one that spoke of enjoyment, satisfaction, and fulfillment. Several of the most influential critics of advertising—including Vance Packard and Betty Friedan—both relied on and criticized Dichter's work, though they often shared with him a sense that solutions to the problems of consumer culture could be found in one or another form of self-actualizing humanistic psychology.

If Dichter helped businesses understand the psyche of American consumers, more than anyone else George Katona was responsible for surveying the implications of their changing moods. Later in the twentieth century and early in the twenty-first, whenever it was reported that consumers were more or less confident than they had been a month before, people were hearing the results of surveys Katona helped launch at the University of Michigan in 1946. He charted the power of the expanding ranks of middle-class spenders whose disposable income went for durable goods and thus provided the rudder that kept the ship of affluence on course. From the early 1940s until the end of his life, he paid special attention to the question of how to achieve national prosperity without rampant inflation, an issue that his life in Germany in the 1920s had forced him to ponder. In the postwar period, critical of the view that the average consumer was being manipulated into purchasing unwanted goods and experiences, Katona instead found consumers sensible and hopeful. For him, the optimistic American consumer was the hero who would prevent the country from experiencing the inflation, instability, war, and totalitarianism that had ravaged the Germany he'd left behind.

In chapter 3, I show how writers wrestled with the implications of the new middle-class suburban prosperity. David M. Potter's *People of Plenty* (1954), the focus of this chapter, helped define the response to affluence. Most contemporaries read Potter's work as a text that announced America's arrival as the consumer nation par excellence, a city on a hill whose nearby suburbs were a beacon to the world. Yet this was to overlook the fact that *People of Plenty* emerged from the experiences of a man with a Burkean view of the social order. Potter was a southerner by upbringing, a resident in the North almost his entire adult life, and a historian much of whose work focused on the coming of the Civil War. With *People of Plenty*, he offered an analysis of abundance whose cold war celebrations were tempered by a recognition of some of the costs Americans paid for their headlong embrace of a rising GNP. Although his response to affluence was in some ways peripheral to the major issues Potter grappled with during his career, his writing nonetheless reveals the distinctive outlook of a southern white traditionalist in exile, participating in debates over the rising standard of living, predominantly among non-southerners. More deeply than many of his contemporaries, Potter recognized the costs that social and geographical mobility, rapid growth, and the social disruption of affluence imposed on social order and a sense of belonging.

In the late 1950s and early 1960s, John Kenneth Galbraith, Vance Packard, and Betty Friedan perfected the critique of affluence at a time when the excessive embrace of consumer culture among white, middle-class suburbanites was seen as the prime source of the nation's problems. Their critiques from within, the focal point of chapter 4, provided a culmination of the treatment of familiar topics and the introduction of new ones—the public policy for an affluent society for Galbraith, with Packard the class dynamics of affluence and the costs of wastefulness, and for Friedan the impact of suburban affluence on women. As the most intense period of the cold war waned, they offered analyses of consumer culture that were more critical than Potter's. Moreover, on the cusp between the late 1950s and early 1960s, they went beyond Potter's stance as ironic analyst to offer suggestions about how to curb the excesses of affluence through political engagement.

With *The Affluent Society* (1958), the economist John Kenneth Galbraith offered an immensely influential critique. As head of the OPA during World War II, Galbraith exercised tremendous power over people's habits of consumption, restraining them in the name of the war effort much as Mumford had wished. In the early 1950s, Galbraith began to work on a book on poverty. That project turned into *The Affluent Society*, a book whose title he later came to regret. Galbraith encouraged Americans to think about the social imbalance between abundant spending on private goods and pinched resources for public ones. This critique of American priorities undergirded his recommendations that the nation use public policy to counter the excesses of private affluence. If his critique of middle-class affluence was somewhat conventional, his turning that critique into the basis for public policy was pathbreaking.

Beginning in 1957, the magazine writer Vance Packard burst onto the scene with three consecutive best-sellers that explored key aspects of consumer culture. In *The Hidden Persuaders* (1957), he excoriated advertisers for having manipulated American consumers into chasing what he considered the false god of ever higher levels of consumption. In *The Status Seekers* (1959), he exposed how the pursuit of social status in suburbia, as expressed in the purchase of homes, automobiles, and education, revealed a nation in danger of tearing itself apart along lines defined by class and status. And in *The Waste Makers* (1960), he attacked American materialism for its excesses and wastefulness. In all these books Packard relied on a producer ethic that valued meaningful work over empty leisure, moral restraint instead of wanton self-expression through goods, and a moral vision based on an embrace of an earlier America rather than what he considered the immoral chase after satisfaction through empty affluence.

Betty Friedan's book *The Feminine Mystique* (1963), best known for its role in reviving the women's movement, offered a feminist critique of postwar consumer culture. Friedan first began to engage the issues she considered in her book in the early 1940s. As a child growing up in Peoria, she used to listen as her parents fought over the getting and spending of money. As an undergraduate at Smith College in the early years of World War II, she criticized her more privileged peers for not limiting their expenditures in order to fight fascism. When she became a labor journalist in the 1940s and early 1950s, she offered women practical advice on consuming wisely, and she criticized the wealthy and powerful for skewing the distribution of consumer goods. In her 1963 book she lambasted American corporations for trapping women in the "comfortable concentration camp" of the suburban home. Like her nemesis Dichter, she advocated personal self-fulfillment, but in her case as a substitute for consumption rather than, in his, as its handmaiden.

In chapter 5, attention turns to the initial attempt to explore the limits of suburban consumer culture, to speak of its costs, and to make visible both the alternatives coexisting within it and the underside that skeptics from within the confines of the suburban critique helped mask. Paul Goodman, Oscar Lewis, Michael Harrington, and Rachel Carson offered works that grew out of the remnants of political dissent and their own outsider status. Their four books, published in rapid succession beginning in the fall of 1960, recast the discussion of affluence and helped revitalize political insurgency. Goodman's *Growing Up Absurd* (1960), Lewis's *Children of Sánchez* (1961), Harrington's *The Other America* (1962), and Carson's *Silent Spring* (1962) were runaway best-sellers that attacked the focus on middle-class, suburban affluence which had so dominated discussions over the previous decade and a half. Against the background of sustained economic growth, the question of consumer culture in the 1960s became contested. The debates were more contentious, political, and urgent than those of the 1950s. These writers offered powerful analyses of an America others had pictured as an affluent, suburban, middle-class society. Moreover, in distinctive ways they all worked to connect what they wrote about the problems of affluence with the reinvigorated politics of the 1960s.

Each of these books introduced a topic left out of the paradigm that dominated earlier discussions. In *Growing Up Absurd*, Paul Goodman focused on the consequences for young men of the organized society, with its promise of affluence for all and the actuality of poverty for some. Goodman, who embraced anarchism and a life of voluntary poverty, found vacuous the lives of middle-class suburbanites and the ideas of the cultural critics who made them the focus of their work. He feared that the rat race run by the organization man made meaningful work and genuine community impossible to achieve. Like other male writers of his generation, Goodman inspired the youthful counterculture with his rejection of materialism and his emphasis on intense experiences. With *Children of Sánchez*, the anthropologist Oscar Lewis used the voices of his Mexican informants to convey the rich texture of their lives. Although he concentrated on the urban poor of Latin America, his writings—including his notion of the culture of poverty—had immense implications for how North Americans understood their own society. As he introduced his fellow citizens to urban poverty, Lewis called into question the concerns that authors such as Packard had expressed about the well-being of middle-class suburbanites. The picture he drew of poor people living intensely passionate lives under difficult conditions contrasted sharply with the dominant analysis of a nation of affluent, bored, and anxious consumers.

It was Michael Harrington who connected Lewis's view of the urban poor south of the border to the invisibility of poverty in the United States. While working in a soup kitchen as a young man and writing for Dorothy Day's *Catholic Worker*, Harrington had witnessed urban poverty in lower Manhattan, an experience that helped launch his reputation as a rising star among the nation's democratic socialists. In *The Other America*, he stunned a nation used to cold war celebrations of widespread affluence with his revelations of the extent of poverty in America. His work inspired two presidents, John F. Kennedy and Lyndon B. Johnson, to focus on poverty as a public policy issue even as, with some equivocation, he embraced the problematic notion of a culture of poverty.

Rachel Carson turned her attention to another subject celebrants of America's wealth had neglected—the impact on the environment—as she critiqued suburban affluence from a fresh perspective. An unmarried woman who headed an unconventional household, and a professional science writer who had attracted a significant audience early in her career, with *Silent Spring*, Carson wrote an immensely popular book that helped launch the environmental movement—a movement she did not live long enough to witness. Soon after the publication of her book, as she neared the end of her life, she linked suburban affluence, the cold war's legacy, and threats to the environment in ways that called into question the celebrations of the consumer offered by Dichter and Katona and the human-centered concerns of Galbraith, Packard, and Friedan.

In the second half of the 1960s, Ralph Nader, Martin Luther King Jr., and Paul Ehrlich, the focus of attention in chapter 6, stood in opposition to the politics of suburban consensus and the political infrastructure that empowered it. Their writings established a productive dialogue between best-selling books and social movements and legitimated political opposition to mindless affluence, spurring consumer protests. Nader's *Unsafe at Any Speed* (1965) was the pivotal work. Drawing on a radical politics he developed in his hometown of Winsted, Connecticut, as a Princeton undergraduate, and then as a Harvard law student, Nader exposed the dangers posed to Americans by the automobile, the quintessential symbol of 1950s consumer culture. Moreover, unlike the writers of the earlier best-selling books he succeeded in transforming the notoriety his book gave him into a social movement which he was able to lead in its institutionalized form. By late in the decade, others had joined him in developing a politics in which consumer culture occupied a central position. King, steeped in religious and familial traditions of preaching and social activism, extended the focus of the civil rights movement to consumer boycotts, which he justified by deploying morality for adversarial purposes. In the 1950s he emphasized the growing comfort of some African Americans while chastising them for elevating private consumption over public good. Addressing a largely white audience in *Where Do We Go from Here*, in the 1960s King focused on the gap between the poverty of many African Americans and the prosperity of the dominant society, urging blacks to use consumer boycotts to secure or improve their position as workers.

By the late 1960s, the biologist Paul Ehrlich had emerged as a spokesman for a newly invigorated environmental movement. With *The Population Bomb* (1968), he switched from writing specialized scientific books and articles to reaching out to a general audience. His was the most widely read book of the emerging environmental movement, an effort that captured the attention of a nation on Earth Day in April 1970. Interested from an early age in the perils suburban development posed to fragile natural environments, Ehrlich warned Americans of the compounded dangers of increasing population, technology, and affluence. His career illuminates the role of scientific writing in critiques of prosperity. Moreover, like King, Ehrlich reminded Americans of the global perspective in discussions of affluence. Seen from the early twenty-first century, the careers of these three writers—Nader, King, and Ehrlich—afford insights into the relationship between best-selling books and social movements.

In 1970s America, affluence suddenly seemed less certain. Responding to the war in Vietnam, Watergate, and especially the energy crisis, Americans now wondered whether it was possible to sustain prosperity. People were troubled by consumer culture, too, in ways, reminiscent of and yet different from the national mood in World War II. The result, the subject of chapters 7 and 8, was a renewed call by intellectuals, echoed by President Jimmy Carter, for both national and individual self-restraint. If there was a key moment that captured the sense of limits—to the nation's aspirations as well as to its affluence—it was the "malaise" speech Carter delivered in July 1979. As Carter thought about what he would say, he consulted a number of people, including three of the nation's leading intellectuals—Daniel Bell, Robert N. Bellah, and Christopher Lasch. Bell's *Cultural Contradictions of Capitalism*, Bellah's *Broken Covenant*, and Lasch's *Culture of Narcissism* were influential attempts to grapple with the issue of lowered expectations. They shared an awareness that the nation had entered a new age of limits, one best approached by a renewed sense of public good and moral purpose. Their encounters with Carter, and he with their writings, underscore the complex relationship between intellectuals and politicians. Carter's malaise speech, as well as the prefigurations of it in the ideas of Bell, Bellah, and Lasch, also remind us of the persistence in American intellectual and political life of calls for chastened, moral consumption.

The 1980s and 1990s challenged the portrait that Bell, Bellah, Carter, and Lasch had painted of an end to American affluence. Indeed, in the last two decades of the twentieth century, the nation experienced a burgeoning economy and new levels of prosperity, as well as the intensification of inequality. In response, widely read writers of these decades, whose books receive attention in the epilogue, reiterated a full and complicated sense of the challenges and opportunities posed by affluence. Some, in optimistic recovery from the malaise of the 1970s, celebrated the nation's growing wealth and, in a series of wildly popular books, held out the promise that average Americans could obtain untold riches. Others offered a post-moralist defense of affluence. Still others were more skeptical, serving up puritanical critiques of consumer culture or reviving the tradition of simple living. Finally, as we shall see, the response to the tragic events of September 11, 2001, revealed a dramatic and significant change in the way Americans linked a national crisis with consumer culture.

1

Chastened Consumption

World War II and the Campaign for a Democratic Standard of Living

During World War II, millions of American consumers began to put depression conditions behind them and started to look forward to a peace that would enable them to extend their experience of prosperity by spending what they had saved. Government officials and molders of public opinion called on citizens to curtail their expenditures so the nation could dedicate its full effort to winning the war. Some influential social critics went even farther, hoping that the nation would learn from wartime conditions to turn away permanently from the chase after materialistic satisfactions. Lewis Mumford (1895–1990) led the fight for curtailed consumption. Embracing the new moralism, he called on his fellow citizens to sacrifice their standard of living, not only for the sake of wartime exigencies but also for the health of postwar democracy. In the end, he found his hopes for influence over public opinion and policy dashed. The war imposed on him a grave personal sacrifice; in addition, before long he realized that excess rather than restraint would mark the postwar world.

Mumford was fighting an uphill battle. As the historian Thaddeus Russell has demonstrated, during the war the labor leader Walter Reuther unsuccessfully tried to persuade the nation's workers to curb their drive for a more materialistic way of life. Robert Westbrook, Mark H. Leff, and Amy Bentley have noted that during the war, government officials and Madison Avenue typically called on Americans to sacrifice their standard of living by defining war aims, as Bentley has noted, "in private, individualistic terms that dignified and promoted consumption." Indeed, historians have come to identify in the 1930s and 1940s what Jean-Christophe Agnew has called the strengthening of "a far-reaching ideological redefinition of polity and society" which later came to fuller fruition with "the promotion of the social contract of cold-war liberalism." This involved "a state sponsored guarantee of private consumption" that found its clearest expression in the way corporations promoted household appliances, packaged goods, and new forms of leisure. Corporations themselves learned to speak a new communal language, as Mark Weiner has shown in his study of the marketing of Coca-Cola, in campaigns that took advantage of the war to connect purchasing their products with protecting the American way of life by supporting the war effort. Opposition to this identification of social good with private consumption and private enterprise came from several quarters. As Bentley has demonstrated, some Americans, particularly women, faced with government programs for rationing, worked toward a communal vision that linked wartime sacrifice with obligations that were both democratic and patriotic. Although his perspective was hardly gendered in the ways these historians have noted, Mumford also spoke of consumption in terms of democracy and community rather than private satisfaction and corporate gain. The postwar period undermined his efforts and those of others to make a convincing link between democracy, the reform of capitalism, and lessened consumption.[1]

The Depression of the 1930s and Consumer Expectations

In the 1920s, millions of Americans believed that they lived in an era of long-lasting prosperity. In the 1930s, they assumed they were in the midst of a long-term if not permanent economic depression. Looking ahead, few if any observers foresaw the dimensions of the nation's development as a consumer society over the next several decades. The return of sustained economic prosperity seemed always beyond the foreseeable future. Millions of households used short-term measures to hold on to the standard of living they had attained in more prosperous times. Yet for most in the working and middle classes, there was no ignoring how thin was the line between a marginally comfortable and a hopelessly impoverished way of life.[2]

During the 1930s, many influential social critics strengthened their commitment to a moral vision of consumption, believing the nation would turn away from what they saw as corrupt, commercialized patterns of living and opt instead for simple comforts and refined but liberating "culture." Foremost among these heralds of permanently curtailed consumption was Robert S. Lynd. In 1929, Lynd, along with his wife, Helen M. Lynd, had authored *Middletown*, a classic community study in which they expressed their concern with the way radios, automobiles, and movies were undermining face-to-face contact in communities.[3]

Robert Lynd articulated widely shared expectations about the permanence of adverse economic conditions. Writing in *Parents' Magazine* in 1934, he warned those who believed that the depression was temporary against the dangers of instilling in children a false optimism. In 1934, a year after Franklin D. Roosevelt assumed the presidency, Lynd predicted that children would not have as wide a range of career opportunities as their parents. Faced with overcrowded professions and "too few jobs to go round," the younger generation would have to "'count on' less things than we have thought we could." Their future lives would "probably be [defined] less in terms of whopping accumulations of material things and more in terms of more inconspicuous, hard-won personal satisfactions." Lynd, who had serious reservations about the desirability of an ever more materialistic standard of living, preferred a frugal life to an affluent one. Indeed, he argued that without a return to prosperity, the new generation would be "relieved from a part of our irrelevant strain of endless competitive acquisition for its own sake," and could apply its energies toward the "vitalities of personal living" rather than squandering them "in trying to excel in getting ahead." Ironically, Lynd made his cautionary remarks about a generation, born in the decade and a half after World War I, that would benefit greatly from the affluence of the 1950s and 1960s.[4]

Although Americans' expectations during the depression hardly foretold what would occur in the 1950s and 1960s, the earlier period was critical in shaping later changes in ways that Lynd did not anticipate. To begin with, for millions of Americans, the Great Depression, with its enforced experience of retrenched consumption, gave rise to a generation of avid consumers. As Sheila K. Bennett and Glen H. Elder Jr. have demonstrated, the experiences of deprivation in the 1930s later prompted millions of women to pursue "a more prosperous life style," one based in considerable measure on their employment outside the home. After watching their husbands suffer the effects of unemployment and underemployment and their families endure the burden of want, legions of American women took advantage of wartime and postwar job opportunities to strengthen their households' economic position. The effect of the depression on women was hardly unique. Millions of men, also suffering from a decade of deprivation, hoped for a future in which they might realize the promise of affluence their memories of the 1920s had kept alive.[5]

The depression shaped the world that emerged after 1945 in other ways too. The ideological battles of the 1930s and 1940s influenced how American intellectuals later thought about the nature of mass consumer society. Celebrations of the common folk and concerns about totalitarianism during the 1930s made democratic standards and mass culture central issues in American social criticism in the mid-twentieth century. Moreover, the New Deal policies, modest as they sometimes seem in retrospect, and powerless as they were to pull the nation out of the depression, provided important initiatives whose expansion underwrote the emergence of the consumer society. For example, federal support for home mortgages, begun in the 1930s and enlarged in later years, helped create the suburbs so central to American life in the 1950s. Postwar expansion of New Deal social welfare programs, especially social security, minimum wage, and unemployment benefits, assisted families in achieving a more adequate standard of living and producers in reaching a wider market. The shoring up of the banking system gave households a secure way to accumulate savings for homes, automobiles, and education. New approaches to fiscal and monetary policies would offer a later generation stability and confidence in the nation's economy. Indeed, as Alan Brinkley has argued, in the late 1930s a shift in New Deal thinking began to reorient American politics toward a liberalism in which consumption was seen as critical to the economy.[6]

How America Lives: Consumers on the Eve of World War II

Just before the nation's entry into World War II, the standard of living for most Americans stood poised between the stringencies of the depression and the affluence of the postwar world. Examining patterns of household spending helps illuminate this fact. A *Ladies' Home Journal* survey, begun in the summer of 1939 and written (but not signed) by J. C. Furnas—*How America Lives*, published as a book in 1941—shows how Americans reported spending their money. In it we see how the magazine connected its middle-class readers' standard of living with the nation's strength as it prepared to enter the war.[7]

The data the writers and editors of *Ladies' Home Journal* collected, and the assertions they made, were not problem-free. Those who carried out the survey revealed little consciousness of how differentially people from varied walks of life would tailor their responses to the visiting editors' expectations. The editors depicted lives in which neither strong religious nor political commitments commanded their subjects' attention. They also minimized the power of ethnic allegiances. At a time of dramatic gains for labor unions, especially those achieved by the Congress of Industrial Organizations, the editors included no family headed by an employed unskilled or semi-skilled worker. At a time when millions of African Americans and children of turn-of-the-century immigrants were swelling the ranks of industrial unions, the person picked for the study who came closest to being a factory worker was a white-collar Anglo-Saxon tool inspector who stood "halfway between the rank and file on the assembly lines and the crack craftsmen in the plant."

Raising another issue of selectivity, the only black family were dirt poor southerners; one African American reader complained that her people "would feel much happier" had the study also included "a colored family that was doing all right and self-respectingly up north." Also missing from the sample were people who lived alone or couples who cohabited without the sanction of marriage, people whom the editors of a family magazine had little interest in reaching.[8]

Despite their shortcomings, the findings provide a snapshot of how Americans spent their money in a year between the depression and America's entry into World War II. Determined both to attract significant attention and to gather information on a representative sample, the magazine dedicated very considerable resources to the project. Examining the ways in which the editors discussed the households studied reveals the connection some contemporaries made between democracy and the American standard of living, albeit in a way different from Mumford.[9]

Brought together in *How America Lives*, the profiles of sixteen households offer vivid portraits of different American families. They provide detailed budgets for all except the richest and poorest of the families. The editors included four very poor families in their sample, even though "there was no place for the fashion editor to plan a wardrobe," one remarked, "when the problem was to get enough clothes to keep covered." Occasionally they let the subjects speak for themselves, but often they breathlessly summarized the families' worries, hopes, and dreams. The book describes the way of life of a wide range of households—from a wealthy couple earning over $100,000 (about $1.2 million in today's terms) to an African American sharecropping family of sixteen living in Mississippi, a state that provided no public relief, whose cash income was $26 (about $300 today); from a newly married couple in which the husband was in his first job and the wife was pregnant with their first child to two couples who had retired to St. Petersburg, Florida; and from a family in Burlington, Vermont, to one in Cucamonga, California.[10]

Mr. and Mrs. Thomas E. Wilson were easily the wealthiest family the magazine discussed. The son of Scotch-Irish immigrants who settled on a farm in Ontario, Canada, "packing-magnate" Thomas Wilson had risen to the position of chairman of the board of Wilson and Co., a business his thirty years of work had raised "from a pup." His wife, Elizabeth, from an upper-middle-class American family, did not have to worry about budgeting their ample income, although the Wilsons were able to estimate that 29 percent of their income went to charity and 16 percent to taxes. An additional 20 percent went for upkeep of their residences. Only in the fall and winter did they spend much time in their "baronial town house," a "massive, three-story, battlemented and mullioned graystone" building located on Chicago's "conservative old South Side." Mrs. Wilson's ninety-two-year-old mother, "the most ardent moviegoer in the family," spent most of the year there, along with a housekeeper and a "companion-maid." Most of the rest of the time the Wilsons lived in a house on their 1,100-acre "farm" north of Lake Forest, an estate that was like a "private kingdom," with so many "farmers and wives and families, farmhands, stablemen and gardeners" that it had its own school, general store, and railroad station. The Wilsons had a personal staff of six ("butler-houseman, chauffeur, cook, two maids, and a laundress") and three cars (a Cadillac limousine, a Lincoln coupe, and a Packard convertible).[11]

The Wilsons led active lives. Elizabeth Wilson supervised the preparations for the parties they gave and attended a round of club meetings and lectures. When not engaged in corporate affairs or in raising his world-famous herd of shorthorn cattle, Thomas Wilson attended to his charities. His favorite, which combined business, pleasure, and philanthropy, was the 4-H Clubs, the cattle-breeding section of which he presided over like a "patron saint and Lady Bountiful." "Businesslike about his enthusiasms," Wilson vacationed for a month each year on a New Mexico cattle ranch he had purchased as "a further excuse" for continuing to visit the region after he and another corporate president decided that there was no more game to hunt in the area. Thomas considered the ranch both an investment and a means of educating him about the ranchers who supplied his company with beef. Elizabeth spent a month or so during the winter with her mother in Florida. The Wilsons also enjoyed their time with their children, a recently married son who was president of the corporation and a daughter whose husband was now superintendent of the company factory, and four granddaughters.[12]

Ladies' Home Journal pictured the Wilsons as people whose way of life was essentially no different from that of the magazine's middle-class readers. The furniture in their country house was "of prime, sturdy quality but notably haphazard." They did not try "prissily to match" the towels that hung in the bathrooms. The "old-fashioned homeliness" of one room "counteracted" a "suspicion of expensive slickness" in another. The granddaughters, who called Mr. Wilson "Cowpa," knew how to sew, and Mrs. Wilson still did the mending and shopping herself. "If they wanted to keep up with the wealthier Joneses in terms of sables and private planes," the magazine writer noted, "they easily could, for they are definitely rich." Instead, for them "pots of money have meant merely an opportunity to live exactly as they—and not the Astorbilts—like to live; comfortably, that is, sensibly and with a cheering lack of swank."[13]

Alvin Nugent ("Bo") McMillin and his family, though hardly living like the Wilsons, nonetheless got along quite comfortably on the husband's earnings as the football coach at the University of Indiana (see table 1). The son of an unsuccessful shopkeeper who became a day laborer to support his family of twelve, Bo, a former All-American quarterback, had a "stormy" childhood in Fort Worth, Texas. His wife, Kathryn, grew up in Gallatin, Missouri, where her family had produced three generations of successful lawyers. The McMillin household included four children—Fleurette ("Bo-peep"), age seventeen, who attended a boarding school; Jere, age eight; Janey, age seven; and Nugent ("Nuge"), age five. Their nearly $10,000 income came from Bo's salary and speaking fees. The McMillins put the difference between income and living expenses into savings bonds. They lived comfortably on a little over $7,000, an amount that allowed Kathryn never to stint on food and to maintain a "sizeable and smart wardrobe" so she could play her "part in university social life." Their house, purchased for $14,000 two years earlier out of savings, contained a "quietly luxurious" living room and dining room

Table 1. Annual budget of the McMillin family, 1940

Item	Cost	Percentage
Food	$1020.00	14.48
Milk	144.00	2.04
Clothes (except Bo-peep)	750.00	10.65
Furniture (annual replacements)	100.00	1.42
Upkeep of house and lot	100.00	1.42
Maid	384.00	5.45
Laundry	144.00	2.04
Car upkeep	180.00	2.56
Annual payment for new car on trade-in	300.00	4.26
Fuel	130.00	1.85
Electricity	180.00	2.56
Phone	72.00	1.02
Magazines, newspapers, books	75.00	1.06
Medical and dentists' bills	150.00	2.13
Contributions, charities	150.00	2.13
Bo-peep ($5 monthly allowance, transportation, clothes, school expenses)	600.00	8.52
Small children's allowances (Jere $.25 weekly, Janey $.15 weekly, including nickel for church)	20.80	0.03
Entertainment	100.00	1.42
Country-club dues	45.00	0.64
Taxes (real-estate, personal-property, income)	600.00	8.52
Insurance premiums	1800.00	25.55
TOTAL	**$7044.80**	

SOURCE: J. C. Furnas and the Staff of the *Ladies' Home Journal, How America Lives* (New York: Henry Holt, 1941), 219.

and a kitchen that was "a housewife's dream of enameled cabinets and electrical appliances."[14]

Kathryn divided her time between taking care of the children, running the house, and participating in the activities of women's clubs. She and Bo had a full round of social activities, including a neighborhood badminton club, a regular bridge game with a couple from across the street, and university social occasions for which people got "dressed up to the nines." Because he was "too much of a family man," Bo did not often go to the country club, but he did regularly play billiards with two friends who were academic deans. During football season, he went to a movie every night, the only thing that would keep him "from the breaking point of tension." Once or twice a year, Kathryn took the children to visit her family, leaving Bo to wander around Bloomington "like a lost soul, haunting the movies and eating his meals dolefully at the University Union." Occasionally, Bo and Kathryn traveled together, her presence turning a professional trip "into a vacation lark."[15]

The McMillins are presented as a happy American family for whom Bo's football skills made obtainable "necessities, solid comforts and such luxuries as they are able to afford." Like the Wilsons (and unlike most of the other families in the series), they seemed to want for nothing that they did not already possess. Indeed, the only thing that ever prevented Bo from going out and purchasing the latest gadget was his irritation at the fact that it would soon be out of date. Their lives revolved around football, home, family, neighborhood, and community. It did not bother Bo that Kathryn demonstrated no interest in politics. Neither a "comfortable" income nor an active social life, the magazine reported, "weaned any of them away from old-time family living." "Tradition" was the word the writers used to describe their round of life—for Bo, mowing the lawn, voting without regard to party labels, and vowing to fight for his country if called upon to do so; for Kathryn, making those special dishes "that no mere maid can approach." Bo was "a man's man, sure of his niche in the world," who cheerfully admitted that he was "a born family man with the good luck to marry a girl who always had the sole ambition to be a homemaker." For him, "the best place and things in the world are the house he owns and the family that inhabit it." At night, Kathryn would watch the kids squeal and squirm as they romped with their father. Then, "at the proper moment," the writer reported, she "applies the quietus. They make a good team."[16]

If the McMillins represented an all-American family who responsibly handled their notoriety and comfortable income, the magazine picked the Aulden Griffins of Cedar Rapids, Iowa, to fit the formula of typical small city, midwestern America. Neither rich nor poor—an income of $2,000 placed them just below the top third of American households—they were representative of 6 million families at their income level "to whom dimes often seem thicker than the United States mint would approve." Their parents had made the shift from farm to town; Mr. Griffin's father was a dentist in Cedar Rapids and Mrs. Griffin's was a furniture salesman in Marshalltown. They lived with their two young children in a house for which they had spent $7,500, "every penny paid by their own hard work."[17]

They spent $1,860 a year (see table 2); with their income provided by the husband's job in the credit department of an engineering company, a position at which he worked "hard, long and keenly." Exercising prudence and determination, the Griffins were able to get by on such a budget, making major decisions in a family town meeting in which all four members had one vote—demonstrating the "insistence on flexible good manners between parents and offspring." The Griffins paid for automobiles and appliances with cash and did their own housework and repairs. They did not have substantial medical costs, in part because Mrs. Griffin kept "her whole family bursting with health" on a dollar a day for food. Mr. Griffin came home for lunch and had only one week's vacation, which the family used to take a "leisurely motor trip, eschewing the temptation to spend too much time and money at a lake resort." When the depression placed a more remunerative job beyond Mr. Griffin's grasp, they cut back by giving up a maid and their annual party. But hopes for better times kept alive the dream of a higher standard of living: a

Table 2. Annual budget of the Griffin family, 1939

Item	Cost	Percentage
Groceries	$375.00	20.16
Milk	50.00	2.69
Clothing	160.00	8.60
Furniture	35.00	1.88
Taxes	147.00	7.90
Fuel and light	160.00	8.60
Insurance	175.00	9.41
Transportation (gas, oil, depreciation, tires, and other)	250.00	13.44
Maintenance of health	35.00	1.88
Recreation	50.00	2.69
Church, community chest, etc.	18.00	0.97
Telephone	30.00	1.61
Newspapers, magazines	15.00	0.81
Assistance to relatives	360.00	19.35
TOTAL	**$1860.00**	

SOURCE: J. C. Furnas and the Staff of the *Ladies' Home Journal*, *How America Lives* (New York: Henry Holt, 1941), 45.

new tool kit and a woodworking shop for Mr. Griffin and more room to store her collection of vintage clothing for his wife. In the meantime they worked around the house, an activity they found economical, fun, and "happily companionable." Realistic economies made it possible for the family to save money for insurance and to feed the pet alligator, rhesus monkey, guinea pigs, white rats, goldfish, birds, and cats, as well to provide for "other peculiarly important things."[18]

They kept themselves busy in other ways. Irene Griffin did all of the housework, served as president of the local women's club, directed amateur dramatics, chaperoned dances, attended movies, concerts, and civic meetings. Aulden tinkered with cars, worked on home improvements, and listened to popular music, shunning free classical concerts even though he was proud of the "civic spirit" that made them possible. He went in for one sport, "aquaplaning behind a motorboat" on a nearby river. Together they played "homey games like Chinese checkers and jackstraws" and enjoyed the Congenial Hundred, their dancing club which met once a week and whose only rule was one forbidding the drinking of alcohol.[19]

The magazine pictured the Griffins as a typical Middle American couple. They attended church with their children, voted in all elections, and took "a keen proprietary pride" in their city. They tempered their penchant for doing things themselves with an appreciation for the value of their own time and effort. They assumed responsibilities without complaining, confident that they could continue to make their own way in the world. "Just as in aquaplaning" it did not occur to Mr. Griffin that he "might fall off the leaping board," so Mrs. Griffin would "find time and energy—without grim-lipped driving," to do well what she had to do. Like their ancestors who were farmers, they "honored so many of the self-reliant American traditions." The Griffins, Furnas concluded, were "an American family—neither old-fashioned nor new—with a roof over their heads and jobs to do and rich relationships among themselves."[20]

The editors chose the Stanley A. Cases of Dearborn, Michigan, to represent households headed by a skilled worker with middle-class aspirations and an income near the national median. Stanley Case, the son of a skilled carpenter from Plymouth, Pennsylvania, who had tried to launch his own business, earned the automobile industry average wage for his work at the Cadillac plant in Detroit. A loyal and reliable employee, he had steady but not always full employment throughout the depression, bringing in $1,600 a year in 1940, an amount slightly supplemented by income from savings.[21]

Before she married, Edith Case, the daughter of farmers from Perth, Ontario, had worked as a bookkeeper and an assistant buyer in a department store. With the birth of the first of two children, she gave up an income that

exceeded her husband's and began to manage the household budget of
$1,600 with "dash and skill" (see table 3). Edith was able to keep the budget
balanced without skimping on essentials. She put up several hundred cans of
fruits and vegetables, enabling the family to eat well and avoid costly medical
bills. The family paid cash for their appliances—refrigerator, washer, vacuum
cleaner, sewing machine, and radio. They had purchased their furniture in
the early years of their marriage, before they had children and when they were
both bringing home paychecks. Stanley carpooled to work, so the whole
family was able to get by with one seven-year-old Pontiac.[22]

Stanley's principal activities were bowling and going to the movies, pas-
times he had not pursued since the death of his parents. Edith's moments of
relaxation came from her weekly neighborhood handicraft club, which this
year was crocheting rugs. As a result of childhood religious experiences with
"the sternest of old-fashioned traditions" in the Methodist and Baptist
churches, husband and wife relaxed on Sunday mornings rather than attend
church. Likewise, politics remained "outside their immediate realm of values," with their only strong political response being "an instinct against
shouting extremes" like those of the anti-Semitic radio priest Father Charles
Coughlin. Most of their fun came "on the cheap," with "memorable occasions" bearing "no relation to expense." As a family they went ice-skating and
listened to the radio. Stanley and Edith got "plenty of excitement" from board
games, with Chinese checkers their favorite. In the summer heat they'd spend
some time at the cottage of a relative or would go on "modest weekend motor
jaunts." The Cases, however, were hardly without aspirations for a better life.

Table 3. Annual budget of the Case family, 1940

Item	Cost	Percentage
Food	$468.00	29.25
Rent	420.00	26.25
Fuel and light	114.00	7.12
Transportation (family car, $6 per mo., $72; Mr. Case's transportation, $10 per mo., $120)	192.00	12.00
Insurance	120.00	7.50
Maintenance of health (Mr. Case's dental bill)	35.00	2.19
Newspapers, magazines	12.50	0.78
Clothing	150.00	9.37
Miscellaneous (charity, recreation, etc.)	88.50	5.53
TOTAL	**$1600.00**	

SOURCE: J. C. Furnas and the Staff of the *Ladies' Home Journal, How America Lives* (New York:
Henry Holt, 1941), 97.

They planned that some of their insurance would obtain for their children the education their father had missed when he left high school before graduating. Stanley was taking night courses in technical subjects in the hope of raising his rank and pay. The Cases' biggest dream was to move out of their present house, which had only a small living room, two "tiny" bedrooms, and a "minuscule" kitchen that lacked enough "room to swing a cat." To enjoy the comfort of a larger house and to turn rent payments into "an asset instead of just vanishing," they planned to build a home of their own with $4,400 of borrowed money.[23]

The dominant impression the magazine offered of the Cases was of a family who made their own way without complaining and without relying on others for help. Although the new house would "give them a great kick," the magazine reported, "it won't be essential to happiness for these good-natured experts in making do because money has to stretch a long way." When Edith commented that they never used anyone else's money (a statement apparently contradicted by their plans to borrow for a new house) and were "having a perfectly swell time right here and now!" her husband nodded in agreement. "The confident smiles they exchange," the writer noted, made "it plain that fretting for the moon is no part of this family's daily routine." The "mighty warmth and geniality between parents and kids," the author concluded, helped them "get a full year's supply of awfully satisfactory living" on their income, "even in a house too small for the job."[24]

The poorest of the families were the Braceys, a three-generation black sharecropping household of sixteen who lived in a three-room shack just north of Vicksburg, Mississippi. They were one of thirty families living on the ten thousand acres owned by "the man in the big house," which stood "white and shady, with a shiny new car in the driveway." To the sharecroppers, mere survival was a test of endurance. Because the state offered no public relief, Henry Bracey, whom the plantation owner thought was "a sober, hardworking" man, in 1939 had cleared only $26 in cash, a sum he hoped an allotment of extra acreage in 1940 might double. Additional help came from $75 "'furnish' from the plantation" in the winter and occasional labor at the rate of 90 cents per day for the father and his eldest son. Even with cowpeas and cold beancake as their staple daily meal, often the only one they had, Estella Bracey was rarely able to put enough to eat on the table. Only what food they could glean from several pigs, two cows, five hens, and a garden patch kept them from "obvious and literal starvation." Their shack, inadequately protected from cold and insects, was sparse: sixteen people shared four beds and used gunnysacks for blankets. Out in back stood a doorless and almost roofless privy. Their possessions included "an old gutted victrola and an icebox which has never known a piece of ice." A small red truck was the only thing that "even remotely" resembled a toy. Nor was adequate clothing available for the children: the magazine writer noted one young boy "whose miniature black bottom sticks candidly out of a pair of cotton pants that long ago refused to hold together."[25]

"Modern life," the author of the profile commented, "practically never distracts the Braceys from the sheer problem of eating." Few of the children had ever been to Vicksburg, seen a movie, or listened to a radio. Of all the family members, only the older children could read. The lack of shoes prevented the children from attending school in the winter. Going down the road to church on Sunday provided the main contact with the world beyond their home. Yet somehow, the magazine reported, the family went on. Mr. Bracey worried about the children's lack of shoes, "but not fervently," Furnas reported. He "never knew anything much different from this hand-to-mouth existence, with the mouth hungry and the hand slow and fumbling." His wife was still able to "laugh like a reckless girl when the outsider sees nothing whatsoever to suggest laughter." The children remained "astonishingly healthy" and full of "devilment," "tumbling about on the shaky porch like a Stephen Foster song." The inclusion of the Braceys in a book on styles of life in America testified to the impact of the Great Depression on middle-class consciousness. In many respects the article did little to gloss over the harshness of the family's situation. Yet the pictures of the mother laughing like a girl, the father not worrying too much, and the children playing like characters in a Stephen Foster song offered stereotyped images of poor black folk who were too childlike to deal more effectively with their situation.[26]

How America Lives revealed a consumer society in transition. A chasm filled with goods, experiences, and services separated the world the book described and the one tens of millions of Americans would experience sixty years later at the turn of the twenty-first century. In the book there are no television sets, 800 telephone numbers, air conditioners, frozen foods, jet airplanes, theme parks, national credit cards, expensive medical procedures, or computers. Yet in the early 1940s, if the United States was no longer a nation where respectability depended on ethnically based traits and aspirations, it was clearly on its way to becoming a country where possession of a standard package of consumer goods was the key to community membership. To some extent the *Ladies' Home Journal* equated how to live with how to consume and self-respect with the presence of at least the emblems of a middle-class way of life. Yet both new and old elements characterized the dreamed-of, if not the achieved, standard of living of most of the families portrayed: the ownership of a home, automobile, and small appliances; full involvement with a market economy; more limited participation in a mass consumer culture; pursuit of purposeful and "hard-won leisure" that remained centered on the family, neighborhood, and community; participation in face-to-face social life; and enjoyment of recreation and vacations that involved neither considerable time, expense, nor travel.[27]

The authors were aware that consumption patterns were in transition. When the book described how a farm woman and her daughter got "together for a good stint of fine stitching on the old-time patchwork quilt they will show at the county fair next fall—working on it by electric light," the authors returned to a theme that appears again and again: how "inextricably do their busy lives weave old and new together." The families may have been avid consumers, but the study pictures them as mostly debt-free, prudent, self-sufficient, thrifty, careful people who paid cash for major purchases, husbands, wives, and children working cooperatively and amicably in largely democratic households. In a manner doubtless shaped by the depression, the households were as much defensive as they were acquisitive. For the most part, American families seemed, Furnas reported, "almost surprisingly modest in their demands upon life," holding precious what they had and not wanting much more than was obtainable. Both the authors and the families saw new kinds of consumer goods and services not as self-indulgent luxuries but as aids in supporting a family-centered way of life. Indeed, the terms used to talk about expensive items were those of comfort, modesty, and convenience. Thus, in one instance, a large lakefront property where the extended family vacationed was not "an extravagance" but "a kind of patriarchal village" and "as sound an asset as an investor could hope for."[28]

Unlike many earlier household budget studies, *How America Lives* was remarkably free of moral judgments about how people spent their money. The study hardly lacked an ideological strategy, however. While the Nazis were marching across western Europe, the authors hammered home the message that the American way of life was what made the nation capable of resisting the "violence, poverty and spiritually bankrupt hatreds that are wrecking Europe." Although the book contained plenty of evidence of class, regional, gender, and racial divisions, neither the subjects nor the writers acknowledged any social fault lines running through the society. Noting the Griffins' awareness of mansions they would never own and a country club they could not afford to join, a writer stated that "envy apparently never occurs to them."[29]

Rather, the authors tried to depict America, "the last stronghold of democracy," as a nation of neighbors. Indeed, the Office of War Information translated the book into at least eight languages and distributed it to U.S. allies. The fact that everyone knew his or her neighbors, Furnas asserted, was not enough. "Each of us ought to know all his 130,000,000 neighbors in our American democracy," he declared, anticipating charges that the reporters were invading people's privacy. By turning every family into "the family next door," it would be possible to demonstrate what democracy was. "These people are as real, warm and American as pumpkin pie right out of the oven," he commented. "They are yourselves. And you are democracy." Laying bare the lives of a full range of households made it more possible for Americans to "all get along as if they had known each other all their lives. And what's more, feel as if they had." With America as a nation of friendly and familiar households, "the hatredmongers, shirt merchants, class exploiters, race and religion baiters, who are at least symptoms of the same disease that has Europe near death, will find so many fewer likely champs to take."[30]

In portraying how Americans lived, the writers thus revealed what they believed was worth preserving in American life. "The extraordinary mixture of ancestries," the lack of class bitterness, and the assumed absence of privilege would help prevent the nation from becoming a breeding ground for extremists. Nor was it likely that totalitarianism would grow where people were optimistic, self-reliant, cooperative, commonsensical, unpretentious, and mildly apolitical. Above all, it was the strength of American families that knit together the fabric of national life. The editors underscored their belief that it was the "instinct for good-humored family co-operation" which ensured that those portrayed would be "most peculiar citizen[s] of a totalitarian state." The family portraits included wives who, masking their out-of-home achievements, were presented as cheerful, uncomplaining, hardworking, and self-sacrificing homemakers. The study depicted the women of the Minnesota farm family as typical of many others: "brisk workers and proud of their skill in housecraft and anything but sorry for themselves." Husbands worked hard for a living and helped create in the home an atmosphere of "natural harmony." And it was the connection between the family and the community that formed the sinews of democracy. Tempting as it is for us to see them as enmeshed in a mass consumer culture, the study instead pictured its subjects as people whose lives focused on family, friends, neighborhood, voluntary associations, and community. What compensated for the existence of poverty and inequality was the presence of "lots of chins up in these United States and lots of neighborly good feeling."[31]

World War II and the Transformation of the Standard of Living

For most of these families, World War II interrupted their lives and the postwar world transformed their patterns of consumption. The war ended the Great Depression and inaugurated the longest period of sustained economic growth in American history, stretching from the late 1930s until at least the early 1970s. During the early 1940s, the federal government helped bolster the economy by borrowing and spending massive amounts of money to finance the war effort. Between 1939 and 1945, when prices rose 30 percent, the federal budget grew more than tenfold, from $8.8 to $98.3 billion. By 1945, the national debt, which had increased in six years from $40.4 to $258.7 billion, equaled almost thirty times the central government's prewar expenditures. During the war, the GNP increased in real dollars at an average annual rate of 9.2 percent. In current prices, disposable personal income grew from $70 billion in 1939 to $150 billion in 1945. Economic growth, spurred largely by military spending, helped reduce the unemployment rolls from just over 9.5 million to just under 1 million and underwrote the creation of over 17 million new jobs, including those for over 6 million women who entered the paid workforce.[32]

After at least a decade of straitened economic circumstances, millions of Americans were enjoying their newfound affluence. Even though production for military purposes accounted for a significant proportion of economic growth, the nonmilitary sectors improved over their low point in the depression. One community study reported a feeling of exhilaration among most of the local inhabitants, which growing incomes had helped induce. In record numbers Americans were spending their money at grocery markets, department stores, and movie theaters. The greatest increases in expenditures—items for which spending more than doubled between 1939 and 1945—were for food, alcoholic beverages, women's clothing, jewelry and watches, telephone service, private hospitals, health insurance, public transportation, nondurable toys, and sports supplies. Changes in the standard of living, rationing, and rising prices accounted for shifting patterns of consumption.[33]

Throughout the war, budget experts recommended economies that rationing, taxation, and patriotism made necessary or desirable. They especially focused on decreasing expenditures for domestic service, automobile usage, personal care, home entertainment, toll calls, and commercial amusements, and called for less frequent replacement of automobiles, furnishings, appliances, and clothing. Yet, unlike budget experts in World War I who saw the emergency as an opportunity for permanently changing consumption patterns, professionals during World War II tended to view restraint as a temporary expedient—a deferral of purchases of durable consumer goods until the war's end. In addition, experts acknowledged that their recommendations for sacrifice assumed the unlikely situation that longer working hours and overtime pay would not increase household income. Moreover, they noted one ironic effect of rationing: because of the nature of the rationing program, lower income groups had to purchase more expensive food items such as fresh fish and vegetables. Thus, despite shortages, the American diet had improved significantly as millions of families increased their intake of meat, eggs, and fresh foods. Wartime conditions brought about other changes. Gasoline shortages restricted automobile travel and fostered home- and neighborhood-centered entertainments. Friends and family members listened to their radios, went to nearby movie theaters, and played cards and board games. More and more Americans settled down in the evening with a good book. The Pocket Book Company, founded in 1939, made authors from William Shakespeare to Agatha Christie available to masses of readers.[34]

By fostering economic growth and by making income distribution somewhat more equitable, wartime conditions helped ever greater numbers of Americans raise themselves above subsistence level. In 1939, the top 5 percent of the population received almost 27 percent of disposable income, a figure that fell to less than 17 percent in 1945. The poorer the family's status, the greater the wartime percentage gains in income: from bottom to top, the earnings of families by quintile grew 68, 59, 36, 30, and 20 percent. As usually happens in such circumstances, stories circulated about the extravagance of the newly affluent, especially skilled workers. In actuality, of course, economic growth neither turned the United States into an economic democracy nor eliminated poverty. Indeed, one 1944 study estimated that almost one out of every seven Americans lived "constantly in a borderland between subsistence and privation, where even the utmost thrift and caution do not suffice to make ends meet." Another study revealed that 31 percent of American families had "unsatisfactory" nutrition and another 32 percent had diets that were "marginal" in quality.[35]

In important ways, wartime changes started or accelerated the trends that would shape postwar America. World War II was a turning point in the role the military-industrial complex played in the U.S. economy. Military expenditures rose quickly from modest levels to which they never returned after the war ended. Expenditures for national defense, standing at $1.5 billion in 1940, quadrupled by 1941 and then quadrupled again by 1942. In the next year they more than doubled and then reached their wartime peak of $81.6 billion in 1945. As a share of federal spending, the figures are equally dramatic. Starting off at 15.6 percent in 1940, funds allocated to national defense reached 85.7 percent of total federal expenditures in 1945. In percentage terms they did not fall to twice their 1940 level until 1950, then they once again began to rise.

Government expenditures for military installations and production facilities drew hundreds of thousands of families south and west, giving them exposure to the places where they would settle after hostilities ended. Mobile, Norfolk, San Diego, Los Angeles, San Francisco, Charleston, and Seattle were the cities whose surrounding areas experienced the most dramatic influx. The Golden State, with its considerable share of military bases and federal contracts, was especially attractive: between 1940 and 1945 its population increased by almost 2 million, and by the end of the war, its per capita income of $1,740 was the highest in the nation.

Despite these trends, wartime America struggled with issues of sacrifice, obligation, and fairness in myriad ways. Labor and management each asserted its centrality to winning the war. Corporate executives hitched their wagons to claims that their expertise and resources, especially if given both free rein and government contracts, were crucial to defeating the enemy. Unions, fresh from their gains in the 1930s, knew how essential their members were but worried about efforts, in the name of national emergency, to curtail their right to strike. For our purposes, however, what is important is the way in which the government and Madison Avenue linked the preservation of the American way of life to consumer culture. Military necessity forced the government to urge citizens to help the war effort by curtailing consumption and reusing what they did buy. Tens of millions of families saved toothpaste tubes because they contained tin and fat, which were important in making nitroglycerin. In order to save wool for soldiers' uniforms, manufacturers eliminated cuffs on men's trousers and shortened women's skirts. By 1942, the government had adopted a far-reaching policy of rationing, one predicated on what Bentley has described as "the equal distribution of high-status and familiar" goods. The federal Office of Price Administration (OPA) issued coupons that consumers used to obtain shoes, gasoline, sugar, dairy products, canned goods, and alcohol.[36]

The government also used tax policy and bond drives to support the war and curtail consumption. To help finance the war and moderate inflation, the government sold $185.7 billion worth of bonds, which millions of Americans bought instead of new appliances or houses. To persuade Americans to save rather than invest, the government embarked on an unprecedented marketing campaign, selling common sacrifice so that, as Lawrence R. Samuel has noted, it became a "secular religion" which promised to minimize class consciousness, promote pluralism, revive democratic capitalism, and foster postwar affluence.[37]

Mumford's Call for Chastened Consumption

Of all those who wrote about the war as part of a struggle to chasten consumption, no one was more passionate in his commitments or more thoroughgoing in his analysis than Lewis Mumford. On the eve of the war, Mumford was one of the nation's leading public intellectuals, a widely read critic who wrote on architecture, cities, regional planning, and American culture. His *Technics and Civilization* (1934) and *The Culture of Cities* (1938) earned him a well-deserved (and enduring) reputation for his immense learning and trenchant critiques. With his wife and two children, he spent most of his time in the village of Amenia, New York, eighty miles north of Manhattan, although between 1938 and 1945 he also resided in Palo Alto and New York City. As U.S. participation in World War II approached and then intensified, Mumford used an attack on consumer culture and excessive materialism as an essential component of an emerging defense of American democracy and humanistic values. Like the *Ladies' Home Journal* study, he linked self-restraint in consumption with the strengthening of the political order. Unlike the editors of that publication, however, Mumford was critical of the American standard of living and believed that the war provided an opportunity to vanquish excess materialism once and for all. Like other interventionists, Mumford felt that a democratic society, challenged by fascism, had to rest its case on something more heroic and cohesive than a liberalism that placed such heavy emphasis on the pursuit of materialistic self-gratification.[38]

During the 1930s, Mumford had hailed the arrival of a new economy based on restraint, proportion, and stability. In 1930, a year after the stock market crash, he advocated "a basic economic communism" that would provide everyone with elemental physical needs and time for leisure. With life, not comfort, as the primary social goal, people could find meaning in "culture: a maturing mind, a ripening character, an increasing sense of mastery and fulfillment, a higher integration of all one's powers in a social personality; a larger capacity for intellectual interests and emotional enjoyments, for more complex and subtle states of mind." Four years later, in his magisterial examination of world history, *Technics and Civilization*, he envisioned the replacement of an age overcommitted to technology, capitalism, materialism, and growth by the emergence of a humane, life-affirming economy based on the values of regionalism, community, and restraint.[39]

By the spring of 1938, as Hitler threatened to take over the Sudetenland, Mumford had emerged as a passionate advocate of U.S. entry into World War II as the only way to defeat fascism and preserve democracy. In the late 1930s and early 1940s, he cast his response to the world crisis in ways that linked a strengthened democracy to a purged materialism. He shared his commitment to interventionism with other leading intellectuals, including Waldo Frank, Reinhold Niebuhr, and Archibald MacLeish. Puzzled and angered over the reluctance of others on the left to support the nation's entry into the war, Mumford put forth arguments that connected an attack on consumer culture with a call for a toughened liberalism.[40]

An economy built on "the expansion of pecuniary values and private power," he declared in an August 1939 article in the *New Republic*, had to give way to one grounded in "the need for balance, intensive cultivation, stability." He believed that America had already begun to shift from an emphasis on the demands of the individual consumer to a commitment to public well-being, "collective demands, expressed in goods and services that are supplied by the community to all its citizens." Provision of public services and facilities—housing, parks, schools, museums, highways, and theaters— would challenge and eventually displace "capitalist ideology." One consequence would be increased economic equity, "whole milk for everybody" instead of "cream to the few, whole milk to the middle classes, and a blue watery residue to the majority of farmers and industrial workers, agricultural laborers and slaves."[41]

As Mumford became a more outspoken advocate of war, he grounded his case for democracy in the vitality of the "self-governing, self-acting, and self-respecting person." In *Faith for Living* (1940), the first draft of which he composed in ten intense days just after the fall of France in June 1940, Mumford noted that only a democracy could stand against both fascism and communism, since totalitarianism attracted people who had so little sense of themselves that they were "waiting from moment to moment for the party rubber stamp." No longer could the United States justify itself, he wrote, by substituting "bread and circuses" for "justice." The concern for "profits and power and special privileges," rather than for helping to "preserve democratic values and personal liberties," had "vitiated and corrupted and now desperately endangered our whole civilization." His was a vision of the simple, noble life for middle-class Americans, based less on a redistribution of resources than on a vanishing of "all that is represented by" the expenditures of the wealthy on items such as art works, yachts, and lavish entertaining. Being among "the last stout survivors on a sinking ship," Americans had to rediscover or reinterpret their deepest commitments, "to lay the foundations of a world in which life—love, freedom, justice, truth—will once more be sacred." Essential to the task of reinvigorating a democratic faith was the substitution of spiritual for material pleasures. "The fundamental values of a true community," wrote Mumford, reside "in love, poetry, disinterested thought, the free use of the imagination, the pursuit of non-utilitarian activities, the production of non-profitmaking goods, the enjoyment of non-consumable wealth."[42]

Mumford wanted to cleanse America of its materialism. This would serve both to answer those for whom the collapse of Western economies in the 1930s enhanced the appeal of alternative social systems and to counter pacifists who could find no grounds for fighting to preserve a way of life. The commitment to win the war, he hoped, would transform an economy of comfort into an economy of sacrifice. If "in times of peace and plenty" justice demanded "equality of life-sustenance and leisure," then "times of hardship and war" demanded "equality of sacrifice." Moreover, he hoped that wartime conditions might ensure "fruitful and refined leisure" or "the good life itself" in the postwar period. More than emergency conditions, however, justified the abandonment of material pleasure. In a world of monotonous and deadening work, leisure and consumption were chiefly compensations, "modes of passive acceptance and ritualistic vacuity." With "the restoration of manual labor," pleasure and culture would shift from being commercially purchasable to being genuinely enjoyable.[43]

For Mumford, the quest for justice and victory underscored the importance of an economy based on hardship. To strengthen democracy, Americans had to abandon their desire for an illusory affluence that diverted people's attention "from the realities of living." The birthright of the American people was not "a life of material abundance" purchasable in stores but one of "comradeship, art and love," experiences achievable outside the marketplace. "The economy of sacrifice," Mumford wrote, "turns the economy of comfort upside down," as "minus becomes plus" and vice versa. These guidelines were clear: "provide everything that is essential for *life*; but nothing beyond that; nothing for sale, for show, for imitative expenditure of the class above." During the war Americans would have to curb their expenditures on cosmetics, chewing gum, tobacco, advertising, "pulp magazines, high bred dog kennels," refrigerators, automobiles, and amusement parks so that the nation could afford military defense as well as scientific research, "responsible scholarship," education, and facilities for communal recreation. The economy of sacrifice would make life more difficult for the middle class and for the rich. With the survival of civilization at stake, emphasis on "full production and well-apportioned consumption" would lead to "social regeneration" and industrial reconstruction based on commitments to family, land, and an integrated self.[44]

Once the United States entered the war in December 1941, Mumford continued to argue for chastened consumption. He hailed American participation in the war for providing democratic peoples with "the conditions necessary for their regeneration and their renewal." No longer living in an "expanding society," Americans now had to find national self-justification in nonmaterialistic values. World War II provided the preconditions for a new culture "responsive to human needs and human purposes." In contrast to those American leaders who were "already seeking to whet our appetites with visions" of a consumer paradise which would "flow forth" after the war, Mumford called on citizens to give up private comforts so there would be sufficient public funds to "build up the shattered economies of the less favored peoples and equalize advantages of life we can no longer claim for ourselves alone." The regeneration of American democracy had to "substitute for the energy and zeal and self-confidence of the fascist barbarian an even greater degree of energy and self-sacrifice on behalf of all our higher human values." Turning away from the dream of a "deceptive orgy of economic expansion," Americans in the postwar world would have to gird themselves "for at least a hundred years of heroic, unremitting effort, poor in physical comforts, but rich in political inventiveness, spiritual audacity, and human meaning, . . . The luxury liner, that symbol of our past civilization," Mumford concluded, "has been sunk. Mankind has taken to the lifeboats. Only those who can live on hardtack and steer by the stars will reach land."[45]

As one might expect, reality hardly matched his expectations. In many ways, the wartime experience did not provide the model for a postwar America whose polity and economy would be democratic. The nation did not adopt an economy of sacrifice that turned against commercialism and brought about fundamental social reconstruction. Like Americans of earlier generations who were disappointed when a national crisis did not turn their fellow citizens away from materialistic pursuits, Mumford felt saddened when he realized that the nation was about to defeat Nazism without curbing Mammon. Privately, he worried during the war that the pessimism and moralism of his position limited his influence. Yet he persisted in offering his jeremiads. As he observed in *The Condition of Man* (1944), the prosperity America witnessed during the war provided "dubious benefits," an "illusion of health," "an exorbitant demand for machines," and "a ruthless negation of non-mechanical goods, services, arts, interests." In other ways, however, wartime experiences offered a model for the future. His moral equivalent of war was a simplified life that incorporated industrial growth and community involvement. The energy and commitment of nurses, soldiers, and air raid wardens exemplified new definitions of citizenship that, once redirected, would help promote "peace-time co-operation." Americans could now learn how to simplify their lives without rationing, assume public responsibility without being drafted into armed service, and work for the unity of all peoples without seeking power and profit.[46]

As the war proceeded and the victory of the Allies seemed more certain, Mumford remained faithful to his vision of a new economic order. A "life-centered," balanced economy would produce whole, self-fulfilling people and provide real satisfactions and goods. Once again, in 1944, Mumford envisioned a "post-capitalist economy" involving a "better fulfillment of social need: a shift in expenditure from luxury-stimulating industries to the life-maintaining" ones, along with greater commitment to "civic, rather than private consumption." The central task of the postwar world, however, was something much more fundamental than the reconstruction of the Western economies. At an earlier critical juncture, in the middle of the eighteenth century, the Western world had taken a fateful turn. At the very moment when an economic surplus made it possible to satisfy nonmaterial yearnings, "the very ideals of leisure and culture were cast into disrepute—except when they could be turned to profit."[47]

Now, in the middle of the twentieth century, to fulfill the democratic ideal it was necessary to recognize both the limitations of material progress and the possibility of meeting the higher needs of all people. An era of equilibrium had replaced an age of expansion. It was at last possible for all to achieve the kind of human potential once available to only a few, "the fuller contribution of . . . vitalities and energies to the molding of more richly endowed and more fully expressive personalities." Material progress was important only to the extent that it would help "foster spiritual activity and promote spiritual growth" by drawing on the desire for "order, continuity, meaning, value, purpose, and design—needs out of which language and poesy and music and science and art and religion have grown." Protesting, among other things, the Nazi emphasis on efficiency and order, Mumford wrote of the importance of developing balanced, proportioned, and whole personalities, "a new race of pioneers, of deliberate amateurs." Reacting against totalitarianism, he argued that the regeneration of democratic societies must begin with the individual. Secretly longing to place "the burden of their own regeneration upon a savior," people had shied away from the fact that "each man and woman must first silently assume his own burden." Only the initial step, however, was personal. Without individual self-fulfillment, "no great betterment will take place in the social order. Once that change begins," he concluded optimistically, "everything is possible."[48]

Mumford's wartime vision exhibits parallels with what later writers would see as an excessive concentration on individual self-fulfillment. Indeed, compared with what he had written earlier, by 1944 he seems to have developed a concern with promoting individualism, personal growth, and self-expression. Nevertheless, what Mumford meant by self-fulfillment hardly made him a precursor of the human potential movement of the 1970s or an advocate of self-realization through commercial goods and experiences. He feared the stultifying qualities of mass society, which he connected with the rise of totalitarianism. Mumford's ultimate goal was a truly democratic society, peopled by vital and creative individuals who remained committed to "human co-operation and communion." He opposed achieving fulfillment principally through self-satisfaction and instead hoped that people would strive for higher goals, especially a liberating high culture and a democratic way of life. Indeed, if Mumford's writings foretell anything, it is a belief in promoting individualism that was neither selfish nor hedonistic and a commitment to avoid defending democracy on the grounds that it was uniquely capable of producing a high material standard of living.[49]

War and Sacrifice

Mumford was hardly alone in linking the revival of democracy with the curbing of materialism and capitalism. For example, in *The Children of Light and the Children of Darkness* (1944), Reinhold Niebuhr, the nation's leading Protestant theologian and a close friend of Mumford's, lamented the fact that modern capitalism had transformed liberalism's original commitment to "moderate and ordinate desires" into "the temptation to inordinate expressions of the possessive impulse." As the war began, in *Generation of Vipers* (1942), Philip Wylie asserted that "to many, it hardly seems worth while fighting to live until they can be assured that their percolators will live, along with their cars, synthetic roofing, and disposable diapers." Although people in the United States had decried the regimentation of totalitarian regimes, in fact mass production and mass culture had brought about "a national overspread of staleness, repetitiveness and sameness." Americans, "addled with a goods-identification," lacked "a lucid concept of self-preservation."[50]

Bruce Barton added his voice to the counsels of chastened consumption. He was a leading advertising executive whose influential book *The Man Nobody Knows* (1925) portrayed Jesus as a precursor of the modern salesman. Now, in the fall of 1943, Barton offered another of his therapeutic recipes for self-realization that, as Jackson Lears has noted, so typified his outlook. In the middle of the war he was concerned about a future in which the nation would bow "itself low before the twin images of National Income and Purchasing Power." Looking abroad to a postwar world in which Americans would export their gadgets, he wondered if the Arabs, Chinese, and Japanese were "going to enslave themselves to things—they who learned so long ago that through such servitude is found no satisfaction and no peace?" Rather than a materialistic postwar world, Barton hoped for one in which Americans would pursue "inner peace" and "spiritual security" through reading, loafing, thinking, and churchgoing.[51]

In contrast to these male voices, the cultural historian Caroline F. Ware well understood that she had to appeal to women who as consumers were responsible for a large percentage of spending decisions even though she never specifically gendered consumers. In *The Consumer Goes to War: A Guide to Victory on the Home Front* (1942), Ware called on consumers to support those who were risking their lives abroad. As "privates of the civilian army back home," American consumers had to be at their "battle stations twenty-four hours a day." Although they were used to struggling to keep up with the

Joneses, now "both we and the Joneses must 'keep down.'" To support the war effort, Ware urged her fellow citizens to turn their backs on wasteful spending, shop carefully, prefer utility over frills, be wary of the claims of clever advertisements, and work for cooperative housekeeping.[52]

For Mumford and the others, ultimately a faith for living without the excesses of materialism was a faith worth fighting for, something that he realized from the outset but experienced painfully later on. A year before Pearl Harbor, he remarked that he wanted "to have the privilege of sharing the sacrifices" that the Allies were already making. His moment of truth came when his son Geddes went off to fight the war his father, too old and not in sufficiently good health, could only write about. In letters to his parents, Geddes echoed many of his father's concerns about war and sacrifice. Early in 1944 he confessed that, despite his father's years of effort to define why Americans had to fight fascism, soldiers would have to wait until peace came to understand, from those who had stayed at home, why they were in battle. For now, one of them might ask, "'Why should I fight?' and go no further." On July 16, from the front lines in Italy, Geddes wrote his parents that he was "fighting for a new post-war icebox or some such thing. At least," he said ironically, "that's what the ads say." He contrasted this consumerist vision with "the more gruesome side of this man's war." Within days of his nineteenth birthday, he told his parents, he had "felt machine gun bullets" pass his shoulder before some of them went on to hit two of his "buddies." In an August 27 letter, again echoing his father's critique of how consumer culture underwrote selfishness, he contrasted the soldier in battle who "will almost always *give* you half of his last dollar or one of his last two cigarettes" with the person back home who finds "it hard to lend you half of his surplus." Less than three weeks later he was struck down by enemy fire. His death made the war year 1944, his father's biographer Donald L. Miller has written, "the most desolate and emotionally devastating of Mumford's entire life."[53]

What made the news of the death of Geddes particularly painful was that Lewis Mumford knew he was losing the battle to ensure that the war would bring a victory over materialistic consumption. By 1944 it was becoming increasingly obvious that though Americans had fought to halt fascism and preserve democracy, a war against a world filled with more iceboxes, let alone electrical refrigerators, was not in the offing. For tens of millions of Americans, as for the editors of *Ladies' Home Journal,* there was a positive connection between the preservation of democracy and the pursuit of an ever more materialistic way of life. Some observers agreed with Mumford on the necessity for wartime sacrifice but dissented from the long-term implications of his position. For example, the language used to promote sales of government war bonds drew on the reformulation of faith in democracy. Avoiding any suggestion that purchasing bonds was a wise investment or would lessen the risk of inflation, the public relations efforts focused on themes of sacrifice and participation. As one 1946 study noted, the effort to sell bonds, by advocating a modern equivalent of "the old-fashioned barn-raising, cornhusking, or quilting bee," offered "surcease from individuated, self-centered activity." Yet the sales efforts hardly echoed Mumford's position completely. The campaigns did not suggest that the war was a prelude to a longer-term transformation of America into a less materialistic culture. Indeed, unlike in World War I, when there was a puritanical cast to the policies of the federal government, during World War II, Washington generally tolerated pleasure-seeking so long as it did not interfere with military efforts.[54]

When an Allied victory began to seem increasingly likely, most Americans made a mental note of the things they would purchase after the war—especially big-ticket items such as automobiles, houses, and household appliances. Advertisers tried to ensure that consumer goods would constitute an essential part of the American way of life. Although people had enjoyed a new affluence during the war, the combination of taxation, rationing, wartime shortages, government-encouraged savings, and patriotic duty helped to create a tremendous backlog of pent-up demand. Not since the late 1920s had Americans known peacetime prosperity. Those who feared that the end of hostilities would mean a return of economic adversity did not foresee how the $250 billion in savings, reserves, and liquid assets that Americans had accumulated by 1945 would power a recovery.[55]

Yet calls for sacrifice at a time of rising prosperity, as Mark H. Leff has noted, "often involved limits on substantial gains rather than the horrific deprivations and destruction suffered by the citizens of other belligerents." Indeed, as John Kenneth Galbraith, then the first "price czar" for the OPA later remarked, "Never in the long history of human combat have so many talked so much about sacrifice with so little actual deprivation as in the United States in World War II," especially compared with what America's allies and enemies suffered in material destruction and lost lives. During the war, Americans increasingly were told that the reward for any sacrifices they made would come in the postwar period, when at last they could use their savings to buy appliances, homes, and automobiles. As Robert Westbrook has observed, buying bonds during the war involved a version of installment purchasing in reverse, whereby consumers systematically saved before they extravagantly consumed. Even before D-Day, national advertisers began an extensive campaign to win the hearts and wallets of veterans and their families. In an early 1943 *Saturday Evening Post* ad for a Nash Kelvinator refrigerator, a wife promises her soldier husband that when he returns, "Everything will be here, just as you left it, just as you want it," by implication with a new refrigerator in the kitchen. By 1944, advertisers were outdoing themselves in picturing a world filled with shiny new appliances, spacious houses, gleaming automobiles, sleek airplanes, and convenient superhighways, many of them brought to peacetime customers by wartime research. "Just over the horizon," intoned one appliance manufacturer, "looms the promise of a better world." Similarly, the government linked its campaign to sell war bonds with the chance for postwar consumers to catch up on lost opportunities.[56]

For Mumford, not only had the war exacted a severe personal sacrifice, but he had lost the battle for a chastened standard of living and a society based on humanistic values as well. In 1942 he had made clear his hopes for the future. He attacked the "false promises" some leaders offered with "visions of the sleek motor cars and private planes and electric refrigerators and expensive mechanical gadgets." This "stale promise of material satisfaction" reminded him of "the proverbial returning of the sick dog to his vomit." Instead, he called on Americans to "gird ourselves for at least a hundred years of heroic, unremitting effort, poor in physical comfort, but rich in political inventiveness, spiritual audacity, and human meaning." Yet it did not take him long to realize that the war had fostered a pent-up demand and provided the savings to underwrite the postwar boom. During the war, the average real wages of Americans rose by 44 percent. In 1996 dollars, the GDP grew from $903 billion in 1939 to $1,693 billion in 1945.[57]

World War II was a pivotal time in the history of American affluence. The depression of the 1930s had threatened capitalism, including its ability to promote a high and growing standard of living. Americans argued at home over whether the war would advance the relationship between chastened consumption and democratic citizenship. Mumford and the OPA eventually lost in their effort to promote moral spending; indeed, Mumford was neither the first nor the last American intellectual to fail in an effort to persuade the nation to accept the new moralism. Furnas and his households won out as the nation embraced their notion of comfort, which in turn helped underwrite postwar expansion. The blend of old and new in Furnas's study—of living debt-free and moving to a new house, of prudence and new appliances, of family values and movies—muted any hint of the connection between modern goods and psychological self-realization which would play such a major role in postwar thought. Yet in retrospect, it was clear that the war had helped build the conditions for a quarter-century of prosperity. The billions of dollars the government had forced and cajoled Americans to save during the war, along with postwar federal policies and the nation's unchallenged position in the world economy, helped tens of millions of Americans move to the suburbs, buy automobiles and eventually television sets, and enroll their children in newly built schools. In the immediate postwar period, two émigrés who escaped from Hitler's grip on Europe—Ernest Dichter and George Katona—emerged as among the boldest and most influential celebrants of a consumer society. Fascism's ascendancy brought them to America while fascism's defeat, and their own writings, turned their adopted homeland into a consumer's paradise. They understood what it meant to link capitalism, consumption, and democracy, a combination that many Americans would embrace in the postwar world as they confronted the challenges of the cold war.

2

Celebratory Émigrés

Ernest Dichter and George Katona

Beginning in the 1940s, George Katona and Ernest Dichter celebrated the contribution of affluent consumers to American life. Dichter (1907–1991) made a handsome living in the United States helping corporations understand the psyche of shoppers. In the process, he linked democracy with purchasing, redefined the roles of middle-class women, and promoted a distinctly anti-puritanical vision. Katona (1901–1981) relied on his surveys of consumer expectations carried out at the University of Michigan from 1946 to 1972 to assert that the optimistic and sensible American consumer would protect the nation from the inflation and instability that had ravaged Europe in the years between the two world wars. Their writings place them among the many émigrés who found themselves cast in the role of latter-day Alexis de Tocquevilles in their new homeland. They carried out innovative social research and served as "professional explainers" hired, as one historian has noted of intellectuals who arrived from Europe, "to observe American society at its most idiomatic and to analyze its most inarticulate citizens." Dichter and Katona differed markedly from the arguments of the influential émigrés of the Frankfurt school. With its adaptation of Marxism and its emphasis on the role of the mass media, the Frankfurt school provided the most widely recognized analysis of mass culture to come out of Germany in the 1930s and greatly influence American thinking in subsequent decades.[1]

Although the pictures drawn by Dichter and Katona of the American consumer differed in many respects, the two men shared a belief, shaped by their experiences in Europe and then the United States, that American consumers were critical to the promotion of economic growth, democracy, and

48

social stability. In this and other ways they contributed to the cold war consensus, dominant in American social thought for two decades beginning in the late 1940s, that linked consumption not only with private pleasure but also with democratic aspirations and a resurgent capitalism. They both gave a special importance in their analysis to the new middle class of salaried and professional employees and to the leadership of educated experts, especially social and behavioral scientists. These, they believed, were the people who would prevent fascism and communism from coming to America. They connected consumer satisfaction with psychological well-being and criticized the nation's puritanical, morally charged attitudes toward consumption. They believed that the actions of consumers and experts would make state intervention in the economy less necessary. They themselves had more success as experts than as public intellectuals. Their careers remind us of the transatlantic nature of intellectual life in the middle of the twentieth century, how dreams and fears born in central Europe in the 1920s and 1930s made their way into American life beginning in the late 1930s. In the end, both the interwar economic turmoil in Europe and postwar abundance in America undermined any possibility of a critical edge to their views on consumer culture. Yet their gratitude to their adopted homeland and their success as émigrés fully prepared them for the task they would accomplish more successfully than any native-born writer: showing how to bind together capitalism, democracy, and consumption.[2]

The Growth of a Postwar Consumer Society

By the end of World War II, the nation was several years into what would turn out to be three decades of sustained economic growth. To be sure, recessions, unemployment, and uneven distribution of income and wealth marred the picture, especially for African Americans and Mexican Americans. At war's end, roughly 30 percent of the nation's inhabitants lived in poverty. In the late 1940s, 33 percent of American residences lacked running water and 60 percent had no central heat. Most Americans could remember more than a decade and a half of straitened circumstances caused by the depression and World War II. In the immediate postwar years, even middle-class Americans lived by standards a later generation would consider simple. Children's bicycles had only one speed. Most homes, if they had a garage at all, had room for only one car. One radio and one telephone per household was the rule, and television sets and home computers had not yet appeared. Most kitchens and bathrooms were spare and functional. If the family took a vacation, typically they stayed with friends and kin who lived a relatively short distance away but in a different environment. Or they might drive a few hours to a rented cabin in the country or on the water. Rarer was the family that traveled to a resort in a different region let alone a different country.[3]

In the fifteen years after the war, Americans achieved a remarkable degree of affluence—and the highest standard of living in the history of the world. In 1949, per capita income in the United States stood at $1,450, far greater than in the countries next on the list (Canada, Great Britain, New Zealand, Switzerland, and Sweden), where the figures ranged from $700 to $900. By the late 1950s, almost 60 percent of Americans were in the middle class, a proportion that had almost doubled since the prosperous days of the late 1920s. By 1960, three out of five American families lived in homes they—and their mortgage companies—owned, and seven out of eight owned at least one TV set. The GDP had risen about 40 percent, from $1,687 billion in 1950 to $2,377 billion in 1960 (in 1996 dollars). The average worker in the United States earned an income, adjusted for inflation, 35 percent higher than at war's end. By 1960, median family income was 30 percent higher than it had been a decade before. In 1956, for the first time, the nation had more white-collar than blue-collar workers. The United States, with only 6 percent of the world's population, benefited from the use of nearly 50 percent of the goods and services produced on the planet.

What poured forth from factories across the nation and around the world—and filled the new suburban houses inhabited by baby boomers and their parents—were synthetic fibers for clothing and plastic goods for every conceivable use, as well as frozen foods, toys, electric washers and dryers, television sets, stereo systems, ball point pens, transistor radios, and automobiles with automatic transmissions. *Holiday* magazine, founded in 1946, tempted citizens with new opportunities to travel; *Playboy*, which followed seven years later, promised men a more pleasure-filled life. The Diners Club, founded in 1950, made it possible to use one charge card for purchases throughout the nation. Long-distance travel was made easier by the interstate highway system, which the government began to build in 1956, and by jet planes which in significant numbers began to replace propeller planes in 1958. The automobile industry and car culture dominated the economy and society. Cars, festooned with fins, bright colors, and chrome, made it possible for Americans to drive to and from new suburban housing developments (Levittowns began to appear in the late 1940s); to eat at drive-up restaurants (McDonald's, first franchised in 1954); stay at national motel chains (Holiday Inn, incorporated 1954); and visit theme parks accessible only by car (Disneyland opened in 1955). The spread of television, not available in homes at war's end, marked the decade: in 1950, Americans owned 8 million sets; *I Love Lucy* began a five-year run in 1951; *TV Guide* and Swanson's TV dinners appeared in 1953; and by 1956, Americans were purchasing twenty thousand television sets a day. The 1940s and 1950s brought Americans a series of now familiar consumer items: Tupperware (1946) and Barbie dolls (1959) among them. By 1960, Americans ate, lived, drove, slept, dressed, and entertained themselves in ways dramatically different from those that prevailed in 1945.

In response to these changes, those who shaped public opinion and policy hailed the nation's affluence, as in a 1951 book by the editors of *Fortune* magazine, *U.S.A: The Permanent Revolution*. The business community feared an inflationary spiral when labor unions linked citizens with workers and struggles in the workplace with the fight for a rising standard of living. As the historian Meg Jacobs has shown, in the 1930s and 1940s, liberals made an ideology of mass purchasing power a central tenet of their political agenda. The federal government contributed significantly to economic growth— from underwriting the mortgages that fostered the suburban boom to providing research funds for technological advances. The result was a cold war consensus that placed the rising American standard of living in a central position in the nation's identity. Although many influential intellectuals worried about the way consumer culture debased taste, by and large they offered no fundamental challenge to the growing link between capitalism, democracy, and consumption. As much as anyone else, Katona and Dichter both charted the postwar social and economic changes and celebrated the consequences they brought for the nation.[4]

Birth of a Salesman: Ernest Dichter and the Objects of Desire

Ernest Dichter, an émigré psychologist influential in the development of new methods of market research, articulated an unbounded optimism about the affluent consumer culture. Trained as a psychologist in Vienna, after his arrival in the United States in 1938 he made a handsome living by using Freudian methods to help corporations and nonprofit organizations understand the psyche of American consumers. In the years after World War II, he worked to reshape American identity. In the process, he echoed many key elements of the cold war consensus. He linked democracy with purchasing, ascribed considerable power to middle-class consumers, redefined the roles of middle-class women, and asserted that affluence would aid his adopted land in the fight against communism abroad. In books, articles, and thousands of studies carried out for corporations, he promoted a decidedly anti-puritanical vision, as he challenged Lewis Mumford's call for chastened consumption. With the approach of a salesman who could not easily separate the selling of himself from the selling of his product, Dichter offered a vision of a world filled with consumable goods that were symbols of personal growth and creative self-expression. Although several of the most influential critics of advertising—including Vance Packard and Betty Friedan—attacked Dichter's work, they often shared with him a focus on white, middle-class America and a sense that the problems of consumer culture could be solved by self-actualizing humanistic psychology.

Dichter came to maturity under inauspicious conditions in a Jewish household racked by poverty and in a nation traumatized by events stretching from the outbreak of World War I in 1914 to the rise of Nazism. Born in Vienna on August 14, 1907, Dichter left school at age fourteen to help support his family, working from 1924 to 1927 at his uncle's department store. There he developed a fascination with new ideas about merchandising, some of which his uncle brought back from the United States. These experiences helped shape the characteristic features of his ideology especially the emphasis on creative discontent and the pleasure of goods, as well as the quest for security. From his father's failure as a salesman emerged his own success as one. In his uncle's department store Dichter first learned about selling, the presentation of merchandise, and the connection between sexuality and consumer goods. From the tragedies of World War I and the sweep of fascism across Europe, he molded a vision of an America in which democracy and consumer culture were inseparable. His poverty engendered in him a drive for success and an insatiable love of consumer goods.[5]

By 1925, Dichter had resumed his formal education. His studies with Charlotte Bühler introduced him to humanistic psychology, with its emphasis on self-realization, personal fulfillment, and a motivation-based theory of personality. He earned his Ph.D. in psychology from the University of Vienna in 1934 and married Hedy Langfelder in 1935, making a living by the practical application of psychology. As much as any other experience, Dichter's work at the Psychoeconomic Institute in Vienna in 1936 shaped his future. Paul Lazarsfeld was at the institute, beginning the work that would fundamentally redefine market research in America and establish him as an entrepreneur who moved back and forth between the academic and business worlds. By now the fascists had taken over Austria. When the police jailed and interrogated Dichter for four weeks because of the presence of anti-fascists at the institute, he quickly realized that as a Jew and as someone suspected of disloyalty, he would have difficulty securing employment in Vienna. He decided to emigrate.[6]

With his departure from Vienna in early 1937, Dichter began the process of reinventing himself that would be so crucial to his success in America. He and his wife first went to Paris, where he worked as a salesman, learning that his success depended less on a product's quality and price than on his ability to project the power and conviction of his own beliefs. In the spring of 1938, worried about Hitler's expansion across Europe, the Dichters again decided to leave, this time for America. Fearing the denial of a visa, Dichter made what he later called "the best sales pitch of my whole life." He argued that what he could contribute to America was an ability to motivate people to solve problems by using depth psychology to understand why they made the choices they did, especially as consumers. The visa was granted. With only $100 to their name, the Dichters arrived in New York in September 1938, just at the moment when Neville Chamberlain was appeasing Hitler in Munich and six months after the Germans annexed Austria. Members of his extended family who stayed behind perished in Nazi concentration camps. Dichter completed the reshaping of his identity shortly after his arrival in the United States when a professor of phonetics helped him develop "an all-American" accent. "That way," Dichter asserted, people "would not be suspicious of my foreign background."[7]

His success in the United States came quickly and spectacularly. His reinvention of himself had earned him a reputation for using Freudian and sexual references in suggestive and dramatic ways. Lazarsfeld, who had moved to the United States in 1933 and, by 1938, was earning a reputation as America's most sophisticated market researcher, helped him get a series of advertising jobs, the first of which he obtained three days after his arrival. In 1939, Dichter made a study of Ivory soap for an advertising agency. He relied on extensive, non-directive interviews in which people talked about their experience of bathing. Dichter's extended conversations revealed to him an erotic element in bathing, "one of the few occasions when the puritanical American was allowed to caress himself or herself." In addition, Dichter explored the bath as a cultural anthropologist might, as a ritual that involved purification. Finally, the interviews strengthened Dichter's insight into the "gestalt" of a product: the notion that aside from the specifics of price, smell, and convenience, a bar of soap had a personality that advertisements could elaborate upon.[8]

Armed with the insights he was developing and again aided by a stroke of good luck, in 1939, Dichter began a study that brought him national recognition. Hired by the Chrysler Corporation to market Plymouth automobiles, he used interviews with hundreds of consumers to understand the importance of convertibles in selling a wider range of cars. Associating a convertible with the excitement they believed a mistress would give them, once at the dealership men nonetheless bought a more sedate and comfortable sedan, which they associated with their wives. Trade magazines picked up the story of the car as wife or mistress, and *Time* followed, complete with a picture of Dichter, who had been in the United States for only eighteen months. In March 1940 the news magazine accepted Dichter's self-promotion and described him as "the first to apply to advertising really scientific psychology" tapping "hidden desires and urges." By 1940, his salary was $150 a week, over $90,000 a year in 2004 dollars. The Dichters were now secure enough to buy a house and start a family. When his first child was born on the day Hitler invaded Russia, Dichter announced to his wife, "This is it. Hitler has lost the war!" by which he meant both that the invasion was a mistake and that his immediate family was now safe. From 1941 to 1946, Dichter worked for Frank Stanton, the director of research at CBS, where Lazarsfeld was continuing his pioneering studies of consumer behavior. Dichter's experience at the network clarified his future, underscoring as it did his preference for a qualitative approach, as well as his discomfort with bureaucratic restraints.[9]

Selling Motivational Research

On his own in 1946, Dichter established the Institute for Motivational Research, a company that on a contractual basis deployed his own brand of market research for major corporations. He brought energy, drive, willfulness, and a capacity to offer provocative insights. Some of his most telling observations did not rely on research; rather, they were the result of a combination of qualities: the skills of a first-rate copywriter, a large dose of common sense, a debt to Freud, and an ability to see the world through the eyes of the consumer. Dichter offered himself as the nation's leading practitioner of Motivational Research (MR). He packaged himself by using controversial, speculative Freudian remarks to capture the attention of media-hungry clients and consumers. He relied on open-ended, intensive, in-depth interviews, employing both projective techniques and free association. In order to understand the underlying meaning that consumer goods and services had for a person, Dichter focused on hidden, irrational, and often sexualized reasons for behavior. He portrayed himself as a Freudian more for purposes of achieving notoriety and success than because he was one in any strict sense. Indeed, his work reminds us of how American interpreters of Freud turned a pessimistic vision that concentrated on the darker implications of sexuality into an optimistic ideology that equated sexuality with liberation.[10]

In *The Psychology of Everyday Living* (1947), Dichter brought the observations he had made for corporate clients to the reading public, in the process trying to transform himself from a market researcher into a therapist for a troubled nation. Indeed, if ever there was an American who conflated consumption and therapy, it was Dichter. In his mind, his interviews helped not only advertisers in their quest to sell merchandise but also consumers and citizens in their search for self-understanding. Dichter easily jumped to the conclusion that consumer goods, properly marketed, could help people grow in self-awareness and self-esteem. Thus, in 1947 he spoke of how cosmetics provide "a form of psychological therapy," helping women "get rid of an awareness of personal inferiority, real or imagined." What the skillful advertiser did was help "people to build their own *attainable* ideal or wishful self-portrait," presenting, as Dichter saw it in a way that elided a product with its therapeutic value, "step by step, the positive aid which his product can provide."[11]

Dichter also saw himself as a therapist helping a nation come to terms with its fears, a claim that lay at the core of *The Psychology of Everyday Living*. His interviews revealed that underneath the patina of postwar confidence, Americans were frustrated, driven by feelings of "impotence, chaos, and futility." Shrinking from civic responsibility and envisioning the government in Washington as "an invisible, intangible, but immense power" encouraged "repressed feeling of guilt" that might in turn lead to aggression. Previous efforts to calm postwar fears had focused on appeals to "glorified ideals," not "the practical and intelligent application of psychological principles." Instead, Dichter called for the use of "'selling' techniques" as a part of a larger strategy of "social engineering" which would encourage people to live democratically. Relying on a therapeutic model, specialists in mass communication could devise programs that would enable Americans to overcome irrational beliefs that fostered antagonisms among groups as well as the propaganda put forth by demagogues. Dichter compared the challenge of healing a society to the situation of the therapist who treats a child who fears the dark by helping the child understand the beauty of the dark. By showing citizens the beauty of democracy, professionals could aid them in mastering their fears.[12]

As he articulated a role for himself as social engineer/therapist, Dichter demonstrated how easily he could shift from the personal and commercial sphere to the public one. He continually conflated consumer culture and therapeutic well-being, mass communications and democratic culture, market research and social criticism. He yearned for a role for himself as social philosopher, a goal that would elude him for the rest of his life. Yet in his emphasis on the importance of realistic and achievable goals in a democracy, he connected with other writers in the period, such as Reinhold Niebuhr, who responded to the challenge that European totalitarianism posed to American democracy. Having narrowly escaped Hitler's terror in 1938, Dichter now feared the presence in America of a sense of frustration that might threaten his adopted nation. Like others who had witnessed Hitler's rise to power, Dichter worried that the worst of the mass media made a fearful people eager to surrender their freedom to an authoritarian leader. During the early 1950s, when McCarthyism held sway, perhaps sensing a similarity between hysterical anticommunism and Nazism, Dichter considered returning to Europe to live. Instead he remained, and celebrated a democracy that was tough-minded and realistic, more interested in reducing frustration by solving specific problems than in chasing after abstract goals.[13]

Women and the Culture of Consumption

One of the specific problems Dichter tried to solve involved the conditions women faced in postwar society. He persistently linked sexuality, desire, identity, and consumer culture, something that Betty Friedan would attack him for in *The Feminine Mystique*. Although Dichter's relationship with those who hired him necessitated that he pay minimal attention to people who were not white and middle class, he did pay abundant attention to women, who constituted a very large percentage of the purchasers whose sales Dichter worked to promote. Nevertheless, men in the advertising business had traditionally seen female consumers as easily swayed by emotional appeals, a tendency that Dichter's emphasis on the irrational reinforced. Dichter's discussion of the relationship between his work and women's roles was inseparable from his larger vision. Central to his understanding of women's situation was his emphasis on consumption as therapy, his insistence on the centrality of the creative discontent of the consumer, the stress on realistic solutions to relieve frustration, and his belief that his job was to show corporations how to link pleasure with purchases in order to overcome the heritage of puritanical self-restraint.[14]

In the late 1930s, Dichter worked on two studies that laid the groundwork for his attempt to delimit women's roles in the postwar world. In his 1939 work on Plymouth automobiles, Dichter identified women as "psychologically the representation of the MORAL CONSCIENCE" whose "INHIBITION to 'SINFUL EXTRAVAGANCE'" had to be removed by "MORAL PERMISSION." Dichter's first study of housework, done in 1940, makes clear that he was already developing the ideas that would dominate his perspective on women in the postwar period. In a report for a household products company, Dichter argued that since housework was "*filled* with gratifications," women's dislike of it had to be due "to some *outside influence* because it *cannot possibly* be as unpleasant as most women claim." The answer, he found, was that such work lacked "*social approval and appreciation.*" This was in contrast with professional work, which garnered considerable social approbation, even though housework may have been more gratifying than professional work because it provided "women with a feeling of responsibility, organization, and control." The solution was obvious: use advertisements "to give housework *Dignity* and *Social Approval*" by emphasizing efficiency, responsibility and creativity.[15]

Dichter's 1945 study of home appliances offers the initial view of his postwar reconstruction of American womanhood. Here Dichter developed his classification of three types of women, a scheme that would dominate his gendered analysis for at least fifteen years. The first group, "Career Women," felt trapped by domesticity and therefore hated housework. Consequently, they had unrealistic expectations for household products because they sustained "no vital, personal relationships" to what they purchased. Although Dichter did not wish to pursue "the neurotic basis" of their rejection of the role of homemaker, he made it clear that their unhealthy attitudes made them less than ideal consumers. The "Pure Housewife," the second group, was also apt to be too critical of products, but for a different reason. Totally absorbed in housework, Dichter's report noted, she had to prove "that she is absolutely indispensable." As a consequence, she tended to be fearful of new products, nostalgically preferring the familiar ways. Finally, there was the "Balanced Woman," Dichter's favorite, whom he described as the most fulfilled emotionally. What made this type appealing to Dichter was her "feeling of confidence which comes with knowing that she is capable" of both housework and career. For some, career might be in the past or the future; others might be interested in becoming a student or a volunteer. Dichter predicted that this group would become more numerous, principally because two world wars and the depression had convinced Americans that, for economic reasons, women had to do something other than housework. Still, even though the "balanced" type derived pleasure from activities outside the home, she placed considerable emphasis on the home as "a cozy shelter from an indifferent outside world." By 1956, Dichter had come see both the pure housewife and the career woman as relics of the past. The feeling of creativity that he advised advertisers to inspire in the modern housewife would permit "her to use at home all the *faculties that she would display in an outside career.*"[16]

Two years later, Dichter gave the same typologies a different spin. He no longer described the pure housewife as unrealistic; rather, he emphasized her desire to achieve gratification from "creative outlets in domestic interests." His description of the career woman turned harsher, depicting her as often "absorbed" in "competing with and vanquishing men on their own battle-field." Other unhealthy impulses often drove these women, such as feelings of "inferiority" that stemmed from a sense of being "unable to fill the role of wife, mother, parent, housekeeper." Finally, what drove these women was a sense of sexual inferiority and "a desire to imitate and emulate what they subconsciously consider the superior and more privileged sex." In contrast, Dichter now pictured the balanced type in an even more favorable light. He celebrated "a new glorification of intelligent motherhood, an increasing interest in child care, a renewed status for the culinary arts, a stress upon the importance of being a warm, stimulating, encouraging, reassuring mother and wife." He noted that women in this category often worked full-time or part-time and yet ran the house efficiently, "gaining genuine gratification from both areas of expression." As part of "the continuing emancipation of women and acceptance of women in all areas of life," he mentioned their assumption of "formerly sacrosanct male roles" in industry and politics, which had begun during World War II.[17]

These typologies of American womanhood provided the basis of Dichter's advice to corporations. Because the balanced woman was the wave of the future, manufacturers should target her, "educating women to have outside interests and better themselves intellectually" with the extra time made available by labor-saving appliances. Moreover, products should be designed for this type of woman so that a homemaker could lighten her household duties and, at the same time, individualize her house and make it "more home-like." Corporations could thus make it possible for women to fulfill multiple roles, enabling them to find "beauty, sense and balance in housework" through "intelligent planning and organization." Dichter therefore advised his clients to use advertising to teach women that they could "have outside interests and become alert to wider intellectual influences (without becoming a Career Woman). The art of good homemaking should be the goal of every normal woman."[18]

Throughout the 1950s, Dichter focused his attention on teaching American women, especially his favorite "balanced" type, to find creativity in housework. Again and again he advised women to relieve their tensions by solving specific household problems and to accept the challenges of housework. In *The Psychology of Everyday Living*, he suggested that women could make their housework interesting by introducing "numerous variations and surprises." He praised cooking as a task that, compared with career and profession, was "a highly respectable occupation." By organizing kitchen work, using modern recipes, and developing "a production plan," women would be on the road to acquiring their "kitchen degree." As late as 1964, Dichter was urging manufacturers of household products to help women solve the conflicts they faced by accepting their "kingpin role in the family." A woman should be encouraged to identify products as her allies, connecting her with the "physical and spiritual rewards she derives from the feeling of basic security provided by the home." By the late 1950s, Dichter had fully connected women, capitalism, freedom, and consumer culture.[19]

Dichter, Social Criticism, and the Recasting of American Society

If, with *The Psychology of Everyday Living*, Dichter had begun to articulate his social ideology in broad terms, in *Strategy of Desire* (1960), he brought together much of his previous work and provided the most ambitious, if still unsystematized, synthesis of his outlook. Here Dichter moved more fully than he had done before to translate the findings of market research into social philosophy. In the process he articulated how he hoped to recast postwar American society. Dichter wrote *Strategy of Desire* in response to two books he considered puritanical: *The Affluent Society* by John Kenneth Galbraith and *The Hidden Persuaders* by Vance Packard in its critique of Dichter's use of depth psychology and embrace of mass consumption. Ironically, Packard's attack was more successful in bringing Dichter notoriety and business than it was in catapulting him into the ranks of widely read American social critics. Packard gave Dichter celebrity status, with invitations for radio, television, and speaking appearances in the United States and in other parts of the developed world. He established franchises in more than a dozen cities in the United States and abroad. In the late 1950s and early 1960s, Dichter's operation earned about $1 million in annual revenues, equal to roughly $6.5 million in 2004 dollars. He relied on a staff of about sixty-five, on 1,500 to 2,000 part-time interviewers around the nation, and on a consumer panel of 1,000 mostly middle- and upper-middle-class families. From the panel, he selected twelve to sixteen people for a "Living Laboratory," where they watched television in a living room setting and talked, cameras secretly recording their every response. In the late 1950s, Dichter charged his clients between $20,000 and $60,000 for a full-scale study. His Institute for Motivational Research would test Dichter's initial hunches by carrying out interviews with hundreds of consumers. The result was a report that explored the psychological meanings people imputed to products. If the corporation chose to take the next step, Dichter worked with its advertising agency to devise a campaign strategy.[20]

Yearning to realize his desire to become accepted as a social philosopher with a general audience, and to defend MR from its detractors, with *Strategy of Desire*, Dichter sought to prevent America from suffering the consequences of the Nazism which he had emigrated to escape, while at the same time helping his adopted nation fight Soviet communism. He feared that people achieved security through those same mass media that perpetuated "mental laziness, stereotyped reactions, and stock responses," tendencies that might place the nation on the road to a "blind acceptance of Fascist or Communist ideology." To social scientists fell the task of devising the means to prevent the public from oversimplifying issues "in a socially dangerous way." Dichter expressed an anti-utopian impulse that grew out of his assumption that totalitarian governments encouraged a quest for unrealizable goals. To counter the possibility of the emergence in America of what he had witnessed in Austria, and drawing on Freud's notion of the reality principle, Dichter reiterated his call for a focus on specific, achievable goals that would help people reduce the frustration they faced when encountering change. Like other cold warriors, Dichter wanted to shift the competition with the Soviet Union from the military arena to the battlefields of ideologies, values, and economics. One of modern democracy's basic dilemmas, he wrote, involved the rejection of "our own power and importance in changing the destiny of the world." He added, "Among the declarations of faith in the future is the act of buying." Because "our economy would literally collapse overnight" without a continuing high level of consumption, the frontline "defenders of a positive outlook on life, the real salesmen of prosperity, and therefore of democracy, are the individuals who defend the right to buy." In selling us a new car, the salesperson is purveying "*a positive philosophy of life.*" Thus in Dichter's eyes, the fight between free enterprise and communism was one in which Americans had to prove that they controlled their destiny by consuming. Making a purchase was evidence "that we are not living in a world controlled by dialectical materialism" but one "built on individual initiative."[21]

In this epic struggle, what was needed was the social engineering he had envisioned earlier, a strategy that employed consumer goods as therapeutic aids in producing a prosperous society. Social scientists as social engineers carried out "all the therapeutic jobs which must be done to insure the smooth operation of the democratic structure." At its core, this involved getting people to associate buying with creativity and growth. Consuming involved acceptance of what goods did for people psychologically, giving them "the power to express" their "innermost desires by a specific type of merchandise." For example, his interviewing revealed that when a man purchased life insurance, he was moving from childlike self-love to an adult love that involved giving. The market researcher thus served as a therapist who helped people get over their guilt, find pleasure in consumption, and resolve the tensions of their lives. Creative discontent stood in opposition to the status quo, which he identified with "wanting to return to the womb, to hide, to be fatalistic." At times Dichter was positively lyrical about the way people grew psychologically as they gained an increasing intimacy with objects. "What takes place in a few minutes when the new purchase is unwrapped and put to use for the first time, has psychological consequences which last for the rest of our lives." Dichter understood what Marxists call the fetishism of commodities. "We want to know," he wrote, "how we can read into, understand, and interpret the human quality that exists in a piece of furniture." Where Dichter differed from Marxists was that for him the fetishism of an object was laudable, something that the MR practitioner could encourage. He fully celebrated the fact that the automobile was not only a means of transportation but also a symbol of prestige, prosperity, luxury, and, for some, "part of one's woman-hunting equipment."[22]

Central to Dichter's effort to promote the strategy of desire was the assertion of a link between the material and spiritual components of goods, something that enabled him to launch an attack on moralistic and puritanical
skeptics of consumer culture such as Mumford, Packard, and Galbraith. As
early as 1939, Dichter, shaped by his European sensibility, lamented the hold
of "the Puritan period on American life." People needed "moral permission,"
he wrote in a study of breakfast cereals shortly after he arrived in the United
States, to take pleasure from consumer products. As early as 1953, he attacked
social scientists for despising "soap operas, comic strips and popular magazines without analyzing the reason for their success." In the 1950s and 1960s,
Dichter continued to associate moralistic attacks on consumption with a
puritanical Christianity. Like sex, consumption was seen, he wrote in *Strategy
of Desire*, "as an animalistic, undesirable, dirty emotional business." Drawing
on interviews, he concluded that Americans worried too much about the
burdens of the good life, in large measure because of the puritanical tradition
which equated consumption with sin. He questioned the wisdom of social
critics who thought that America was losing to the Russians by pursuing new
consumer goods and forms of leisure. The solution, Dichter argued, was to
enjoy life more. He called on Americans to develop a "morality concept"
based not on the rejection of self-indulgence but on the "idea that the basic
goal of life is human dignity, the ability to achieve self-realization through
leisure." In the cold war with the USSR, the true test of "the American way
of life" was whether it provided a "feeling of growth, self-realization and
achievement."[23]

Dichter thus offered the business community ways to give the consumer
"moral permission" to purchase products, ostensibly as part of a larger social
vision that undergirded democracy with abundance. He saw his task as liberating people's desires and showing them how to achieve spiritual ends
through material means. By attacking puritanism, Dichter hoped to provide
a basis for what he called appreciatively the new hedonism, "the morality of
the good life." To overcome this sense of guilt and immorality, he argued,
Americans had to accept pleasure as moral by seeing that objects led to
idealistic ends. "If the desire for freedom and discovery can be expressed
through the glamor of a new convertible," he remarked in *Strategy of Desire*,
"I willingly accept responsibility for combining two strong human desires for
the benefit of the car advertiser—and ultimately for the benefit of both the
national economy and the creative happiness of the individual."[24]

Dichter emphasized new patterns of consumption among what he saw as
an expanding middle class. It was these people whom the MR practitioner
could help persuade to associate self-realization with consumer goods and
experiences. Dichter believed that the American middle class was "taking over

and engulfing all other classes." Because those new to middle-class status had no prior experience with "traditions which are symbolized by such products as sterling silver, furs, good furniture," market researchers had to devise strategies to make clear to them through advertisements the importance of new patterns of consumption. Consequently, Dichter advised advertisers how to market luxury goods to the wives of plumbers and daughters of day laborers who lacked the "background which would enable them to judge style, quality or artistic work and buy with competence." He emphasized the functional qualities of refined goods rather than their prestige and stressed the tradition that children would inherit rather than the tradition their parents lacked. Dichter identified another change in patterns of middle-class consumption, too: the inconspicuous consumption of what he called the "inner Jones." For people who wanted to keep their neighbors guessing about their social status by not displaying "it too openly," the new way to buy status was "to resort to individuality." The switch from the outer Jones to the inner one meant a change in emphasis from success to happiness, a shift in which the market researcher could play a critical role. If people made purchases to impress others, then the objects possessed them. If, however, people bought items to express themselves, then they mastered the object.[25]

With *Strategy of Desire*, Dichter defended himself against his critics and made extravagant claims for the power of his version of MR to reshape society. He did so by linking the spiritual and the material. In the process, he emphasized the importance of self-fulfillment, creative discontent, and self-discovery, almost always in connection with the consumption of new goods and services. He thus fully discharged the émigré's obligation to his adopted land. Dichter was not just earning a living by promoting his services and specific products. He was also participating in the reconstruction of American society in the postwar world. He emphasized key elements of the cold war consensus. He celebrated the broadening of the middle class in a way that minimized the importance to America of those beyond the pale. He defined the American dream in opposition to what he saw as the Soviet nightmare and attacked what he saw as the nation's excessive commitment to a puritanical moralism. And he linked the consumption of goods not just with psychological well-being but with participation in a democracy and a free economy.

The Death of a Salesman

By the early 1960s, MR and Dichter were past the heyday they had achieved in the late 1950s. On Madison Avenue, new approaches usually have a short life, and MR was no exception. Computers were beginning to give corporate research directors renewed confidence in statistical data and mathematical projections. At the same time, the academic study of consumers, increasingly located in business schools, came to rely on quantification and social-science theory. Although Freudianism had lost its appeal in market research circles, what persisted of Dichter's legacy was the use of the depth interview and the notion of lifestyle segmentation based on psychological typologies. After the early 1960s, Dichter shifted the emphasis of the services he offered. He changed his focus from advising corporations to helping nonprofit organizations, from working in the United States to offering his services abroad, and from carrying out market research to focusing on the problems of management, packaging, and society.

In 1970, Dichter suffered a heart attack in a setting fraught with significance about the meaning of his work and his identity. He was on a platform with a Black Nationalist who called for $150 billion in reparations to compensate for the oppression of slavery and racism. Throughout his career, Dichter had paid minimal attention to African Americans, focusing instead on the groups his clients targeted: white, mostly suburban, middle-class Americans. When in his writings he turned to the issue of diversity, reacting against the notion of separatism that he associated with Nazism, his cosmopolitanism minimized racial and ethnic differences. On this occasion Dichter rejected his opponent's call for government compensation. In reply, his adversary called him a racist. On the podium, Dichter suffered a heart attack.[26]

The combination of illness and opportunity prompted Dichter to cut down on his obligations. Twice he sold his business and, when the arrangements did not work out, twice he took it back. Well into the 1980s he maintained a hectic schedule as a lecturer, adjunct professor, consultant, and author. In 1989 he was hired to travel to the Soviet Union, at the moment of its demise, to carry out what the advertising columnist of the *New York Times* described as "what may be the first study of what motivates Soviet consumers." Before his departure, Dichter remarked that "for 50 years, Soviet citizens have been told, 'Don't buy from capitalist devils! They will tempt you with hidden persuaders!'" And then he added, "*I'm* the hidden persuader!" Dichter died of heart failure on November 21, 1991.[27]

Although the 1960s critique of materialism and the onset of the energy crisis in 1973 troubled him, to the end Dichter remained optimistic in what he wrote. He believed that the energy crisis, and the inflation and drop in disposable incomes that accompanied it, "most likely will have the same effect on us as the discovery that the Russians had gotten ahead of us with Sputnik." He hoped that the new crisis would not tempt Americans to "switch over to a rigid, timid, and planned economy" and lose "our verve, ingenuity, and daredevil philosophy." Dichter ended a talk on the energy crisis with the words that he wanted engraved on his tombstone. It was a phrase that brought together his European education and the émigré's boundless faith in his adopted nation: "Why Not?"[28]

George Katona and the Heroic American Consumer

If Ernest Dichter probed the psyche of the American consumer, George Katona took her temperature. As much as anyone else, Katona was responsible for tracking the changing mood of his adopted nation's shoppers. The director of the Survey of Consumer Finances at the University of Michigan for twenty-six years beginning in 1946, Katona was ideally situated to study the expectations of American households. For Katona, who came to the United States from Germany in 1933, the optimistic and sensible consumer was a hero who would save America from the inflation, instability, and depression that ravaged Europe in the years between the two world wars. Drawing on his experiences in Germany in the 1920s and early 1930s, on what he had learned from his mentors, and on his own life as an émigré, Katona was able to explain the changes in the American standard of living that were reshaping his adopted nation. From the early 1940s until the end of his life, he paid special attention to how Americans achieved prosperity without rampant inflation. Contrary to the view that the average American was being manipulated into purchasing unwanted goods and experiences, Katona found the consumer to be sensible and optimistic. His celebration of the consumer's ability to keep inflation in check provided an alternative to the attack by business leaders on labor unions for creating a wage-price spiral. He charted the emergence and expansion of middle-income families, whose discretionary spending for durable goods provided the rudder that kept the ship of affluence on course. Like Ernest Dichter, Katona contributed to the cold war consensus that celebrated the burgeoning of a middle-class consumer society. He also, though less vehemently than Dichter, questioned America's moralistic attitudes toward consumption.[29]

Katona characterized the consumer as someone who aspired to a higher standard of living and worked hard in order to achieve it. Optimistic, confident, and yet reasonable, the American consumer was continually discovering new desires, thus shifting the United States from a needs-based economy to one based on wants. Like Dichter, he celebrated consumer culture, which had made his adopted homeland a prosperous and free nation. Only during the last decade of his life—as Americans responded to Watergate, the war in Vietnam, and increasing rates of inflation—did his confidence, like that of the consumers he surveyed, begin to wane. Throughout his career, this sophisticated European émigré emerged as one of the most sympathetic and knowledgeable experts on the changing American standard of living.

From Businessman to Émigré Intellectual

Born in Budapest on November 6, 1901, Katona grew up in a prosperous Jewish household.[30] In 1919, the communist takeover of Hungary prompted him to move to Germany, where in 1921 he earned a Ph.D. in experimental psychology. The hyperinflation that roiled Germany in the early 1920s inspired him to examine how psychology and economics together shed light on the dynamics of rapid price increases. In 1926 he settled in Berlin. There, from Max Wertheimer, one of the founders of Gestalt psychology, Katona learned about the psychology of perception. Gustav Stolper provided much of Katona's training in economics and, at the *German Economist*, a forum for his ideas. Stolper fostered in Katona an interest in inflation, business cycles, emotional moods, and consumer behavior, as well as a belief in a public role for the scholar, an appreciation of the power of capitalism, and a dislike of excessive state expansion. Katona first became fascinated with America as a modern consumer society during the late 1920s and early 1930s. He appreciated the efficiency and flexibility of its businessmen and applauded the spread of prosperity across social classes. In particular, what compelled his attention were the inventiveness and the extent of consumer credit mechanisms, the power of marketing, the importance of brand recognition, and the tendency toward conformity. Shortly after Hitler came to power in 1933 and banned the *German Economist*, Katona emigrated to the United States, where he worked in Stolper's investment office on Wall Street until illness cut short his business career.[31]

Recovering fully in 1939, the year in which he became a U.S. citizen, Katona returned to his long-standing academic interests in psychology, economics, and inflation. Especially formative in his thinking were the debates at the New School for Social Research, where Katona taught in the early 1940s, on democracy, totalitarianism, mass culture, and class relations. The books he published over a five-year period beginning in 1940 launched his career. In *Organizing and Memorizing: Studies in the Psychology of Learning and Teaching* (1940), he made clear his debt to Wertheimer while at the same time he laid the groundwork for his own later work on psychological understanding. *War without Inflation: The Psychological Approach to Problems of War Economy* (1942) was Katona's first extended exploration of the connections among psychology, economics, and inflation. Assuming the reasonableness of the consumer, and putting aside his reluctance to sanction government intervention, he argued that the prime factor in waging the war without bringing about inflation was the role of the state in creating a "gestalt," a comprehensive set of cultural expectations that would influence group psychology and moderate price increases. In *Price Control and Business: Field Studies among*

Producers and Distributors of Consumer Goods in the Chicago Area, 1942–44
(1945), Katona, relying on the work of Lazarsfeld, first used survey methods
based on open-ended interviewing to obtain information that would explain
the impact of household behavior on the economy.[32]

Katona did not agree with those who believed that the war's end would
bring a return to depressed prewar conditions. Rising levels of aspiration, he
argued, would emerge from the public's sense of their contribution to the war
effort, encouraging people to aspire "to a higher social and economic status."
Moreover, wartime shortages would "create an emotional halo round the
goods and activities of which one is deprived." He remained confident that
"public and private agencies" could maintain an atmosphere that would keep
inflation in check. Like other professionals who were confident that their
expertise could guide democracy, Katona allotted to the expert the task of
helping the public develop "frames of reference for new experiences."[33]

By 1945, Katona had developed much of the framework he would use to
understand consumers in the ensuing years. He already believed that under
the right circumstances, consumers would act to contain inflationary pressures. His outlook broadened in the late 1940s and the 1950s to emphasize
rising levels of aspiration and the nature of social learning, but even these
concepts had a place in his pre-1945 outlook. Well trained in economics and
psychology, possessing a commitment to making his expertise intelligible to
a broad public, and already widely published, at the end of the war George
Katona was at a turning point in his career.

Surveys of Consumer Finances and Expectations, 1946–1972

In 1946, Katona moved to the University of Michigan to conduct pathbreaking surveys of consumer finances and expectations. His wartime work on
price controls was critical in creating this opportunity. As the end of the war
neared, economists and policy makers feared that Americans, by spending
their enormous wartime savings, would intensify inflationary pressures. Before hostilities ended, Katona had joined a research team, sponsored by the
Federal Reserve Board, that was studying the implications for prices of these
savings. In Ann Arbor, he joined the group that established the Survey Research Center (SRC) at the Institute for Social Research (ISR) of the University of Michigan, where he also served as professor of both economics and
psychology. One of the SRC's major projects was the Survey of Consumer
Finances, which continued the study of liquid assets he had undertaken during the war. The Federal Reserve Board supported the survey until 1959.
After that, underwritten by corporations, foundations, government agencies,
business magazines, and the ISR, Katona continued his investigations into

the dynamics of the consumer economy. He helped assemble staff members from a variety of disciplines. A prolific writer who sought a hearing from academics, government officials, business executives, and the public, Katona presented his findings in official reports, professional papers, and a series of books. He influenced consumer surveys worldwide, saw his books translated into many languages, and earned a reputation as the dean of behavioral or psychological economics. His work won him the American Psychological Association's Distinguished Professional Contribution Award and honorary degrees from universities in the United States, Germany, and the Netherlands. Although he never reached a general audience, Katona had a following among influential figures in the government and business communities who grew to trust his evaluation of consumer sentiment and among social scientists interested in survey research, consumer behavior, and the application of psychology to economics.[34]

Throughout the postwar period, Katona felt a tremendous sense of gratitude to the institutions and people who supported him. His wife, Marian Katona, whom he had married in 1929, did her best to shelter him from the day-to-day concerns of the domestic world. They lived together, without children of their own, in a comfortable house near the campus. His sense of gratitude extended to his colleagues and to the university, and he felt a special sense of indebtedness to and love for America. He appreciated the lives of ordinary middle-class Americans and expressed an affinity for them, although Katona himself was frugal when it came to spending money on the consumer durables, gadgets, and big-ticket items that those about whom he wrote seemed to pursue with such eagerness. Katona's gratitude to America never turned him into an incautious celebrant of the American way of life. A liberal Democrat, he voted for Adlai Stevenson, John F. Kennedy, and Lyndon B. Johnson. Although corporations provided some funds for his research, he retained some antagonism to big business, in particular the large automobile companies.[35]

Katona's surveys and writings had considerable influence, though not as much as he claimed or hoped for. Many decision makers in government, business, and finance closely followed the reports. If imitation is a form of flattery, Katona should have felt flattered: the European Common Market, the federal government, and the business-sponsored Conference Board, as well as the Gallup organization and several other private polling groups developed consumer sentiment surveys. In 1989, the Department of Commerce included the Survey of Consumer Finances' data on its Index of Leading Economic Indicators. Although orthodox economists remained skeptical of Katona's emphasis on the psychological and his ability to predict long-term trends, Katona received ample recognition from professional psychologists.[36]

The Survey of Consumer Finances provided Katona with the context in which to bring together his interests in research techniques, inflation, American society, psychology, and economics. His position at the juncture of various academic disciplines allowed him to understand how people made decisions on what and when to consume. Applying to the study of consumer attitudes what he had learned in Germany during the prewar period and in the United States during the war, he was able to explain critical aspects of America's emergence as an affluent society in the postwar period. In his study of consumers, Katona found an opportunity to define how postwar America was different from interwar Germany. Like many others who worked for research institutes connected with universities, Katona was in a position to build bridges—between American and European perspectives, social sciences and public policy concerns, psychological and economic approaches, pure and applied research. While developing an influential survey, he also helped develop the field of behavioral economics.[37]

Aggregate data on consumer savings and expenditures had long been available, but with the Survey of Consumer Finances, Katona provided something else: a unique combination of information on economic conditions and psychological expectations at the household level. The investigations focused on how consumers evaluated their own and the nation's financial prospects. The interviews concentrated on questions about why people saved, the nature of each household's liquid assets, and the plans for spending each kind of holding. Over time the surveys became more extensive and elaborate, with interviewers asking more than 150 questions. After obtaining information on the demographics and finances of the households, they urged respondents to reflect on their own and the nation's economic prospects. They probed expectations about general business conditions, price changes, employment, domestic and international turmoil, government spending, and interest rates. The study then turned to specific kinds of spending. After securing data on rents and mortgages, the survey focused on plans for buying and improving the home. Next, accounting for about 30 percent of the survey, came questions about durables such as major appliances, furniture, television sets, and cars. Here the data were most specific. The survey also sought information on installment debt. Finally, the interviewers noted demographic characteristics, including the sex of the head of the household and of the respondent, as well as the "race" of the family unit.[38]

Over time, important changes appeared in the surveys. What started out as a study of plans for using savings quickly turned into a more general examination of spending, especially on consumer durables as well as vacations. Naturally, as patterns of spending changed, so did the kinds of purchases inquired about. Always focusing on consumer durables, eventually the survey included color television sets, air conditioners, freezers, and stereo equipment. Moreover, with the emergence of new policy questions and sources of funding, in the 1960s, Katona's colleagues turned to questions of welfare and poverty. Building on the work of those who had gone before, Katona and his colleagues made important advances in sampling and interviewing techniques. One of the survey's most important contributions involved the use of the fixed question/open response approach, in which the interviewer not only asked specific questions but also probed for full answers. The hour-long interviews of more than a thousand people, initially carried out in the homes of the consumers, had "a conversational character" so that the interviewers could establish "*rapport*" with the people interviewed. With these methods, the survey helped close the gap between psychology's focus on the individual and the concentration of economics on the aggregate and on policy issues. The scale of the project grew apace, from one survey of about eight hundred people in two communities in 1945 to a quarterly nationwide investigation that interviewed well over a thousand families beginning in 1960, and then on a monthly basis in 1978.[39]

In the years after 1945, advocates of the survey argued for its record of prescience and reliability. As an Allied victory seemed more likely, many knowledgeable observers expected either a repeat of the sharp inflation of 1918 and 1919 or a return to the economic conditions of the depression. To such Cassandras, Katona's first study, carried out in 1945, should have been reassuring. In that year, when prices rose by 8.5 percent, the report indicated that Americans did not seem about to liquidate the considerable assets they had accumulated during the war, which would have fueled runaway inflation. Consumer credit and income, not liquid assets, would fund consumer purchases. Potential consumers were still defensive, giving little indication of the booming consumer culture that lay ahead. Most of those who held war bonds and time deposits said they intended to use them for long-term purposes rather than for buying luxuries or consumer durables.[40]

Katona had reason to have confidence in his work and in the future of the American economy. In the next few years, as inflationary pressure increased, the investigation provided some cause for a moderate amount of alarm, but the annual reports nonetheless remained optimistic that consumers were sensibly balancing saving and spending. The reports highlighted a pronounced increase in the optimism of American consumers. As early as 1946 and 1947, Katona was able to predict many of the major components of consumer attitudes that would help underwrite postwar prosperity. What was already emerging, the 1946 report noted, was a cohort of young prospective purchasers, over 40 percent of whom were "skilled and unskilled workers" and about 33 percent of whom were "professional, white-collar, or business people."

Their positive attitudes would prevent both excessive inflation and a return to the depression. Americans, Katona found, were willing to spend because they believed that the nation's and their own financial situations were improving. The only danger in sight was that top-heavy income and asset distribution meant that prosperity might run out of steam. Nonetheless, Katona concluded in 1947, if optimistic attitudes continued to prevail, they would help to "counteract unfavorable tendencies" that often appeared following a sustained period of prosperity.[41]

As time went on, with both justification and some exaggeration, Katona could praise the ability of his surveys to explain the relationship between consumers' attitudes and economic activity. His surveys, he continually asserted, had revealed that the sensible and appropriately optimistic attitudes of consumers were both the engine and the rudder of national economic wellbeing. For example, when war in Korea broke out in 1950, economists and business executives expected a period of sustained inflation. After an initial increase in prices, however, consumers decided to save rather than spend. Similarly, although some expected a deep recession and even a depression in 1953–54, the nation experienced only a mild downturn in economic activity. Millions of Americans, Katona reported, remained confident and planned to buy more durable goods, despite the bad news they read about in the newspapers and saw on television. Just as critics of the survey's approach began to argue that its reports of sustained consumer optimism merely stated the obvious, the survey seemed to confound skeptics. It revealed that the recession of 1958 came about because, even though Americans still had money to spend, "cumulative adverse expectations" prompted them to cut back on their purchases. Finally, when respected business analysts in the same year claimed that the postwar prosperity had ended, the survey data indicated that American optimism remained strong enough to prevent a deepening of the recession into a more serious depression.[42]

From Survey Researcher to Social Commentator

Building on his success as an economic analyst, Katona hoped to claim an audience as a social commentator as well. In doing so, like Dichter, he presented an optimistic vision of America as a middle-class consumer society and critiqued moralistic attitudes toward affluence. He offered his most sustained celebration of the affluent society in *The Powerful Consumer* (1960), *The Mass Consumption Society* (1964), and *Aspirations and Affluence* (1971), although, unlike writers who were more critical of affluence, he never succeeded in commanding a wide or general audience. Compared with books by John Kenneth Galbraith and Vance Packard, Katona's relied heavily on statistics, lacked human interest, and often used the language of professional social science. Moreover, in the late 1950s and early 1960s, the educated public actually preferred jeremiads that warned of the dangers of an excessively high standard of living to celebrations of middle-class consumerism.[43]

Yet few other writers of his generation captured as well as Katona the emergence of that middle-class consumer society. Using 1961 data, he described the basis of the new social order. The "backbone of the mass consumption economy," controlling more than 50 percent of all personal income, was the 40 percent of American families in the "upper-middle" or "discretionary-income group" with before-tax incomes between $6,000 and $15,000. Below this group, with incomes under $3,000, were the poor, most of them elderly, nonwhite, or widows; earning between $3,000 and $6,000 was "the lower-middle-income group," including many "younger people who have every reason to expect their income to rise substantially in the future." One of the things that made the discretionary income group so important was that, adjusted for inflation, it had grown from 12 percent of the population in 1929 and 25 percent in 1945 to 40 percent in 1961. Indeed, he noted, in 1961 almost half "of American spending units in their main earning period belonged to the upper-middle-income group." According to Katona, their spending of discretionary income for items such as automobiles, appliances, and leisure-time activities was flexible and powerful enough to have an impact on the nation's economic activity.[44]

For a quarter of a century after 1945, Katona's outlook remained remarkably consistent. Drawing on his pre-1945 experiences as well as on what the surveys revealed, between the end of World War II and the early 1970s he described a society in which the consumer played a heroic role. By moderating inflation and promoting prosperity, he asserted, consumers helped keep America a stable society. A broad middle class that aspired to ever greater levels of affluence provided the engine of a booming American economy. Discretionary spending on durable goods was the backbone of postwar economic growth. Drawing on his earlier work in psychology, Katona pictured the American consumer as optimistic, reasonable, and intelligent. Consumers were realistic, expecting "only *slightly* more than they have." When people made important purchases under new circumstances, they were acting as problem solvers. Neither manipulated nor unthinking, consumers were capable of learning, of transferring knowledge from one situation to another. No one, he wrote in criticism of Galbraith's *Affluent Society* and Packard's *Hidden Persuaders*, "attributed greater power to Madison Avenue than its critics."[45]

The power of mass communications could cause opinions to change simultaneously among large numbers of people, Katona acknowledged, but "experiences shared with neighbors and friends" also helped determine how consumers would use information to shape their purchases. Although both the media and one's peers could cause opinions to spread like "a contagious disease," only in extreme situations would this tendency destabilize the economy. What stood between order and disorder was the ability of the consumer to understand economic and political events. "The economic thinking of the masses is fundamentally conservative and sane," Katona remarked. "People resist speculative fever as well as despondency," he wrote in 1958, perhaps with the German inflation of the 1920s in mind, "unless their sanity is crushed by a series of repeated shocks." By regulating themselves, a notion that reflected Katona's exaggeration of their autonomy, consumers provided stability to the economy "either by serving as a brake to inflationary trends or by stepping up their demand when the economy needed new incentives so as to emerge from a plateau."[46]

Katona also took issue with Galbraith's contrast between private wealth and public poverty. He argued that Americans had in fact spent money for public purposes. "The necessity of fighting the cold war," he argued in 1964 (only confirming the wisdom of what Galbraith had said), had persuaded taxpayers to increase the government's share of GNP to a peacetime high. Katona acknowledged that additional public funds had to be spent on education and health care, but he emphasized that the development of more positive attitudes toward spending on social needs would be possible only when further economic growth had allowed consumers to feel that they had all the goods they believed necessary for their "basic comfort." To solve domestic problems by redistributing resources, thereby diminishing consumer expenditures, "might easily plunge the economy into stagnation or recession." Echoing a widely shared notion of the cold war consensus, Katona believed that "the solution to mass poverty is not cutting the pie into different-size slices, but rather exerting every effort" to increase the size of the pie.[47]

For Katona, serious inflation remained the greatest threat to prosperity and social order. In a 1952 government publication designed to persuade Americans to resist rising prices during the Korean War, he called inflation "a national calamity" which fostered "an atmosphere of mutual mistrust and conflict" among social groups. A stable currency, he wrote, was "the financial backbone of the free world." Eight years later, pointing to the individual "misery" and social "disorganization" that inflation caused, he said, "Runaway inflation is one of the greatest possible evils." Serious inflation results, he noted, drawing on his knowledge of Gestalt psychology, "when there is a break with the past that compels us to reorganize our field." That is, in difficult situations, usually prompted by war, military defeat, or governmental change, people find that their old ways of behaving no longer work, and they struggle to understand the world in new ways. Consumers would save the day, he believed, by curtailing their spending when they feared rising prices and thus preventing their fears from becoming reality. Indeed, only once in the quarter-century after World War II did his surveys reveal the kind of anticipatory buying that fueled inflation. From the end of the war to the early 1970s, Katona remained convinced that consumer behavior, though not sufficient "to avert creeping inflation," would help "arrest galloping inflation."[48]

Above all, for Katona, the rising aspiration of American consumers was a critical factor in the health of the postwar economy. Drawing on the work of the émigré Kurt Lewin, Katona stressed how group experiences foster positive changes in attitudes. The writings of the psychologist Abraham H. Maslow strengthened his belief that people desire to fulfill themselves. With increased achievement came greater levels of aspiration. Countering those who believed that prosperity was "its own gravedigger," Katona argued instead that the ability to satisfy wants "makes life easier but does not necessarily result in soft living and waste." On the contrary, with affluence came optimism and aspirations to more. Although Katona concentrated primarily on purchasable pleasures, on occasion he argued that a rising standard of living also enhanced "cultural aspirations." Yet where Maslow emphasized the emergence of non-materialistic needs, at least until the early 1970s, Katona tended to focus on new but not necessarily higher needs. Like Dichter, Katona thus questioned the puritanical and anti-materialistic streak in American culture, envisioning a society based on expanding wants and increasing pleasures. He recognized a rising standard of living as a force that provided the United States with the stability and direction that Germany in the 1930s lacked. Although he wrote relatively little about work, what he did say underlined the importance of consumption. People labor in order to consume, he argued; they decide on the level of consumption they want and then work in order to pay for it.[49]

For Katona, the United States was capable of achieving even higher levels of affluence. American optimism, especially the "discontent with low status," represented "the heart of the psychological climate in which prosperity flourished." Much more so than his counterpart in western Europe, the American, "confident of his own power to advance his well-being, steps up his wants at an equal pace with, or even faster than his accomplishments." Moreover, the "ideal of higher living standards and consumer comforts" was expansive, "penetrating into Europe, Asia, and Africa." Even communist countries "are not immune to the sweet poisoning emanating from America." The spread of prosperity represented "our best hope for peace," since "unscrupulous leaders" would find it difficult to "create war frenzy" among people who "had a decent standard of living" and looked forward to even better conditions.[50]

Whether trying to reach a wider audience as a social commentator or sticking close to his empirical data, Katona revealed both the origins and the limitations of his analysis. His optimism, arising from his personality, his data, and his gratitude to the United States, served a number of purposes. It discharged his debt to his adopted country, it helped in convincing funding agencies of the importance of his studies, and it contributed to the reigning cold war consensus. But an examination of what Katona neglected or minimized, in both his surveys and his more general writings, also reveals the implications of his perspective. Until changes in public policy and funding directed attention to households for which the American dream was out of reach, the survey concentrated on people with incomes large enough to buy consumer durables and to affect significantly the overall level of national economic activity. Consequently, millions of people remained outside the scope of Katona's studies. As late as 1964, as other Americans were rediscovering poverty, he could still insist, "Ours is a middle-class society with middle-class comforts."[51]

The survey authors made other assumptions, too. They reflected the male bias of the social sciences when they interviewed the male " 'head' of the spending unit, usually the husband," even though advertisers and social critics had long since recognized the importance of women in consumption. "Only if the wife had adequate knowledge of the family's financial situation and the husband was not available was she interviewed," noted the 1946 survey. Even in 1970, only when interviewers got around to asking about durables other than automobiles were they instructed to "encourage wife to help with this section."[52]

Also reflecting the biases of social science in the 1950s, the survey implicitly envisioned a society in which income mattered but ethnicity and social class did not. The surveys asked about age, education, occupation, race, and income but not about religion, ethnic identification, or political orientation. Despite Katona's emphasis on the influence of social groups and the media, the household appeared relatively isolated from advertising, community, friendship networks, and other mediating institutions. Katona's surveys assumed a relatively direct relationship between the individual household and the marketplace, with national economic and political events serving as the principal determining factors. Moreover, dichotomies of optimism and pessimism, on the one hand, and good times and bad times, on the other, may have captured people's attitudes toward politics and economics, but the interviews were hardly capable of giving a full sense of how people felt about what and how they consumed.[53]

In his attempt to reconstruct liberal economic theory, Katona resurrected Adam Smith's rational man, this time in the guise of the sensible consumer. He expanded his lifelong focus on the consumer into a generalized theory that missed a larger set of actors and issues. His American writings revealed his lack of formal training in and attention to the macroeconomic forces that economists of all stripes considered critical. Because of his failure to broaden his focus, he could not develop a comprehensive theory. He tended to separate work from consumption. To a considerable extent he neglected the contributions to the economy of workers and entrepreneurs. He minimized the power of corporate capitalism to shape patterns of spending. Moreover, he underemphasized the contribution to the postwar economy of the full range of government activities.[54]

In fact, although Katona distanced himself from the libertarianism of many émigré economists, in important ways his celebration of the consumer as the critical element in the economy served as an argument against government intervention. During the heyday of Lyndon Johnson's Great Society, he seemed to endorse government intervention that went "beyond the economic into the areas of physical and mental health, education, and social welfare." Yet he returned to his central position that these wider social obligations "can best be provided for if the economy is soundly based on a large, optimistic mass of consumers constantly seeking to improve their way of life." In postwar America, he believed, the "countercyclical effect of consumer behavior" lessened the need for government intervention to steer the economy. "It would be consistent with the American preference for voluntary and private action in maintaining our system," he concluded in 1964, "if we give increasing thought to the reinforcement of the stabilizing role that may be played by consumers." Implicitly helping to build the cold war consensus in his new homeland, Katona was refuting those who had once thought that totalitarianism would come to the United States. The consumer was a free representative of democracy, he believed, whose independence and power made the totalitarian control of government pointless. The American way was superior.[55]

By the early 1970s, Katona had discharged his debt to his mentors and to his country. From the late 1940s until his retirement, Katona's professional world flourished. The University of Michigan, the ISR, and his own survey grew in prestige and resources, in large measure because of the accomplishments of the generation of researchers and scholars who came to Ann Arbor around the time Katona arrived. Optimism and gratitude dominated his personal perspective during these years. Although inflation was a significant and growing concern during the postwar period, Katona usually looked on the brighter side of things. He persisted in focusing on the present and future, emphasized the positive, and avoided worrying about or even looking back on the past. To be sure, he had not lived through the worst horrors of Nazi Germany. Even so, it is surprising that either in person or in writings, he almost never mentioned Nazism or 1930s Germany. Perhaps this had some-thing to do with the fact that he was an agnostic and a non-observant Jew whose beliefs remained a private matter.

Katona began an active retirement in 1972, a turning point that coincided with the worst postwar economic crisis, one marked by significant inflation. Escalating prices, the war in Vietnam, environmental awareness, and Water-gate shattered his optimism—and provided just the kind of disruptive break in the gestalt that he had long feared. Nine years later, on June 17, 1981, Katona received an honorary doctorate in economics from the Free Univer-sity of Berlin. He died the next day. In remarks he prepared for delivery in Berlin, Katona still saw rapidly rising prices as the most serious threat to economic well-being, and was less hopeful than he had been at any time since the 1940s. Katona ended his remarks by emphasizing other elements of his faith which his experiences in Germany and the United States had strength-ened. The scholar's dedication to truth, Katona remarked, might "compel the researcher to abandon his adherence to cherished hypotheses and theo-ries," something Katona himself had not experienced in a major way for at least sixty years. "A great university," he said, perhaps recalling his personal victory over the Nazis, his debt of gratitude to the University of Michigan, and his commitment to social science expertise, "must transmit these char-acteristics of research to its students and through them to the wider world."[56]

Ironically, Katona died in Berlin, the city from which he had emigrated almost half a century before. In the intervening years he had come a long way, and yet in some sense he had also stayed in the same place. For it was interwar Germany that had given him the experiences and education that caused him to focus on social cognition, inflation, and the consumer. In his reminiscences, Katona called Béla Kun and Adolf Hitler his "benefactors," an odd word to describe one man who drove him out of his homeland and another who forced him to emigrate once again and who was responsible for killing millions of Jews. Nevertheless, the University of Michigan, various foundations and corporations, and the U.S. government also served as his benefactors. Above all, it was American consumers who caused his career to flourish. Or, to put it in a different way, his gratitude to America and his achievement there gave him the passion of a convert. Katona displayed none of the irony or sense of betrayal by a new homeland that was characteristic of other émigrés. His writings revealed no sense of feeling marginal to American life. Throughout most of his career in the United States, Katona thus was that paradoxical figure: the sophisticated European who became so captivated with America that he identified with his audience.[57]

Central to Katona's vision, as we have seen, was the notion that the con-sumer heroically prevented inflation, totalitarianism, and economic instability from reaching America. Here, with his emphasis on consumer power, he articulated a distinctive concept of civic duty. The American consumer made state planning unnecessary. In many ways Katona continued to participate in the debates among New School émigrés, maintaining that consumer culture was the source not of civilization's demise but of its revitalization; that mass society promoted not stultification but satisfaction. He thus contributed to the celebration of American exceptionalism which so dominated American social thought in the years after World War II. Like many contemporary social critics, he appreciated the expertise of social scientists, remained confident about the effects of affluence, emphasized a psychological outlook, celebrated an expanding middle class, paid little attention to issues of equity and poverty, hoped for the achievement of social justice through economic growth, celebrated America in contrast to life in the Soviet Union, and expressed reservations about government intervention in the economy. Bent on self-improvement, aspiring to an ever higher standard of living, embracing the benefits of materialism, embodying bourgeois values, Katona's consumer provided the engine and the balance wheel of the postwar U.S. economy. Consumer sovereignty is a cliché among economists, but in Katona's hands this notion became something more. His picture of the consumer as a sensible social learner in effect became a defense of what he saw as the essential elements of the American way of life: democracy, middle-class prosperity, and individual economic effort.

The Émigré as Celebrant of American Affluence

Historians usually see émigré intellectuals, especially members of the Frankfurt school, as critics of consumer culture. What has not been so apparent is the crucial role of certain émigrés in shaping a positive view of America's quest for a rising standard of living. Dichter and Katona articulated an American ideology of consumption as an essential component of people's aspirations for psychological well-being. As much as anyone else in the postwar world, Katona was responsible for surveying the changing mood of the American consumer and Dichter for teaching Americans how to consume. A number of factors which influenced how émigré intellectuals, most of them Jewish in ancestry, came to terms with life in America help explain why the stories of Katona and Dichter were marked more by success and optimism than by struggle and bitterness. They were both adaptable men who came to the United States early in their careers after having experienced little or nothing of Europe's pre-1914 heyday and much of its post–World War I turmoil. Nor did they leave well-established and prestigious positions from which their initial situation in the United States would inevitably involve a decline. By and large, the émigrés who had the greatest success in America were those who, like Katona and Dichter, eschewed a sense of European superiority and readily appreciated American values and institutions. As individuals who achieved considerable success in their new homeland, they used their skills more to appreciate than to criticize what they found.[58]

In Berlin and Vienna of the 1920s and 1930s, two European cities in the forefront of the development of mass culture, Dichter and Katona had already encountered societies fascinated by innovations in consumption even as they looked to America to see what the future held in store. Even before emigrating, they had developed an appreciation of American consumer culture because the United States offered what Germany and Austria lacked: a link between new products, economic freedom, and political democracy. Looking at the world from Berlin and Vienna in the 1930s, they understood their own emigration as a path to enjoying both the fruits of affluence and a world safe from the threat of Nazism.

Katona and Dichter had much else in common. They offered an ideology that enabled Americans to overcome their depression-born fears and understand the connections between democracy, capitalism, and affluence. They believed that professional experts played critical roles in helping Americans come to terms with consumer culture in positive ways. Having achieved considerable success in their fields, they tried to write books that would reach a wider audience. They attacked puritanical restraint and celebrated the middle-class consumer. They connected consumer culture to a series of larger personal and social goals. They fueled the cold war consensus. They saw America as a white, middle-class society whose strengths would prevent the emergence of totalitarianism and would underwrite restraint of state intervention into the economy. They bought the American ideology of consumption as an essential component of national aspiration. They emphasized the psychological dynamics of the pleasures of consumption. Their adopted country inspired in them the passion of converts and, in doing so, helped shape their lives.

3

A Southerner in Exile,
the Cold War, and Social Order
David M. Potter's *People of Plenty*

George Katona and Ernest Dichter believed that middle-class consumers would make their adopted nation safe for democratic capitalism. In the 1950s and early 1960s a series of native-born writers cast a more skeptical eye on the effects of affluence. In the mid-1950s the most influential of these critiques was *People of Plenty: Economic Abundance and the American Character* (1954) by the historian David M. Potter (1910–1971). His book differed from the celebrations that Dichter and Katona offered as well as from the more insistent and forceful critiques that John Kenneth Galbraith, Vance Packard, and Betty Friedan would soon provide. A southerner by upbringing, a northerner by residence, and a historian much of whose life's work focused on the coming of the Civil War, with *People of Plenty*, Potter offered an analysis of abundance whose cold war celebrations were tempered by an acknowledgment of the costs Americans paid for their headlong embrace of prosperity. What shaped Potter's view was a complex of factors that included his southern heritage, his life in the North, and his generational experience as an academic. As a white, upper-class, uprooted southerner, he had an appreciation of the virtues of a cohesive, ordered society which in turn gave him a distinctive outlook on the disorderly, anomie-provoking consequences of a society of plenty.[1]

Potter's outlook rested on a set of traditional values that stood in opposition to the emphasis that Dichter and, later, Betty Friedan placed on psychological self-realization and national prosperity. He believed in human weakness, expressed skepticism toward unbounded individualism, and remained horrified by the power of unbridled capitalism to dissolve traditional social relations. Instead, he preferred the organic ties of family and community, accepted social stratification, and recognized the distinction between moral and material progress. In some ways his views resembled those of certain northern-born peers of his generation—academics turned public intellectuals, such as Richard Hofstadter, Oscar Handlin, Daniel Bell, David Riesman, and Edward Shils. In other ways his southern heritage gave his ideas a distinctive cast. The most significant difference between Potter and his northern-born contemporaries was that his commitment to traditional values developed earlier and ran deeper than theirs. Though related to his southern origins, his traditionalism was more Burkean than anything else.[2]

In the mid-1950s, without claiming the tradition as his own, though in fact describing his worldview, Potter explored aspects of what he called "the conservative position." He talked about "the importance of experience over theory," of "organic growth over logic," and of "the whole complex of existing values over the promise of potential." Opposing individualism, the conservative saw people as "beings in relationship." The conservative, for Potter, defended not the status quo but "status" itself, along with "social habits." What killed status in the United States between 1800 and 1830, Potter wrote, was "the double impact of polit.[ical] demand for equality & economic demand for mobility." From the Jacksonian era on, he noted regretfully, "conservative thought had to go underground." "A great conservative," Potter remarked, referring to Edmund Burke, "will accept change, and will even sympathize with revolution." Like Benjamin Disraeli, a true conservative "will accept democracy."[3]

Potter's task was to bring these values aboveground, use them to criticize society rather than to defend vested interests, and in the process underscore the importance of experience, tradition, status, leadership, and responsibility. As he defended these values, Potter stood in sharp contrast to major southern conservatives of the twentieth century such as Donald Davidson, William Watts Ball, Richard M. Weaver, Lewis Simpson, and M. E. Bradford. Unlike Potter, they never left their beloved South to live in the North. Unlike the more extreme among them, Potter defended neither the master class as a bulwark against the rabble nor a southern way of life with segregation at its core. Like northern academics, and unlike true southern conservatives, Potter avoided dogma and relished irony and paradox. In the 1950s he offered a qualified celebration of American democracy and prosperity as he made clear his opposition to the Soviet way of life. Yet he did not let his appreciation of life in America prevent him from criticizing advertising, the growth of suburbia, and mass culture. He worried about rootlessness and anxiety and yearned for a community that relied on feelings of belonging and on a stable sense of status. Yet unlike northern-born intellectuals who cherished the social mobility available in America, something that many of them as Jews experienced at firsthand, Potter honored stable status more than social opportunity. His vision relied less on the new moralism than on a love of social order. During the 1960s, like his southern counterparts, Potter felt that his ancestral home was under attack; like his peers among northern academics, he veered to the right. More than anything else, this complex heritage shaped Potter's views on affluence.

A Southerner on the Move

Born December 6, 1910, in Augusta, Georgia, Potter came from a very successful, well-established, upper-class mercantile family. Sickly as a child, he did not attend school until he entered high school. Instead, "he spent most of his boyhood in bed reading," a colleague later remembered, and by age fifteen "had been through the memoirs of every Confederate leader and every Southern politician of consequence." His class status, his mother's commitment to Christian Science, and his long exemption from the pressures of school gave him a critical distance from the region whose history he would ponder as an adult. In a talk at his high school commencement, he revealed some of the issues that compelled him at an early age and would shape his perspective on Americans as a people of plenty. In the context of defending a classical education against vocational training, young Potter pondered the meaning of work and wealth. He honored those who labored hard and remarked that he did not despise the "material values of life." Yet he found "contemptible . . . the parasite who cherishes lofty ideals and lives by the sweat of another's brow." Above all, he cast a skeptical eye on people who used a monetary yardstick as their standard of value: "When worth is to be measured by wealth, mental ability by money, and greatness by gold, it is time to take stock of our educational ideals." Potter left Augusta in 1928 to attend Emory University. As an undergraduate he read H. L. Mencken's critiques of southern mores and institutions, from lynching to sharecropping, peonage, illiteracy, and bigotry. Potter and the fellow members of his Emory debate team, including C. Vann Woodward, were coached by Glenn Rainey, "whose probing questions," Potter later recalled, "led a good many Southern youths to reflect for the first time that segregation was perhaps not a necessary part of the order of nature, like sunrise and sunset."[4]

After earning his B.A. in 1932, Potter entered graduate school at Yale, having gone there to work with Ulrich B. Phillips. When Phillips died during Potter's second year, Potter went on to write his dissertation under Ralph Henry Gabriel, an intellectual historian who was laying the groundwork for the newly emerging field of American studies. He earned his Ph.D. in 1940 with a thesis that served as the basis for his first book, *Lincoln and His Party in the Secession Crisis* (1942). While working on this project, he taught at the University of Mississippi (1936–38) and Rice Institute (1938–42). Then he returned to Yale, never to live in the South again. At Yale he rose quickly through the ranks, from assistant professor in 1942 to an endowed chair in 1950. His leadership of the American studies department and his editorship of *Yale Review* expanded his vistas and spurred his interests in wider questions of interpretation and in new approaches developed by social and behavioral scientists.[5]

Throughout his life, Potter remained very conscious of the contrast between his southern heritage and his northern lifestyle. In New Haven, he surrounded himself with physical reminders of the South. "A native Southerner who transcended his southern heritage but never disclaimed it," as colleagues once remarked, Potter concentrated his writing and teaching on southern history. Conscious as he was of his regional heritage, he was also acutely aware that he had chosen to leave the South. In 1965 he called himself and Woodward "ex-Confederates." A colleague recalled that though Potter never expressed "nostalgia for the South or any interest in returning there to live," he was nonetheless "the most intensely Southern man" he had ever known. Potter, another colleague commented, had a "bifocal view: he kept the South and left it." Potter himself emphasized how his complicated relationship to the South shaped his outlook. He was aware that he had resided "longer outside of the South than in it," he remarked in 1968, "and hopefully have learned to view it with detachment, though not without fondness. Certainly no longer a Southerner, I am not yet completely denatured." What particularly haunted him was the Civil War. As a child he had seen Confederate veterans march in Memorial Day parades. He had lived, he remembered, "in the long backwash of the war in a land that remembered the past very vividly and somewhat inaccurately." Born forty-five years after its conclusion, Potter noted, he could remember references to "what was still called 'The War'—as if there had been no other." As a historian, Potter wanted to face the region's past realistically. "For two generations after Appomattox," he wrote in 1969, "the compulsive memories of the Lost Cause had held the Southern mind in thrall; myth had grown like ivy over the brick and mortar of Southern historical experience; sentimentality and veneration had inhibited realism." Indeed, Woodward credited Potter, along with W. J. Cash and Howard Odum, with having exposed the South's defensiveness and conformity, or what Potter called its "siege mentality."[6]

Especially during his Yale years, Potter prided himself on being a realist opposed to ideological stances. Almost all of his work was nuanced and deliberate, and in most of his scholarly writing he tended to mute his personal politics. Yet his experiences and commitments as a southerner fundamentally shaped his outlook. Potter said of Woodward that he faced an "inner struggle in which his historical realism was pitted against his liberal urge to find constructive meanings in the past for the affairs of the present." It is possible to turn the tables and say of Potter that he faced an inner struggle in which his historical realism was pitted against his Burkean urge to find problematic meanings in the past for the affairs of the present. Central to his work was his assertion, common among historians of his generation from North and South, that "the Civil War was the great trauma in the American experience," a subject on which he focused in both his first and last books. A leitmotif of *Lincoln and His Party in the Secession Crisis* was that in the years before the Civil War, northern Republicans had shown a capacity for misconceptions, mistaken judgments, miscalculations, and unrealistic beliefs. His monumental Pulitzer Prize–winning study *The Impending Crisis, 1848–1861*, begun in 1954 but left unfinished at the time of his death seventeen years later, was likewise an extended meditation on the failure of statesmanship at a moment of crisis.[7]

If for Potter the coming of the Civil War underscored the tests leaders faced when confronted with insoluble problems, southern history also presented the historian with impossible dilemmas. As he noted in 1968, the history of the South was "the focus of two of the most profound and most difficult problems in the American experience." One was the "enduring distinctiveness and combative sectionalism" of the South within a nation that had grown from "a loose confederation" into "a consolidated, homogenized nation." The other was the tension between the professed commitment to equality and the fact that the South "has clung to racial distinctions."[8]

His pessimism had personal origins as well. For a man who cherished a sense of place, Potter was constantly uprooting himself. He continually faced tragedies in his private life. His father, a wholesale grocer, died in the late 1930s. His first marriage, in 1939, to Ethelyn E. Henry ended in divorce six years later. He married Dilys Mary Roberts in 1948, but when their only child was born in the early 1950s, Dilys suffered a nervous breakdown and Potter's mother came up from Georgia to help out. Potter's relationship with his mother was tense, in part because the son had broken with the mother's religion. During her stay in the North, Potter's mother was diagnosed with cancer. As a Christian Scientist, she refused medical treatment. In the fall of 1952, while on a walk, she was struck and killed by a truck. Dilys took her own life in 1969.[9]

These historic and private tragedies shaped what his Yale colleague Howard Lamar called Potter's "deep pessimism about the social fabric and cynicism about human nature." Contradictions marked his politics, but throughout his life the issue of how leaders handled crises remained a central force in his social vision. Two critical moments in U.S. history, which he explored in books that he edited in 1949 and 1950, captivated his attention: the conflicts between section and nation that resulted in the Civil War and the struggles to define the relationship between the government, corporations, and the individual which came to a head in the New Deal. In both instances, he believed, the nation suffered from a crisis of statesmanship. In 1936, a "conservative outraged by the New Deal," as a colleague later described him, Potter voted for the Socialist candidate Norman Thomas as a protest against what he saw as the failure of Roosevelt's leadership, which he considered as blundering as that of the generation he was studying in his thesis. Whether labeled a "Conservative or realist," his Stanford colleague Don E. Fehrenbacher remarked, Potter "lived with limited expectations concerning human capacity to understand social reality and control social forces." As a result, he had a "keen eye for paradox and dilemma. To be faced with a choice between unsatisfactory alternatives was, in Potter's view, the characteristic condition of man."[10]

Mobility and Social Order: Potter's Writings of the 1940s

Before he began work on *People of Plenty*, only once during his career did Potter write on affluence. He did so in an unexpected place, in the introduction to a book he edited, *Trail to California: The Overland Journal of Vincent Geiger and Wakeman Bryarly* (1945). The immediate context was Potter's discussion of what happened when the travelers realized that they were carrying too much with them on the overland trail: "greater quantities of foodstuffs than it was practicable to carry, . . . heavy mining equipment or valued personal effects such as feather beds, stoves, and other articles of furniture." Because it gives us clues to some themes in *People of Plenty*, Potter's observations are worth quoting at length:

> Ultimately, of course, this vast surplus was thrown overboard, with the result that for hundreds of miles, the trail was littered with articles of value. Traveler after traveler recorded his astonishment at the abundance of this jetsam and at the magnitude of the waste, and at the same time, almost every one told of his own company's adding to the accretion. Yet, while everyone deplored the loss of goods, few perceived the most tragic aspect of it—namely, that most of the excess was hauled for hundreds of miles, constantly retarding the journey and weakening the teams, before the penny-wise emigrants could bring themselves to face the inevitable. The waste of energy of mules and oxen, rather than the waste of goods, was the significant loss.

Like the travelers themselves, many American intellectuals, when faced with such information, would have lamented the needless waste of material. Yet here was Potter, writing in 1945, at a time when the nation had experienced more than a decade and a half of scarcity, not recognizing that "the significant loss" was in fact "the waste of goods." Potter's concern instead for the "waste of energy of mules and oxen" is at first glance puzzling. Perhaps the situation evoked for him the carnage of the Civil War, with the animals serving as some sort of correlative for the people who had borne a heavy burden amidst the waste of material. Maybe what we are reading here, if it is possible to see the animals as symbols of human labor, is Potter's concern for the way in which wasteful consumption forces people to work harder, in the end draining both work and consumption of positive meaning, a theme he would articulate fifteen years later.[11]

Potter's remarks bear comparison with "A Statement of Principles," which the Nashville agrarians issued in *I'll Take My Stand* (1930), lamenting that though contemporary Americans had more time to consume a greater number of goods than before, "the tempo of our labors communicates itself to our satisfactions, and these also become brutal and hurried." Defining consumption "as the grand end which justifies the evil of modern labor," the agrarians asserted that "the constitution of the natural man probably does not permit him to shorten his labor-time and enlarge his consuming-time indefinitely. The modern man," they noted with regret, "has lost his sense of vocation." In words that Potter would echo almost a quarter of a century later, they decried how advertisers "must coerce and wheedle the public into being loyal and steady consumers, in order to keep the machines running." Advertising "consults the happiness of the consumer no more than it consulted the happiness of the laborer. It is the great effort of a false economy of life to approve itself." Although Potter rejected agrarianism, it is possible to see his thinking as a part of a southern tradition that identified affluence as degrading both work and the values of a supposedly organic society.[12]

In light of what Potter would write in *People of Plenty*, several things are clear. When considering affluence, a word he used in the quoted passage, Potter worried less about the morality of spending than the implications of mobility and excessive abundance for the quality of human life. Unlike that of Katona or Dichter, Potter's background prepared him to cast a skeptical eye on the unbridled enthusiasm for abundance. Above all, the theme of mobility connects the passage from *Trail to California* with Potter's later work. Americans, he was writing as he pondered the consequences of the westward movement (and perhaps his own geographical and professional mobility), paid a heavy price for their restlessness as they set out to achieve a dream of improved social position.

Before turning to *People of Plenty*, let us examine one more article that Potter wrote in the 1940s which reveals not only what he thought about race relations, the article's ostensible subject, but also how the racial situation in the South affected his view of the fragility of the social order. In 1948, while he was Harmsworth Professor of American History at Oxford, Potter wrote an article titled "The Future of the Negro in the United States" for the BBC publication *The Listener*. Here Potter was responding to President Harry S. Truman's proposed civil rights legislation, the first such presidential initiative since the end of Reconstruction more than seventy years earlier. With this bill, which focused on housing, public facilities, voting, and anti-lynching legislation, Truman was calling for the strengthening of federal protection for African Americans. Potter's response shows what a moderate he was on race relations. At the same time, he expressed his fears about the fragility of the South's social cohesion.[13]

He began on a skeptical note, calling into question American boasts about the rapid growth of racial equality. In the process he made clear his commitment to incremental change that recognized the hold of tradition. Potter hailed the progress that African Americans had made, much of it, he emphasized, with the support of southern white liberals, southern state governments, northern philanthropists, and the Supreme Court. He agreed that improvements in the nation's race relations were "urgent." He worried, however, that African Americans in the South, supported by northern politicians beholden to racial militants, would insist on too rapid a pace of change. The resulting pressure from the federal government might provoke a reaction among white southerners. This would be a strong possibility if the nation employed force and government intervention that ignored regional folkways, rather than "moral pressure and political suasion." If there had to be intervention from Washington, it "should be applied in such a way as to reinforce rather than to destroy the indigenous growth within the South of a movement that has worked steadily toward more just and less antagonistic race relations."[14]

This was the faith of a southern white moderate of the 1940s, a faith that rested on traditional values. There was a certain degree of noblesse oblige in Potter's position. He assumed that an improved racial situation in the South would come from the efforts of white liberals, and he thought unfavorably of or simply neglected the contribution of the NAACP nationally and African Americans in the South. Indeed, in his historical work, Howard Temperley has remarked, Potter "had remarkably little to say about African Americans," a lack that reflected his perspective as a southern white man, his preference for a traditional style of political history, and his relative lack of engagement with the emerging fields of African American and social history. In 1948, however, he further framed his thinking within a cold war context, eager, as he said, "to disarm Soviet critics who have followed the example set by the Nazis in seizing upon the Negro question as a convenient stick with which to beat the United States." He feared the possibility of social disorder, which he identified with a leadership that resorted to coercion and militancy. Using phrases like "voluntary" change, "regional folkways," "personal good-will," and "indigenous growth," Potter made clear his commitment to organic community, social cohesion, responsible leadership, and a pace of change that would not disrupt the social fabric. He hailed progress in race relations while at the same time he worried about the consequences of changes that might threaten the fragile social order of an unprepared nation—or, more precisely, section.[15]

Potter's view of the South and of the section's race relations both resembled and differed substantially from the outlook of Phillips, his mentor and fellow Georgian. As a historian, Phillips took as his life's work the task of defending slavery, the social order of the antebellum South, the legitimate rule of a white patriarchy, and racial segregation. Potter wrote about Phillips on several occasions. His first scholarly article, authored when he was twenty-one, revealed his debt to his mentor. His second scholarly publication was a bibliography of Phillips's work, which appeared right after his mentor's death. In 1967, Potter responded to Eugene D. Genovese's landmark reassessment of Phillips, admitting that his mentor was a racist but insisting that northern liberals failed to acknowledge that "Phillips' most formidable quality . . . was his realistic recognition of the potency of racism as a factor in Southern life." Moreover, he congratulated Genovese for having brought "into excellent focus the question of the values of a patriarchal or paternalistic system as opposed to a system, which exalts competition, minimizes the responsibilities of the individual to the group, and denies the principle of social order." However much Potter distanced himself from these commitments, he carried over from Phillips, and more generally from southern tradition, commitments to elitism, racial peace, social order, organic community, a sense of place, and noblesse oblige.[16]

Yet the student's vision differed from that of his mentor in major ways. Unlike Phillips, Potter relished paradox, irony, and complexity. As a southerner who spent his adult life in the north, and a moderate on race, he was attentive to the possibility that northern attacks on southern traditions might actually impede racial progress. Yet he believed that blacks and whites were inherently equal and remained skeptical of the claims of southern whites that their color entitled them to special privileges. He felt that northern and southern leaders shared the blame for slavery, the Civil War, and the persistence of racial problems. As a southerner living in New England, Potter was intensely interested in the question of what constituted a distinctive regional character. He greatly respected W. J. Cash's classic *Mind of the South* (1941), a fact that underscores his distance from Phillips and, more generally, from those southern conservatives who took for granted the attraction of the Lost Cause and a way of life built on racism and nostalgia.[17]

People of Plenty: Social Order, Mobility, and Affluence

People of Plenty, which relied for its critique of affluence on notions of social order and community, had complex intellectual and institutional origins. Potter began work on the book not long after he returned from Oxford, where he had been struck by the contrast between war-torn Europe and an unscathed and dramatically more prosperous America. As he worked on the book, he kept before him a quotation from the introduction to *I'll Take My Stand*. In a world of underconsumption, the southern agrarians asserted, producers, "disguised as the pure idealists of progress," had to "coerce and wheedle the public into being loyal and steady consumers." Modern advertising, along with salesmanship, they had noted in 1930, "is the most significant development of our industrialism."[18]

The postwar celebrations of America's unique destiny increased Potter's skepticism about the claims made during the cold war for a moral basis of American exceptionalism. As a historian trained in the 1930s, he had to come to terms with the frontier thesis of Frederick Jackson Turner, about to reach the height of its influence. Teaching the survey course on U.S. history at Yale in the 1940s sparked Potter's interest in questions of national character, an issue very much on the mind of social scientists as they worked to shift the focus in their field from racial to cultural attributes. His involvement in American studies connected Potter to scholars who were exploring questions of American distinctiveness, an issue central to the "myth and symbol" school that dominated the emerging interdisciplinary field in the 1950s.[19]

The invitation to deliver the Walgreen lectures at the University of Chicago in 1950 afforded Potter the opportunity he needed to develop his ideas and commit them to print. Charles R. Walgreen, who made his fortune developing a chain of drug stores, had endowed the series in 1937 after a niece told him that some of her professors at the university were communists or communist sympathizers. Walgreen complained to the president, Robert Maynard Hutchins, that he was unwilling to have his niece "absorb the Communistic influences to which she is so insidiously exposed." Don't you realize, Walgreen asked his niece, that communism involved "the abolition of the family, the abolition of the church, and especially do you realize it means the overthrow of our government?" Her reply hardly allayed his fears: "Yes, I think I do; but doesn't the end ever justify the means?" Hutchins eventually turned the ensuing attack on the university by the state legislature into a fund-raising opportunity by persuading Walgreen to counteract the damage his accusation had caused, as well as any subversive faculty influence, by endowing a series of lectures on the American way of life. For Potter, the opportunity to deliver the Walgreen lectures was irresistible, involving as it did prestige, a handsome stipend, and publication. Above all, it afforded him the occasion to work out his ideas on the relationship between abundance and national character.[20]

In *People of Plenty*, Potter expressed less criticism of American society than he actually felt. Referring to the sponsorship of the Walgreen lectures, his Yale colleague Paul Pickrel speculated that Potter "undertook to give full value—to fulfill the announced terms of the endowment." In addition, there is some evidence in the book of Potter's concern that the reader might believe he sided with unthinking anticommunists who celebrated America's distinctiveness as a moral attribute. His materialistic explanation of the origins of America's uniqueness, perhaps itself an ironic play on Marxist determinism, cautions us not to assume that he too ascribed America's virtues to moral superiority.[21]

People of Plenty was a bold, original, and complicated book. Written in a clear and accessible style, it was one of those pathbreaking works through which historians after 1945 reached an audience outside their field. The book was simultaneously analytic, historical, and topical. Like Hofstadter and Handlin, Potter explored how historians might benefit from the conceptual advances of social and behavioral scientists. His central task was to explore the relationship between national character and abundance. As he proceeded with the book, issues surrounding the concept of national character, as well as the process of establishing the connections between the work of historians and behavioral scientists, grew more important than the original question about the impact of abundance on American national character.[22]

In the first part of the book, he pondered the issues raised by the extensive literature on national character. As he examined the ways in which historians had employed the concept, Potter noted a gap between the importance of the notion to them and "the inadequacies, the abuses, and the confusion" with which they actually deployed it. He then turned to three non-historians who, relying on the concepts of culture and personality, had written suggestively on national character: Margaret Mead, David Riesman, and Karen Horney. Noting that all three posited "the competitive spirit" as a distinctly American quality, Potter argued that they had failed to draw with adequate precision the connection between character traits and the changing conditions in which the development of distinct national features took place.[23]

This was the task Potter tackled in the second part of *People of Plenty*, admitting as he went along that it was not easy to explain the connection between history, national character, and affluence. He began by discussing the nature of American abundance. Countering those who ascribed the nation's economic success to a surfeit of natural resources, he emphasized the distinction between potential and actual abundance. Denying that he had any desire "to bring in a verdict on the free-enterprise system," Potter nonetheless argued that what had enabled the United States to actualize its potential was its people's industry and creativity, "the ventures and struggles of the pioneer, the exertions of the workman, the ingenuity of the inventor, the drive of the enterpriser, and the economic efficiency of all kinds of Americans, who shared a notorious addiction to hard work." What Turner had seen as unique to the frontier was but one instance in a larger story of American achievement.[24]

To Potter, the results of this transformation of resources were clear. The hourly wages of unskilled American workers were 60 percent higher than for their counterparts in other industrialized nations. Only a handful of nations achieved more than half the American level of per capita income, and the richest of these did not reach two-thirds of the U.S. standard. Moreover, the nation's "unprecedented riches" were "very widely distributed." Potter did not present statistics on the distribution of wealth or income in America, however, for that would have revealed a greater inequality than he acknowledged. Instead, he boasted that "we can afford college educations and T-bone steaks for a far higher proportion of our people than receive them anywhere else on the globe."[25]

Though at times Potter could seem positively celebratory about what the United States had accomplished, he went to great lengths to question the grounds on which some of his contemporaries praised American exceptionalism. He poked fun at those who worshipped America as a freedom-loving nation, as if such a designation implied a free and morally superior choice. Instead, he argued that nations could afford only those political systems that economic conditions made possible. Thus it was just as inadvisable to attribute American democracy "to sheer moral and ideological virtue" as it was for an aspiring democracy to raise expectations which its lack of economic achievement made it impossible to fulfill. Therefore, rather than exporting democracy to the world, which he felt America had tried to do but failed to achieve, he called on the nation to export the economic conditions that would eventually make democracy possible. America's redemptive message for the world was that abundance, not democracy, was the truly revolutionary force.[26]

If Potter wished to argue that abundance was the key to the nation's history and character, then he had to identify its central institution, which he found in modern advertising. Under conditions of abundance, advertising performed an essential economic function "for instilling new needs, for training people to act as consumers, for altering men's values, and thus for hastening their adjustment" to those conditions. There was ample evidence of the power of advertising: the fact that the nation spent more on advertising than on primary and secondary education, the way advertising was transforming the mass media for its own purposes, its pressure to accentuate the lowest common denominator, and its avoidance of the controversial. Potter lamented that advertising lacked any larger social purpose to balance its unquestioned power. Unlike the key institutions of an earlier age, the school and the church, which instilled beliefs that had social value, advertising lacked such positive goals. Instead, what it sought was "the stimulation or even the exploitation of materialistic drives and emulative anxieties and . . . the validation, the sanctioning, and the standardization of these drives and anxieties." In the end, what made advertising problematic was that it did not try to "impart qualities of social usefulness, unless," Potter noted skeptically, "conformity to material values may be so characterized."[27]

To fill out his argument, Potter had to show how abundance had actually shaped national character. With great ingenuity he focused on the conditions of child rearing which he believed abundance underwrote. He argued that modern wealth made possible the substitution of breast-feeding by bottle-feeding, the replacement of the extended family by the nuclear one, and the provision of separate bedrooms for children. Improved economic conditions also brought about the provision of warmth not by constricting clothing but by central heat, encouraged permissive toilet training, and led to the substitution of a peer group's control for family governance. All of these phenomena, Potter argued, fostered in American children from their early days a sense of separateness and individuality. To Potter, the new position children occupied provided no cause for celebration, since abundance made it possible for a larger number of the young to postpone economic responsibility at the same time that they were more rapidly achieving social maturity.[28]

Potter further connected abundance and national character in his discussion of the modern American family. By encouraging parents to have fewer children, by making it possible for them to have children at an earlier age, and by enabling people to live longer, affluence made it more likely that parents would raise their own children. Yet by making the wife less dependent on her husband, the new economic conditions made divorce more common. The effects of changes in the child's relationship to the parents were also mixed. Potter argued that the new economic order, by giving the father "lucrative opportunities through work outside the home," made it less likely that he and his children would work side by side as they had on farms, but more likely that the father, with increased leisure, could devote more attention to his offspring.[29]

For Potter, the most important transformation had to do with women's roles. The extension of economic independence to women had "enabled them to assume the role of partners rather than of subordinates within the family." If Potter minimized the extent to which women had worked outside the home in an economy of scarcity, he also exaggerated the degree to which affluence had eased the burden on mothers. The nation's wealth, he argued pointing to the introduction of labor-saving devices, "very nearly exempts a very large number of mothers from the requirement of economic productivity," leaving them free to devote "an unprecedented share of their time" to taking care of a much reduced number of offspring. With "fewer physical distractions in the care of the child," Potter asserted, the mother "is more likely to be restive in her maternal role because it takes her away from attractive employment with which it cannot be reconciled."[30]

The changes brought about by abundance were thus a mixed blessing. Some of his concerns focused on how surfeit shifted the nature of family relations from the economic to the emotional. With "emotional harmony" as "the principal criterion of success," marriages had become more unstable. Moreover, just as he lamented the demise of a status-based society, he also lamented the disappearance of the strong father. He doubted that the rise of the permissive family was due to "our more enlightened or progressive or humanitarian ideas." It troubled him, too, that "the principle of authority [had] lost some of its majesty" as "the only true criterion of domestic order," something he ascribed in part to abundance undermining the worker's docility. Consequently, authority was no longer an end in itself but a means to an end as workers embraced self-reliance and independence rather than obedience.[31]

Central to *People of Plenty* was Potter's constant assessment of the benefits and costs of abundance. Because "an economic surplus was available to pay democracy's promissory notes," Americans had been able to achieve equality of opportunity. Although America's "somewhat disillusioned intellectuals" emphasized the gap between reality and ideals, in fact, he argued, the nation's circumstances had brought about a degree of social mobility and equality unprecedented in world history. "Certain conspicuous exceptions, such as the treatment of American Negroes," he admitted, "qualify all these assertions but do not invalidate them as generalizations." Despite the facts that contradicted the myth that every man was responsible for his own fate and that America was a classless society, these dreams nonetheless had "immense moral power" because "they approximate reality closely enough to be convincing."

The belief in full equality in a classless society was responsible for all that Potter found decent in American culture. It underwrote the optimism, confidence, commitment to merit, and "respect for the human dignity of any man or woman, regardless of that person's social credentials."[32]

One of the ironies of Potter's position was that in assuming that abundance shaped national character, he overlooked the historically exceptional experience of his native region. Writing in 1958, Woodward reminded his former debate partner of this fact. Though acknowledging the South's recent "taste" of abundance, Woodward paid more attention to the region's "long and quite un-American experience with poverty." The experience of southerners with want and scarcity, Woodward pointed out, "was too deeply embedded in their memory to be wiped out by a business boom and too deep not to admit some uneasiness at being characterized historically as a 'People of Plenty.'" Woodward concluded his gentle questioning of Potter's book by suggesting that "in a nation known around the world for the hedonistic ethic of the American Standard of Living, the Southern heritage of scarcity remains distinctive."[33]

Although Potter failed to acknowledge southern poverty, he was too much of a southerner and a Burkean—and too fascinated with paradox—not to recognize the drawbacks of abundance. Unlike those who embraced the cold war consensus and celebrated the demise of social classes in America, Potter emphasized the persistence of class divisions and social inequalities. He feared that the gap between ideals and reality would attract idealists to Marxism. More important, the gap left many people "personally broken and defeated." In addition, because the indicators of social differences were "relatively intangible" in the United States, class distinctions seemed "doubly unfair and discriminatory."[34]

Even more serious to him was that the dream of social equality had destroyed the sense of status, "the one value which seemed inherent in the traditional class society—namely, that sense of the organic, recognized relationship between the individual and the community." Burke and Disraeli had recognized true status of a sort available only to members of the American upper class and long out of favor even among conservatives. Status as "fixed differential social position" meant "a condition of corporate membership in the group and thus a sense of belonging in the community." It implied "a condition of dependence by the group upon the individual for the performance of certain specific work and thus makes possible a sense of worth for the individual and a pride in performance, no matter how humble his labor." Genuine status "assures the individual that he may lead a meritorious and respected life in the station where circumstances have placed him, regardless of what that station may be." To Potter, the benefit of a status-conscious society, characteristic of an era of economic insufficiency, was that "under a system of subordination transmitted by heredity, social competition, with its attendant loss of energy through friction, was avoided." The status-bound individual "often gained a sense of contentment with his lot and even of dignity within his narrow sphere, and all that he sacrificed for this psycho-logical advantage was a statistically-negligible chance for advancement." In such a society, the tasks of government are simple, since the qualities needed for leadership are minimal and therefore the necessity to recruit widely is unnecessary.[35]

Potter hoped that Americans were beginning to recognize the adverse con-sequences of denying the importance of social status, which since the Ameri-can Revolution had "borne the hateful implications of privilege and subser-vience." Drawing on the writings of Erich Fromm and Theodor Adorno, two émigrés of the Frankfurt school, Potter insisted that Americans still had "a deep psychological craving for the certitudes." Craft-based work and the production-based family once offered the status that abundance had now undermined. The result was a fragmented status rather than "one of a single, homogeneous social relationship." The emphasis on social mobility and equality, whose excesses he believed Americans were now coming to realize, had generated "tensions too severe for some people to bear." The belief in equality meant that "even the least invidious form of subordination comes to be resented as carrying a stigma," and as a result people performed some kinds of work "grudgingly." Individuals, ever restless for advancement, often felt "stress and insecurity," without a sense of belonging or where they had come from or where they were heading, a sentiment Richard Hofstadter would echo in his discussion of status anxieties in his 1955 *Age of Reform*.[36]

In the end, once again relying on his capacity for paradox, a penchant he shared with Riesman and Hofstadter, Potter drew back from the pessimistic conclusion to which his argument seemed to be driving him. Ironically, abundance in a mature economy, he suggested, might enhance the very circumstances it had earlier undermined. Having destroyed the balance be-tween mobility and status in an earlier period, now, when "there were fewer undeveloped opportunities demanding to be exploited," American society no longer needed such a mobile population. "The wide prevalence of a high standard of living" meant that people no longer had to be mobile in order to share in the nation's abundance. This might make it possible for the nation "to relax the tensions of mobility, keeping it as an instrument for the self-fulfillment of the individual but dispensing with it as a social imperative." Moreover, "the fulfillment of abundance" could "free status of its one great historic blemish—its condemnation of the vast majority to a life of want." As a result, "a more beneficent form of status" might emerge "which would emphasize the concepts of membership, of identity, of place in the community."[37]

People of Plenty: Consensus and Dissent

In some important respects, with *People of Plenty*, David Potter participated in the cold war celebration of America as an affluent society. Like Katona and Dichter, he offered a vision of a white, middle-class world in which abundance was widespread and an increasing standard of living was transforming the society, often in positive ways. At moments, his argument that technology, hard work, and enterprise made possible the realization of the full potential of natural resources sounded like an unproblematic evocation of the American way of life. If his book was any guide, poverty had virtually disappeared, the wealthy had decreased in numbers and impact, work had become less irksome, women were more liberated, leisure was more prevalent, family life was more cooperative, and America could still stand as a model to the world.

Potter's exploration of the social implications of abundance also served to reaffirm America's uniqueness. His argument that abundance produced "the distinctive system of voluntaristic relationships" reverberated with what he had written in his 1948 article "The Future of the Negro," gave evidence of Potter's admiration for Alexis de Tocqueville, and connected his thinking with the descriptions of America as a pluralistic society which other leading intellectuals offered. Potter shared with those who articulated a consensus ideology a belief that what was distinctive about American egalitarianism was the process by which an increasing standard of living had made Americans hostile "to the class-struggle concept" and rendered social conflict unnecessary. Whereas in Europe, he wrote, the redistribution of wealth relied on "the expropriation of some and the corresponding aggrandizement of others," America "had conceived of it primarily in terms of giving to some without taking from others."[38]

Likewise, to Potter, as to many leading northern intellectuals, the nation's wealth helped explain central qualities of politics in America, including "the relative lack of intellectualism in its reform or radical movements." For example, he found the Populists and Progressives "incredibly muddled, sentimental, and superficial in their thinking," especially when compared with European radicals, whom he found more articulate and doctrinaire. Affluence had made it possible to "overleap" difficulties rather than solve them, because "the social problems of America were not at all fixed, and their mutability has made logical solutions unnecessary." Pointing to late-nineteenth-century problems with the currency, monopoly, and regulation, Potter argued that "in each case technological change interposed to relieve the acuteness of the problem or even to make it obsolete."[39]

Although Potter in many ways welcomed affluence, he also provided a cautionary tale. The book can be read as an assertion of the nation's mission as a purveyor of know-how; but Potter also warned against being carried away with paeans to the wonders of American democracy. Moreover, although he was an anticommunist, he cleverly distanced himself from the excesses of those who saw evidence of American superiority everywhere. At one point in *People of Plenty* he cites American expressions of sympathy for the underdog as evidence of the "desire to see the creed of equality proved by the success of those who appear less than equal," a statement that it is possible to construe as indicating that a pluralistic America was superior to an authoritarian Soviet Union. Perhaps with tongue in cheek, Potter then adds a footnote mentioning a newspaper article, which had appeared under the headline "Something the Russians wouldn't Understand," which reported that the son of a janitor had defeated the son of a very wealthy man in a golf tournament.[40]

The most interesting thing about Potter's dissent from celebration is his argument that abundance, far from being beneficent, is problematic because it undermines status. Most American analysts of consumption had worked within a moral tradition that emphasized the dangers of conformity and profligacy. Though he now expressed some concern about materialism, as he had in his high school graduation speech and in his essay on *Trail to California*, he seemed not at all troubled by the waste of goods. Unlike those of most northern-born leading intellectuals, Potter's concerns for standardization and conformity were mild, especially compared with his anxiety about the loss of a cohesive, hierarchical society based on status.[41]

It is on this issue that Potter's perspective as a southerner shows most clearly. On the surface, this is an odd claim. For one of the striking things about *People of Plenty* is that, although Potter was aware of how regional distinctiveness cut across and qualified national character, he never even hinted that American abundance affected the South differentially, an especially telling lapse given the region's historic poverty. Nonetheless, Potter's southernness shaped his outlook. With full, albeit implicit, consciousness of the South, Potter lamented the destruction of an organic society based on a clear sense of hierarchy and the corrosive effects of the individual's craving for acquired status. Even his reasons for optimism revolved around the restoration of balance, order, and a sense of belonging. With Americans no longer condemned to a life of want, it was now possible, he hoped, to minimize the power of hierarchy and maximize the positive qualities of status.[42]

The remarkable and all but unnoticed aspect of Potter's critique of affluence was that it rested on a traditional, even Burkean, set of values derived from a number of sources, including his view of the southern tradition as seen from his position in exile. In 1955, Louis Hartz argued in *The Liberal Tradition in America* that the nation lacked genuine radical and conservative traditions. *People of Plenty* was Potter's attempt to make a case for a critical stance toward affluence that relied on traditional values. For example, after a discussion of abundance as it involves competition, efficiency, and aggression, Potter issued a warning. Although these qualities were necessary "for the sake of the system," he wrote, "aggression at its maximum violates Christian ideals." Excessive appetite for rewards "outstrips the possibility of attaining them." The overweening quest for freedom and mobility "clashes with the real responsibilities and limitations of life," and the lure of riches tempts people "to abandon the system of status," opening themselves up to lives of insecurity and anxiety. Seen in conjunction with his early writings on California and civil rights, *People of Plenty* makes clear that his attention to status rested in part on his regional heritage. If earlier he had associated social fragility with race relations, he now feared that abundance undermined social cohesion. The themes that ran through much of what he had written since the mid-1940s emphasized the difficulty people faced when they were unprepared for change, the danger of rising expectations, and the celebration of a status-based organic community.[43]

Although the book focused on the implications of affluence, it was even broader than it claimed to be. It was, in many ways, a meditation on how modernization—characterized by social and geographic mobility, the widespread distribution of wealth, the transformation of work, and the demise of the nuclear and patriarchal family—threatened the social order. Potter's model for an admirable society, based in good measure on his southern identity, was a small, organic, socially cohesive community. This was what he believed prosperity and its attendant forces had done so much to undermine. Potter found it difficult to join in the celebrations of the 1950s, for it seemed to him that American abundance threatened the social order. He did his best to reassure himself that affluence might foster a new basis for cohesion, status, and belonging, but his sense of loss was palpable.

After the publication of *People of Plenty*, Potter continued his career as a distinguished historian. He remained at Yale for seven more years, leaving for Stanford in 1961. In the years between the publication of *People of Plenty* and his death, he pursued a two-track career. He kept at work on a history of the events leading to the Civil War. At the same time, the success of *People of Plenty* opened up to him the possibility of a career as a public intellectual, a historian with a considerable audience outside his profession of choice. He died of cancer in Palo Alto on February 18, 1971, while serving as president of both the American Historical Association and the Organization of American Historians. He may have been, the historian Martin Duberman said a few years before Potter's death, the "greatest living historian of the United States."[44]

Beginning in the early 1960s, Potter, like many of his leading northern-born academic counterparts such as Bell, Handlin, and Hofstadter, took a turn to the right and experienced a deepening pessimism. The radicalism of the 1960s, including the Black Power movement, seriously undermined his commitment to realism, to a non-ideological stance, and to understanding before making judgments. What especially sharpened the edge of his despair was that as a white southerner, he felt his region was under attack. He feared that a host of forces were arrayed against the place he loved and the best of the values it represented. His worst fears, first articulated in his 1944 article "The Future of the Negro," were coming true, especially with the rise of African American militancy and the federal use of force, both increasingly visible by 1963. The South was so important to Potter's view in general, and his view of affluence specifically, in large measure because it represented the values and way of life that modernization was destroying. "Even in the most exploitative economic situations," he wrote of the South in 1961, "this culture retained a personalism in the relations of man to man which the industrial culture lacks." Perhaps southern nostalgia, he remarked, "was the yearning of men in a mass culture for the life of a folk culture" that still existed. Perhaps, he concluded, even with its inequalities, life in the South "still had a relatedness and meaning which our more bountiful life in the mass culture seems to lack."[45]

Potter's increasing pessimism involved a reconsideration of the issues he explored in *People of Plenty*. Freed from the constraints of the Walgreen lectures, and perhaps worried about the use to which others had put his work, Potter acknowledged that he was more concerned about the implications of abundance than he had been willing to admit in 1954. Nothing captured this concern so well as his response to the writings of John Kenneth Galbraith. When Potter read *The Affluent Society* (1958), in the margins he noted that Galbraith "has not entered upon a consideration of the vital question whether our present production has reached the level at which further increases will have minimal social value." In reviewing Galbraith's *Liberal Hour* (1960), he asked rhetorically, was it necessarily true that "a nation with two cars in every garage" was "better equipped to fight Communism than a nation with one?"[46]

In the ensuing years, Potter grew more troubled about the promise of American life even as he asserted ever more strongly his commitment to traditional values. In 1959 he criticized the cold war celebration of American life by pointing out that those who focused on suburban life were neglecting "the poor, the dispossessed," prefiguring arguments made a few years later by Michael Harrington and Oscar Lewis. To the extent that the standard of living had improved for the poor, he noted in a speech at Smith College, this had been accomplished by economic growth rather than "by solving the problem of the distribution of wealth." Above all, it was America's wastefulness ("the residue of our own devastation" in nature and cities) and willingness to walk away from problems that most bothered him. The real source of America's malaise lay not in the suburbs but in the failure to create true community, especially in the nation's cities. Agricultural communities fostered continuity, a sense of belonging, and organic relationships, whereas aggression, anxiety, challenges to authority, and alienation were endemic in modern America.[47]

His deepening despair became clear in several essays he wrote in 1963. In one, not published until after his death, Potter argued that America's great success "in approaching the goals of mobility, of individualism, of permissiveness, of equalitarianism has not produced the society it was expected to produce." Perhaps it was time, he argued, to look beyond proposals for social reform and understand how widespread aggression, anxiety, and alienation were in America. Moreover, he suggested that Americans consider "the possibility of serious shortcomings in the organic structure or the intrinsic nature of the society itself." In the same year, in lectures delivered at his alma mater, Potter argued that the very factors that he had connected with abundance ten years earlier—the increasing impact of the mass media, the decline in breastfeeding, the development of new technologies, the heightening of egalitarianism and individualism, and the rise in rates of mobility—were responsible for alienation. Similarly, in lectures delivered in 1963 but only published posthumously, Potter worried about forces in American society that were bringing about the demise of authority, the threat to distinctiveness, the tyranny of the majority.[48]

By the late 1960s, abundance—accompanied as it was by technology, large-scale enterprise, and the breakdown of small institutions—no longer seemed to him worth the price. "High productivity," he wrote in an unpublished 1969 manuscript, "brought a material standard of living which, at one time, appeared to validate the society completely. But it is now evident that all the gains were at a high price not yet paid, and they created problems not yet solved," such as overpopulation, devastation of the environment, and the development of warfare based on atomic, chemical, and biological weapons. "Many human values," he argued, "have been sacrificed to technological values," as he lamented the "rigorous psychological demands upon human beings, that they be achievement-oriented and consumption-minded."[49]

In the end, Potter's response to affluence drew on his identity as a southerner in academic exile, his debt to a strand of the southern tradition that was skeptical of modernization, and his sense of being trapped by dramatically changing circumstances. His influential book, which differed so significantly from his scholarship on the Civil War, marked a major excursion into the arena where public intellectuals debated issues surrounding the cold war consensus. His critique signals the beginning of a long process of deligitimization of that outlook, though more ironic and subdued than those that came later. His warnings about the impact of affluence drew less on the new moralism than on distinctive southern traditions. What Allen Tate said of the Southern Renaissance applies to Potter as well: that his "backward glance" derived from the tension between a traditional past and a modernizing present. Indeed, what the historian Daniel J. Singal said of Ulrich Phillips might, with some qualification, apply to Potter as well. "In the sharp, assertive, occasionally bitter tone Phillips sustained in his last publications, one detects a pained reaction on his part to the intellectual changes then underway in the country, which brought him in turn to a fervent affirmation of those values under challenge." The key values Potter asserted in *People of Plenty* and elsewhere— commitment to an organic community in which people had fixed status but corporate membership; to the pride in meaningful labor performed within one's station; to skepticism about the virtues of competition and mobility that undermined a sense of place; to individuals unalienated by modernization; and to order, proportion, and belonging—derived from his being, though no longer a southerner, "not yet completely denatured."[50]

4

Critique from Within

John Kenneth Galbraith, Vance Packard,
and Betty Friedan

In the late 1950s and early 1960s, a series of best-selling books transformed the discussion of American affluence. They can be divided into two groups. The first—John Kenneth Galbraith's *Affluent Society* (1958); three books by Vance Packard, *The Hidden Persuaders* (1957), *The Status Seekers* (1959), and *The Waste Makers* (1960); and Betty Friedan's *Feminine Mystique* (1963)— launched critiques of American society even as they continued to assume that the affluence of the middle class was the chief problem facing America. The second group—Paul Goodman's *Growing Up Absurd* (1960), Oscar Lewis's *Children of Sánchez* (1961), Michael Harrington's *The Other America* (1962), and Rachel Carson's *Silent Spring* (1962)—offered a head-on attack against the very notion that middle-class, suburban affluence was itself an urgent issue. Both groups of books, the second more than the first, contributed to unlinking the connection Ernest Dichter and George Katona had made between democracy, capitalism, and consumption.

In this chapter I focus on the books by Packard, Galbraith, and Friedan, immensely influential works that critiqued middle-class affluence even as they reaffirmed its centrality as an object of social criticism. Each of the authors made distinctive contributions that set them apart from the writers who preceded them. Galbraith deployed the familiar formula when he gave his book its title, *The Affluent Society*, but broke new ground by introducing the idea that public policy could counter the excesses of affluence. He called on the federal government to play a key role in addressing what he saw as the imbalance between the prosperity of private households and the poverty of the financially strapped public sector. Packard's trilogy offered an accessible picture of the way advertisers secretly tricked the public into buying goods, suburbanites sought to assuage their status anxieties through shopping, and manufacturers planned obsolescence which wasted resources. In all three he asserted that the excesses of affluence were undermining a producerist ethic and enshrining a consumerist one. With *The Feminine Mystique*, Friedan at once worked within the formula Packard and others had established while breaking new ground in her analysis of the impact on women's lives, a subject other authors had largely neglected in their critiques of suburban affluence.[1]

Like their émigré peers, Galbraith, Packard, and Friedan focused on middle-class consumers, though they rejected the anti-puritanism that Dichter and Katona had advocated. Their books shared with Potter's *People of Plenty* a belief that affluence was a problem, although, unlike Potter, Packard and Friedan linked lessened materialism with psychological self-realization, and Galbraith connected chastened consumption with a revived public sphere. In different ways, they breathed life into the new moralism. Their tone was less ironic and their stance less detached than Potter's. Their analysis of affluence, its origins and consequences, was more scathing, insistent, even conspiratorial. Their solutions were often problematic; nonetheless, unlike Potter, they more fully positioned themselves as interested in public policy as they went beyond an analysis of affluence to suggest some ways of lessening its cultural and social impact. Between 1954, when Potter's book was published, and the time when those by Galbraith, Packard, and Friedan appeared, the hold of the cold war on Americans had begun to loosen. The battles over civil rights, the repudiation of Senator Joseph R. McCarthy in 1954, and the launching of *Sputnik* by the Soviets in 1957 were just a few of the many events that, by undermining the complacency that had shaped American politics and culture in the immediate postwar years, began to make room for a more critical assessment. Unlike Dichter, Katona, and even Potter, these three writers strongly dissented from key elements of the cold war consensus. Their writings marked a major turning point in the nation's response to affluence. Other writers in the late 1950s and early 1960s would turn this shift into a floodtide of skepticism about the benefits of consumer culture and would even call into question their focus on the affluence of the middle class.

John Kenneth Galbraith: Private Affluence and Public Poverty

Galbraith came to the writing of *The Affluent Society* after more than two decades of involvement in economics and politics. Born in 1908 to a family of Scottish ancestry on a Canadian farm, he received a degree in agricultural economics from Ontario Agricultural College in 1931 and his Ph.D. in the same field three years later from the University of California at Berkeley. Between 1934, when he first arrived at Harvard as a young faculty member, and the fall of 1949, when he was granted tenure as a full professor, Galbraith gained the experience that turned him from an academic economist working in a specialized field into a public figure of great intellectual range. While in Cambridge, England, in 1937–38, he encountered Keynesian economics. He served as a speechwriter for Franklin D. Roosevelt in the 1940 presidential campaign. From 1941 to 1943, he worked in Washington, D.C., at the Office of Price Administration (OPA), charged with rationing goods, controlling prices, and making consumption more efficient, a moralist's dream job worthy of Mumford's hopes. This position, a biographer has remarked, gave Galbraith the second "most powerful civilian post in the wartime economy." His stint in Manhattan as a writer for *Fortune* (1943–48) was interrupted by government service in Washington and abroad. By 1952, when he published *American Capitalism: A Theory of Countervailing Power*, his graceful writing style, prodigious output, frequent movement between Washington, New York, and Cambridge, and controversial ideas had earned him a wider audience among policy makers and general readers than among academic economists. After the publication of *The Affluent Society*, he maintained a formidable career as a writer, public figure, and politician.[2]

In *The Affluent Society*, Galbraith, more brilliantly than any other contemporary, combined a critique of consumer culture with an insistence that the federal government restore the balance between private spending and public needs. What he called the conventional wisdom, the outmoded ideas of the dismal science of economics shaped in the eighteenth century when poverty was the norm, was irrelevant to Americans living in a society suffused by affluence. What was for others mainly a cultural critique of affluence became in his hands explicitly political. He drew on a long-standing skepticism among intellectuals on the left about the morality of unbridled spending by middle-class consumers but linked that outlook to public policies designed to curb what he saw as involuntary and excessive spending. Drawing on calls for increased funding for education and research in the wake of the Soviet Union's launching of *Sputnik* in 1957, and on the debate over national purpose and the uses of leisure that emerged in the closing years of the Eisenhower administration, Galbraith offered to a wide audience a sophisticated argument for federal intervention in the public realm. As he noted in 1969, the USSR's success prompted millions of Americans to realize that the Russians "were using their more meager resources more purposively" than the United States.[3]

For Galbraith, a number of forces had come together to make America an affluent society, or more precisely a society virtually obsessed with maintaining a rising standard of living. Like many social critics of the 1950s, Galbraith defined widespread affluence as a problem. From the vantage point of a broadening middle class, more and more people on the lower margin had entered the consumer mainstream, while at the other end of the social scale, the wealthy were becoming less visible and less ostentatious, their prominence challenged by the managers of large corporations and by a federal government strengthened in the Great Depression. Advertising and salesmanship had virtually conspired to persuade Americans positioned between the wealthy and the poor to identify pleasure with the acquisition of an unending series of goods and services. Increasing levels of consumer debt, the cold war linkage between production of goods and national security, and the inflationary pressures that resulted from a constantly rising standard of living all signaled dangers on the road to prosperity.[4]

As a consequence of these pressures, millions of Americans were working harder and spending more, with neither activity, according to Galbraith, consistently providing genuine satisfaction. Americans, he noted with considerable skepticism, had come to enshrine a rising standard of living and increased production as social goals in good measure because they were feeling less urgency about dealing with thorny issues of inequality and redistribution. This had given the nation, including liberals, the false reassurance that poverty was disappearing. The fact that "increasing aggregate output leaves a self-perpetuating margin of poverty at the very base of the income pyramid" went "largely unnoticed" because poverty was "the fate of a voiceless minority." He estimated the proportion of Americans living in poverty at just under 8 percent. Most of the poor, he wrote, fell into one of two categories. The first he called "case poverty," the situation of individuals or families with "some quality peculiar" to them, such as "mental deficiency, bad health, inability to adapt to the discipline of modern economic life, excessive procreation, alcohol, insufficient education." The second he labeled "insular poverty," social islands in which nearly everyone was poor, usually in a rural or urban environment that "perpetuates its handicaps through poor schools, evil neighborhood influences, and bad preparation for life."[5]

Yet though Galbraith acknowledged the existence of poverty in America (which, as a farmer's son and an agricultural economist, he saw as more rural than urban), his focus was on its opposite. He later came to regret what the book's title implied, yet it was America as an affluent society that worried him. While he acknowledged the existence of poor people in affluent America, for him the real poverty was that of the public sector. At the core of his critique was the assertion, commonplace among contemporary social critics, that consumption, especially by the middle class, was vacuous, forced, and ultimately unsatisfactory. "As a society becomes increasingly affluent," he wrote, "wants are increasingly created by the process by which they are satisfied." He called this the "dependence effect." Advertising played a critical role in this process. In the affluent society, advertising fostered a "craving for more elegant automobiles, more exotic food, more erotic clothing, more elaborate entertainment—indeed for the entire modern range of sensuous, edifying, and lethal desires." Similarly unexceptional was his more muted suggestion that "more esoteric desires," such as the arts, were superior to the more ordinary commercial pleasures that relied on "mass appeal." The goal, he argued, was to break the link between "the identification of goods with happiness."[6]

What made his argument innovative was how he linked his critique of the pursuit of a higher standard of living to his advocacy of fundamental changes in public policy. In contrasting what he saw as an "opulent" supply of "privately produced and marketed goods and services" with the "niggardly" provision of public services, he argued that private affluence actually caused the poverty of public sector services. In the immediate postwar period, shapers of public opinion attributed "a certain mystique . . . to the satisfaction of privately supplied wants" while at the same time, in the name of productivity and freedom, they launched "a remarkable attack on the notion of expanding and improving public services." Meanwhile, advertisers assailed "the eyes and ears of the community on behalf of more beer," though "no similar process operates on behalf of the nonmerchantable services of the state." A number of factors intensified the pressures against increasing public services, including inflation, the nature of federal and local tax systems, unrelenting calls for defense spending, and what he saw as a truce on discussions of inequality.[7]

Again and again, Galbraith portrayed Americans bowing down before the gods of consumer pleasures while finding public spending "an incubus." The result was dirty air and dirty streets, overcrowded urban schools, juvenile delinquency, a fragile infrastructure for housing, underpaid police officers, inadequate public transportation, and insufficient recreational facilities. "The family which takes its mauve and cerise, air-conditioned, power-steered, and power-braked automobile out for a tour," Galbraith wrote, with the love of contrast and ease of expression that made his book so compelling, "passes through cities that are badly paved, made hideous by litter, blighted buildings, billboards, and posts for wires that should have long since been put underground." Then they'd picnic "on exquisitely packaged food from a portable icebox by a polluted stream and go on to spend the night at a park which is a menace to public health and morals." Although Galbraith never systematically spelled out what enhanced spending in the public sector would involve, scattered throughout the book were references to federal funding for urban renewal, scientific research, education, housing, health, the environment, and transportation.[8]

To remedy the social imbalance between the private and public realms, Galbraith offered an extended discussion of specific policy proposals. Reductions in expenditures on defense and national security would make money available for domestic purposes. By breaking "the nexus between production and income security," a system of unemployment compensation would lessen pressure to consume, make work less onerous, and lower inflationary pressures. This would ultimately lead, Galbraith wrote in what was an exceptional and cogent dethroning of work from its pedestal, to the elimination of "toil as a required economic institution." The centerpiece of his proposals was a national tax on consumption, "which automatically makes a pro rata share of increasing income available to public authority for public purposes." The result would be to distribute the increased revenues "in accordance with relative needs. Schools and roads will then no longer be at a disadvantage as compared with automobiles and television sets in having to prove absolute justification." A national sales tax would restore social balance. "By making private goods more expensive, public goods are made more abundant." Thus, forcing people to spend less money on cigarettes, television sets, movies, and vacuum cleaners would make more funds available for supporting schools and cleaning up cities.[9]

The Affluent Society had considerable impact on national debates and, eventually, national social policy. Yet in the short and even the longer term, most of Galbraith's specific policy recommendations fell on deaf ears. As he well anticipated, his advocacy of a tax on consumption met with great resistance—from liberals and labor union leaders who feared the regressive effects of a sales tax (an issue he did not adequately address) and from conservatives who wanted to reduce income taxes rather than adopt new taxes of any kind. Nor did the shapers of public policy give much credence to his critique of work and his suggestions for non-stigmatized unemployment compensation. Moreover, as he no doubt expected, economists paid remarkably little attention to his assault on their "conventional wisdom." As a member of the administration of President John F. Kennedy, he fought unremittingly but largely unsuccessfully for increased spending on domestic social programs.[10]

What Galbraith did accomplish was to help reshape the framework in which discussions of social policy took place. *The Affluent Society*, the historian Loren J. Okroi has remarked, was the first of his books that "would irritate and antagonize most sectors of the business community and the economics profession, find a mass readership both in the United States and abroad, and establish Galbraith as one of the most important and prolific social theorists and critics in modern America." The timing of the book's publication was fortunate, appearing as it did right after the Soviet Union launched *Sputnik*, an event that caused millions of Americans to question how successfully the United States was achieving its national purpose. His book gained an enormous readership; it quickly reached the *New York Times* best-seller list, where it stayed for about a year, and continued to sell well over a long period of time. Academic economists criticized Galbraith, often sharply, calling into question his evidence, his reasoning, and his conclusions. Yet non-economists appreciated what he had accomplished. Writing in the *Saturday Review*, David Potter declared that Galbraith's book "ranks as a work which, Utopian or not, ought to contribute in the long run to the reshaping of some of our basic ideas."[11]

Potter was right. Beginning with *The Affluent Society*, Galbraith made a series of important contributions. He joined with others, most notably his Harvard colleague and Cambridge neighbor Arthur M. Schlesinger Jr., in promoting a qualitative liberalism. Distinguished from the quantitative liberalism of the New Deal in the 1930s and from unflinching support for labor unions, this approach promised to use government programs to deal with what Schlesinger called "the miseries of an age of abundance" in America, "so rich and overflowing a society" in which problems nevertheless remained in education, health care, urban renewal, opportunity for minorities, and the quality of the mass media. In the early 1960s, this emphasis provided a basis for public sector commitments to the arts, education, and science, and, in the mid-1960s, to public housing and health. In addition, in the early days of the Johnson administration, what little Galbraith did have to say about poverty in *The Affluent Society* became one of many influences that shaped the nation's poverty programs. Over the long run, Galbraith's insistence on the environmental costs of increased production helped shape the national consciousness on this important issue. Finally, his critique of affluence intensified what he had called "an incipient revolt against goods or at least a refusal to allow competitive emulation to be the source of wants, something that emerged in full force in the 1960s counterculture."[12]

Yet his greatest contribution was his introduction into national discussions of the idea of correcting the social imbalance between private affluence and public poverty. The headline for a February 7, 1960, front-page story in the *New York Times* announced, " 'Great Debate' in Capital: Is U.S. Misusing Wealth?" The reporter, Edwin L. Dale Jr., called Galbraith and Walter Lippmann the writers most responsible for inspiring "politicians, civil servants, intellectuals, and many plain persons" to consider "that the basic trouble with American society" was the imbalance between private consumption and public services. Evidence for this conclusion, Dale noted, came from the disjuncture between "bigger and better tailfins" and the lack of adequate health care, education, and urban renewal. Five weeks later, again giving Galbraith the lion's share of credit, Dale noted that "more and more people in the capital are convinced that the most important continuing issue of American policy and politics over the next decade will be the issue of public spending—what share of America's total resources should be devoted to public as distinct from private purposes." In his speech accepting the presidential nomination of the Democratic Party in 1960, John F. Kennedy had noted that Americans faced the choice "between the public interest and private comfort." Two years later, the founding document of the New Left's Students for a Democratic Society (SDS) acknowledged the impact of Galbraith's ideas while at the same time dissenting from his exaggeration of affluence and his relative inattention to poverty. "We live amidst a national celebration of economic prosperity," wrote the authors of the Port Huron Statement, "while poverty and depriva-tion remain an unbreakable way of life for millions in the 'affluent society.' "[13]

Galbraith helped transform the debate over American affluence, most no-tably by insisting that it was possible to use the public sector to redress the shortcomings of private prosperity. Potter, Packard, and Friedan, among oth-ers, agreed that affluence was a problem but offered few solutions that called for actions beyond those of individuals or relatively small scale organizations. To a certain extent, Galbraith's argument succeeded. Although the nation did not adopt a tax on consumption or a radically different plan of unemploy-ment insurance, American politics did fully engage the central issue Galbraith raised: how to use government policy to restore a balance between private wealth and public poverty.

Vance Packard's Trilogy on Affluence

Born on May 22, 1914, in Granville Summit, Pennsylvania, Vance Packard spent his early years on his parents' farm. The experiences and memories of the world of his youth provided a set of values that shaped what he wrote, in particular his vision of an America based on family, community, hard work, and individualism. Growing up in a Methodist household gave him a moral basis for judging postwar affluence. As a writer, he romanticized the con-ditions that existed during his childhood. Much of his critique grew out of his heartfelt appreciation for the virtues of the life he had left behind. When he was around ten, his family moved to State College so his father could take a job at Penn State. Packard himself entered the university as an undergraduate in 1932. There he sharpened his skills as a journalist. When he graduated in 1936, he enrolled in the Graduate School of Journalism at Columbia University. During the late 1930s and early 1940s, he married, started a family, moved from New York City to the suburbs, and held a series of jobs as a journalist. He eventually landed a position at *American Magazine*, a mass-circulation family publication for a middle-class audience. From 1942 until 1956, under pressure from advertisers and editors, Packard wrote articles in which he celebrated the spread of affluence throughout America and exaggerated the extent to which the United States had become a middle-class society. By the mid-1950s, he was growing increasingly restive about the constraints he faced as a writer, a feeling that intensified as *American Magazine* was forced to compete with television for advertising revenue. His years as a journalist nevertheless gave him an intuitive sense of what appealed to the largely suburban, white, middle-class generation that created the baby boom and populated the burgeoning suburbs.[14]

With the collapse of *American Magazine* in 1956, Packard found himself having to earn a living as an independent writer. With the publication of *The Hidden Persuaders* (1957), *The Status Seekers* (1959), and *The Waste Makers* (1960), he quickly emerged as one of the nation's most widely read authors. This trilogy secured Packard's position as a popular social critic, giving him what few if any other American authors achieved before or since—three different number-one nonfiction best-sellers in a period of four years. In the trilogy, Packard brought together his life experiences, the lessons he had learned from his youth on a farm and his young adulthood during the depression. He relied on the skills he had honed in his twenty years as a journalist, as a keen observer of American life, a writer of human interest stories in mass-circulation magazines, an author fascinated by the social and behavioral sciences, and a critic with an interest in developing a comprehensive picture of what he observed. Undergirding his books was his commitment to "producer values"—a moral economy based on hard work and anticommercialism. Though his later books did not have the impact of his trilogy, he nonetheless carried on as a writer and social critic.

The Hidden Persuaders was a response to those who claimed that advances in advertising were fundamental to the national well-being. Expenditures on advertising in America had grown from less than $2 billion in 1939 to nearly $12 billion by the late 1950s. With the increasing use of installment payments and credit cards, consumer debt was rising at three times the rate of personal income. Ads had become more sophisticated, visual, and subtle in approach and more pervasive in reach. Especially significant were the ways in which practitioners had learned to take advantage of the new medium of television and new methods, such as motivational research (MR), which Dichter and others promulgated. Until Packard's book appeared, however, these new techniques had remained largely immune to public criticism.

Packard began *The Hidden Persuaders* with a warning that ominous changes were taking place in the United States. Invoking a better past, a time when producer values reigned, he argued that in the early 1950s, corporate leaders had shifted "from being maker-minded to market-minded." As executives realized that there might be a limit to how much consumers would buy, they turned to advertising and market research for help. New kinds of appeals offered a way out of the dilemma caused when increased production met a potentially stable demand. With the aid of the social and behavioral sciences, motivational researchers such as Dichter were developing techniques that promised to "channel our unthinking habits, our purchasing decisions, and our thought processes." By appealing to the fears of psychological obsolescence, sexual inadequacy, and the loss of social status, advertisements were fundamentally reshaping everyday life and threatening to undermine individualism. At the heart of this assault on the psyche was an attempt by "depth merchandisers" such as Dichter to promote self-indulgence. Packard also warned of the consequences of extending new methods of persuasion into personnel management, public relations, and politics. He resented corporate intrusion into the lives of executives and their wives through the hiring and evaluation processes. He worried about the use of advertising methods in American politics, noting how candidates for public office appealed to the irrational, emphasized the role of personality, and treated public issues like items in a supermarket.[15]

The use of MR, he argued, prompting a critical response from Dichter, relied on the exploitation of feelings below the conscious level. Packard's ideal was the growth-seeking, self-determined individual suggested by humanistic psychologists. He feared that "hidden persuaders" were moving the nation closer to the world that George Orwell had described in *Animal Farm* and *1984*. The danger was that Big Brother, represented by psychologists, market researchers, advertising agencies, and corporations, would invade people's privacy and erode their self-determination. Relying on the producer ethic, Packard expressed concern about the morality of a society built on happiness derived primarily from consumer goods. He bristled at Dichter's attempt to make hedonism seem moral by undermining the "old-fashioned puritanism of the average American" and by helping people overcome the guilt attached to conspicuous consumption. Although he remained mute on the alternative to affluence, he took issue with the promotion of a rising GNP that rested on maintaining "a confidence-inspiring viewpoint, come hell or high water." The broader question of the future of an economy based on consumerism, he believed, was "destined to become one of the great moral issues of our times."[16]

In important ways, Packard dissented from the celebratory mood established by the mass media, the business press, and some consensus intellectuals. What was responsible for the postwar equation of spending and pleasure, he argued, was not the irrational female consumer, as many suggested, but the manipulative powers of those who exploited the nation's fears and dreams. Himself playing on what a critic has called "overanxious fears of manipulation," Packard exaggerated the power of advertising, especially of MR. He also overemphasized the degree to which advertising agencies accepted MR, an approach that remained controversial in the industry. Taking the self-promoting claims of Dichter and others at face value and quickly passing over contradictory evidence, Packard both criticized and unintentionally promoted them. As a Harvard professor of marketing stated in 1958, though the "'hidden persuaders' in their exaggerated form are, in fact, made of straw," the most tangible result of Packard's book was "an increased and unrealistic demand for motivational research." Ironically, Packard's book allowed advertising agencies to complain bitterly about his criticism while they called on people like Dichter to help them take advantage of the authority that *The Hidden Persuaders* had given them.[17]

The ambiguity of Packard's book stemmed from a number of sources. *The Hidden Persuaders* suffered from a tension between its critical framework and the often humorous stuff of its case studies. With the larger argument, Packard sounded an alarm about the relationship between capitalism, democracy, individualism, and morality. When he focused on specific examples, however, he seemed more fascinated than worried. In addition, he did not always make clear which was problematic, the means or the ends. Although some read the book as a sweeping attack on Madison Avenue, Packard found fault mainly with anyone who exploited the new manipulative approaches. Moreover, he offered few remedies. His principal solution—greater consumer awareness—involved both demystification and self-help.

In writing *The Status Seekers*, Packard was reacting to the claims of those who asserted that affluence was increasing social mobility in America and decreasing class and ethnic divisions. To the contrary, he claimed, "under its gloss of prosperity" the nation was becoming more socially divided as people scrambled "to find new ways to draw lines that will separate the elect from the non-elect." Thus in 1955 the editors of *Fortune* hailed "the rise of the great mass into the new moneyed middle class" as a change that was "erasing old class lines" and elevating "proletarians" into "America's booming new middle-income class." The lines between income groups were becoming "remarkably penetrable," they wrote; "inconspicuous consumption" was making spending patterns more uniform, and people were trying "to keep *down* with the Joneses." Against this background, Packard argued that by strengthening the "barriers and humiliating distinctions of social class," the nation's "fantastic" level of affluence was intensifying social striving. Whereas liberal intellectuals traced the problems of mass society to mindless consumption, Packard blamed capitalists for developing the consumer culture.[18]

At the heart of the book lay evidence, drawn mainly from market research and social science, on the relationship between consumption and status. Here

Packard again displayed his ambivalence between what he found both fasci-
nating and preposterous. His commitment to producer values was expressed
in his preference for workmanship and in his hostility to status based on
materialism. But *The Status Seekers* also provided readers with material they
could use in their own quest for higher social status, as Packard educated
them about occupations that offered the greatest financial rewards and explained how different choices in cars, house styles, and colleges provided
markers of social status. Nowhere was this more vivid than in the chapter
titled "Snob Appeal = Today's Home Sweet Home." There he analyzed the
symbols used to distinguish homes, from key words such as "estate," "exclusive," and "executive" to touches such as gas lanterns and colonial décor
suggesting that the occupants had roots in the nation's past. Top executives,
he wrote, lived on estates "beautifully manicured on the outside, highly pol-
ished on the inside," with period furniture, family portraits, books bound in
leather, and a paneled den with leather chairs and old sporting prints. Houses
for those who lacked money but not aspirations displayed air conditioners,
television aerials, monogrammed towels, antiques, and classical records.[19]

A series of factors, he argued, had transformed modern American society.
With work in large national corporations increasingly fragmented and imper-
sonal, employees derived less social prestige, satisfaction, and self-esteem from
their jobs. As opportunity became blocked and status striving exaggerated,
Packard argued, millions of Americans were suffering emotionally. Frightened
"by the anxieties, inferiority feelings, and straining generated by this unending process of rating and status striving," Americans were constantly trying
"to surround themselves with visible evidence of the superior ranking they
are claiming." Shut off from social advancement and bored with their jobs,
blue-collar and white-collar workers alike could feel they were getting somewhere by shopping. Consequently, people consumed "flamboyantly, much as
the restless Roman masses found diversion in circuses thoughtfully provided
by the emperors." Advertisers and market researchers were foremost among
the villains who persuaded people to seek satisfaction through buying, not
working. While promoting the vision of a classless society, advertisers exaggerated the importance of specific status symbols.[20]

Like Potter in *People of Plenty*, Packard emphasized the costs of mobility
and explored the benefits of a more integrated and stable life. What Potter
took from his origins as a southern gentleman, Packard derived from his
evocation of the farm and small town where he had grown up, but also from
his own social ascendancy. Unlike Potter, Packard embraced the fullest measure of social mobility. He spoke out against a social system based on "ascribed status" as running counter to American ideals—and to his own preference for a society that encourages talent. Packard worried that a decline in

social mobility might undermine what he saw as the American dream of abundant opportunity, a vision that at moments rested on a nostalgic view of America's past. Although he understood the importance of ethnic divisions and social class, he saw the real chasm as that between the "diploma elite" and the "supporting classes." It was becoming increasingly difficult for a person to rise in big business without an education beyond high school. He cautioned against exaggerating the extent to which members of the working class had entered the middle class, noting that "many of the new white-collar jobs are essentially manual or require little skill," and observed that blue-collar workers, especially union members, had made gains in income or social position significant enough to threaten the middle-class status of some white-collar workers. "The better-paid blue-collar working people such as craftsmen and foremen," he argued, "are coming to dominate the middle-class positions in our society." He reserved some of his ire, usually muted, for organization men, "who have successfully shed their rough edges of individualism," especially those who "manage to become rebels at night," turning into "wicked wits and flaming liberals in the safety of their patios and favorite bars."[21]

Packard's critique of a status-driven present rested on a naïve vision of the past. He recalled his own experiences as a child "attending Protestant churches that drew their congregation from virtually the entire community." He remembered a time when neighbors knew one another well enough to "be judged for their personal worth rather than by the trappings of status they exhibited." In contrast, most contemporary suburbs lacked class and ethnic diversity, though he did not explore how this might be true of New Canaan and Chappaquiddick, the wealthy suburb and summer community between which he divided his time. Most American suburbs, he noted, offered only "a synthetic, manipulated quality of community life."[22]

One of his principal solutions to the problems of a status-conscious society was to enhance one group's understanding of another. By comprehending the entire society and not just their own particular place in it, Americans might "lead more effective lives, and probably more serene ones." Packard's second solution was to open up opportunity. He criticized college-educated and economically comfortable Protestant men, who should have the least cause for concern about social position, for erecting barriers against Jews in corporations, clubs, and neighborhoods. Packard's solution to the problem of blocked mobility was to make class distinctions less burdensome by ensuring that the society would discover people of real talent and then help them fulfill their potential. He advocated open access to higher education, especially for "all of high native ability" and those discouraged by the high cost or by "an environment of resignation, ostracism, and hedonism."[23]

With *The Waste Makers* (1960), the third of the best-sellers that established his reputation as a social critic, Packard was responding to the increasing pace of technological innovation and the rapid shifts in styles and fashions. Though these were hardly new phenomena, Packard correctly understood that manufacturers and advertisers had devised strategies to tempt consumers to buy products they did not necessarily need. "The challenge to business," remarked the editors of *Fortune* in 1955, "is to keep up with the market's potentialities not only by making and selling more of everything but by improving, varying, adorning everything—by blurring still further the already blurred line that distinguishes Americans' luxuries and Americans' necessities."[24]

Here Packard offered his most thoroughgoing critique of America as an affluent society. The nation's enormous productivity had forced the business community to invent new means to sustain the economy. The result was a widespread commitment to an increasing GNP as the mark of national success. He argued that the United States faced the problem not of scarcity but of overabundance. Regardless of whether they needed these goods, Americans had learned that continual prosperity demanded that they consume more and more. Although he acknowledged that millions of Americans lacked adequate food, clothing, and shelter, he nonetheless concentrated on prosperity, which seemed "to spill over into the aisles of stores, spread along the highways, and bulge out the doors, windows, and attics of houses." Hardly blind to the Soviet Union's faults, Packard nevertheless disapproved of the way the mass media, politicians, and members of the business community used competition with the USSR to justify more rapid economic growth, a focus that he felt distracted the United States from grappling with issues more central to the quality of life.[25]

At the outset, Packard stated, "If I can help it, there will be no villains in this book." But in fact he laid the blame at the feet of boastful businessmen, laborers who lacked a sense of workmanship, and politicians like Eisenhower who implored citizens to help the nation buy its ways out of a recession. He was especially critical of conniving market researchers and advertising executives. The former, he argued, systematically developed techniques to transform millions of Americans "into voracious, wasteful, compulsive consumers." Packard devoted almost half of the book to an examination of the new strategies that companies had developed to encourage spending. Corporations persuaded people to buy more goods, or goods with more frills and accessories, when simple items would suffice. They promoted planned obsolescence by introducing products that broke down easily or whose style became quickly outmoded. In addition, the business community relied on installment debt to enable consumers to pay for present purchases with future income, packaged goods in a wasteful manner, and encouraged a hedonism that undermined the commitment to hard work and self-restraint.[26]

Marketing experts, Packard reported, dreamed of a "Cornucopia City," where buildings were made of papier-mâché, where every week a rocket would be launched into outer space, where the military could dump excess goods into the ocean, and where it would be "unpatriotic" for homeowners to think of repairing "an ailing appliance that is more than two years old." The future was a place where citizens would be able to pass "their lifetime electronic credit cards in front of a recording eye" to facilitate their purchases in a "titanic push-button super mart built to simulate a fairyland," a place "where all the people spend more happy hours a week strolling and buying to their heart's content." Succumbing to the campaigns of marketing experts who had promoted a morality of hedonistic consumption, people now spent more on "frivolous" private goods than on worthwhile public ones. Americans, increasingly seeking "their main life satisfaction" as consumers rather than producers, were becoming pleasure-minded, self-indulgent, materialistic, and passive. Whereas in his earlier books Packard had blamed advertisers and market researchers for foisting goods upon an innocent public, in *The Waste Makers* he argued that the consumers were culprits as well.[27]

Packard went against the grain of 1950s celebrations of prosperity built on rapid innovation and changes in taste. He echoed instead the concern about national purpose, arguing that the implications of affluence for American society were profound. Excessive fascination with consumer goods had begun *"to make Americans look a bit fatuous in the eyes of the world."* The Soviet Union, for example, was puzzled by the sense of values of a nation that placed so little emphasis on education and health care. By concentrating on obsolescence, marketing, and advertising rather than on technology, skills, and resources, the nation had begun to lose its competitive edge, thus opening itself to a flood of goods from abroad. Moreover, he argued that increasing attention to promotion and display encouraged "the rise of business oligarchies." The affluence that marketers promoted threatened to bring a real decline in the quality of American life, a judgment that reflected his concern that many middle-class Americans were losing the ability to resist the consumer culture.[28]

Other consequences of affluence troubled Packard. The combination of more consumption and more people was forcing Americans to exhaust vital resources. In its search for raw materials, the United States was colonizing other nations and helping to develop friction among countries. He also lamented the way the commercialization of American life was "becoming so all-pervasive that at times it seems to be getting into the air the public breathes," causing "an unprecedented saturation of American life with pleas, hints, and other inducements to buy." His analysis of the impact of these changes on women, primarily those in the upper reaches of the working class and the lower reaches of the middle class, was especially telling in terms of both his commitment to traditional roles for women and his ability to spot major social trends. The purchase of household appliances and prepared meals, he wrote, "tends to disenfranchise the wife by depriving her of many traditional, time-consuming homemaking functions." Pinched budgets and diminished domestic challenges, Packard concluded with regret, "tended to send the wife out looking for a job."[29]

Above all, the waste makers threatened to change the American character, undermining what Packard saw as values that had long stood the nation in good stead. Americans used to think of themselves "as a frugal, hard-working, God-fearing people making sacrifices for the long haul." Early in the nation's history, "puritanical traits" had been essential to "settlers struggling to convert forest and prairie into a national homeland." In the nineteenth century, how-ever, as growing numbers of Americans settled in urban areas, "hedonism as a guiding philosophy of life gained more and more disciples." Packard noted that "quite possibly, the environment of thickly settled areas brought a less-ening of serenity and a feeling of being swallowed up that impelled people to strive for distinctive emblems and gratification through consumption." In-creased concentration of population, Packard argued, reflecting his anti-urban bias, meant crowds, ugliness, noise, pollution, and threats to individual liberty. He attacked urban blight, "the growing sleaziness, dirtiness, and chaos of the nation's great exploding metropolitan areas."[30]

As for solving the problems that the new affluence caused, Packard warned that over the long run, Americans had to learn to balance "a satisfying way of life" with the preservation of "a reasonably thriving economy." He opposed what he saw as the two alternatives that dominated American politics: the "business-Republican-conservative" emphasis on increased population and the "liberal-Democratic-labor" commitment to economic growth. Drawing on a tradition that went back at least to Stuart Chase's *Tragedy of Waste* (1925), he called on Americans to seek other choices. To begin with, they ought to take "pride in prudent buying." They should follow the advice of the Consumers Union and demand, as shoppers, "to be approached on a rational basis, and protest" when they were not. Selecting plain and func-tional goods while avoiding the new and fashionable, buying generic drugs, and learning how to repair broken items would help "restore today's consumer-citizen to this sovereignty he has lost." Packard also urged manu-facturers to emphasize quality and resist the guidance of marketers who pro-moted gimmicks and evanescent fashions.[31]

But beyond these steps, Packard called for even more fundamental changes. By curbing population growth, recycling materials, changing tax laws, and rejecting planned obsolescence, the nation could begin to restore the balance between growing population and diminishing natural resources. With considerable accuracy he predicted that the United States would experience an oil shortage in 1973. He tempered his advocacy of shorter work hours because he feared that people might use their free time to consume more. "In terms of life satisfaction," he warned, "acts of consumption are no adequate substitute for acts of individual productivity." Packard also toyed with the notion of having the nation "tune down the economy somewhat, even if it meant settling for a more modest level of living." He encouraged his readers to avoid superficial changes in living standards, such as buying multiple items of clothing when one would do or frequently trading in automobiles. He urged the nation to work instead toward historic innovations that, like the automobile, radio, refrigerator, and jet airplane, "would fill a genuine need and represent a real breakthrough for technology." Finally, Packard hailed the coming dominance of a service economy because, unlike mining and manufacturing, "travel, cultural, or educational activities" made only a "modest" claim on natural resources and were "capable of greater reasonable expansion."[32]

Ultimately, Packard's vision of a better society relied on a restoration of the balance between public and private needs and an enhanced opportunity for individual fulfillment through nonmaterial pleasures. Drawing on the writings of Reinhold Niebuhr, Schlesinger, and Galbraith, he called for a reversal of the trend toward "private opulence amid public poverty." He hoped that the reduced commitment to unnecessary goods and services would enable the nation to devote more of its creativity to improving the quality of life. Although he remained skeptical about the benefits of economic growth, much of what he wrote paralleled a liberal consensus emerging in the late 1950s concerning the agenda of American politics. Packard mentioned some of what in the early 1960s would become essential elements of the New Frontier and the Great Society, focusing on air pollution, conservation, urban slums, education, health care, public amenities, and the needs of the elderly. He joined others, including Galbraith, in calling for a turn away from military expenditures, which were an example of what he considered government prodigality. Beyond that, he called for "a more mature citizenry" and a "more painless" way of collecting taxes, such as through payroll deductions before the taxpayer saw the income.[33]

At the end of the book, Packard looked forward to an America that would offer more moral kinds of pleasures. The benefits of "ardent materialism" and "superabundance" had reached their limits. To encourage "self-respect, serenity, and individual fulfillment," it would be necessary to lift "the all-pervading smog of commercialism." He asked Americans to counter the pressure to define life's satisfactions in terms of material possessions and develop an opposition to the merchants of discontent. In the construction of urban cultural centers, and especially in the grassroots revival of music, art, and reading, he found signs of "a cultural renaissance in America." He believed that "such reflective, private pursuits . . . may help Americans gain a new perspective on their possessions in relation to other life satisfactions." He hoped that greater numbers of Americans would come "to see that cherished values and integrity of the soul have more to do with a well-spent life than self-indulgence." He admitted that he felt "a freshening of the spirit" whenever he would stroll "about the tree-shaded village green, peer into the lovely old spired, clean-lined churches, visit the still picturesque stores, chat with the natives, and walk among their two-century-old homes." Contemporary hucksters, "with all their huffing and puffing to sell their packaged dream communities," had not been able to match the "spiritual and political environment" of these small New England villages.[34]

In the final analysis, Packard's answer to the problems of affluence in *The Waste Makers* was more personal than political. His solutions relied as much on individual effort and the work of nonprofit organizations as on government action. Perhaps adversity, Packard speculated, would be necessary to bring Americans to appreciate nonmaterial values. "The central challenge," he wrote in the book's final sentence, was that "Americans must learn to live with their abundance without being forced to impoverish their spirit by being damned fools about it." Moreover, as was true in his other books, at critical moments Packard often undercut his own recommendations. "Perhaps the United States has no acceptable alternative to ever-rising and wasteful consumption," he noted at one point, and then went on to say that "this viewpoint deserves respect," though it was a position with which he did not agree. Characteristically, just when he seemed to be reaching a crescendo of analysis and recommendation, he failed to deliver a strong punch line. Finally, Packard seemed unwilling to answer the question of how to provide "a sane, intelligent and satisfying way of life while preserving a reasonable thriving economy."[35]

In this last book of the trilogy, Packard offered a forthright statement of his faith. Though not without equivocation, he vigorously exposed some of the worst excesses of American industry and called on the public to respond in a variety of constructive ways. As in *The Status Seekers*, here too Packard exaggerated affluence and minimized poverty. "Haunting anxiety about where one's next meal or pair of shoes is coming from," he commented, "has become a memory for all but a small proportion of the population that is unemployed or lives in rural slums or is engaged in migratory work." In the next sentence, he offered an example that illustrated his confidence in America as well as his own naïveté. "A Negro bootblack in Oklahoma," he noted, "proudly showed me his pair of thirty-dollar cowboy boots." He also remained ambivalent about the products of affluence. Though he extolled the simple life, he hailed the invention of jet planes. Similarly, in a way that reflected his fascination with new technologies and his ambivalence toward plenty, he recommended helping other countries develop nuclear energy as one way of enabling "the people of friendly nations [to] enjoy a little more of the fabulous abundance attained in the United States."[36]

Packard's trilogy of best-sellers had an immense impact on his life and on America's consciousness. Facing an unsure future in 1956, by 1960, Packard had emerged as an immensely successful writer and a national celebrity. Each of his three books reached the top of the best-seller list, together selling perhaps 5 million copies in the United States and abroad. Packard introduced key phrases into the American language: hidden persuaders, status seekers, planned obsolescence. Advertisements for goods he abhorred played on themes he had introduced. If academic reviewers criticized him for being shallow, popular, simplistic, and nostalgic, readers responded with great interest and members of the business community with vitriolic attacks.

Although his influence is harder to track than that of Galbraith or Friedan, there is nonetheless clear evidence that his books made a difference. *The Hidden Persuaders* affected attitudes toward advertising and helped prompt the federal government to curb some of the industry's excesses. Editorial writers and columnists echoed his call for protection of the individual from motivational research, the invasion of privacy, and pressures for conformity. Packard "helped to make consumerism a household word," remarked one reporter. *The Hidden Persuaders* and *The Waste Makers* were among the many factors that persuaded President Kennedy to create an office of consumer affairs. Among government officials and shapers of public opinion, Packard's exposés intensified interest in curbing excessive advertising and materialism, in protecting the environment, and in redressing the imbalance between public squalor and private wealth. All three books taught consumers how to buy wisely and protect themselves from the actions of corporations. From the pages of these three books, members of the reading public came to understand the imbalance between public and private needs, the values of self-realization, and the evils of advertising. Packard helped call attention to pervasive doubts about the benefits of suburban living, growth of the GNP, and the social and psychological costs of affluence.[37]

Scathing, nostalgic, humorous, moralistic, ambivalent, and influential, Packard's books offered a critique of the experts and powerful institutions that manipulated Americans into pursuing false pleasures. Packard's ambivalence, which many of his readers shared, led him to express both fascination and horror over advertising, social status, and the consumer culture. He advocated individualism, creativity, hard work, authentic personal relationships, and respect for the environment. His three best-sellers were stronger on diagnosis than on strategies for change. Yet they awakened millions of Americans to the dangers of corporate power, the divisions among social groups, and the threats that economic growth posed to natural resources and national character. However attenuated at times, his articulation of a producer ethic evoked a better world, one characterized by honest work, simple living, and community cohesion, but constantly threatened by the corrupting power of wealth and commercialism. Opposing avarice and luxury, Packard stood for a virtuous life based on civic responsibility, unalienated labor, widespread property ownership, and personal independence. He remained skeptical about the benefits of material progress, which he believed threatened to undermine a moral economy.

Betty Friedan, *The Feminine Mystique,* and the Impact of Affluence on Women

At a meeting of the Society of Magazine Writers in the late 1950s, Betty Friedan heard Vance Packard explain that he had decided to write *The Hidden Persuaders* when *Reader's Digest* turned down a controversial piece on advertising. She listened attentively because she was having a similarly difficult time getting articles accepted which challenged the reigning consensus. Packard provided Friedan with both a positive and a negative example—positive because he helped her understand how, by making the shift from magazine writer to book author, she could get her social criticism published, and negative because Packard, like other male critics of suburban conformity, painted a generally unfavorable picture of career women, emphasized women's role as sex objects, and imagined suburban women as gracious helpmates for their organization-men husbands. Betty Friedan exploded these and other myths about women, in the process offering a critique of affluence that was at once familiar and distinctive.[38]

By personal background and political education, Friedan was in an ideal position to launch such a critique. The household in which she grew up, the education she received at Smith College and later as a labor journalist in Manhattan, the articles she wrote for women's magazines in the 1950s and early 1960s, and the contradictions in her own experience as a suburban housewife enabled her to write a book that in turn helped launch the women's movement. As much as any book written in the mid-twentieth century, *The*

Feminine Mystique changed the course of America's political and social history. It was a key factor in making the nation aware of the challenges that middle-class women faced and in reviving the women's movement. By extending to women many of the ideas about the implications of affluence that widely read male authors had developed for white, middle-class men, Friedan's book translated into feminist terms the social criticism of suburban life which Packard and others had offered. She attacked the picture that male social critics had drawn and presented an alternative to the vision of women as frustrated housewives and consumers. At the same time, she shared with Galbraith and Packard the limitations of an analysis that saw the pervasive affluence of middle-class suburbanites as the central problem facing the nation.

Friedan was born February 4, 1921, in Peoria, Illinois, into a middle-class Jewish household wracked by protracted fights between a mother who spent money too freely and a father who, as the owner of a jewelry store during the depression, struggled to be an adequate provider. By the summer of 1938, when she graduated from high school and left Peoria for good, Friedan had developed an interest in becoming a writer and an awareness of herself as an outsider and of issues of social justice, including the limited choices available to educated women. As a student at Smith College, from which she graduated in 1942 with a string of stunning achievements, Friedan found her voice. She advocated trade unions as the herald of a progressive social vision, gained exposure to feminist concerns, and fiercely questioned the way her wealthy peers expressed their social privilege through conspicuous consumption. Like Lewis Mumford, who launched a similar campaign, as the editor of her college newspaper in 1941–42, Friedan grew pessimistic about the possibility of linking wartime sacrifice with chastened consumption.

After a year of graduate school in psychology at the University of California at Berkeley, from 1943 until 1952, Friedan worked as a journalist for two radical labor union publications. As a labor writer she continued commenting on the perils of consumer culture, while she extolled the consumer savvy of ordinary women, attacked the extravagance of the wealthy, and called on Americans to share their bounty with poorer nations. She criticized men in corporations for turning women into objects for their consumption, and reported on working women who struggled as both producers and consumers to make sure their families had enough to live on. Unlike Katona and Dichter, Friedan did not see America becoming a satisfied middle-class society, nor did she envision American women as lulled into complacency by the surfeit of consumer goods. In 1952, now married and well on her way to building a family, fighting with her husband, Carl, over the getting and spending of money, Friedan lost her job at the union paper. This ended her career as a labor journalist.

In the mid-1950s she turned to writing for mass-circulation magazines, focusing on issues facing middle-class women in the suburbs which were familiar to her as a housewife and journalist. She offered a picture of suburban America that contradicted the cold war hosannas to life in an affluent society. She focused on women, emphasizing their assertiveness, their sense of community, their desire to build a cooperative household with their husbands, and their ambition for careers—all themes that ran counter to the mainstream view of the impact of affluence on housewives. The articles Friedan wrote were not naïve celebrations of the pleasures of suburbia; rather, she offered a critique, albeit a muted one, of the isolation and conformity of suburban life in the 1950s. When she read Paul Goodman's *Growing Up Absurd* (1960), an influential investigation of the problems young men had in developing an authentic sense of self within the confines of a society dominated by large organizations, she pondered the distinctive situation faced by young women in suburbia. She contrasted his assumption about the intrinsic meaningfulness of men's work with women's labor in the home. She offered a vision of how to enhance the creativity and identity of teenage girls while encouraging them to avoid the twin traps of, on the one hand, a peer culture that relied on conformity and, on the other, a rebellion that tempted them to follow the example (and apparent resignation) of the Beat Generation.

In *The Feminine Mystique*, Friedan brought together all of her life's experiences to shape a powerful critique of the lives of women in affluent cold war America. She painted a searing picture of the constricted lives of suburban women. With affluence underwriting a sense of self that no longer depended on necessity, Friedan argued, consumer culture had filled the void created by women's lack of identity. The suburban home had become a "comfortable concentration camp" which fostered "passivity, softness, boredom" in American children and, for their mothers, false promises of abundance. Consumption, mechanized housework, and unsatisfying marital sex offered women only false and unsatisfactory experiences. In the pivotal chapter, titled "The Sexual Sell," Friedan sought to explain the forces that generated the feminine mystique. What, she asked, undermined the power of feminism and fueled the retreat of women into the privatism of the suburban home? Given that women were mainly responsible for shopping, she argued, "somehow, somewhere, someone must have figured out that women will buy more things if they are kept in the underused, nameless-yearning, energy-to-get-rid-of state of being housewives." Having hinted at the possibility of a conspiracy to oppress women, but determined not to reveal her own radical past, Friedan concluded that she "had no idea how it happened. Decision-making in industry," she wrote, contradicting her earlier attacks on corporations, "is not as simple, as rational, as those who believe the conspiratorial theories of history would have it." Friedan instead relied on the work of Dichter to show how corporations used marketing strategies to convince the suburban wife that she could seek fulfillment by baking a cake or polishing a floor. He had used motivational research to generate advertisements that he fancied would give American women a sense of identity, self-realization, and sexual pleasure through participating in consumer culture. Friedan, who gave moralism a feminist cast, pulled no punches as she explored the dangers of Dichter's approach. He and his colleagues, she wrote, "are guilty of persuading house-wives to stay at home, mesmerized in front of a television set, their nonsexual human needs unnamed, unsatisfied, drained by the sexual sell into the buying of things." By equating satisfaction with consumer goods, market researchers had locked millions of women into the home and prevented them from achieving a more genuine happiness that could lead to growth and self-development. Friedan made clear her animus against the toil of housewives whose freedom Dichter had proclaimed, whose spending Katona had charted, whose liberation Potter had emphasized, and whom Packard told to stay at home. Pessimistic about the life of the housewife-volunteer, she preferred that women enter the paid workforce. Hinting at the reluctance of husbands to help with household chores, the domesticity that Dichter had promoted, Friedan charged, demanded the unrecompensed labor of white, middle-class women to complete the Herculean task of keeping their suburban homes spotless.[39]

Friedan never mentioned her adversary by name, referring to him only as "the manipulator." Dichter returned the favor when he attacked women's liberation without using the name of the person whose book and whose organizing had revived the women's movement. Clearly there were very important differences between Dichter and Friedan, most notably in their attitudes to the condition and aspirations of women. Yet there were similarities as well. Although Dichter linked women's satisfaction to consumption and Friedan to careers, they shared a belief in the centrality of self-realization as well as a tendency to psychologize social problems. They had both absorbed these ideas from European psychologists who emigrated to the United States, Charlotte Bühler in Dichter's case and Kurt Lewin and others in Friedan's. Moreover, both of them focused almost exclusively on white, middle-class suburban women, an approach characteristic of much social observation and criticism of the 1950s.[40]

Sustaining her interest in her undergraduate major, Friedan turned what humanistic and ego psychologists had written about men, and occasionally women, to feminist purposes. Abraham Maslow, for example, believed that women would achieve self-actualization primarily as wives and mothers. They held such notions despite evidence from the Kinsey Report that proved to

Friedan the link between women's emancipation and the capacity for sexual fulfillment. Friedan, however, hardly wished to rest her case for women's enhanced self-esteem on the likelihood of more and better orgasms. Rejecting a narcissistic version of self-fulfillment, she argued that people develop a healthy identity not through routine work such as that of the housewife but through purposeful and committed effort "which reaches beyond biology, beyond the narrow walls of home, to help shape the future."[41]

She acknowledged the importance of child care and continuing education; but personal growth, self-determination, and human potential were central to her solution to the problems women faced. Here Friedan was participating in one of the major postwar cultural and intellectual movements, the incorporation of the therapeutic mentality into the discussion of public policy and social issues. In the process, she joined others in using humanistic psychology and neo-Freudianism to ground a powerful cultural critique at a time when other formulations, especially Marxist ones, were politically discredited. She offered what the historian Ellen Herman has called a "postmaterial agenda," which employed psychological concepts to undergird feminism. In doing so, Friedan was responding to other writers who used psychology to suggest that only the acceptance of domesticity would cure women's frustrations. Friedan's contribution was to turn the argument around, declaring that women's misery resulted from the attempt to keep them in "their" place. Rather than persuading women to adjust and conform, psychology ought to foster their personal growth and encourage their fuller embrace of non-domestic roles. Other observers concentrated on the troublesome nature of male identity. Friedan also gave this theme a twist, reiterating the problems posed by "feminized" men and "masculinized" women while promising that the liberation of women would strengthen male and female identity alike.[42]

What Friedan accomplished in *The Feminine Mystique* was a powerful translation into feminist terms of concerns that popular social critics had articulated. She criticized affluence for trapping women, in the process dissenting from Katona, Dichter, and Potter while drawing on an analysis, developed by male social critics such as David Riesman, William H. Whyte, and Vance Packard, which blamed life in the suburbs, jobs in large organizations, and consumer culture for the failure to promote healthy masculinity. By and large, works of fiction and social criticism by male authors paid minimal attention to women, or else stereotyped them as maladjusted career women or as housewives, mothers, and consumers who were helpmates to husbands striving to be status seekers or organization men. Friedan applied what these authors had written about suburban, middle-class men to their female counterparts.

Friedan's focus on identity rested on an assumption, shared by other widely read social critics of her generation, that the main challenge facing American society was affluence, not poverty. In opposition to all that she had learned as a labor journalist, she asserted that America had become a middle-class society and that the group suffering the most serious problems was white, middle-class suburbanites, not inner-city African Americans, poor rural whites, or working-class union members. Like Packard, Friedan adopted the new moralism, a view of consumer culture that rested on the assertion that new goods and services provided the middle class with false satisfactions while distracting them from solving the more authentic problems of love, work, and politics. Though articulating sympathy for the plight of African Americans, hers was decidedly a lily-white book. Overall, Friedan offered little awareness that millions of Americans, herself included, had to work in order to make ends meet or to support a family under intense pressure from an escalating standard of living. Nor, as others have noted, did she seem to have much sympathy for women who struggled under objectively difficult conditions and were not fortunate enough to worry about self-realization and fulfilling careers. In her attempt to emphasize the horrors of household work and to appeal to middle-class women who did not have jobs outside the home, Friedan largely ignored women who had paid employment. She also devalued middle-class women who worked, both because the notion of professionalism was so important to her personally and because it was in the professional ranks that women's workforce participation had taken a dramatic downturn since the 1920s.[43]

The Feminine Mystique simultaneously reflected 1950s discussions and reconfigured them by focusing on suburban women. Central to the book were warnings that Friedan's male counterparts had also issued but on which her personal history gave her a different perspective. Faced with the pressures for conformity, she believed, Americans (and in her case specifically American women) had to go against the grain and seek personal autonomy. Like her male predecessors, Friedan held a mirror up to Americans, urging them toward that shock of recognition that combined personal insight and social analysis. Like Riesman, Whyte, and Packard, Friedan psychologized social problems and considered identity and mythology but not social structure the principal impediments to a fully realized self. C. Wright Mills went further in identifying the scope and power of undemocratic elites, but Friedan nonetheless suggested the existence of a male power elite that systematically suppressed women. Her emphasis on self-realization rather than on hard social experiences echoed Riesman's focus on problems of autonomy, Whyte's insights on how to cheat on personality tests in order to maintain a modicum of psychological independence, and Packard's advice on countering status seeking by returning to an earlier type of individualism. Like Riesman, Packard, Galbraith, and others, Friedan defined the good life not in terms of increased material possessions and commercial services but in the language of personal growth and a vaguely articulated commitment to solving social problems. She followed others by writing a book that was longer on analysis designed to shock readers than on public policies and solutions.[44]

By framing her argument in psychological terms, Friedan enabled women to analyze their situation in ways that might enable them to resist the lure of consumer culture. She mixed personal testimony with psychological concepts to offer the self-help her readers could use to their advantage. With its dramatic interviews and stories of frustration, self-knowledge, and recovery, the book thus provided its audience with the same therapeutic insight Friedan had benefited from. The incorporation of firsthand personal narratives also brought to fruition a kind of journalism Friedan had been struggling to give birth to since the mid-1950s and that the New Journalists of the 1960s would develop into an art form. These approaches enabled her to convey the drama of the lives of American women. What made her writing so convincing was that it involved narratives of conversion—her own and that of her readers. After all, she portrayed herself as someone who, once trapped by and complicit in the creation of the feminine mystique, had now seen the light. With examples of small groups of women who had suddenly come to a common understanding, she offered a preview of what women in consciousness-raising groups of the late 1960s and after would profit from: self-knowledge obtained in the company of other women. If the stories of women who were suffering under the feminine mystique enabled her readers to understand what they felt but could not easily articulate, the stories of triumph gave them models to emulate.

The power (and limitations) of her book came from her insistence that the feminine mystique was a mental construct characteristic of an affluent society and as such something that women could alter with equally powerful ideas. As Donald Meyer has pointed out, Friedan argued that women could discover the answers in themselves and not through religious, economic, political, or social change. If they had the wrong ideas, all they needed was the right ones, which her book provided. Since the feminine mystique as a series of myths rested on the scientific claims of its proponents, she marshaled equally authoritative scientific evidence to expose and contradict what mystique makers, including Dichter and Katona, celebrated. Yet hers was also the authoritative voice of the expert who knows best. Her writing resonated with the same warnings that male critics of affluence had raised in widely read books, but what made *The Feminine Mystique* different was her sense of personal urgency and her presentation of authentic voices. Her career in Old Left journalism, her experiments with new forms, her long-held feminism, and her personal experiences made it possible for her to write a social critique that changed her readers' lives.[45]

Friedan's emphasis on education, like her emphasis on therapy, had immense appeal to a generation that, having put the contentious political issues of the 1930s aside and moved to the suburbs, was enjoying the fruits of the postwar economic boom. *The Feminine Mystique* itself was like an adult education course that reminded women of what it meant to wrestle with ideas. An intensely intellectual book, it displayed the agility of the author's mind, her skills as a researcher, and her ability to make difficult ideas easy to understand. Reading *The Feminine Mystique* helped millions of women comprehend, and then change, their conditions. The book has had a commanding impact on historical scholarship, cultural memory, and American feminism. It awakened hundreds of thousands of women to what they had long felt but been unable to articulate—how the mystique of suburban womanhood and the obligations of a housewife smothered their aspirations for a more fulfilling life. For good reason, historians have credited the book with playing a key role in the emergence of second wave feminism. The book's reception also transformed Betty Friedan's own life. Within three years of its publication, she had emerged as a leader of the feminist movement. Friedan's notoriety and success turned her into a significant breadwinner, heightened the tensions in her marriage, and played a role in leading to her divorce in 1969. She became one of the founders and the first president of the National Organization for Women. Formed in 1966, NOW fought for equal employment opportunities for women, equitable marriage and divorce laws, provision for equal treatment of female athletes, and fair treatment of women in textbooks and on television. Eventually, her manner, tactics, and commitments embroiled her in controversy. After the early 1970s, Friedan never again provided leadership of the women's movement from a base in a major national organization. Although she continued her work as an activist, in many ways it was as a speaker and a writer that she maintained her place in American public life.[46]

In 1969, Stephan Thernstrom, a historian then on the left, noted that "the myth of American affluence has become the new conventional wisdom, and it constitutes a formidable obstacle to understanding our present condition." The myth, he wrote, "mirrored the dominant political and social tendencies of the Age of Eisenhower." Not only did it detract attention from poverty, but it also "provided the well-to-do with an intellectually respectable vantage point from which to criticize the materialistic strivings of the vulgar masses rather than the American social order itself." Those who fostered this myth, along with readers who accepted it, "were far more distressed by the vulgar barbecue pits, television sets, and tailfins of the vast majority than by the sufferings of what they took to be a tiny minority. Conspicuous consumption," Thernstrom concluded, "not economic deprivation, was the real villain." He was speaking here of Galbraith's *Affluent Society*, which had just appeared in a new edition that more fully acknowledged the existence of poverty than the original one. But he could have been talking as well of the books by Packard and Friedan. As social criticism, these books relied on the new moralism, a self-righteous critique of the pursuit by middle-class Americans of the materialistic pleasures of an affluent society. His comments remind us how far the nation had traveled from 1963, when Friedan's book appeared, to 1969, the date of Thernstrom's comments.[47]

To be less harsh on these authors is to acknowledge that they served as scouts or negotiators in the shift from 1950s to 1960s America. Their books were as much a part of the earlier as of the later decade. Coming to terms with postwar affluence, they prodded the complacent to think about their apathy and the restive to shed their reserve. They reflected the tone of social criticism of the 1950s while heralding and influencing the bolder politics of the 1960s. In its earliest stages, this renascent sense of social responsibility often lacked specific programmatic content, appealing to readers dissatisfied with the complacency of the 1950s but unsure how to create a better society. All of the books under consideration in this chapter had shortcomings that remind us of their location in time. Galbraith started out to write a book on poverty but ended up focusing on affluence, thereby minimizing the extent of economic deprivation. Readers were more likely to hear his acknowledgment of the nation's prosperity than to embrace his call for new social and economic policies. Packard and Friedan, in their emphasis on a psychology of self-realization, were closer to Dichter's vision than they might have cared to acknowledge. Moreover, they were more effective in analyzing the costs of affluence than in suggesting remedies, which often seemed both timid and at odds with the thrust of their critiques.

Above all, these books shared an assumption that the affluence of white, middle-class suburbanites was one of the nation's most compelling social problems. The conditions facing African Americans, the poor, and disaffected youths, as well as environmental problems, were not among their primary concerns, though they would soon become the focus of national attention. Despite the challenges these books posed to the placid consensus of the 1950s, their central focus was the impact on the nation of the choices made by middle-class suburbanites. Even before the appearance of *The Feminine Mystique* in 1963, new issues had begun to command the attention of Americans. In the early 1960s, a series of books appeared that challenged the assumption that the nation's principal problem was the affluence of the middle class.

5

From the Affluent Society to the Poverty of Affluence, 1960–1962

Paul Goodman, Oscar Lewis, Michael Harrington, and Rachel Carson

If Vance Packard, Betty Friedan, and John Kenneth Galbraith offered perspectives on affluence that were at once familiar and challenging, then Paul Goodman, Oscar Lewis, Michael Harrington, and Rachel Carson broke new ground by turning their attention to people and issues missing from works on the perils of middle-class affluence. In *Growing Up Absurd: Problems of Youth in the Organized Society* (1960), Goodman focused on the adverse impact of postwar prosperity on young men. The anthropologist Lewis, in *The Children of Sánchez* (1961), his dramatic portrayal of a family living in Mexico City, focused not on suburban affluence but on urban poverty. With *The Other America* (1962), the democratic socialist Harrington alerted his readers and policy makers to the existence of millions of Americans who did not lead comfortable lives. And Carson, in *Silent Spring* (1962), warned of the dangers that the pursuit of affluence posed to the natural environment. Thus, in a brief two years, a series of widely read books awakened Americans to issues to which cold war celebrants and social critics alike had failed to pay adequate attention.[1]

Throughout most of the 1950s, the discussions that dominated the public arena assumed that consumer sovereignty and the wisdom of social scientists and market researchers obviated the need for the federal government to provide public services. The issues highlighted by Goodman, Lewis, Harrington, and Carson, along with those addressed by consumer activists discussed in the next chapter, transformed American views of affluence. Together these authors reflect what Albert O. Hirschman has called "a turn by the disappointed and hostile consumer-citizen to public action." These writers turned

129

moralism from a cultural critique of excessive consumption to a political assault on the excesses of a prosperous society. By addressing neglected subjects, the four authors examined in this chapter reshaped discussions of affluence. They did not believe that white, middle-class suburbanites were the tragic victims of a burgeoning GNP. Nor did they agree with social critics who saw organization men and their wives as the emblematic representatives of an affluent society. By and large, they thought in terms that were less limited, and more political, cultural, and social than psychological. They dissented from the cold war liberalism that suffused the nation's politics and even widely read works of social criticism. They suggested, with some uncertainty and hesitancy, what it might mean to move toward a more radical analysis, political activism, and a renewed sense of what public policy can accomplish. Their analyses of the effects of consumer culture were more probing, suggestive, and critical than those of their predecessors. Yet their efforts exposed the perils awaiting anyone who would use a pathbreaking book as an entry point for political activism.[2]

Paul Goodman: Disaffected Youth in an Affluent Society

When Paul Goodman's *Growing Up Absurd* appeared in the fall of 1960, on the eve of the election of John F. Kennedy to the presidency, Galbraith hailed the book as "a highly serious effort to understand the relation between society and the disaffected youngster." Summarizing Goodman's argument and connecting it to his own work, Galbraith noted that "everywhere the diminishing marginal urgency of goods . . . is robbing work of its purpose." Goodman brought attention in particular to young men, a group that previous critics of affluence had neglected. Like Galbraith, he breathed new life into the familiar critique of consumer culture in ways that were both distinctive and complex. As with Packard on the publication of *The Hidden Persuaders* and Friedan with *The Feminine Mystique, Growing Up Absurd* thrust Goodman into the national limelight.[3]

Yet Goodman's life differed dramatically from that of Galbraith, Packard, and Friedan. Goodman (1911–1972) was born in Manhattan into a Jewish household transformed just before his birth by his father's abandonment of the family. With his mother often on the road as a traveling saleswoman, Goodman was raised by his aunts and a sister. He completed public school in Manhattan and earned a B.A. in 1931 from City College of New York (CCNY). Five years later he began graduate school in philosophy and literature at the University of Chicago, returning to New York in 1940. He did not receive his Ph.D. until 1954. In 1938 and then again in 1945, he entered successively into two common-law marriages, but throughout his adult life he remained bisexual. An antimilitarist, anarchist, and pacifist, he opposed U.S. entry into World War II, a stance that, along with his very public bisexuality, cost him his job as film critic for *Partisan Review*. In the 1940s, Goodman published in obscure anarchist journals such as *Why?* and *Retort*, as well as in Dwight Macdonald's *politics*, an important postwar radical publication whose authors were coming to terms with the consequences of the collapse of the Old Left. Given his politics and his sexuality, the 1950s were a difficult time for Goodman, but he survived the decade by practicing and writing about Gestalt therapy. Until 1960, he subsisted on a household income below the poverty line, earned mainly by his wives but also by his own occasional teaching, by his persistent but generally unremunerative publishing, and, during the 1950s, by his work as a therapist. Novelist, psychologist, poet, playwright, social and literary critic, urban planner, and education reformer, Goodman was, as Alfred Kazin noted, "the nearest thing to an eighteenth-century *philosophe* any of us had ever seen." Throughout his adult life, Goodman remained steadfastly committed to a set of principles. He was a "conservative anarchist," as he said of himself two years before his death of a heart attack at sixty.[4]

Goodman's writing in the mid-1940s prefigured much of what he would have to say about affluence in his 1960 book, most clearly in *Communitas*, the highly original work on architecture and planning that he authored in 1947 with his brother, the architect Percival Goodman. At a time when others on the left either hoped for or feared a return to scarcity, the Goodmans believed that World War II had shown the power of the U.S. economy to produce in ways that were both abundant and wasteful. Indeed, they estimated that for Americans to live on a decent subsistence level, people would have to work only one day a week. As would be true later, too, here Goodman and his brother made explicit their preference for a world that would reconnect what modern capitalism had torn asunder: country and city, work and leisure, means and ends, social relations across class lines. They sketched out three paths American society might take. One was "A City of Efficient Consumption," in which the department store was the key institution. (Although they tried to be neutral in discussing this option, "facts kept slipping into satire and ridicule," as Paul Goodman's biographer Taylor Stoehr has noted.) The Goodmans employed a moralist vision to imagine a dystopian world of expanded production, decreased satisfaction from work, and a depoliticized public sphere. The dominance of the department store ensured that emulation and fads would rule. Every so often such a society would erupt into a "Carnival," with installment debts forgiven, schedules forgotten, capital goods spent, inefficient consumption indulged in, huge but perishable floats prepared, and families returned to self-sufficiency. The next day, people would awaken to stores "cleared for the spring inventory" and debtors "given new heart to borrow again."[5]

In *Growing Up Absurd*, edited by Jason Epstein at Random House, Goodman focused on the problems that riddled America's affluent society, making it difficult for young men to lead meaningful lives and achieve genuine manhood. In the process, as the historian Kevin Mattson has shown, Goodman "politicized the cultural critique that dominated so much of American intellectual life in the 1950s," a critique articulated by David Riesman, William Whyte, and Vance Packard, but whose central themes of alienation and conformity "had political roots and demanded serious social reform." The central issue for Goodman was that the work men engaged in so as to produce a high standard of living was fundamentally unsatisfactory. For him, genuine work, which involved the production of "necessary food and shelter," was creative, dignified, and essential, characteristics he could not apply to the activities of those involved in "salesmanship, entertainment, business management, promotion, and advertising." Lacking meaningful work, men sought what he saw as false satisfactions, including consumption and role playing. Yet if worthwhile work was hard to find in America, so was genuine consumption and leisure in a society he saw as more committed to public relations than to the public good—and one, moreover, in which popular culture was trivialized and consumer culture false.[6]

In important ways, Goodman dissented not just from the cold war celebration of affluence but even from other critics' dissent. The problem for him was not so much the excess of affluence but the banality of the work necessary to create it. His critique of meaningless jobs and vacuous consumption thus raised questions about affluence that others ducked. As Mumford had done during World War II, Goodman called for "a more sensible abundance, with efficient production of quality goods, distribution in a natural market, counterinflation and sober credit." As a consequence of the nation's commitment to an ever-growing GNP reliant on what he saw as false work, the nation could not grapple with the key issues of labor, pleasure, and leisure that affluence made possible. Yet if Goodman saw excessive affluence as a problem, more so than any other widely read writer of his time, he also emphasized the persistence of poverty and class distinctions in America. He pointed to a bulge in the income pyramid composed of the lower middle class. Below were "those at the bottom," whom others would later identify as the underclass, who "tend to fall out of 'society' altogether." Echoing President Franklin D. Roosevelt's estimate during the depression of a third of a nation living in want, Goodman wrote of bringing "back into society the 30 per cent who are *still* ill fed and ill housed, and more outcast than ever." Although at times he came close to romanticizing the outcast, he had no illusions about the relationship of the poor to consumer culture. "Our present poor," he asserted, "are absolute sheep and suckers for the popular culture they cannot afford." Unlike Galbraith, who saw poverty as primarily rural, situational, and isolated, Goodman asserted that it "now consists mainly of racial and cultural minorities, including migrant farm labor."[7]

Goodman made psychological processes central to a social analysis. "*Growth, like any ongoing function,*" he asserted, relying on his training as a psychologist, "*requires adequate objects in the environment* to meet the needs and capacities of the growing [person]." "In terms of Gestalt theory," the historian Richard King has noted of Goodman's vision, "American society frustrated the natural desires of its youth and prevented them from following through or completing a situation on their own terms." For Goodman, growing up was absurd because, with society blocking the fulfillment of basic human needs, socialization to false ideals produced alienation. It was precisely its affluence and organization that underwrote the nation's failure to provide young men with role models and conditions for growth. Only a decentralized society that did not worship an ever-expanding GNP could foster satisfaction of authentic human longings for love, patriotism, work, faith, honor, and community. For Goodman, the solution was the completion of what he called the "missed revolutions," which ranged from technocracy, the New Deal, and syndicalism to democracy and agrarianism.[8]

Goodman believed that the burdens of an affluent society suffused by the frustrating pursuit of false pleasures fell most heavily on its young men, not, as Friedan would claim, on its women. "A girl does not *have* to, she is not expected to, 'make something' of herself," he wrote, celebrating motherhood while denigrating a full range of women's aspirations. For him, producing and raising babies was an "absolutely self-justifying" act "like any other natural or creative act," which exempted women from the grind of meaningless work. Goodman's picture of the problems men faced echoed William H. Whyte Jr.'s exposé *The Organization Man* (1956), which emphasized the psychological trials of middle-class men who worked in large bureaucracies. Goodman's central metaphor was that of the "apparently closed room in which there is a large rat race at the dominant center of attention." The genius of Goodman's book was that where others saw diverse groups of men—those who worked in bureaucracies as well as youthful dropouts and rebellious teens—pursuing radically different lives, he saw them all as fundamentally shaped by the dominance of the organizational rat race. For example, he detected an unacknowledged "alliance between juvenile delinquents and the middle status of the organized system, exchanging cultural heroes, norms of cool behavior, and the values of cynicism."[9]

A wide range of men peopled his book, all joined by the way the system forced them into role playing and being cool. Organization men, lacking satisfaction from their jobs and personal relationships, became cynical and resigned. Non-delinquent boys, "mesmerized by the symbols and culture of the rat race," would eventually end up in factory jobs once they decided to stop hanging out on street corners and instead follow their parents in pursuing lives on the installment plan. For Goodman, juvenile delinquents were the "Early Fatalistic" types who learned to desire what society offered through their exposure "to expensive glamour" but found they could obtain worldly goods only by stealing them. What deepened their anger was the "inner conflict between their dreams of American glamour and their own impotent resources." Likewise, hipsters exuded a sense of disengagement as they played it cool and "warded off surprise by being ahead of every game." Finally, the Beat Generation, whom he called "The Early Resigned," enacted "a critique of the organized system" by participating in a "major pilot study of the use of leisure in an economy of abundance." Yet in the end, Goodman found the Beats too disengaged and their culture too ephemeral to convince him of their importance or vitality.[10]

Like *The Hidden Persuaders* and *The Affluent Society*, *Growing Up Absurd* transformed its author's life. With more than 100,000 copies sold in the first year, Goodman "achieved a public visibility and influence" that no other New York intellectual, save perhaps Norman Mailer, equaled. The reception of the book marked a turning point, for whatever Goodman wrote now was sure to find an eager audience. He used the early proceeds from the book's sales to buy a modest farm in northern New Hampshire. This made it possible for him to achieve for himself the balance between city and country living which he had advocated for so long. Although his new circumstances enabled his wife to quit her job as a secretary and for them to have another child, Goodman remained committed to what he had described as decent poverty, the condition of people who needed to remain in society but lived with very little money. In other respects, things remained much the same as he continued to cherish his economic freedom and modest way of life. Swept away by the fact that there were now people who would listen to, and perhaps even act upon, what he had to say, Goodman spoke on college campuses and on occasion accepted invitations for stints as a visiting professor. Publishers rushed to get his books into print, with at least one coming out every year throughout the 1960s. His articles still appeared in *Liberation* and *Dissent*, though he now broke into print in more mainstream publications as well.[11]

Growing Up Absurd, noted Theodore Roszak, himself a chronicler and celebrant of the youthful revolt of the 1960s, transformed Goodman into "the foremost tribune of our youthful counter culture." The young, Stoehr has noted, "gave him his subject, his audience, his troops." In the 1960s,

Goodman worked on public issues through the Institute of Policy Studies in Washington, D.C. Throughout the decade he supported, criticized, cajoled, and engaged the New Left. If his relationship to a new generation of activists was a complicated one, his writings nonetheless inspired rebellious youth in innumerable ways. He was one of the first in a series of older men who played a key role in articulating the dreams of America's counterculture, emphasizing noncommercial experiences rather than empty materialism. His commitment to open sexuality, his opposition to the war in Vietnam, his role as an intellectual who thrived outside the academy, and his vision of the inseparability of politics and culture all fostered the youthful rebellion of young men, from the hippies to the New Left. In the late 1960s, the death of his son and his own objection to what he saw as the violence, naïveté, and apocalyptic vision of antiwar protesters widened the gulf between Goodman and those he had inspired. He nevertheless influenced a wide range of people with a practical utopianism that centered on restoring the balance between urban and rural living and stressed the need for a moral vision to guide the role of technology in American life and the importance of decentralizing institutions. He was also a prominent and articulate advocate of a new vision of education, laying the basis for alternative, progressive education from grade school to graduate school. Above all for our purposes, he provided middle-class youth with a defense against consumer culture and a celebration of its opposites—meaningful work, intense experience, and authentic community.[12]

Oscar Lewis and the Poverty of Affluence

Born on Christmas Day, 1914, as Yehezkiel Lefkowitz, Oscar Lewis spent his early years in Manhattan, where his parents had recently arrived after fleeing pogroms in Poland. When Oscar was about five, poor health forced his father to give up his career as a rabbi and relocate the family to a farm in the Catskills, which over time became a small hotel that enabled his family to live modestly. While still a teenager, at the suggestion of a Communist Party organizer who worked at his parents' hotel, Lewis started reading books by Marx and Lenin. Using the name Oscar, which his parents had also given him at birth, he entered CCNY in 1930 when he was only fifteen. One teacher who influenced him was the Marxist historian Philip Foner, who taught Lewis about trade unions and African American slavery, emphasizing in both cases the struggles of oppressed people to achieve dignity and power. After graduating in 1936, he became a student in anthropology at Columbia. In 1937 he married Ruth Maslow, sister of the humanistic psychologist Abraham Maslow. The income that allowed him to marry came from his work with the WPA (Works Progress Administration), in which he examined the contributions that African American culture made to the nation. Lewis's principal professor at Columbia was Ruth Benedict. Although she focused on culture and personality, Oscar continued to pursue issues that had interested him in college—class, stratification, and the relationship between economic forces and cultural processes. In 1939, under Benedict's supervision, he made his first field trip, to Blackfoot reservations in Montana and Alberta, which resulted in the dissertation he completed in 1940, the same year he legally changed his last name from Lefkowitz to Lewis. During his years as a graduate student, he maintained an interest in politics. Like Friedan, he focused on support of trade unions and the fight against fascism, though, unlike her, he saw the USSR as a bulwark against Nazism. As with Friedan, anti-Semitism was never out of his consciousness, an awareness intensified in his case by the loss of fifty-five relatives in the Holocaust.[13]

As happened to so many of his generation, federal employment in World War II proved crucial to Lewis's career. Work on a series of government projects enabled him to produce *On the Edge of the Black Waxy: A Cultural Survey of Bell County, Texas* (1948). Government programs also made it possible for him to learn Spanish and to carry out his first significant fieldwork, a study of a Mexican community which resulted in the publication of *Life in a Mexican Village: Tepoztlán Restudied* (1951) and *Tepoztlán: Village in Mexico* (1960). After the war, he spent two years on the faculty of Washington University in St. Louis, and then in 1948 he accepted his second and final academic position, in anthropology at the University of Illinois. He took a leave of absence for two years (1952–54) to participate in a Ford Foundation project on India. As he had done in Mexico, Lewis worked on a community study, publishing *Village Life in Northern India* in 1958. From the beginning of his academic career to the end, Ruth Maslow worked closely with her husband on every project, though as was true of many scholars' wives of her generation, she never received public recognition equal to the importance of the work she did. Throughout his university career, accompanied by his wife and two children, Lewis was away doing fieldwork almost as much as he was in Illinois. Socially insecure, with a prickly personality, and feeling himself very much an outsider, Lewis preferred being in the field among poor people to being in the classroom or in polite, middle-class Gentile society. Culturally a Jew who had rejected his father's Orthodoxy, he did not hide his ethnic identity, although he strained to suppress evidence in his speech of his origins in a Yiddish-speaking New York household. In the 1950s, he also had to be careful about revealing his history of commitment to an albeit vaguely defined and undogmatic socialism. "The vicious and arbitrary anti-leftism of the McCarthy era compounded his fear of anti-Semitism," his biographer Susan M. Rigdon has written, "so that he came to speak frankly to almost no one outside his family." Instead, he would find an outlet for his commitments in his writing.[14]

In his research and writing on Tepoztlán, Lewis was laying the basis for the distinctive work that would sustain him from the late 1950s until his death. Starting in the 1940s, he developed his methods for collecting the life histories of Mexican families. He used intensive, open-ended interviews to record the stories of a few families and experimented with carrying out interviews using a tape recorder. Lewis derived considerable satisfaction from direct, one-on-one, highly personal interchanges. He focused on the historical factors that shaped the lives of the people he studied and systematically collected data on the economics of their households. He cast his net wide as he tried to understand all aspects of his subjects' lives and the relationships among them. Using grants and networks of scholars and researchers, he developed entrepreneurial techniques that resulted in the amassing of more data than he could control or explain. In the 1950s, when most academic fields relied on a vision of smoothly functioning societies based on a consensus model, Lewis remained committed to a positive view of the centrality of conflict in society. Thus, in *Life in a Mexican Village*, he criticized Robert Redfield, a more senior anthropologist, for painting a romantic picture of village life in Mexico, minimizing the costs of economic backwardness, and giving short shrift to social conflict.[15]

By the late 1950s, Lewis had reached a major transition in his career. Until then, though he continued to play by the rules of academic research, he increasingly chafed at the restrictions those rules imposed. In his movement toward what he called "ethnographic realism," he was reacting especially to what he considered the false divisions among disciplines and between art and science, participation and observation, subjectivity and objectivity, detachment and involvement, intellectual work and its application to policy. The occasion for resolving these tensions was his study of the urban poor in Mexico City. When he returned to Mexico in 1956 on a Guggenheim fellowship after completing his work for the Ford Foundation in India, he made a number of critical innovations. Improvements in the technology of tape recording transformed the nature of his interviewing and thus his relationship with the people he interviewed. No longer concerned with writing down information accurately and focusing on specific questions, he could engage in a personal conversation. As he listened to the tapes afterward, he could pay attention to inflection and language. As a result, what became the focus of his work were the stories people told him rather than the historical and demographic data he unearthed or the academic analysis he developed. In addition, he had now conclusively shifted the locus of his work from relatively stable rural areas and villages to more dynamic city settings, a move that intensified his sense of urgency and clarified his political mission. He completed the shift, long under way, from his emphasis on community to a concentration on families. This enabled him to reach a broader audience as he communicated what he called "both the suffering and the humanity of the urban poor." Lewis also drew inspiration from *Rashomon*, the Japanese film released in the United States in December 1951, which told a single story from multiple perspectives. Before long, he discovered subjects whose compelling stories called forth his best efforts.[16]

In *Five Families*, Lewis wrote almost like a novelist, telling those stories as an omniscient narrator. With the multiple autobiographies of the Sánchez family, he let his subjects speak in their own voices, leaving his comments to the introduction, a style that is familiar today but then represented a dazzling innovation. As one reviewer noted, Lewis "blazed a new trail for what the 19th Century called naturalism and the 20th Century Joyceanism." Eliminating his voice from the narratives, he let those whose words he recorded speak directly to the reader in vivid, dramatic prose.[17]

With the publication of *The Children of Sánchez* in 1961, Lewis achieved his goal of giving voice to the urban poor of Mexico City, and of doing so in a compelling manner. Jesús Sánchez and his four children lived in the Casa Grande *vecindad* in the heart of Mexico City in a "large one-storey slum tenement." On most nights, ten or more people slept in the Sánchez's single room. Jesús, the father, born in 1910, had grown up in an Indian village in Veracruz. Illiterate, he worked in Mexico City for thirty years as a purchasing clerk for a restaurant, supplementing his income by raising pigs and exotic birds. In what spare time remained, he was building a home away from the center of the city. His life revolved around hard work, responsibility, and persistent conflicts with his children. The four children mentioned in the book were the products of his common-law union with Leonore, who died shortly after the birth of the youngest. Jesús considered most of them ungrateful. He was painfully aloof from them, rejecting their pleas for affection.[18]

Manuel, age thirty-two, was the eldest child. Hard-hearted and self-righteous, after failing to make a go of running a small shoe factory, he went to the United States, where he worked as a farm laborer. A drifter, gambler, and talented storyteller, he eventually became a hawker of stolen goods. Manuel neglected his two wives and six children. As one of his sisters said of him, "He reminded me of a person walking backwards in darkness, without setting foot upon solid ground."[19] Next in line was Roberto, twenty-nine, a small, dark-skinned young man who thought himself ugly. Uneducated except for one year in school, he was a brawler and a thief who served time in a penitentiary and retained a hatred for the police. Idealistic and a devout and mystical Catholic, he went through life in a state of confusion. Consuelo, the elder of two daughters, poetic and brittle, served as the chorus to the book's dramas. Plagued by physical and mental illnesses, she gave up her dream of becoming a nun and struggled to obtain an education and values that would bring her into the middle class. She lost her job as a stenographer when she refused to give in to the sexual demands of her boss. She responded frigidly to her brutal lover and left home because she hated her father's fourth wife. Marta at twenty-five was the youngest. A tomboy, she left school after the first grade and joined a gang of young girls. Initiated into sex at fourteen, she bore children early and often. Leaving the man with whom she'd had her first child at sixteen, she married another who was an alcoholic. She was the only one of the four children whom her father liked, and she remained dependent on him.

Jesús and his children told about their lives in a series of dramatic stories that Lewis orchestrated with a skilled editorial hand. Early sexual encounters, feuds with family members and others, alcohol and marijuana, violence, encounters with corrupt government officials, and seemingly unstable family and conjugal relationships marked their existence. Yet there was also in their lives, and in their telling about them, abundant dignity and courage. This complexity and individuality defied easy ideological conclusions. The Sánchezes struggled against enormous odds to sustain themselves, physically and spiritually. As they told their stories of hardship, they suggested that they could not help themselves, making it easy for unsympathetic readers in the United States to dismiss their troubles as stemming from character flaws. Some people in the *vecindad* were disciplined and lucky enough to enter the middle class. Nevertheless, the four Sánchez children had failed to fulfill their aspirations because complex combinations of sexism, poverty, self-doubt, and corruption were working against them.

The epilogue, in which Jesús contemplated the meaning of his life as he spoke to the reader, revealed the book's many and often contradictory meanings. At one point, he talked of his two sons in terms that any North American advocate of free enterprise could have articulated. "They don't have the will-power to get a job and stick to it," he remarked, "an honest job so that they can go out into the street looking decent and feel proud of themselves." Yet elsewhere in the epilogue Jesús spoke of the corruption of the Mexican government and labor unions, wondered if things were any better in the United States or the Soviet Union, and decried the fact that those who "rule over us have expensive cars and many millions in the bank, but they don't see what's underneath where the poor people live." Lewis chose to end the book with Jesús evoking his aspirations to be a good provider for his grandchildren, a sentiment that both reverberated with and remained distinct from the 1950s American dream of providing a suburban homestead: "I want to leave them a room, that's my ambition; to build that little house, one or two rooms or three so that each child will have a home and so they can live there together. But they don't want to help me. I asked God to give me the strength to keep struggling so I won't go under soon and maybe finish that little house. Just a modest place that they can't be thrown out of. I'll put a fence around it and no one will bother them. It will be a protection for them when I fall down and don't get up again."[20]

To North American readers who lived in the suburbs and had absorbed *The Organization Man, The Man in the Gray Flannel Suit, The Affluent Society*, and *The Status Seekers*, the lives of Jesús and his children provided a dramatic contrast. By and large, Lewis left implicit his critique of other writers who explored the lives of the affluent, disdaining their comforts and their smugness. Yet in the introduction, where he spoke directly to his readers, he underscored his intent. He noted that although sociologists had once written pathbreaking studies of urban poverty, they were "now concentrating their attention on suburbia to the relative neglect of the poor." Novelists, for their part, were "so busy probing the middle-class soul that they have lost touch with the problems of poverty." Perhaps answering those who saw a direct relationship between character, ambition, and success, Lewis noted that Jesús was not at the bottom of Mexico City's economic ladder. Growing up in a world with neither modern consumer goods nor "the hope of upward mobility," he had "managed to raise himself out of the lower depths of poverty." In contrast, his children, exposed to the values of individualism and social mobility, had remained poor.[21]

The Sánchez family enjoyed pleasures and pains unknown to Whyte's, Packard's, and Friedan's suburban subjects. Providing an alternative to moralism, Lewis pictured a vibrant world, filled with pageantry and a strong sense of community. The members of the Sánchez family were able to derive pleasure from satisfying their basic needs in a world marked by poverty, not affluence. "Except for an old radio," Lewis wrote, "there were no luxury items in the Sánchez home in the Casa Grande, but there was usually enough to eat and the family could boast of having had more education than most of their neighbors." The lives of the people in the book were filled with violence, pain, corruption, and cruelty. Yet their stories revealed "an intensity of feeling and human warmth, a strong sense of individuality, a capacity for gaiety, a hope for a better life, a desire for understanding and love, a readiness to share the little they possess, and the courage to carry on in the face of many unresolved problems." Gaiety, genuine individuality, intense feelings, and an ability to enter imaginatively into the world others inhabited: these were not qualities popular writers had ascribed to member of the lonely crowd who worked as organization men and sought social status through consumer goods and experiences.[22]

If, with *The Children of Sánchez*, Lewis offered a critique, albeit a largely implicit one, of the poverty of the affluent society and turned ethnography into a riveting genre, over the long haul the book has been best remembered for its discussion of the "culture of poverty." Indeed, in writing on this topic, Lewis became unwittingly responsible for introducing into social-scientific discourse one of the twentieth century's most influential and problematic concepts. In *Five Families*, he used the phrase in the subtitle, but his introduction offered neither explanation nor analysis. As Rigdon has noted, the concept served many purposes. It made sense of a massive amount of testimony and thereby offered the kind of authority valued by professional anthropologists. It provided what Rigdon has called a culture façade for Lewis's radicalism, a way of hiding his controversial political history behind a more respectable front. Lewis increasingly believed that people's stories were more important than any social-scientific generalization he could make about them. "I'd hate to spoil it," Lewis said to a colleague, referring to *The Children of Sánchez*, "with questionable models like the culture of poverty. But I've found nothing better to explain the similarities."[23]

The Children of Sánchez was the first book in which Lewis paid more than minimal attention to the concept. He was less interested in the culture of poverty than he was in culture, in poverty, and in what a book about these two subjects might accomplish. Ambivalent about the thesis, he was unable to resolve the contradictions inherent in the meanings he gave it. What remained central to him was to write a book that would help in the struggle to eliminate poverty. Although the book ends with the testimony of Jesús about his dream of passing property to his children, Lewis concluded the introduction on a very different note. Lewis had wanted the stories to stand by themselves, but his editor at Random House, Jason Epstein, insisted that he explain their significance. Lewis therefore spoke of the people in the book as "badly damaged human beings" who were nonetheless "the true heroes of contemporary Mexico," for they revealed a "great capacity for misery and suffering" without which the Mexican political system would have no stability. "But even the Mexican capacity for suffering has its limits, and unless ways are found to achieve a more equitable distribution of the growing national wealth and a greater equality of sacrifice during the difficult period of industrialization," Lewis wrote, "we may expect social upheaval, sooner or later." He wrote this at a time when other social scientists, such as Walt Whitman Rostow, were celebrating the possibilities of economic development in the Third World.[24]

With *The Children of Sánchez*, Lewis fulfilled his dream of reaching a wide audience. The book garnered enthusiastic reviews. On the front page of the *New York Times Book Review*, Elizabeth Hardwick declared that Lewis "has made something brilliant and of singular significance, a work of such unique concentration and sympathy that one hardly knows how to classify it." Writing in *Commentary*, the education critic Edgar Friedenberg called the book "altogether superb" with "an immediacy and vividness that are completely compelling." The reviewer in *Time* hailed it as "extraordinary" and "a work of art created by reality itself." Some observers, doubtless unaware of Lewis's background, correctly linked the book to 1930s genres: the reviewer in the *New Republic* labeled it "'proletarian literature' with a vengeance." When reviewers tried to think of authors of comparable imaginative power, they mentioned Kafka, Dostoyevsky, Tolstoy, Shakespeare, Lawrence, Joyce, Dante. Appreciative readers ascribed varied meanings to the book: an exploration of life in developing nations; a prediction of revolutions to come or an understanding of those already in the making; a chronicle of the struggle of ordinary people against injustice; evidence that foreign aid had divided rather than united the comfortable West and the impoverished nations of the world; an emphatic, unsentimental view of the poor; a psychodrama worthy of Freud. Most reviewers found the culture of poverty concept interesting and persuasive, though they offered a variety of contradictory responses to it. As the sociologist Mirra Komarovsky wrote, Lewis made "no systematic attempt to discern the influences which have molded the Sánchez family," among which she listed the Mexican heritage, the impact of poverty, and distinctive family relationships, including the father's combination of responsibility and harshness. Overall, reviewers treated the thesis as but one of the book's many contributions, with its literary and imaginative powers deserving more attention and certainly greater accolades.[25]

Quickly, however, the ground shifted. Lewis and his book became best known for the concept of the culture of poverty when Michael Harrington popularized it and applied it to the United States. Indeed, Lewis had sparked a debate of immense importance and duration. For the rest of his life he defended, refined, qualified, and at times moved away from his thesis. As Rigdon has noted, the term was a slippery one, and Lewis's formulation was full of ambiguities and contradictions. "The convenience of the phrase," she has noted, "is that it contains something for everyone; in using it to describe the life-style of the poor, one can attach to it the causation of one's choice"— on the left, the power and structures of capitalism; on the right, the flawed character of the poor themselves. Especially surprising to Lewis was that, by not emphasizing how terrible poverty was, he had allowed the left to attack him and the right to misuse what he had written. Over time, especially after the political terrain shifted in the mid-1960s and the hold of McCarthyism waned, he more frankly revealed his radical commitments.[26] In 1966 he offered one of his clearest statements. The culture of poverty, he wrote, was a method of coping with hardship that one generation passed along to another. Mobilization from below, expressed through pride, class or race consciousness, and organization, would erode its power, a process most visible in the U.S. civil rights movement or in revolutionary societies such as Cuba.[27]

For the rest of his career, Lewis continued to produce in the same genre, once sales and accolades had convinced him that he no longer had to write for academic audiences. *Pedro Martínez: A Mexican Peasant and His Family* appeared in 1964. *La Vida: A Puerto Rican Family in the Culture of Poverty—San Juan and New York* won him the National Book Award in 1968. Many others followed: *A Study of Slum Culture* (1968), *A Death in the Sánchez Family* (1969), *Anthropological Essays* (1970). After his own death, *Living the Revolution: An Oral History of Contemporary Cuba* was published in three volumes with the assistance of Susan Rigdon and Ruth Maslow Lewis. Lewis's productivity was shaped by dramatic changes in the conditions under which he worked. In the Kennedy and Johnson administrations, funding to explore the culture of poverty thesis was readily available, especially for someone with his talents and record of achievement. For six years, beginning in 1963, Lewis worked in San Juan, New York, and Champaign-Urbana under the auspices of a series of federal grants, totaling in excess of $400,000 (roughly $2.5 million a year in today's dollars). Ironically, the success of his work on the culture of poverty distanced him from the poor people whom he had enabled to speak for themselves to a wide audience, as he found himself spending more time doing administrative work than fieldwork. Diagnosed with heart disease, his body wracked by illnesses dating from childhood and from years of fieldwork in the tropics, but unable to abandon the habits of a workaholic, Lewis brushed aside the warnings of doctors who urged him to change his diet, stay away from extreme climates, and slow down. He died on December 16, 1970, a few days before his fifty-sixth birthday.[28]

Michael Harrington and the Rediscovery of Poverty

When *The Children of Sánchez* appeared, most reviewers did not relate what Lewis had written to poverty in the United States. For instance, the author of the review in *Time* remarked that it had no "compelling social and political significance to the U.S." It was Michael Harrington (1928–1989), writing in *The Other America*, who made that connection. "The first thing which struck me," Harrington wrote in a 1961 review in the Catholic magazine *Commonweal*, "was the similarity between the Mexican and the American poor." What had prepared Harrington to recognize the existence of poverty in North America was a complex combination of circumstances, including education, experience, religion, and ideology. Born into a comfortably middle-class Irish American family in St. Louis, Harrington was educated at local Catholic schools before graduating from the College of the Holy Cross in 1947 at nineteen. In college, casting himself as a rebel and an outsider, he penned stories that joined issues of race and poverty to Catholic social teaching. After college he floundered briefly, spending a year (1947–48) at Yale Law School and another (1948–49) earning an M.A. in English at the University of Chicago, punctuated by visits to his home in St. Louis. In 1949 he moved to Greenwich Village in the hope of becoming a poet. Instead, he ended up on the staff of *Life* magazine. A conscientious objector during the Korean War, he worked in 1951–52 at the *Catholic Worker* on the Lower East Side of Manhattan. There he pursued a life of voluntary poverty and communal living, helping out at the soup kitchen and writing for the anarchist, pacifist, and radical publication inspired by Dorothy Day. While there, he wrote an article on poverty in America that countered the widespread celebration of affluence. For a decade to come, he spent almost every night participating in wide-ranging discussions at the White Horse Tavern, a bar that, as his biographer Maurice Isserman has noted, was a "hangout for a variety of grizzled longshoremen, accomplished writers, aspiring folk singers, would-be revolutionaries, gay intellectuals, and assorted other bohemians."[29]

By late 1952, chafing at the saintly role he had to assume at the Catholic Worker house, he broke with that organization and with the Roman Catholic Church, shifting from leftist Catholicism to a mixture of existentialism and Marxism. Involved in sectarian debates during the 1950s, he opposed both Stalinism and McCarthyism. He developed a determination to build a political movement that would fight for social justice. By the mid-1950s, he was traveling tirelessly to university campuses, recruiting students into what would soon become known as the New Left while at the same time writing for *Commonweal*, the leftist Catholic monthly, and two influential journals, the democratic socialist *Dissent* and the more centrist *Partisan Review*. He was what Isserman called a "premature sixties radical." By 1960, Harrington had spent time with Martin Luther King Jr., participated in civil rights protests, and served as editor of the Socialist Party's *New America*. He was thus a key figure at the extraordinary point in the late 1950s when American culture and radical politics were opening up. The Old Left had collapsed, while at the same time the civil rights movement was suggesting what a new politics of protest might look like. Harrington remained a socialist but was more skeptical than others around him about sectarian disputes. Hailing from the American heartland, at least a decade younger than his more embattled elders, and a captivating speaker, he was one of the key figures in the transition from the quiescent 1950s to the insurgent 1960s.[30]

With *The Other America*, Harrington helped change the nation's attitude toward poverty. Between the publication of Galbraith's *Affluent Society* in 1958 and Harrington's book four years later, the tide had already begun to turn. In 1960, Edward R. Murrow's TV documentary "Harvest of Shame" focused on migrant workers. John F. Kennedy's presidential campaign exposed poverty-stricken areas of West Virginia to the nation's view. Articles in middlebrow and leftist publications, as well as critiques of Galbraith's assumptions, were challenging cold war complacency. Yet it is difficult to realize now how invisible poverty was to most middle-class Americans and to policy makers on the eve of the publication of Harrington's book. Most liberal intellectuals, caught up in analyses of America as a middle-class society, accepted that the nation had solved basic problems such as poverty. They followed the lead of Arthur Schlesinger in believing that what the age demanded was not an expansion of New Deal social welfare policies but a vaguer "qualitative" liberalism.[31]

The Other America was one of those rare books, not unlike *The Feminine Mystique*, which dramatically changed the way Americans saw the world around them. Harrington explicitly and forcefully rejected the picture that Whyte, Packard, and others had drawn of the psychological suffering of middle-class organization men and status seekers. He believed that people had "misinterpreted" Galbraith's message in *The Affluent Society* and as a result had underestimated poverty. Harrington opened his book with the observation that America's "anxieties were products of abundance." As examples he pointed to the hand-wringing about Madison Avenue, the excesses of automobile design, and "the emotional suffering taking place in the suburbs." He attacked key elements of the consensus, especially the assumption "that the basic grinding economic problems had been solved in the United States," making it possible to focus on the "qualitative" issues Schlesinger had defined, such as "learning to live decently amid luxury." In contrast to these misplaced concerns, Harrington pointed to "the huge, enormous, and intolerable fact of poverty in America," which he estimated as affecting 40 to 50 million people, or about 30 percent of the nation's population. These people, he argued, lived "at levels beneath those necessary for human decency" in a condition that "twists and deforms the spirit." Pessimistic and defeated, the poor were victims of "mental suffering to a degree unknown in Suburbia." To such a fact, he concluded, "the truly human reaction can only be outrage."[32]

Harrington cited several unique characteristics of American poverty. Following Galbraith, he acknowledged that America's poor were "the first minority poor in history, the first poor not to be seen, the first poor the politicians could leave alone." Members of no major institutions, geographically isolated, they were voiceless and atomized. A number of factors rendered the poor invisible, among them the natural beauty of poverty-stricken areas such as the Appalachians, the segregation of the urban poor into districts suburbanites rarely if ever saw, the sleight of hand of urban renewal, the isolation of the elderly, and the "well-meaning ignorance" of Americans who lived in comfort. Moreover, in a bitter twist on celebrations of contemporary progress and prosperity, Harrington asserted that what had made the postwar middle class comfortable had impoverished those below. Federal welfare and housing programs, the expansion of education, automation of factories, and mechanization of farms helped the wealthy and the middle class but caused many poor people to "view progress upside-down, as a menace and a threat to their lives." Harrington offered two explanations for the persistence of American poverty. The first involved what he called "the vicious circle of poverty": born under inauspicious circumstances, the poor faced a complex of objectively difficult conditions that kept them down, such as substandard housing, health care, and education. Second, without acknowledging that he had borrowed the term from Lewis, Harrington spoke of a "culture of poverty" which dominated the lives of America's disadvantaged and threatened to keep them poor. Poverty, he asserted, was "a culture, an institution, a way of life." To be poor in an affluent society meant more than the lack of material goods; it meant entering "a fatal, futile universe, an America within America with a twisted spirit." It was the nation's poor, "not the quietly desperate clerk or the harried executive," Harrington concluded, who were "the main victims of this society's tension and conflict." Unlike conservative users of the term, in referring to a culture of poverty he was countering the image of the poor as lazy welfare cheats who had no desire to pull themselves up by their bootstraps by earning a living.[33]

Harrington offered his readers a comprehensive, compelling view of the varieties of poverty in America. Among the "Rejects" were the semiskilled and unskilled workers who faced unemployment or underemployment when factories closed and they lost union jobs. "Humiliated and downgraded," they went to work in hospitals, sweatshops, restaurants, and private homes. Their lives contradicted the widely accepted notion of America as a classless society whose democratic capitalism had enabled industrial workers to enter and remain in the middle class. In addition, on America's farms, millions more were trapped in poverty—migrant workers as well as small farmers living in the shadow of large-scale and corporate farms. He included other groups as well: intellectuals and bohemians in big cities; the Skid Row alcoholics he had encountered during his year at the Catholic Worker settlement house;

the rural poor who had migrated to urban slums; and men and women in their "golden years," 50 percent of whom, he estimated, led lonely, impoverished lives in a youth-obsessed society. Although Harrington noted that poverty cut across racial lines, he nonetheless was especially passionate in describing the plight of African Americans in inner cities. At a time when civil rights advocates were fighting to end discriminatory laws, a fight Harrington supported, he believed racism to be so inbred that enacting laws against discrimination was only a partial solution. "The American economy, the American society, the American unconscious are all racist," he asserted, with what was exceptional bluntness at the time, though within a few years such remarks would become commonplace. He pulled no punches when he described the "interlocking base of economic and racial injustice" that white Americans imposed on blacks. Showing how racism reinforced "institutional patterns of the economy," Harrington took aim at "liberal rhetoric" that denied the existence of "racist practices."[34]

In seeking a solution, Harrington maintained the centrality of the culture of poverty. With the poor enmeshed in an interlocking set of conditions that destroyed their aspirations and left them trapped "at a level of life beneath moral choice," society had to "help them before they can help themselves." Only a "war on poverty," a massive, comprehensive, and coordinated federal program, would reverse the tragic and equally comprehensive problems afflicting America's poor. Such a program would destroy the fatalism that dominated their lives by changing "the social reality that gives rise to their sense of hopelessness." What such a program required was a spirit of commitment that would suffuse American society. Although he did not spell out specific proposals, Harrington called on the nation to extend to the poor the same provisions for social welfare that the upper two thirds already enjoyed through legislation on health care, the minimum wage, social security, and public housing.[35]

Yet he had something more in mind, too. Coordinated at the federal level, programs should be locally organized, with professionals such as "housing administrators, welfare workers, and city planners" taking the lead. He recognized that the civil rights movement provided examples of grassroots organization, for creating "a vast social movement." Yet the thrust of Harrington's argument was based on earlier philanthropic and welfare models. Because the other America could not speak for itself, "the poor, even in politics, must always be an object of charity." The most significant impediment Harrington saw to a new politics had to do with the structure of the political party system: given the presence in the Democratic Party of southern conservatives, the poor would remain invisible and real issues submerged. Only a political realignment would bring "a new mood of social idealism." Beyond that political shift, what was necessary to generate such a federal program was for affluent Americans to overcome the "indifference and blindness" that immobilized their consciences, to "see through the wall of affluence and recognize the alien citizens on the other side." Given what he saw as the political voicelessness of America's poor, their fate rested in the hands of the nation's better-off citizens, who should feel "anger and shame" over what his book revealed.[36]

Harrington skillfully captured the hearts and minds of those in his audience who had benefited from living with prosperity. He made his readers feel the pain of poverty. He crafted a book that was readable, vivid, learned, and persuasive. Realizing that his opponents might contest his estimates of the extent of American poverty, but not wanting to bore readers with dry data and analyses of their meaning, he confined his presentation of statistics and methods to an appendix. The text of the book itself was a compact and fast-paced 175 pages. He used a variety of strategies that cumulatively made the book both appealing and compelling. He threaded *The Other America* with quotes from the prose, lyrics, and poetry he had immersed himself in since entering college—from W. H. Auden, George Eliot, and Woody Guthrie to Ralph Ellison and Sigmund Freud. He enhanced its authenticity by telling of his encounters with the alcoholic poor during his days at the Catholic Worker house. He used government reports, historical references, academic studies, and journalistic reporting to give his controversial conclusions credibility. He was simultaneously reasonable and passionate. He avoided romanticizing poverty or those it afflicted. He appealed to the emotions of a range of middle-class readers, especially privileged youth and liberal professionals. He never used the word "socialism" or identified himself as a socialist, though he made clear where his political sympathies lay. He denounced the "ignorant, smug moralisms" of opinion leaders who enjoyed comfortable lives, while at the same time he avoided attacking groups other than conservatives. With moral passion, he told Americans that it was "an outrage and a scandal that there should be such social misery" in an affluent society. He strove to rally a comfortable audience by asserting that the question was not how much worse things had been in previous generations but "how much better they could be if only we were stirred."[37]

And stir America he did. The initial response was quite favorable but limited in impact, as appreciative reviews appeared in daily newspapers and weekly journals of opinion such as the *New Republic* and the *Nation*. Radicals felt that the book's publication marked the arrival of Harrington as successor to Norman Thomas as the nation's leading socialist. Then in January 1963 his life suddenly changed. Dwight Macdonald published an essay-review of unprecedented length on *The Other America* in the *New Yorker*, which soon appeared as a pamphlet. Harrington sold the paperback rights to the book and used the proceeds to take a long-dreamed-of trip to Paris. In May he married the American journalist Stephanie Gervis and remained in Paris to work on his next book, on cultural decadence. If Galbraith had started out to write about poverty but completed *The Affluent Society*, Harrington wrote the book Galbraith never completed but then began to work on a book that might have amplified the one Galbraith actually wrote.[38]

The political impact of *The Other America* was felt in the presidential transition from John F. Kennedy to Lyndon B. Johnson. Harrington's book had caught the attention of Kennedy's advisers as they formed a task force to work on a program called "Widening Participation in Prosperity," which met in the summer and fall of 1963. The book had been critical in shifting their attention to an approach to poverty that went beyond piecemeal programs. On the eve of his assassination, Kennedy, who had most likely read Macdonald's essay but not Harrington's book, expressed interest in a poverty program. On November 24, 1963, on his first full day in office, Johnson told an aide that he wanted to move ahead with an antipoverty program. Harrington returned from Europe on December 12, 1963, to find that he had become a celebrity, as rumors swirled that Johnson was about to announce a major effort. In his January 1964 State of the Union address, Johnson proclaimed that his administration "today, here and now, declares unconditional war on poverty in America." Quickly, Harrington was much in demand for interviews and speeches, with one New York newspaper calling him "The Man Who Discovered Poverty." *The Other America*'s readership grew apace, attracting a wide audience not only of policy makers but also among liberal reform-minded Democrats.[39]

Then came one of those extraordinary but ultimately complicated turnabouts when an author becomes a policy adviser. Called to Washington by Sargent Shriver, Kennedy's brother-in-law and the head of Johnson's antipoverty effort, Harrington spent twelve days in early February 1964 working on a presidential task force, writing memos and attending meetings with cabinet members. Although his book remained a goad to action, Harrington nonetheless had little impact on legislation and programs. After those heady February days, fearful of his radicalism, Johnson and his administration snubbed Harrington. Harrington, in turn, applauded what the president and Congress had done, all the while insisting that a more massive program was needed.

The legacy of *The Other America* was considerable but complex. Harrington had succeeded in awakening the conscience of a nation. The Economic Opportunity Act of August 1964 probably would have passed even without the impetus of *The Other America*. Yet as Isserman has noted, though the book had little impact on policies, it bore "a great deal of responsibility for how those policies would be justified to the public." For the rest of his life, though in some ways he worked in the shadow of his most successful book, Harrington used writing, speaking, and teaching to maintain his position as the nation's leading socialist. Though he no longer lived in voluntary poverty, he continued to fight for social justice. Especially critical was Harrington's notion of a culture of poverty, a phrase he used variously and imprecisely, often interchangeably with the idea of the vicious cycle. Although he neither fully understood nor was fully committed to the idea of a culture of poverty, he was credited with making it a well-known concept. In fact, as Isserman has shown, Harrington did not really believe that the poor had developed an unshakeable set of cultural and personality traits; rather, as a socialist and something of an economic determinist, he understood inadequate employment, housing, and health care as conditions imposed by insufficient income and remedied by adequate income. Indeed, Harrington expressed concern that conservatives might translate the idea of a culture of poverty "into the moralistic language so dear to those who would condemn the poor for their faults." That is exactly what happened when conservatives and neoconservatives in the 1970s built the groundwork for the Reagan revolution of the 1980s.[40]

In other ways, Harrington's analysis proved problematic. He correctly foresaw a political shift that, especially with the realignment of southern voters along racial lines, would make the Democratic Party liberal and the Republican Party conservative, a process that in some ways began as early as 1964. Yet over the longer haul, rather than a clear left-right division, the nation ended up with a centrist Democratic Party that was hard to distinguish from the Republican Party. Although he seemed to understand the social potential embodied in the civil rights movement, in his book he did not envision the poor as principal actors in a social movement that would transform their lives in positive ways; rather, he kept the focus on middle-class professionals. Unlike the anarchist Goodman, who was so inventive when it came to envisioning new organizations and programs, Harrington, very much a democratic socialist, seemed less imaginative. In the early 1960s, none of these problems was apparent to Harrington or to most of his readers. Nor, over the longer term, do these problems diminish the importance of the contribution he made. In 1998, *Time* magazine listed *The Other America*, along with *Silent Spring*, as one of the ten most influential nonfiction books of the twentieth century.[41]

Rachel Carson and the Environmental Costs of Affluence

When *The Feminine Mystique* appeared in 1963, Gerda Lerner wrote a letter to Betty Friedan. At the time completing her Ph.D. but before long one of the leading women's historians in the United States, Lerner told Friedan that she had "done for women what Rachel Carson did for birds and trees." What neither Lerner nor anyone else in 1963 could have foreseen was that *Silent Spring*, like *The Feminine Mystique*, would play a key role in starting a social movement.[42]

Rachel Carson (1907–1964) grew up in a financially strapped middle-class home in a rural area outside Springdale, Pennsylvania, a small town eighteen miles from Pittsburgh, whose landscape the spread of mining and industry was destroying. As a child, she published stories and poems in national publications. She loved to walk through the orchards and fields of her family's farm. After graduating magna cum laude from Pennsylvania College for Women (later Chatham College) in 1929, she entered Johns Hopkins University the following fall, earning her M.A. in marine zoology in 1932. Beginning in the mid-1930s, she held a series of U.S. government jobs that combined science and writing, principally at the Fish and Wildlife Service (FWS), an agency that until the Eisenhower administration was home to public servants deeply committed to conservation. At the same time, she began writing about science for a general audience, a calling that a female faculty member at college had inspired her to pursue.[43]

From the mid-1930s on, her concerns remained largely consistent: to make a general audience aware of the beauty, harmoniousness, interconnectedness, and fragility of the natural world (the oceans especially) and, often more implicitly, to remind her readers of the threats posed to these qualities by the quest for profits, by government policies, and by reckless human intervention. Fascinated by the sea since childhood, she did not actually see it until she had a summer fellowship in 1929 at the Marine Biology Laboratory at Woods Hole in Massachusetts. In her first book, *Under the Sea-Wind*, which appeared in 1941 to enthusiastic reviews and a place on the national bestseller list, she explored how fish and birds lived in and over the sea. In the late 1940s she published a series of government pamphlets, titled "Conservation in Action," in which she supported preservation of the natural world through wildlife refuges, an issue that increasingly commanded her attention both as a writer and as a supporter of organizations. Like Packard and Friedan, Carson had difficulty getting her controversial articles published in mass-circulation magazines; in her case, *Reader's Digest* in 1945 turned down a proposal to write an article on the effects of DDT on the environment.[44]

The publication of *The Sea Around Us* in 1951 established Carson's national reputation as a major science writer and transformed her life. Serialized in the *New Yorker* and selected by the Book-of-the-Month Club, it won the John Burroughs Memorial Medal for nature writing and the National Book Award for nonfiction and was adapted into a movie. Appearing on the best-seller list for eighty-six weeks, it was translated into forty languages. *The Sea Around Us* turned the reticent and private Carson into a reluctant media star. Her book earned her enough awards, contracts, and royalties to give her freedom to write once she resigned from her government job. A single woman responsible for the economic well-being of her multigenerational household, which at various times included her mother, two nieces, and an adopted grand-nephew, at last she was free of financial worries. By 1952, she could devote herself full-time to writing. She built a cottage on the seacoast of Maine and a house in Silver Spring, Maryland, outside Washington. Her next book, *The Edge of the Sea*, an evocative discussion of the mysteries of tidal areas, appeared in 1955 after being serialized in the *New Yorker*. As with *The Sea Around Us*, *The Edge of the Sea* earned acclaim from readers and a place on the best-seller list.[45]

Carson was beginning to become more aware of herself as a public figure. She was also becoming increasingly aware of women's networks. In the late 1950s and early 1960s, Marie Rodell, the literary agent for both Betty Friedan and Rachel Carson, was having difficulty placing controversial articles by her two authors at *Ladies' Home Journal* and *Women's Home Companion*. Beginning in 1961, groups of women around the country organized Women Strike for Peace to protest in materialist language the pollution of the milk supply by strontium 90 and fallout from atomic testing by the United States and the Soviet Union, among other things. It was also during this period that her friendship with her Maine neighbor Dorothy Freeman intensified.[46]

Since the late-1930s, Carson had been interested in the effect of poisons on the environment. During her years of government work, she knew that some federal scientists were concerned about the use of pesticides and herbicides, while others sanctioned their use. She was understandably upset to learn that the U.S. Department of Agriculture (USDA) was promoting the use of pesticides and herbicides and that the Food and Drug Administration (FDA), in offering reassurances about the safety of chemicals, was siding with farmers and not with consumers. As early as 1951, worried about the possibility of the destruction of the environment, Carson had begun to transform herself from a nature writer into an environmental critic. She linked concerns about the cold war, atomic weapons, and an affluent nation's priorities. She started to speak out at a time when peace efforts in Korea were stalemated, when the government's testing of atomic bombs on the Bikini Islands in the South Pacific in 1946 was still fresh in her memory, when other nations were developing atomic weapons, and when the spread of affluence threatened the environment.[47]

Her commitments emerged in her efforts to encourage conservation. In

1951, speaking at a lunch for supporters of a symphony orchestra, she remarked that orchestras were "not luxuries in this mechanized, this atomic age. They are, more than ever, necessities." Several months later, Carson questioned the culture of a scientific elite, "isolated and priestlike in their laboratories," and called for the joining of science and literature as interdependent ways of discovering the world. She also warned of the danger that human beings, ignorant of the interconnectedness of their universe and driven by "vanities and greed," did not realize they were planning "for our destruction." In a 1953 letter to the editor of the *Washington Post*, she protested the dismissal of the director of the Fish and Wildlife Service, a committed conservationist, to make way for a pro-business nonprofessional. Carson used the occasion to turn the tables on anticommunist rhetoric. "It is one of the ironies of our time," she remarked, fearful that a new Republican administration might reverse hard-fought gains in protecting the environment, "that, while concentrating on the defense of our country against enemies from without, we should be so heedless of those who would destroy it from within." By the mid-1950s, her biographer Linda Lear has noted, "the very existence of the atomic bomb forced Carson to the ugly realization that human beings truly had the power to destroy all the beauty, mystery, and wonder that she knew for herself and communicated to others in her writing." Gone, Lear noted, was her "belief in the ultimate sanctity of nature." She was becoming increasingly concerned that the dumping of radioactive refuse in the seas threatened not only the oceans but also life itself. She read *The Affluent Society* shortly after it came out in 1958 and acknowledged that the ways in which it had inspired her would become clear in her next book.[48]

For Carson, it was not just nuclear waste but affluence itself that threatened the environment. In 1954, speaking before a thousand women journalists, drawing on the moralist tradition, Carson contrasted the beauty of the natural world with the ugliness of a materialistic society. She felt that women had a "greater intuitive understanding" of beauty and the threats to its existence than men. She spoke to her female audience as professionals who could write about such subjects but also as mothers who would "want for their children not only physical health but mental and spiritual health as well." She perceived the destruction of the beautiful in a number of settings. One of her concerns was the consequence of suburban development—not, as with Packard, for raising social anxieties or, with Friedan, for its effect on women, but because of its impact on the human and natural environments within which Americans lived. The spread of "man-made ugliness" and the "trend toward a perilously artificial world" heralded the "destruction of beauty and the suppression of human individuality in hundreds of suburban real estate developments where the first act is to cut down all the trees and the next is to build an infinitude of little houses, each like its neighbor." She also saw threats to the serenity of urban oases such as Washington's Rock Creek Park, near which she lived, where planners proposed to build a six-lane highway. For her these were places where people could go to escape "man-made confusions," to enjoy nature and "a little interval of refreshing and restoring quiet." She feared the invasion of "commercial schemes" into national parks. Did "our generation, in its selfish materialism," have the right "to destroy these things because we are blinded by the dollar sign? Beauty—and all the values that derive from beauty—are not," she insisted, "measured and evaluated in terms of the dollar." She envisioned a dramatic questioning of the actions of human beings, who were increasingly insulating themselves "with steel and concrete, from the realities of earth and water," which for her were the true sources of pleasure. She suggested that perhaps man (a word she used in its gender-neutral sense common at the time) was "intoxicated with his own power, as he goes farther and farther into experiments for the destruction of himself and his world." The antidote to this dire situation, she remarked, was that "the more clearly we can focus our attention on the wonders and realities of the universe about us, the less taste we shall have for destruction."[49]

By the late 1950s, Carson's concerns about the threat of atomic power, the misuse of science and technology, and the spread of materialism had inspired her to begin work on *Silent Spring*. Most frightening to her was the increasing evidence of the dangers posed by chemicals used as pesticides and herbicides. In her book she documented the impact of chemical poisons on the oceans, trees, soil, plants, animals, the food chain—and the health of human beings. Between 1947 and 1960, the production of synthetic pesticides in the United States increased from 124,259,000 to 637,666,000 pounds a year. She watched in horror as government agencies indiscriminately sprayed thousands of pounds of poisons on suburbs and farmers used DDT, chlordane, and malathion on crops. She carefully tracked and supported citizen protests, usually led by women, against government spraying of pesticides to control insects.[50]

In *Silent Spring*, published in 1962, Carson restated many of the themes she had developed in her earlier writings. She emphasized the long "history of interaction between living things and their surroundings." It had taken "eons of time," she noted, for the earth to reach "a state of adjustment and balance." As in her previous books, she waxed lyrical as she described the beauty, harmony, and interconnectedness of the natural world. For example, she told of the "web of inter-woven lives" of earthworms and mites, "each in some way related to the others—the living creatures depending on the soil, but the soil in turn a vital element of the earth only so long as this community within it flourishes."[51]

If in her previous books Carson had emphasized the wholeness of nature and only hinted at the dangers posed by human intervention, in *Silent Spring* the balance, and with it her tone, shifted. In her earlier writings, using what a later generation would recognize as a feminist perspective (*Silent Spring* appeared five months before *The Feminine Mystique*), she tried to heal the division between the personal and the scientific in a way that enabled her readers to see the natural world from the perspective of the environment itself. Her insights were poetic, even spiritual. In *Silent Spring* she balanced those qualities with hard scientific data and warnings whose import was as much political as moral. What happened, she asked, to the integrity of the natural world when human beings intervened with poisonous chemicals? As Vera Norwood has suggested in her rich feminist reading of Carson's works, she had come to understand "the limitations of human trespassing on nature," whose protean force she increasingly appreciated. The result, she warned, would be catastrophic. With the delicate balance upset, the interconnectedness that once underwrote the vitality of nature now led to devastation. Human intervention initiated a "chain of poisoning" when "the solution of an obvious and trivial problem," she wrote, describing the disastrous consequences for flora and fauna that ensued when the government used chlorinated hydrocarbons to control small but harmless gnats living in California's Clear Lake, "creates a far more serious but conveniently less tangible one." Only recently had human beings "acquired significant power to alter the nature of the world." To Carson, human intervention, principally through the use of chemicals, had increased so dramatically that its unprecedented consequences were nearly irreversible. Where she had once written lyrically of nature's beauty, now she spoke with equal grace of man's destructiveness:

> The world of systematic insecticides is a weird world, surpassing the imaginings of the brothers Grimm—perhaps most closely akin to the cartoon world of Charles Addams. It is a world where the enchanted forest of the fairy tales has become the poisonous forest in which an insect that chews a leaf or sucks the sap of a plant is doomed. It is a world where a flea bites a dog, and dies because the dog's blood has been made poisonous, where an insect may die from vapors emanating from a plant it has never touched, where a bee may carry poisonous nectar back to its hive and presently produce poisonous honey.[52]

A vision of death and destruction suffused *Silent Spring*, reflecting Carson's own battle with illness as well as the seriousness of the environmental issues she described. In the dedication to Albert Schweitzer, she quoted him as saying, "Man has lost the capacity to foresee and to forestall. He will end by destroying the earth." She spoke of the "shadow of death" advancing across the landscape. The attempt of human beings to control and even conquer nature had backfired, with nature fighting back in ways that circumvented human intervention. "The question is whether any civilization can wage relentless war on life without destroying itself," she asked rhetorically. The silence of the book's title evoked for her a world in which spring never came, "unheralded by the return of the birds," its "early mornings . . . strangely silent where once they were filled with the beauty of bird song."[53]

The book's message was an especially ominous one, for several reasons. For one thing, the insidious costs of poisons were often hidden from view. Relying on innovative research in genetics and cellular biology not widely available to the public, Carson explained how chemicals in pesticides and herbicides passed secretly through the food chain, altering people's hereditary makeup. "Beyond the dreams of the Borgias," she called these threats, referring to the tyrants of the Italian Renaissance who fed their enemies ground-up diamonds that would eventually kill them without their knowing what had happened. Like the natural world in general, she argued, our bodies had their own ecologies which the intrusion of dangerous chemicals threw out of balance. She struck a second frightening note when she linked atomic warfare and the use of chemicals. Both had been developed at the end of World War II out of scientific research impelled by a desire to stop the Axis powers. "In this now universal contamination of the environment," she wrote, "chemicals are the sinister and little-recognized partners of radiation in changing the very nature of the world." Thus, "along with the possibility of the extinction of mankind by nuclear war, the central problem of our age has therefore become the contamination of man's total environment with such substances of incredible potential for harm."[54]

Among the heroes of Carson's book were scientists in government agencies and universities who, along with public health officials and conservationists in organizations such as the Audubon Society, had sounded warnings and fought to reverse the increasing use of chemicals against nature. Deserving special note were two national figures: E. B. White, who had written a series of pieces for the *New Yorker* in which he warned of environmental degradation, and William O. Douglas, the Supreme Court Justice who had fought tirelessly to protect the natural environment. In addition, she credited citizen activists, most of them women, who were fighting to halt the spread of pesticides. On the other side was a coalition of chemical manufacturers and government scientists in the Forest Service and especially the USDA, whom she accused of recklessly developing, sanctioning, and applying poisons to nature in order to advance the short-term interests of industrialists, cattlemen, and developers. Drawing on the absurdities captured by Lewis Carroll, she described a system in which government officials permitted the poisoning of the food supply and then policed the results.[55]

At times Carson saw larger forces at work. If Packard and Friedan had pictured the suburbs as places of psychological and social anxiety, Carson recognized affluent suburban life as a source of ecological danger. She devoted a whole chapter to exploring items of consumer culture—from food off the shelves of supermarkets to garden gadgets—that contained dangerous compounds which threatened the well-being of consumers and the environment. Advertisers and packagers, so central to the work of Dichter, she condemned for making poison attractive. She cast a skeptical eye on the "mores of suburbia" which underwrote a war on crabgrass; yet she also laid blame at the feet of advertisers who hid deadly chemicals behind pictures showing "a happy family scene, father and son smilingly preparing to apply the chemical to the lawn." She pointed to the "fanatic zeal on the part of many specialists and most of the so-called control agencies" which she held responsible for the worst offenses. Wary of lawsuits as well as personal attacks, she took pains to avoid criticizing specific chemical manufacturers, but the targets of her ire were clear. She chastised the chemical industry for supporting university research that resulted less in the production of socially useful knowledge than in academically sanctioned green lights for manufacturers.[56]

She also took on the basic premises of the cold war consensus. An underlying but not very well hidden theme of her book was a critique of the modern commitment to the sanctity of corporate autonomy, the smooth working of democracy, the beneficent power of scientific experts, the dream of technological progress, and the advantages of living in an affluent society. She spoke of "an era dominated by industry, in which the right to make a dollar at whatever cost is seldom challenged." Then, when citizens did question threats to the environment, they were "fed little tranquilizing pills of half truth." Those who supported the use of chemical pesticides branded "as fanatics or cultists all who are so perverse as to demand that their food be free of insect poisons." The effort to substitute grasslands for sage in the West, she noted, involved an "unthinking bludgeoning of the landscape." Mocking the corporations that advertised "Better Living through Chemistry," she cautioned against dangerous chemicals that had "become an accepted part of our economy and our way of life."[57]

To some extent, Carson's outlook rested on the gendered dimensions of her own world. As a government official and a writer, she had relied on the help and support of male scientists, but especially during her years as a full-time writer, she was increasingly involved in a network of female friends and supporters. Indeed, she scattered throughout her book reports of women environmentalists heroically challenging a world dominated by avaricious male manufacturers, scientists, and government officials. The gendered nature of this struggle always remained implicit, though at times Carson verged on using maternalist language, for example, warning women about their responsibility to their children. "The breast-fed human infant," she noted in her discussion of the dangers of insecticide residues, "is receiving small but regular additions to the load of toxic chemicals building up in his body." In talks she gave to women's groups shortly after the publication of the book, the gendered aspect of her analysis and appeal was markedly stronger. Speaking in October 1962 to the National Council of Women, she insisted that mothers had a special responsibility for protecting nature and their children in a world of "push-button conveniences" and dangerous chemicals. In the spring of 1963, she reminded the women gathered at a meeting of a garden club of the consequences of their personal choices for future generations. "The exhaust from the cars we drive, the detergents that ease our work in kitchen and laundry, the chemical sprays we use in gardens and homes," she said, employing common references to suburban life, contributed significantly to environmental pollution.[58]

Yet holding the citizen responsible was as central to her task as blaming government officials, scientists, and manufacturers. In an especially stirring section of the book she asked rhetorically, "Who has decided—who has the *right* to decide—for the countless legions of people who were not consulted that the supreme value is a world without insects, even though it be also a sterile world ungraced by the curving of a bird in flight?" Ultimately, she argued, people were responsible for their own fate and for the fate of the earth. Using a phrase Packard popularized, Carson called on citizens not to be "lulled by the soft sell and the hidden persuader." She believed that "the authoritarian temporarily entrusted with power" had made key decisions "during a moment of inattention by millions to whom beauty and the ordered world of nature still have a meaning that is deep and imperative." The facts about the dangers of pesticides, which she presented with scientific precision in language a layperson could understand, would enable the public to take action. Once aroused, they would demand research to discover less harmful pesticides and laws requiring chemical manufacturers to test for the genetic effects of new compounds. She advocated not a total ban on harmful pesticides but careful use along with a search for alternatives. In the end, the choice was between working with or working against nature. Referring to the national system of interstate highways, which was rapidly nearing completion as the biggest public works project in the nation's history, she cautioned her readers against taking a "deceptively easy" ride on "a smooth superhighway on which we progress with great speed," urging them instead to work *with* nature to control nature. Citing examples in which natural predators and prey had restored balance, often with human help, Carson concluded that only by relying on "living populations and all their pressures and counter-pressures, their surges and recessions," would it be possible to "guide them into channels favorable to ourselves" and even "hope to achieve a reasonable accommodation between" the human and natural worlds.[59]

More so than any of the other books discussed in this chapter, *Silent Spring* had an immediate, long-lasting, and momentous impact. Controversy arose even before the book's publication, when, in response to revelations in a series of excerpts from it which appeared in the *New Yorker*, a chemical company threatened a lawsuit. The *New Yorker* series inspired more than fifty newspaper editorials. The chemical industry launched an expensive and aggressive attack on Carson's credibility. Detractors suspected her of being under communist influence and accused her of being just another hysterical woman. This attack only helped *Silent Spring* attract an enormous and varied audience, in the United States and abroad. Significantly, Carson's most political and tough-minded replies to her critics came when she spoke before women's organizations. Carson was able to get her word out in other ways, too. In 1963, CBS turned the book's findings into a documentary, "The Silent Spring of Rachel Carson." Kennedy's Science Advisory Committee issued a report in May 1963 that endorsed the book's findings and, countering USDA recommendations, called on federal agencies to reconsider their policies on pesticides. Carson testified before congressional committees that summer in which Senator Abraham Ribicoff of Connecticut played a key role. She died a year later at age fifty-six, having hidden from the public the cancer that threatened her life because she feared that the chemical industry would have used this information to undermine her credibility and question her motives. Like other public figures in the early 1960s, Carson was making the private political, albeit not fully public.[60]

Although toward the end of her life she witnessed some of the book's impact on Americans' responses to environmental degradation, she did not live to see, as Friedan and Harrington did, the way her book fundamentally changed how a nation thought and acted. As was true of *The Feminine Mystique* and *The Other America*, with *Silent Spring*, Carson unwittingly started a social movement whose power was long-standing. In 1964 came the passage of the Federal Insecticide, Fungicide, and Rodenticide Act; the Environmental Protection Agency was established in 1970; and the federal government banned the use of DDT two years later. Carson's contribution, however, was in many ways unique. She linked the American suburbs, long the focus of social critics' attacks for their costs in aesthetic taste and social well-being, to environmental threats. Her fear of the dangers posed by the misuse of radioactive and chemical substances impelled her to critique scientific elitism, the malfeasance of government agencies, the deadly imperatives of technology gone wild, corporate greed, and the excesses of affluence. Passionate and angry, she nonetheless made her case in a careful and even under-stated way. Lewis used the concept of the culture of poverty to mask a radical agenda. Harrington avoided the word "socialism" in *The Other America*. Friedan did not reveal her radical past. Galbraith shifted his attention from poverty to affluence. Goodman did not explicitly connect his bisexuality with his book's arguments, even though a later generation placed sexuality at the center of social criticism. So too did Carson work more implicitly than ex-plicitly. Only a year after the publication of *Silent Spring*, in the last speech she ever gave, did she identify herself in public as an "ecologist."[61]

From the Affluent Society to the Poverty of Affluence

The four key books discussed in this chapter dealt telling blows to the cold war consensus. They cast a skeptical eye on government and corporations and revealed that democracy was not working effectively to protect the pub-lic's interests. They helped pierce the myth that affluence made it possible to divide an expanding GNP equitably, to create a harmonious world, to enable all to participate equally in democratic capitalism. The books raised troubling questions about the consequences of affluence for America's youth, its poor, and its environment. They also made it possible for millions of Americans to wonder if the psychological well-being of middle-class suburbanites should monopolize the attention of social critics. Goodman used humanistic psy-chology to critique an affluent society, while Harrington, Lewis, and Carson, by departing from the psychologizing of social problems, suggested that the goal of prosperity should be something greater than self-realization. All four authors deployed moralism to radical ends—Goodman by using the celebra-tion of authentic work and community to critique the vain chase after satis-faction through consumption; Lewis by using the vital culture of poor urban folk to suggest that people could lead passionate lives despite a low standard of living; Harrington by showing how the comforts of affluence helped hide poverty; and Carson by contrasting a genuine natural world with an artificial commercial one.

These books appeared at a time of major shifts in American culture and politics. Between 1958 and 1962 came the collapse of the labor-liberal alli-ance which had tried to make the purchasing power of unionized workers a keystone of national policy. With the waning of that possibility, those inter-ested in probing the connection between affluence and public policy had to look for a willing audience to whom they could introduce new perspectives. This was a unique moment, underscoring the difference between the 1960s and The Sixties. On one side of the divide stood the liberal realism of Presi-dent John F. Kennedy, an integrationist civil rights movement, and an American presence in Vietnam dwarfed by that of the war in Korea. On the other side was a massive American presence in Vietnam and the emergence of social movements that had a greater range, variety, and radical insistence than seen a few years earlier: Black Power, feminisms, environmentalism, and gay rights. The books discussed in this chapter exemplify the distinctiveness of that earlier period, a time when best-selling books laid the groundwork for social movements that would emerge with full force only later. Most strikingly, these were transformative books that helped start social movements. Moreover, the necessity their authors felt to maintain a certain silence reminds us of the persistent hold of fears generated during the cold war. Above all, what they share is that they broke away from the criticism of suburban affluence offered by authors such as Packard, Friedan, and Galbraith and introduced new issues into the bill of particulars against the affluent society. They laid the groundwork for the shift from the mild protests of the 1960s to the insurgency of The Sixties, something that would become evident in the social protests over consumption that emerged after 1965.[62]

6

Consumer Activism, 1965–1970

Ralph Nader, Martin Luther King Jr., and Paul R. Ehrlich

In the late 1960s, a group of writers went beyond the influential books by Rachel Carson, Paul Goodman, Michael Harrington, and Oscar Lewis. Among others, Ralph Nader, Martin Luther King Jr., and Paul R. Ehrlich not only critiqued affluence but also turned their critiques into vehicles for consumer activism. Vance Packard and Betty Friedan had inspired activists, but neither through their books nor in their own activity did they lead consumer movements. Other writers—Galbraith, Goodman, Harrington, Lewis—had tremendous impact, but more in shaping public discussion than in fostering consumer insurgency. Carson presents a more complicated case of the connection between the writing of an influential book and the launching of a mass movement. Eight years separated the publication of *Silent Spring* in 1962 from the emergence of an organized social protest inspired by her writings.

The careers of Nader, King, and Ehrlich, and the books they wrote, mark a major turning point in the criticism of affluence. With their emphasis on the adverse impact of prosperity, they intensified the process by which the cold war consensus was increasingly being discredited. They broke the connection that Dichter, Packard, Friedan, and others had made between social problems and psychological self-realization. More emphatically than those who went before them, they harnessed a moralist perspective to activism. Moreover, their work marks an important shift in the relationship between books, their authors, public policy, and social movements. Significantly, Nader was the first postwar social critic to write a book and then successfully develop and sustain institutions to fight for the changes he had proposed in it. Of equal importance is that with King, and to a lesser extent Ehrlich, it was social movements—of African Americans and environmentalists, respectively—that inspired their books, not their books that inspired activism. Words still mattered, but the relationship between pathbreaking books and social movements was changing.[1]

The Revival of Consumer Activism

As often happens, consumer activism arose during a time of prosperity. Technological developments of the 1960s increased productivity and laid the basis for dramatic changes that became fully visible later in the century. In the early 1960s, advances took hold in laser technology, and communications satellites began to dot the sky. Scientists had recently cracked the genetic code, and Xerox manufactured the first production-line copying machine. Corporations, governments, and universities were increasingly putting computers to use. Color television sets made their first appearance in American homes, and by 1967 the networks were broadcasting all their programs in color. At the same time, S. S. Kresge began to close its downtown five-and-ten-cent stores and in 1962 started to open its Kmart discount stores in the suburbs. This was the same year Wal-Mart opened its first store. During the decade Visa and Master Charge made their debut, and the use of credit cards increased rapidly. Goods imported from abroad—especially cars from Germany and electronic goods from Japan—began their transition from objects of curiosity to essential items of American consumer culture. The combination of government policy and economic boom, and the doors that opened up as a result of the fight against discrimination and poverty, helped bring millions of African Americans and others into the middle class. The percentage of women in the paid workforce continued to grow, helping to swell the ranks—and the expenditures—of the middle class.

The decade witnessed the continuation of a wave of sustained prosperity. In 1963, two thirds of the world's automobiles were driven by Americans. The GNP was increasing substantially, and both unemployment and inflation remained low. In 1996 dollars, the GDP grew from $2,377 billion in 1960 to $3,578 billion in 1970, a rise of about 50 percent. Meanwhile, in 1973, the poverty level reached a postwar low of 11 percent. Nonetheless, warning signs of more troubled economic times were not hard to spot. By the late 1960s, inflation had picked up. In 1965, for the first time in its history the United States had a trade deficit with Japan. The fruits of affluence remained unevenly distributed. In 1964, almost two thirds of whites said they were satisfied with their income, compared with less than one third of nonwhites.

The consumer protests that Nader, King, and Ehrlich represented grew out of the adversarial politics of the 1960s, shaped initially in the cauldron of the civil rights and antiwar movements. America's economic well-being was but one of many factors that helped bring consumer activism to prominence. Consumer protests took many forms, among them boycotts in support of union organizing, collective buying by union members and others, claims by women on welfare that participation in consumer culture was a right and not a privilege, efforts to explore the relationship between commercialism and feminism, and, if it does not drain the word "activism" of meaning, the attempt by members of the counterculture to live simpler lives.

César Chávez's development of a consumer boycott in support of union organizing represents one very important strand of consumer protests. In 1965, under the banner of the Farm Workers Association (which in 1966 changed its name to National Farm Workers Union), Chávez led a strike in Delano, California, of Mexican American migrant laborers. Along with his co-leader Dolores Huerta, Chávez created a nationwide movement to boycott grapes sold by growers opposed to the unionization of migrant laborers. If Chávez used an age-old tactic to organize the purchasing power of middle-class consumers in support of unionization, groups of women developed newer forms of consumer activism. As the historian Felicia Kornbluh has demonstrated, beginning in the late 1960s, when welfare activists focused on securing income rather than jobs, they relied on the widespread understanding of the centrality of American affluence to social policy in the postwar period. As a result, in the late 1960s and early 1970s, women on welfare started to demand decent treatment from welfare officers as well as fuller participation in consumer culture than meager welfare budgets allowed. As they transformed a minimum standard of living from a privilege the state granted to a right of citizenship, they insisted on access to credit cards as well as better housing, furniture, and clothing for themselves and their children. In other words, as Kornbluh writes, they were demanding to "participate fully in the post–World War Two consumer economy."[2]

If welfare women wanted in, then many middle-class feminists wanted out. They developed a series of strategies to combat what they saw as the dangers of excessive commercialism. In *The Feminine Mystique*, Betty Friedan had blamed women's magazines for fostering a limited sense of options for women. In 1969 two feminists denounced corporations for promoting the "wasteful consumption" of products such as new television sets and automobiles by claiming they would "add to their families' status and satisfaction." Women also opposed the use of cosmetics that promised to "increase their desirability as sex objects." In May 1970 a group of feminists took direct action, sitting in at the offices of *Ladies' Home Journal* to protest advertisements they believed demeaned women. The editors responded by including an eight-page insert on women's liberation in the August issue. Other feminists also struggled with the relationship between the media and women's issues. While the feminist editors and publishers of *off our backs* and *No More Fun and Games* eschewed commercial venues, the founders of *Ms.* magazine, launched in 1972, wrestled with the question of what kind of advertisements they were willing to accept in order to reach a wide audience of women. In the process they articulated what Amy Farrell has called "popular feminism."[3]

While consumer activism was growing, quite a different trend emerged as advocates for and participants in the counterculture adopted a critical stance toward affluence. In a series of widely read books, a number of older male writers—Paul Goodman, Herbert Marcuse, Norman O. Brown, Charles Reich, Theodore Roszak, Philip Slater—urged young people to value intense experiences rather than the pleasures of consumer culture. The counterculture also drew on Eastern philosophers who emphasized the connection between simple living and spiritual well-being. Hundreds of thousands of young people—from hippies to university students to young professionals—used sex, drugs, clothing, and music to counter the conventional routines of suburban, middle-class life, even as they indulged in an increasingly commercialized alternative culture. A smaller but still significant number of the baby boom generation sought the simple life in urban or rural communes, in the process challenging the hold of commercialism on American life.[4]

Amidst all these political, social, and cultural changes, Nader, King, and Ehrlich were among the period's leading consumer activists. Their writings provide significant entry points into the critique of affluence. In *Unsafe at Any Speed*, Nader exposed the built-in design dangers of the automobile, one of the central items of consumption in postwar America. Nader also offered a moral critique of consumer culture by living simply as a way to oppose capitalism's profusion of consumer goods. As a lawyer, he initially assumed that the best means of protecting consumers from dangerous goods was through public interest legislation and regulations to counter the activity of corporate lobbyists. Over time, he supplemented this Washington-based, top-down approach by inspiring and providing institutional support for grassroots consumer protection movements. In the 1950s, King emerged as a leader of the Montgomery bus boycott, a protest against segregation by African Americans who relied on public transportation. In sermons in the 1950s growing out of a moral tradition deeply embedded in African American religion, he urged middle-class and well-to-do blacks to stop consuming conspicuously and instead use their discretionary income to advance the cause of racial justice. Shortly before his death in 1968, King shifted his attention to the urban ghettoes in the North and fought to deploy African American purchasing power to secure employment for blacks. At the same time, now addressing a largely white audience, King called on the affluent to stop their conspicuous consumption and instead spend their tax dollars in support of federal programs to make America a more egalitarian society. Throughout his career, he drew on Christian traditions to remind audiences that spiritual goals were more important than material ones. Ehrlich was a scientist and environmentalist who emerged as a social critic and a consumer activist. Until 1967 he reached an audience primarily of fellow scientists. With *The Population Bomb* (1968), connecting science, activism, and environmentalism, he brought to the fore concerns he had long held but was only now presenting to a lay audience.

Nader, King, and Ehrlich represent three important forces that transformed public awareness into consumer protests against the problems created by affluence. Unlike many earlier writers, they were unconcerned with psychology and self-realization. They intensified the attack on the cold war consensus even as they suggested new ways to understand the relationship between democracy, capitalism, and politics. For them, writing successful books was central to their activity as activists. Finally, they continued what Goodman, Harrington, and Lewis had begun when they turned their moralist critiques to radical ends.

Ralph Nader: From Author to Activist

With *Unsafe at Any Speed: The Designed-In Dangers of the American Automobile* (1965), thirty-one-year-old Ralph Nader initiated a controversial career as a consumer activist by reenvisioning a cherished status symbol as a dangerous weapon. The youngest of four children of Arab American parents, Nader was born and raised in Winsted, Connecticut. His parents, Nathra and Rose Nader, who had emigrated in the early 1900s from Lebanon, ran a restaurant in a small mill town in the northwestern part of the state. Inspired by their experience as immigrants, they fostered in their children strong commitments to family, education, democracy, citizenship, and social responsibility. The parents conveyed to their children a passionate concern for social justice and a suspicion of power. At the restaurant, Nathra would engage customers in animated discussions about politics. Around the family dinner table, he presided over sustained, intense discussions of social issues in which he prodded his children to defend their positions. At his graduation from eighth grade, Ralph Nader gave a speech on the environmentalist John Muir. A year later, he began devouring issues of the *Congressional Record*. As a teenager, he read classic muckraking books by Ida Tarbell, Lincoln Steffens, and Upton Sinclair.[5]

Building on his family's heritage, Nader garnered from his college and law school education the perspectives that would shape much of his later career. He graduated magna cum laude and Phi Beta Kappa in 1955 from Princeton, where he took several courses with H. H. Wilson, a professor of political science who described himself, as Nader might well have said of himself later on, as a "conservative, anarchist and socialist." In the early and mid-1950s, Wilson published a series of articles in the *Nation* in which he articulated many of the themes that later animated his student's work: the corruption of the political process, the capture of regulatory agencies by the interests they supposedly regulated, the hiring by major corporations of ex-FBI agents to suppress civil liberties, and the call for a new, post–labor union source of political protest. Wilson taught a course called "Political Power in the U.S.," in which he relied heavily on the works of C. Wright Mills. Wilson emphasized the invisibility and irresponsibility of the powerful as well as the tension between democracy and capitalism. He also underscored how an ambitious foreign policy diverted attention from the problems of a society in which social class played such a prominent role.[6]

At Princeton, Nader was a loner on a campus that, in its wealth and clubbiness, differed dramatically from Winsted. His politics emerged most clearly in his undergraduate writing, and less so in thwarted political action. Before the publication of Carson's *Silent Spring*, Nader had protested the university's killing of birds by its use of DDT but was unable to persuade the editors of the student newspaper to take an interest in the subject. After traveling to Lebanon in the summer after his junior year, Nader wrote a 203-page senior thesis on Lebanese agriculture, in which he called on that nation's government to take an active role in modernizing this crucial sector. In the spring of his senior year, he also wrote on Puerto Rico, confident that democracy would open up economic opportunity. In the summer after graduation, Nader traveled to Native American reservations in the West and then published his first significant article, emphasizing the terrible living conditions there, which a paternalistic federal government showed no interest in remedying.[7]

Since childhood Nader had wanted to be a lawyer working for the public interest. At Harvard Law School, where he received his degree in 1958, he was often a disengaged student, though he found his voice in a series of articles on issues of social justice. They appeared in the law students' newspaper, the *Harvard Law Record*, which he served as president, resigning when his peers voted not to allow him to turn the publication into a crusading journal with a national readership. He authored articles titled "The Commonwealth Status of Puerto Rico," "Legislative Neglect Keeps Migrant Workers Mired in Asiatic-Type Poverty," and "Do Third Parties Have a Chance?" At Harvard, as at Princeton, Nader wrote about fostering democracy and the general welfare, which he believed a committed individual could accomplish by awakening an apathetic public and by countering a conservative government dominated by special interests. Such actions would make it possible to narrow the gap between the nation's ideals and its practices.[8]

In law school he also first began to think about the issue of auto safety. What shaped his concern was a 1956 *Harvard Law Review* article by Harold Katz on the liability of automobile manufacturers for faulty design and congressional hearings in the same year on the toll that auto design was taking on drivers and passengers. Also influential was his own seminar paper in his final year on the legal and moral obligations of auto makers to design cars with safety as a priority, in which he lamented the wreckage of human life he had observed while hitchhiking home. One scene remained especially vivid to him. In 1956, he reported later, he "saw a little girl almost decapitated in an accident when the glove compartment door flew open and became a guillotine for the child as she was thrown forward in a 15-mile-an-hour collision."[9]

For seven years after law school, 1958–65, Nader explored a series of career options until his book's impact enabled him to focus his energies. Following a brief stint in the army, he worked for a small law firm in Hartford. He taught some courses at the University of Hartford and testified before the state legislatures in Connecticut and Massachusetts. He also focused on consumer protection and auto safety bills in the Connecticut state legislature and helped draft for his home state one of the nation's first ombudsman bills, which did not, however, become law. In April 1963 he published an article in the *Christian Science Monitor* titled "An Ombudsman for the U.S.?" an issue he had explored while visiting Scandinavia in 1961. In the early 1960s he traveled as a freelance journalist in Europe, the Soviet Union, Latin America, and Africa. In 1964, Nader moved to the nation's capital, where he worked in the office of Assistant Secretary of Labor Daniel Patrick Moynihan on a critique of the government's highway safety programs. In an April 1959 article in the *Reporter* titled "Epidemic on the Highways," Moynihan brought the issue to public attention.[10]

During the late 1950s, Nader increasingly focused on automobile safety. He published a series of articles, including several on the hazards of automobile design. In December 1958 the *Harvard Law Record* printed his essay "The American Automobile: Designed for Death?" Here the recent graduate lamented the public's apathy in the face of a "highway blood bath" caused less by incautious drivers than by automobiles designed not for safety but "for style, cost, performance, calculated obsolescence." Seeing death and injuries from automobile accidents as a public health issue, he called for legislation to give the federal government the kinds of control over auto design that it already had for drugs and railroads. A few months later, less than two weeks after Moynihan's article appeared, Nader published a piece in *The Nation* lambasting the "widespread immorality of our scholarly elite" of experts who allowed corporations to undermine their investigations of auto safety and thus were "insensitive to the increased responsibility as citizens which their superior knowledge should require them to shoulder." He again called for federal legislation, which he saw as necessary to protect consumers from their "indiscretion and vanity." As with Vance Packard and Rachel Carson before him, the editors at *Reader's Digest,* who had already published one article by Nader, made it clear that they had no interest in anything he might submit for publication on auto safety.[11]

Nader then took the same path as Packard, Carson, and Friedan, responding to the magazine's rejection by publishing a book, *Unsafe at Any Speed.* Best known for questioning the safety of the Chevrolet Corvair, the book was a far-ranging critique that raised fundamental questions about corporate secrecy, government supervision, nongovernmental organizations (NGOs), and scientific expertise. To recapture the book's power and scope, it is necessary to recall the place of the automobile in 1950s consumer culture, politics, and society, a place not unlike that of the computer, the Internet, and wireless communications decades later. In the 1950s, automobiles constituted the nation's premier industry. Three U.S. corporations—General Motors, Ford, and Chrysler—were yet to be seriously challenged by German and Japanese imports. Annual design changes (at their most baroque in the late 1950s and early 1960s) captured the imagination of an eager public, and advertisements equated cars with power, sexuality, and patriotism. Celebrants and critics of affluence alike focused on the automobile. Dichter had achieved the major breakthrough of his career by designing a new marketing strategy for the Plymouth. Katona gave automobile purchases a central role in measuring consumer expectations. Packard considered cars key examples of hidden persuasion, status seeking, and waste making. Friedan criticized the necessity for suburban women to chauffeur their children to school and other activities in the family station wagon. Galbraith used car travel as his most powerful example of the disjuncture between private affluence and public need.[12]

Nader's book, dedicated to a law school classmate seriously injured in a car accident in 1961, began: "For over half a century the automobile has brought death, injury, and the most inestimable sorrow and deprivation to millions of people." It sounded a familiar theme of conspiratorial collusion. President Eisenhower in his valedictory speech had warned of the dangers of a military-industrial complex. C. Wright Mills in *The Power Elite* (1956) had explored the parallel power of leaders of government, the military, the media, and industry. Rachel Carson had alerted the nation to the disastrous consequences for the environment of cooperation between industry and government. Sim-

ilarly, Nader emphasized the perils of a government–industry–university–
traffic safety establishment complex that failed to protect the nation's citizens
from the consequences of automobile accidents. He called on his investigative
experience as he combined the methods of a lawyer arguing a brief with the
outrage of a citizen at what he discovered. He framed his analysis of auto
safety in terms of a series of "assaults on the human body." Linking his efforts
to the struggles of African Americans then commanding national attention,
Nader remarked that "our society's obligation to protect the 'body rights' of
its citizens" deserved the same commitment, resources, and leadership that
were "being devoted to civil rights."[13] In one of the book's few literary references, Nader evoked Walt Whitman's line, "If anything is sacred, the human
body is sacred."[14]

Throughout the book, Nader detailed the tragic costs of built-in design
flaws. For him, the situation was far more consequential than social critics
had acknowledged. The problem with automakers' emphasis on advertising,
style, and status, he wrote, was not just that this was the work of "hidden and
subliminal persuaders," implicitly critiquing Packard. In 1964, Nader noted,
almost fifty thousand Americans died in auto accidents and over 4 million
were injured. Although he singled out the Corvair, in fact Nader saw all
automobiles as instruments of pain and death. Automobile companies focused on preventing accidents, not injuries. He was especially interested in
the "second collision"—what happened inside the car after the initial impact,
when poorly designed steering wheels, instrument knobs, glove compartment
doors, and dashboards wreaked their havoc on driver and passenger alike. He
exposed how corporations hid behind issues of style and cost, to say nothing
of corporate collusion, as they fought against measures to control environmental pollution.[15]

At the heart of the book was Nader's analysis of the way industry, professionals, the government, and nongovernmental organizations all perpetuated
dangerous design, a line of analysis that echoed what Carson and Mills had
written. The executives of major automobile corporations had allowed de-
signers to triumph over engineers, and thus style, profits ("that bitch-goddess,
cost reduction"), and obsolescence over safety and efficiency. Professional
scientists and engineers who worked for universities and supposedly independent laboratories, as well as government officials and organizations of engineers, remained silent on safety flaws, making consumers the captives of the
industry's focus on style. Like Carson, Nader laced his book with calls on
scientists and engineers to live up to their professional obligations. Thus,
though he lauded doctors who had recently picketed an automobile show to
protest a lack of attention to safety, he castigated other professionals who
"have failed in their primary professional ethic: to dedicate themselves to the

prevention of accident-injuries." Implicated as well were private organizations that constituted what he called "the closely knit traffic safety establishment"— the American Automobile Association, the National Safety Council, and the insurance industry's Institute for Highway Safety. Like professionals and government agencies, they had become the captives of the very industry for which they were supposed to serve as watchdogs. Governed by "existing business values," this unholy alliance undermined democratic processes. The secrecy of corporations and professionals made informed consumer decisions impossible.[16]

Nader showed how deeply embedded in the political and economic system was the refusal to make cars safer. Auto companies were especially negligent, he asserted, when they resisted attempts to require use of seat belts and blocked the introduction of safety technology such as air bags. At issue here was the decision of government, industry, and NGOs made earlier in the century to emphasize driver education and safe highways over the manufacturer's responsibility to develop safe design. As early as the 1920s, with the help of the federal government and the agreement of the auto companies, "the traffic safety establishment" had developed "an ideology guarded and perpetuated by a network of trade associations, tax exempt organizations, and other groups professing an interest in traffic safety." In 1935, when *Reader's Digest* published J. C. Furnas's article "And Sudden Death," which it reproduced in 8 million copies, the auto industry had turned the ensuing cry for reform to its own purposes. The emphasis on consumer education and driver responsibility, which placed the burden for avoiding death and injury on the driver, freed corporations from their own responsibilities. In the postwar period, the President's Committee for Traffic Safety offered an example of the way businesses used government's aura to advance their own interests and create a false sense of public good, though this could have hardly surprised someone like Nader, who studied Mills as an undergraduate.[17]

Having spelled out the immense costs that auto accidents inflicted on people and on the economy, Nader insisted that the solution would come "only by the forging of new instruments of citizen action." The neglect of safety, he asserted, was "a rebuke to an affluent, technologically advanced society." He certainly did not underestimate the obstacles. "Like a Molloch," he wrote, "the automobile makers press for an increasingly larger share of everything economic," with the result that the national economy "is being distorted by tendencies strikingly similar to those that operate in one-crop economies." With the federal government's commitment to the safety of drugs, airplanes, boats, and railroads in mind, Nader's goal was to make safe auto design a public health issue by filling what he called "that dreaded chasm, public regulation."[18]

Like Harrington, who envisioned for professionals key roles in poverty programs and minimized the contribution of the poor themselves, to a great extent Nader emphasized a top-down, Washington-based, and lawyer-instigated approach. He gave few hints of the consumer activism that his work would soon help bring into existence. "Only the federal government," he noted, "can undertake the critical task of stimulating and guiding public and private initiatives for safety." Although he understood the place of "public awareness," Nader also heralded the power of the professional expertise of lawyers, doctors, and engineers, who would "assume the role of leadership that their superior knowledge makes available to them." He acknowledged that federal action was necessary to provide balance against the enormous power of automobile corporations. This would mean putting an end to the blurring of the connections between government and corporate power. He called for a national policy on automobile pollution. He advocated enforcement of safety standards, preferably through the establishment of a federal agency responsible for auto safety but protected from control by auto manufacturers. Indeed, threaded throughout the book were many of the elements that would dominate the fight over auto safety in the ensuing decades, especially the call for the federal government to force automobile companies to design safer cars.[19]

After it appeared in November 1965, *Unsafe at Any Speed* initially achieved moderately good sales. It was General Motors' investigation of Nader, however, that brought him national attention. Soon after the book's publication, GM hired a private investigator to gather information that the corporation could use to undermine Nader's credibility. (GM's legal staff had wondered, incorrectly it turned out, whether Nader was trying to line his own pockets as a lawyer representing Corvair drivers in their suits against the auto maker.) As often happens in such cases, these efforts backfired, especially when an FBI agent turned private investigator overstepped the boundaries of legitimate tactics. A March 12, 1966, *New Republic* article by James Ridgeway exposed GM's investigation to discredit Nader, finally persuading newspapers to pay attention to what Nader had written. The news helped catapult the book on to the best-seller list. Senator Abraham Ribicoff, a Connecticut Democrat who had been the key senatorial ally of Rachel Carson, played a crucial role in Nader's case as well. Ribicoff had fought for auto safety as governor of Connecticut and as a U.S. senator. In 1965, Nader had helped Ribicoff's staff prepare for hearings on auto safety. Now, in 1966, Ribicoff called the head of GM before a Senate hearing to explain the corporation's investigation of Nader and its own record on auto safety. At the hearings, with Senator Robert F. Kennedy asking the most insistent questions, GM admitted that in a typical year, with $1.7 billion in profits, it had spent only $1.5 million designing safer cars. The president of GM publicly apologized (albeit in carefully guarded terms) for improperly investigating Nader, and Ribicoff's subcommittee vindicated Nader. As Nader's biographer Charles McCarry notes with some exaggeration, the committee hearings "did something for Nader that the Senate had never done for an individual in the history of the nation. It certified his virtue, gave birth to him as a public figure, and equipped him with an image that has remained a combination of the best qualities of Lincoln of Illinois and David of 1 Samuel 17."[20]

The eventual sale of sixty to seventy thousand copies of *Unsafe at Any Speed* in hardback and several hundred thousand in paper, as well as its translation into seven languages, only begins to convey the book's notoriety and impact. At the end of the 1960s, in a list of the ten most notable nonfiction books of the decade, *Time* included *Unsafe at Any Speed*, along with *The Children of Sánchez* and *The Other America*. By 1970, Nader had already made crucial contributions to the revival of consumer protection laws and the consumer movement itself. What was true of Betty Friedan's role in the revival of feminism and Michael Harrington's contribution to the rediscovery of poverty was nevertheless true of Nader as well: forces were already in motion that would have brought new protections for the consumer had Nader never come onto the scene. The consumer cornucopia of the postwar world had brought forth a plethora of increasingly complicated and often dangerous goods. After a long period of relative inactivity, for the first time since the 1930s, calls for consumer protection returned in the 1960s.[21]

As with any social movement, the sources of the pressure for consumer rights built on the efforts of more than one person. In 1963, Jessica Mitford's exposé of funeral practices in *The American Way of Death* captured national attention and a place on the best-seller list. In the early to mid-1960s, books and articles were appearing on the dangerous consequences of faulty automobile design which in many ways paralleled Nader's work. Also critical was a cadre of public interest lawyers and medical doctors interested in issues of public health. Carson, Friedan, Galbraith, and Packard had contributed to the revival of interest in consumer issues, though more as authors than as activists. At least since 1956, when Alabama congressman Kenneth A. Roberts held hearings on auto safety, members of Congress, their staffs, and labor unions had played increasingly vital roles, as did Moynihan. In 1960, President Kennedy delivered a campaign speech that focused on consumer issues. Once in the White House, he was the first president to deliver a message on consumer issues, when, on March 15, 1962, he called for a Consumer Bill of Rights. President Johnson considered consumer protection part of the Great Society, and in 1964 appointed Esther Peterson the first special presidential assistant for consumer affairs. The Consumers Union had long campaigned for safer cars. In 1965, public television stations aired a program, "Death on the Highway," that detailed the dangerous aspects of car design. In the 1960s and 1970s, congressional leaders helped pass a series of consumer protection bills, which had the advantage of costing the government relatively little and of identifying the consumer with the public interest. These bills aimed to protect citizens from dangerous products ranging from tobacco, automobiles, and toys to flammable clothing, and to provide consumer protections for other items such as packaging, product descriptions, and financial products.[22]

If Nader was but one of many who fostered the revival of a consumer movement, he nonetheless made major contributions. A skillful, passionate advocate and public conscience, Nader helped Americans connect their roles as consumers and as citizens. He energized disparate forces and put his unique stamp on consumer protection. Nader himself filled a series of unique and in some ways contradictory roles. A loner who projected the image of standing above politics, he was a Washington resident who fought in the halls and hearing rooms of Congress for consumer interests. He was simultaneously a solitary, outraged citizen and an organizational entrepreneur who created and financed an infrastructure that fostered a burgeoning movement. He combined the muckraker's ability to make boring and technical details compelling with the lawyer's knowledge of details of legislation that proved critical in changing the balance of power between corporations and consumers. He built an ideology and institutional structures that enabled him to equate his vision with the public interest. In some ways radical and revolutionary, in other ways he evoked traditional moralistic values of chastened consumption, hard work, and engaged, individual citizenship.

What distinguished his book from the best-sellers that preceded it—and thus marks 1965 as an important turning point—was that Nader was able to use his critique of consumer culture to launch a social movement. In addition, this movement relied in good measure on his ability to institutionalize organizational efforts in which he played a key role over a long period of time. Here comparisons with Packard, Friedan, and Harrington are instructive. Lacking the temperament of an activist, Packard used his books to awaken a nation's conscience. After helping to found the National Organization for Women in 1966 and then serving as its first president, Friedan quickly lost her organizational base in the feminist movement, though she remained an influential writer and speaker. Despite the considerable impact of *The Other America*, Harrington rapidly lost influence in policy formation and lacked a strong organizational base. After the mid-1960s, like Friedan and even Oscar Lewis, Harrington was often at odds with the people his work had initially inspired. In contrast, Nader developed an elaborate organizational structure over which he retained control.

The structure of Nader's activism took shape very soon after his book's publication. He played an important role in a series of major victories for consumer protection. In September 1966, ten months after the publication of *Unsafe at Any Speed,* Congress unanimously passed and President Johnson signed the National Transportation and Motor Vehicle Safety Act, which for the first time in the nation's history placed automobile design and safety under federal regulation. Seat belts, padded dashboards, headrests, and collapsible steering wheels were among the specific results which, over time, helped reduce dramatically deaths and injuries from automobile accidents. Nader also played an important and at times critical role in the passage of a series of consumer protection laws, including the Wholesale Meat Act (1967), Wholesale Poultry Products Act (1967), Natural Gas Pipeline Safety Act (1968), Radiation Control Act (1968), Coal Mine Health and Safety Act (1969), and Occupational Safety and Health Act (1970). In congressional testimony he warned of the dangers of mercury in fish, asbestos in ventilation systems, and tobacco smoke in public spaces. He called for the establishment of offices of consumer affairs in federal, state, and local governments. He promoted the use of class action suits, encouraged whistle blowers, product recalls, and product testing. In the last third of the twentieth century, few other individuals (especially if one excludes elected officials) had as much impact on American politics, business, and society.[23]

As a person Nader remained remarkably consistent over time: intense, passionate, focused, serious, and private. Unlike the other authors whose books catapulted them to national fame and lucrative speaking engagements, Nader continued to lead a life of voluntary simplicity. He lived by himself in a small apartment in Washington, D.C. He did not partake in the consumer culture to the extent that his income could have allowed. He did not own a car and did not eat processed foods. His clothing remained spartan, crumpled. Shopping was peripheral to his life. He evinced no interest in acquiring the growing number of gadgets that came to define the way of life of so many of his fellow Americans. With a high income and considerable net worth, he lived on a small percentage (at times as little as 5 percent) of what he earned, using the rest of his income to underwrite the investigative and advocacy groups he founded. He presented himself as someone who intensely disliked his celebrity, even as he parlayed his fame into his status as an anti-celebrity icon. In the early 1970s, he received seventy thousand letters a year, mostly from citizens who supported his efforts.[24]

Yet as tempting as it is to see him as a solitary fighter for other people's rights, he was extraordinarily skilled in using the levers that shaped public policy. By the mid-1970s, the patterns of Nader's consumer activism were well established, his organizational base secure. He quickly developed the full arsenal of weapons in the consumer movement. He persuaded journalists to play key roles in his crusades. Before long, Nader had established his organizational base. He quickly found inventive ways of funding his efforts, using a combination of student fees, citizen contributions, foundation grants, proceeds from lawsuits and speaking engagements, and royalties from publications. In 1968 he created the first in a series of Nader's Raiders, groups of college students and young lawyers whose investigations exposed the inadequate consumer protection provided by federal agencies—initially the Federal Trade Commission and soon after the Interstate Commerce Commission and the Food and Drug Administration. These investigations explored issues such as air pollution, airline safety, and the provision of health care by nursing homes and the medical profession. Beginning in the late 1960s, he established in Washington a complex and largely decentralized series of organizations that carried out investigations, advocacy, lobbying, and litigation. The first, founded in 1969, was the Center for the Study of Responsive Law. In 1970, he used the $425,000 from the settlement of his suit against GM for invading his privacy to establish the Public Interest Research Group (PIRG), essentially a law firm that would file suits and carry out lobbying programs. By the early 1970s, he had helped form PIRGs on university campuses, supported by student fees. In 1971 he started Public Citizen. Thus, within a few years of the publication of *Unsafe at Any Speed*, he had helped found, fund, and inspire a series of centers or groups that bore the stamp of his vision, focusing on corporate accountability, clean water, auto safety, health research, and tax reform.[25]

Unlike the 1950s critics who emphasized the way affluence eroded the moral and psychological dimensions of the lives of middle-class suburbanites, Nader mobilized the moralist critique of consumer culture into the basis for a passionate politics of consumer protection. Consumer goods were dangerous, he argued, the products of corporations and governments that, caught up in greed and bureaucratic imperatives, made affluence toxic rather than vacuous. He led a life of voluntary simplicity and agreed with Paul Goodman, Michael Harrington, Rachel Carson and Oscar Lewis that middle-class Americans had an excess of useless consumer goods. Yet for Nader, in *Unsafe at Any Speed*, and in much of his early activism, it was the dangerousness of consumer goods that was the problem, not their surfeit. Moreover, unlike earlier influential writers, Nader was able to use his notoriety as an author to build a popular movement. For decades, he maintained institutional control over the movement he helped create. Nader was one of the first to shape a stream of consumer protests that would become a powerful river.

Martin Luther King Jr. and African American Consumer Protests

The first time Martin Luther King Jr. appeared in the national media was in 1939. Then ten years old, he was sitting in front of a replica of Tara costumed as a member of the "Slave Chorus" that sang at a Junior League gala held to celebrate the Atlanta premier of the movie *Gone With the Wind.* The organizers of the event invited the white actors in the movie but not their African Americans counterparts. King next came to national attention in 1955 when, with the Montgomery bus boycott, he led an effort of African Americans to demand rights equal to those of whites in the use of public transportation. The victory in that protest catapulted him onto the national stage. Initially in sermons and speeches to African American audiences in the mid-1950s, and later in a 1967 book explaining his shift to a new set of issues, King articulated a view of consumer culture that was simultaneously moralistic and radical.[26]

Born in Atlanta on January 15, 1929, King grew up in a world steeped in African American religious traditions and social activism. His maternal grandparents were leaders of Ebenezer Baptist Church, an institution they had transformed into a prominent presence in Atlanta's African American community. His father, the minister at Ebenezer Baptist, protested segregation and led African Americans in voting rights drives. Martin Jr. grew up on and around Auburn Avenue, which the historian David Levering Lewis has called "the spine of this remarkable affluence" of the African American community of Atlanta, where his father was a prominent public figure.[27]

King earned his B.A. from Morehouse College in 1948, his B.D. from Crozer Theological Seminary in 1951 (where he was valedictorian), and a Ph.D. in systematic theology from Boston University in 1955. Ordained and serving as associate pastor at Ebenezer Baptist during his senior year in college, he began his ministry in a world shaped by family, African American, and Baptist traditions. He married Coretta Scott in 1953. In 1954 he assumed the pulpit at Dexter Avenue Baptist Church in Montgomery, Alabama, several months after the Supreme Court's landmark decision in *Brown v. Board of Education of Topeka.* His involvement in the Montgomery bus boycott in 1955, a movement he neither began nor controlled, thrust him into national prominence, placed him in a leadership position among African Americans, and put into practice his commitment to nonviolent protests influenced by Christian and Gandhian principles. In 1957 he became a founder and first president of the Southern Christian Leadership Conference (SCLC) at a time when he was achieving a position of national and international recognition. In 1960 he returned to Atlanta and became co-pastor with his father of Ebenezer Baptist Church. He delivered his "I Have a Dream" speech at the March on Washington in 1963 and won the Nobel Peace Prize a year later. Until he was assassinated on April 4, 1968, he continued his struggle for civil rights and social justice. The sites of his protests constitute a road map of the 1960s' most important battles: Albany, Georgia; Birmingham and Selma, Alabama; Chicago; the Mississippi Delta; Washington, D.C.; and Memphis.

The Montgomery bus boycott was one in a series of civil rights actions that was also a consumer protest. Indeed, the historian Robert E. Weems has called consumer activism "the most potent nonviolent strategy employed by African Americans" in the civil rights movement. "Don't Buy Where You Can't Work" was a slogan used extensively in the 1930s which, along with black cooperatives and Buy Black campaigns, placed social activism at the nexus of work and consumption. In the 1940s, when African Americans participated in "Double V" campaigns to fight for victory against racism at home and abroad, they continued to use their power as consumers as a tactic of activism.[28]

In the 1950s, the Montgomery bus boycott was but one of many such efforts to link patronage with campaigns against segregation, a tradition whose lineage stretched back at least to the early years of the century. The protests against segregation in the 1950s were genuine grass-roots movements, sparked not by a widely read book but by organizing that grew out of experiences in the community. Rosa Parks, carefully selected and trained within her community, was well aware of the struggle against the treatment of the Scottsboro defendants in the 1930s. In February 1960, when four students from North Carolina A&T College sat down at a segregated lunch counter in a Woolworth's in Greensboro and demanded service, they were underscoring their insistence on being treated equally not only as African Americans but also as consumers. In the spring of 1961, when a coalition of whites and blacks moved through the South protesting the segregation of interstate travel facilities, they were calling attention to one aspect of racial segregation. In 1962 an Easter boycott of stores in Birmingham caused a 90 percent drop in purchases by blacks. The Civil Rights Act of 1964 included provisions that made discrimination illegal in accommodations, in restaurants, and at sites of entertainment. In the early 1960s, African Americans also stepped up their campaigns to have blacks represented in advertisements more frequently and in a nonracist manner. They protested, for example, the derogatory depiction of the African American woman as Aunt Jemima and of the African American man as Uncle Ben. In the mid- to late 1960s, with the emergence of Black Power, African Americans used consumer culture to express race pride: they donned dashikis, wore their hair in Afros, and ate soul food. By the mid-1960s, Black Muslims and other black nationalists were connecting separatism and consumption. They built a series of African American–owned and operated stores. With a constituency that was lower on the economic scale than King's had been in the 1950s, and with goals very different from his, they articulated, like King, a vision of moral consumption that banished vice and materialist excesses.[29]

Family tradition, personal experiences, and wide reading shaped King's beliefs about consumer culture. His experience of racism and his awareness of his father's social activism constantly reminded him that he was an outsider to sources of power and prestige in the white community. His absorption of the Baptist tradition instilled in him a sense that spiritual goals were more important than material goods. King admired his father's careful managing of the household's budget and celebrated the "unsophisticated simplicity" of the community in which he grew up, one his parents did not abandon for the more prestigious areas to which many of Atlanta's well-to-do African Americans were moving. Coretta Scott King remembered that soon after she met her future husband, he told her that he did not want to be a "thorough-going capitalist." "I think a society based on making all the money you can and ignoring people's needs is wrong," he told her. "I don't want to *own* a lot of things."[30]

His memory of people standing in bread lines during the depression had encouraged him to develop what in 1950 he called "my present anti capitalist feelings," to which his engagement with the works of Karl Marx during his Crozer years and those of Reinhold Niebuhr at Boston University gave intellectual heft. He recalled that his reading of Marx in 1949 intensified his concern "from my early teen days about the gulf between superfluous wealth and abject poverty." He feared that "we are prone to judge success by the index of our salaries or the size of our automobiles, rather than by the quality of our service and relationship to humanity—thus capitalism can lead to a practical materialism that is as pernicious as the materialism taught by communism." Although he rejected Niebuhr's anti-pacifism (which Niebuhr shared with his friend Lewis Mumford), King drew on Niebuhr's early 1930s radicalism. He and his wife argued over his decision to give away the money he won with the Nobel Peace Prize and to continue to live in modest circumstances, for he gave a higher priority to the social movement he led than to his family's economic well-being.[31]

In the mid-1950s, King first articulated his views on affluence as he spoke before audiences of middle-class and working-class African Americans. An early critique of consumer culture is a sermon he delivered at an African American church in Detroit in 1954, when he warned the assembled congregants that "it's wrong to throw our lives away in riotous living." He noted how materialism had prompted people to leave behind spiritual and religious values. "We became so involved and fascinated by the intricacies of television," he remarked, "that we found it a little more convenient to stay at home than to come to church." He urged his audience to choose going to church over participating in consumer culture. Some of what he said was less institutionally self-serving. "All of our gadgets and contrivances and all of the things and modern conveniences"—such as "luxurious cars" and television sets—threatened to turn people's attention away from God. Money and the things it bought were useful, "but whenever they become substitutes for God, they become injurious." Using the cadence and contrasts so typical of his ministry specifically and of the African American religious tradition generally, King intoned that he was "not going to put my ultimate faith in things . . . in gadgets and contrivances" but in "something eternal and absolute." He would not place his faith "in the god that can give us a few Cadillac cars and Buick convertibles, as nice as they are, that are in style today and out of style three years from now," but in "the God who threw up the stars, to bedeck the heavens like swinging lanterns of eternity."[32]

By 1956, King, fresh from victory in Montgomery, had come to link the fight against segregation with his opposition to excessive materialism, citizenship with the suppression of desire. As he noted in an address to a black fraternal organization in August 1956, he did not wish to give priority to "extravagances" in the fight for civil rights. "We must spend our money not merely for the adolescent and transitory things," he cautioned his audience, but for "this eternal, lasting something that we call freedom." Then, in December 1956, on the first anniversary of the Montgomery boycott, he clarified the connection between prosperity in the African American community and financing the struggle for civil rights. "Statistics," he told his African American audience, "reveal that the economic life of the Negro is rising to decisive proportions." He underscored his point by noting that the annual income of blacks in the United States was roughly equal to the Canadian national income. "It would be a tragic indictment on both the self-respect and practical wisdom of the Negro," he continued as he called on his audience to give money for the freedom struggle, if members of the community "spent more for frivolities than for the cause of freedom . . . more for the evanescent and ephemeral than for the eternal values of freedom and justice."[33]

In December 1957, speaking in Montgomery on the second anniversary of the bus boycott, King returned to these issues. How, he asked, were African Americans going to spend the money they were now earning? His own preference was for "cooperative enterprises that will make for economic security for the race" rather than for "meaningless things." He acknowledged that African Americans often lived beyond their means because, having been discriminated against, they purchased things they could not afford "in order to feed our repressed egos." Not able to buy the home he wanted because of discrimination, the African American instead purchased "a Cadillac because it's as big as the white man's Cadillac and it can pass his on the highway, and when he sits up there, they're there together." Yet, calling on his audience to live on what they earned, he urged them not to "let our psychological situation cause our values to be distorted." He asked his listeners to stop spending on "frivolities" and instead save their money and "invest it in meaningful ends." A good Baptist, he picked as one example the money African Americans spent on alcohol, money that could be better spent, he argued, to endow black colleges or make contributions to the United Negro College Fund or the NAACP. "Oh, it would be one of the tragedies of this century," he concluded, "if it is revealed that the Negroes spent more for frivolities than we spent for the cause of freedom and justice and for meaningful ends."[34]

As the anthropologist Paul R. Mullins has noted, there is a long tradition of black leaders who believed that "consumption forebode the erosion of communal moral standards, a focus on individual desires over group needs, and the decline of their own personal influence." Standing before members of African American churches and fraternal organizations in the 1950s, King offered a moral critique of affluence shaped by his family heritage, his position as minister and social activist, the prominence of his Baptist Christianity, and his strategically muted Marxism. He understood that buying a Cadillac, especially if it meant violating the careful spending he so much admired in his father, originated in feelings of emptiness and doubt spawned by racial discrimination and segregation. But such excess undermined communal values and self-respect. The alternative, he asserted, was to curtail expenditures for "frivolities" and instead spend money to advance the race through education or through campaigns of social justice. He thus linked affluence to the resources and self-confidence on which the African American community could draw.[35]

During the 1950s, as the historian Thomas Jackson has noted, King focused as much on the growing wealth of one sector of the African Americans community as on the persistence of poverty in another. He believed that the political and economic action of an elite was necessary in order to secure gains for the less fortunate. He hoped to use the purchasing power of the African Americans who had benefited from postwar prosperity to gain employment (and thus the power to consume) on behalf of those an increasing GNP had left behind. He understood that the economic gains made by the black middle class, and some members of the working class as well, undergirded their self-confidence, which he hoped to persuade them to use for public protests rather than private purchases. Jackson has written that King's "analysis paralleled and drew on the optimism of the popular and intellectual celebration" of American affluence in the 1950s. Indeed, King's sermons preceded by several years the publication of Galbraith's *Affluent Society*. Yet more than Galbraith, King emphasized the extensiveness of poverty and its rootedness in capitalism.[36]

Writing in *Where Do We Go from Here: Chaos or Community?* (1967), his fullest statement on affluence and consumer activism for a later period, King offered a very different critique from the one he had presented to African Americans in the 1950s. A number of factors explain the change. As the historian Thaddeus Russell reminds us, such moral sermonizing met resistance among ordinary African Americans. This made it necessary for King to recognize the materialistic aspirations of his audience and shift his attention elsewhere. In the 1960s, more impelled to express his radicalism, and with searing personal experiences having deepened his Christian faith and his political ideology, King now linked a questioning of affluence with morality, politics, and protest. Writing for a white audience, but with his attention nonetheless riveted by the poor blacks and whites whom he strove to help with his consumer activism, King now offered a critique of affluence that was morally infused in a different way from the one he had developed in the 1950s. He now gave minimal attention to excesses within the African American community and focused instead on the gap between black poverty and white prosperity. Convinced that the best way to counter white backlash was by calling for an interracial struggle against poverty in which income and work would no longer be connected, he linked his analysis of consumer culture to a national politics rather than a politics of advancement within the black community. He harnessed his moralism to a radical analysis and politics.[37]

When King was writing *Where Do We Go from Here*, the African American struggle for equality and his own leadership position both stood at critical junctures. Not long after the ink was dry on the Civil Rights Act and the legislation creating the War on Poverty, all passed in 1964, the triumph they represented for King and others seemed to fade. Resistance to the African American struggle, first among southern segregationists and then among white liberals, intensified. The assertiveness of blacks—whether at segregated lunch counters in the South or public schools in the North, in the Black Power movement, and in the urban riots of the mid-1960s—intensified white backlash. But "cries of Black Power and riots," King noted in 1967, "are not the causes of white resistance, they are the consequences of it."[38]

Youthful insurgents in the southern civil rights movement, especially in the Student Non-Violent Coordinating Committee (SNCC), challenged King's leadership and his commitment to interracial cooperation. In northern cities, Malcolm X and the Black Muslims did the same. The escalation of the war in Vietnam and the draining of resources from the war on poverty that resulted, as well as the challenges from SNCC and Malcolm, impelled King to a more oppositional and radical stance. By 1965 he had begun to proclaim his opposition to the war and to criticize the Johnson administration for reneging on its commitments to fight poverty. By the time he began writing *Where Do We Go from Here*, King had shifted his attention from South to North, from desegregation to poverty, from a faltering middle-class and interracial coalition to the promise of a more class-based Poor People's Campaign.

King noted in the book that the first phase of the struggle, culminating in the Voting Rights Act of 1965, was easier than the challenges blacks now faced. For ten years, he wrote, most whites supported "the demand that the Negro should be spared the lash of brutality and coarse degradation." By the mid-1960s, King believed, the situation was more problematic because most whites "had never been truly committed to helping him [the Negro] out of poverty, exploitation or all forms of discrimination." Without broad-based support from whites, African Americans faced a difficult situation in "the second phase, the realization of equality." This involved a shift in emphasis from enhancing the dignity of African Americans to changing the social, political, and economic structures of the nation. "The persistence of racism in depth," King wrote, "and the dawning awareness that Negro demands will necessitate structural changes in society have generated a new phase of white resistance in North and South." Although the events that began in Montgomery had removed "a caste stigma" and "elevated the spiritual content of our being," he remarked, "to sit at a lunch counter or occupy the front seat of a bus had no effect on our material standard of living."[39]

King's experiences, along with the shifting tides of racial and national politics, had always shaped his ideological positions. As Thomas Jackson has convincingly demonstrated, by 1957, King had "privately developed a radical egalitarian framework of analysis, and a dream of far-reaching social change transcending the immediate goals of winning civil rights in the South." Now his radicalism was strengthened, or, perhaps more precisely, it came more fully into public view. Two efforts in 1968 just before his death—his work on the Poor People's Campaign and his support of the strike by sanitation workers in Memphis—make evident his affirmation of a militant direct-action insurgency based on a class-focused, interracial, and democratic social-ist vision. The war in Vietnam, the Johnson administration's backing off from commitments to the war on poverty, white backlash, Black Power, the urban riots, his own experience with poverty and racism in northern cities all impelled him toward an increasingly adversarial stand.[40]

In *Where Do We Go from Here*, published in the summer of 1967, King pondered the meaning of affluence for the United States and the world. Although it would be wrong to say that consumption stood at the center of his analysis and his activism, it nonetheless played an important role in both. King used his discussion of African Americans and the culture of affluence to offer a complex critique of the drive toward a higher standard of living. At the same time, he advocated consumer activism as one of the several tactics in an expanding struggle for social justice. Moreover, more so than any of the writers on affluence in postwar America discussed so far, King placed his considerations within a global framework. In the end, his commitments and experiences as a Christian and as an African American undergirded his powerful moral vision of an alternative to an affluence that mistook material means for spiritual ends.

King understood how severe were the consequences of the war in Vietnam for the African American community specifically and the fight for social justice more generally. He dwelled not at all on the toll American firepower took on the people of Vietnam, however, and paid relatively little attention to the disproportionate deaths and injuries that black soldiers suffered in the conflict. Rather, he focused on the impact of increased military expenditures on domestic policy. In 1964, he noted, Johnson's proposal for a War on Poverty made "the bold assertion that the nation would no longer stand complacently by while millions of its citizens smothered in the midst of opulence." Three years later, "in the wasteland of war," military expenditures were vastly outstripping those to fight poverty.[41]

Moreover, with the shift of the quest for racial justice to the North and the breakdown of the interracial coalition that was so important in the civil rights movement until the mid-1960s, King reminded white Americans that their affluence helped make poverty invisible. Echoing Galbraith and Harrington, King wrote that especially with the new interstate highway system, which he might have noted had been built with federal funds, white Americans could "speed from suburb to inner city through vast pockets of black deprivation without ever getting a glimpse of the suffering and misery in their midst." With the importance of American Jews to the civil rights struggle very much in mind, King alluded to the recent trial of Adolf Eichmann, asking, "How responsible am I for the well-being of my fellows?"[42]

If white affluence made the dire conditions of the African American community invisible to wealthy Americans, it also intensified the sense of deprivation in the black community. Countering stereotypes in the white community that African Americans were profligate or lazy, King explained how patterns of discrimination in housing, banking, and shopping made homes and food more costly and less safe for African Americans than for their white counterparts. Again and again, he pointed to the way money and possessions dominated the lives of well-to-do-Americans, at one point asking why 40 million poor people had to live "in a nation overflowing with such unbelievable affluence." He persistently emphasized the psychic costs for African Americans of living in poverty in an affluent society, a dilemma that had eluded other observers from Katona and Dichter to Potter, Packard, Galbraith, Friedan, and even Harrington.[43]

In January 1966, King moved to Lawndale, an inner-city African American neighborhood in Chicago which he described as "an island of poverty in the midst of an ocean of plenty." What tormented African Americans, he noted, again, was not just poverty but poverty amidst affluence. The mass media gave dominant groups a vision of America that reinforced their sense of the centrality of whiteness. For African Americans living in ghettoes, the affluence of suburbia constantly reminded them of their deprivation. "Their television sets bombard them day by day with the opulence of the larger society," King noted. He underscored the impact on the African American of the differences between "the misery generated by the gulf between the affluence he sees in the mass media and the deprivation he experiences in his everyday life." King was right. In the 1960s "the country's mass-communicated culture of material consumption," as the historian Carl H. Nightingale has shown, "thoroughly inundated American inner cities." The "*inclusion* in mainstream America's mass market," he has argued for young African Americans in ways that can be extended more broadly in the community, helped determine their "responses to the economic and racial *exclusion* they face in other parts of their lives."[44]

King advocated a number of tactics, including consumer activism as a form of mass nonviolent action, to redress the social imbalances marked by poverty in the midst of plenty. He called on the federal government to undertake bold, ambitious social programs. Speaking against advocates of Black Power who rejected working together with whites, King reminded his readers, black and white alike, of the importance of a political coalition of white liberals and African Americans. He formulated his position in opposition to Black Muslims and other advocates of Black Power who called for programs that emphasized Buying Black. He also urged African Americans to use labor unions to improve their conditions at work. If consumer activism was but one of many policy initiatives he envisioned, it was nonetheless an important one.

In *Where Do We Go from Here* King sketched out the rationale and strategies of consumer activism. The annual income of the African American community, which he estimated at $30 billion, gave blacks "a considerable buying power that can make the difference between profit and loss in many businesses." Although he mentioned the work of Mahatma Gandhi, he drew even greater inspiration from Niebuhr's advocacy in *Moral Man and Immoral*

Society (1932) of boycotts against banks, stores, and public services that discriminated against African Americans. "One waits for such a campaign," Niebuhr had written prophetically, referring to nonviolent protest by blacks, "with all the more reason and hope because the peculiar spiritual gifts of the Negro endow him with the capacity to conduct it successfully. He would need only to fuse the aggressiveness of the new and young Negro with the patience and forbearance of the old Negro, to rob the former of its vindictiveness and the latter of its lethargy." King recalled that the civil rights struggle in the South in the early 1960s had involved protests against white store owners, educating "them forcefully to the dignity of the Negro as a consumer." That experience had led SCLC to launch Operation Breadbasket in 1962, which used the purchasing power of the better-off members of the black community as leverage to assuage the unemployment and poverty of the less well off.[45] "If you respect my dollars," African Americans told shopkeepers, "you must respect my person." The larger goal of consumer protests was respect, dignity, and jobs. African American ministers played a key role in this struggle, a reliance on elites somewhat analogous to Harrington's preference for professionals and Nader's for experts in law and science. The way these protests worked was that clergymen collected data about the number and quality of jobs in a corporation, then requested that the corporation hire more African Americans and ensure their employment in nonmenial positions. These negotiations were educational as well, for they revealed how immoral it was for corporations to earn income from selling to African Americans while denying them employment. If negotiations did not succeed—and they usually did—then the SCLC would launch a boycott. Begun in Atlanta, Operation Breadbasket moved to Chicago in 1966 with twenty-five-year-old Jesse Jackson as its leader.[46]

For King, the purpose of consumer activism was not to ensure that African Americans could participate more fully in consumer culture. Work, community, identity, and spiritual values were far more important to him than acquisition of finery or the latest appliance for the home. For King, consumer protests stood at the nexus of production and consumption. Thus, his goal was not so much to obtain the right to consume equally as it was to achieve a stronger foothold for African Americans in the job market. King also offered a penetrating critique of the impact of increasing affluence within the African American community. Black people undermined their own dignity, he asserted, when they used creams to lighten their skin and chemicals to straighten their hair. He chastised members of the black middle class who, having "forgotten their roots," were "more concerned about 'conspicuous consumption' than about the cause of justice."[47]

Indeed in a book intentionally laced with dichotomies, none was more telling than the tension between integration into existing society and transformation of that society, King noted that the "racial revolution has been a revolution to 'get in' rather than to overthrow," but the movement he led was not one "that seeks to integrate the Negro into all the existing values of American society." As a Christian and a moralist, he could hardly claim that the goal of his struggle was simply to enable African Americans to indulge themselves with more goods. But though he realized that spiritual values mattered more than material conditions, he never advocated a return to a simpler way of living or extolled the virtues of a folk culture. Dignity, he remarked, was "corroded by poverty no matter how poetically we invest the humble with simple graces and charm." Yet his crusade went further. With his eye more on whites than on blacks, he called on Americans to be more concerned with justice than with wealth for "a withered sense of justice in an expanding society leads to corruption of the lives of all Americans." Indeed, "material abundance has brought us neither peace of mind nor serenity of spirit."[48]

King's farthest-reaching and most profound critique of affluence occurs at the end of the book, in a chapter whose position is prominent and whose focus is global. In order to understand the significance of his contribution here, it is important to recognize again that among the critics of affluence, with the exception of Oscar Lewis, King's perspective was the most transnational. Although the books of Packard, Carson, Friedan, and Nader reached audiences outside the United States, the focus of their work was on the nation itself. And though he wrote much of *The Affluent Society* while living in Switzerland, Galbraith gave little attention to the international context. Harrington understood some dimensions of the relationship between the situation of the poor at home and abroad even as he focused primarily on the conditions facing America's poor. Lewis wrote about urban poverty in Third World nations even as both he and his audience were thinking about the situation in the United States. Central to King's critique of American affluence however, was his awareness of the gap between the world's rich and poor. He called on the United States to move beyond its focus on the struggle between capitalism and communism. Yet just as his efforts to improve the condition of America's poor went hand in hand with an acknowledgment of the emptiness of affluence, so did he underscore the need for a revolution in values that would not confuse material abundance with spiritual well-being. "The richer we have become materially," he noted, "the poorer we have become morally and spiritually." Evoking Henry David Thoreau and Eastern philosophy, he warned that Americans were so focused on the means of achieving satisfaction through consumption that they had lost sight of the nonmaterial ends of life. In one of the book's most penetrating turns of phrase, he remarked that "when scientific power outruns moral power, we end up with guided missiles and misguided men." With the injustice of the global gap between poverty and wealth keenly in mind, King concluded, "We must rapidly begin the shift from a 'thing'-oriented society to a 'person'-oriented society." As he remarked elsewhere in 1967, "When machines and computers, property motives and property rights are considered more important than people, the giant triplets of racism, materialism and militarism are incapable of being conquered."[49]

Because an assassin's bullet cut short King's life in 1968, we will never know what success he could have achieved in his effort to link spirituality, a critique of affluence, and radical politics. In the late 1950s he identified the growing affluence of the black middle class as a source of funding for the fight against discrimination and segregation as he called on African Americans to avoid the excesses of affluence. In contrast, in 1967 he emphasized the consequences of the disparity between black poverty and white affluence while at the same time calling on the nation to repent of its materialism and join him in a battle for social justice. He worked to break the link between democracy, capitalism, and consumption. In both instances he connected consumer activism with a call for chastened consumption—a connection environmental activists in the late 1960s and early 1970 were also beginning to make.

The Reemergence of Environmentalism

The work of Paul Ehrlich underscores the importance of science and environmentalism in consumer consciousness and protests in the late 1960s and early 1970s. *The Population Bomb* (1968) represents the work of a scientist long concerned with environmental issues who only in the late 1960s came to address a popular audience. Written before the environmental movement emerged with full force, Ehrlich's book sounded ominous warnings about the consequences of the nexus of technology, population, and affluence.

In important ways, Ehrlich was following in the footsteps of Lewis Mumford, who influenced the environmental movement that originated in the 1960s and emerged fully in the 1970s. In 1967, Mumford published the first of his two-volume study *The Myth of the Machine*. Almost forty years before, he had hoped that America's entry into a war that he supported would help counter overconsumption. Indeed, the 1967 book opens with a quotation from *The Condition of Man* (1944), in which he had celebrated poetry, drama, and music as "the symbolic activities which give significance both to the processes of work and their ultimate products and consummations." Now as the nation was waging a war in Vietnam which he opposed, Mumford warned about the dangers of too great a commitment to means rather than ends. Advances in science and technology, he wrote, were proceeding at such a rapid pace that man had "detached himself as far as possible from the organic habitat." The result was the impending transformation of the human being into "a passive, purposeless, machine-conditioned animal whose proper functions, as technicians now interpret man's role, will either be fed into the machine or strictly limited and controlled for the benefit of de-personalized, collective organizations." In the second volume, published in 1970, he inveighed against modern consumer culture. He believed that technology and the economic system were capable of producing goods that were durable and a system that was efficient. Instead, what modern America had were overdrawn consumers chasing shoddy goods packaged in glitzy wrappings and designed not to last or please. "Every member of the community," he asserted as he echoed what he had written thirty years earlier, "must, in duty bound, acquire, use, devour, waste, and finally destroy a sufficient quantity of goods to keep its increasingly productive mechanism in operation."[50]

A number of forces shaped resurgent environmental activism. The writings of Rachel Carson played a pivotal role. The critique of technology, rationality, and authority by the New Left and the counterculture inspired old activists and new ones as well. Interest in Eastern religions and Native American cultures fostered a growing respect for nature. Above all, the costs that economic and technological change exacted eventually alerted citizens to how high the stakes were. It turned out that nuclear power, pesticides, new compounds (chemicals in plastics and in laundry detergents, to name a few) had their costs as well as their benefits. Moreover, suburban developments gobbled up land, as did the clear-cutting of forests needed to produce the wood to construct houses, and the interstate highway system so central to developing new residential areas. The increasing use of cars and trucks—especially gas-guzzlers that had few or no emission controls—produced pollution, with smog in Southern California the most infamous result. The nation seemed to be changing from the affluent society to the effluent society, as people grappled with the problem of what to do with the waste products of nuclear energy, automobiles, and new industrial and household goods.[51]

People became increasingly aware of the dangers of excessive consumption and environmental degradation as pollution of air and water worsened and threats to the natural wilderness and to endangered resources increased. Several incidents provided vivid reminders of the danger. In the summer of 1966, air pollution was held responsible for the deaths of eighty people in New York City. The following year a tanker, the *Torrey Canyon*, spilled over a hundred thousand tons of crude oil into the English Channel. As Americans used more oil, the consequences of offshore drilling became apparent. In 1969, leaks from a rig in the Santa Barbara Channel despoiled beaches and killed fish and fowl. In the same year, Cleveland's Cuyahoga River caught fire as a result of chemical pollutants. Americans were learning firsthand of the importance of limits, the necessity to tame technology, and the virtues of human coexistence with, rather than domination of, nature.

This growing consciousness of the need to protect the environment began to foster watershed changes in activism. An older generation of conservationists consisted of elite groups that focused on protection of the wilderness. During the 1960s, David Brower, the executive head of the Sierra Club, urged the club to shed what was then its constricted vision and tame tactics. Instead, he called on the organization to use mass mailings and media-savvy advertisements to build a broader base for an emerging environmentalism opposed to pollution, population growth, and economic development that threatened the environment. His efforts came to a head in the fight against building dams on the Colorado River that would have radically changed the ecology of the Grand Canyon and for the passage of the Wilderness Act of 1964.[52]

By the mid-1960s, momentous shifts were under way—from conservation to environmentalism, from elite to mass-based organizations, and from wilderness protection to improvements in areas of intense settlement, including cities and suburbs. The economic boom of the postwar period had fostered among white, middle-class Americans an interest in leisure pursued in suburban parks and in more far-flung recreation areas. In some ways this was the kind of qualitative liberalism that Schlesinger and Galbraith had articulated in the 1950s. By this point the new environmentalism had produced some results. Lady Bird Johnson had launched her campaign to "Keep America Beautiful," and in 1965 President Johnson signed the Highway Beautification bill. Other legislative victories came with the strengthening of existing laws such as the Clean Air Act of 1955 and the Clean Water Act of 1960. In the late 1960s, the Native American Iron Eyes Cody appeared in a famous advertisement, shedding tears over environmental degradation.

If there was one moment that marked the emergence of environmental activism onto the national stage, it was the first Earth Day, April 22, 1970. As many as 20 million Americans attended teach-ins, signed petitions, planted tress, and cleaned up their neighborhoods. The same year brought the Water Quality Improvement Act and Clean Air Act, as well as the signing of the National Environmental Policy Act, which created the Environmental Protection Agency. During the 1970s, publications that linked environmentalism with chastened consumption appeared in abundance, among them the periodicals *Mother Earth News*, *Green Revolution*, and *Organic Gardening*. Although environmentalism in its milder forms often seemed as exempt from criticism as motherhood, it nonetheless did not go unchallenged. The FBI closely monitored the new movement. Many in the business community opposed restrictions on their activities. Some radicals schooled in the civil rights and antiwar movements worried that new concerns about the natural environment might distract attention and resources from the fights for racial justice and against an unjust war. Some feared that any pressure to slow economic growth would adversely affect the poor.[53]

Most critics of affluence—such as Friedan, Harrington, Lewis, and King—had focused on its impact on people but not on the planet. Carson had blazed the path toward a different perspective. Now a number of books appeared that were influential among environmental activists, among them works by Garrett Hardin, Barry Commoner, E. F. Schumacher, Roderick Nash, the Club of Rome's Project on the Predicament on Mankind, and, later in the 1970s and early 1980s, works by Annette Kolodny, Carolyn Merchant, Jonathan Schell, Amory B. Lovins, William Ophuls, and Bill McKibben. Consumer activism focusing on the environment sprang from other social movements and from changes taking place throughout the world. As expected for a largely middle-class movement, books also played a critical role, including works by Henry David Thoreau and Aldo Leopold as well as Rachel Carson. With environmentalism, the relationship between books and the movement was largely reciprocal. An important new trend was seen as self-help books enjoyed their heyday among environmentalists.[54]

Nowhere is this clearer than with Frances Moore Lappé's *Diet for a Small Planet* (1971), one of the period's best-selling books on environmental concerns. Married to an experimental pathologist who studied environmental contamination, Lappé was inspired to publish this book of recipes because of her concern about worldwide food shortages. Until she started working on it, she noted, whenever she went to "the supermarket, I felt at the mercy of our advertising culture." Evoking the dual roles of woman as nurturer and consumer, she wrote, "Food, instead of being my most direct link with the nurturing earth, had become mere merchandise through which I fulfilled my role as a 'good' consumer." As she studied the subject, she learned how environmentally inefficient it was to produce meat. She set out to identify alternative sources of protein in order to counter "our heavily meat-centered culture that is at the very heart of our waste of the earth's productivity." She hoped that teaching people about the connection between what they ate and the well-being of the natural world might be "the first step toward changing our cultural pattern of waste." By modifying their diet so as to get their protein from grains, people could expand their sense of choice, consume lower levels of pesticide residue, and use the earth more efficiently.[55]

Paul R. Ehrlich: *The Population Bomb*

There was at least one widely read book that appeared before Earth Day: Paul Ehrlich's *Population Bomb* (1968). A capsule review of his life illuminates the process by which this research scientist became a critic of affluence and an environmental activist. Born in Philadelphia on May 29, 1932, into a middle-class Jewish household, Ehrlich grew up in suburban New Jersey. As he commented later, "It was my good luck that my mother got me interested in nature, that a camp counselor got me interested in butterflies, and that butterfly taxonomy got me interested in evolution and thus ecology." Ehrlich published his first scientific paper in 1948, when he was still in high school. Fascinated by how different types of butterflies had evolved, he began to collect them, a process that grew increasingly difficult during his teenage years, he later recalled, when "my collecting sites were disappearing under subdivisions, and my efforts to raise adult butterflies from caterpillars were frustrated by the ubiquitous presence of DDT residues on their food plants." The suburban growth that inspired Vance Packard's critique of status seeking and Betty Friedan's on behalf of trapped housewives also laid the groundwork for Ehrlich's environmental activism. The reckless use of DDT, which impelled Rachel Carson to write *Silent Spring* and Ralph Nader to attempt to limit pesticide use when he was still an undergraduate, also raised Ehrlich's consciousness about the fragility of the natural world.[56]

Ehrlich graduated with a degree in biology from the University of Pennsylvania in 1953, where he read Fairfield Osborn's *Our Plundered Planet* (1948) and William Vogt's *Road to Survival* (1948). Both books emphasized human cooperation with rather than domination of nature, the interdependence of all living things, conservation of natural resources, and recognition of the impact of population growth on the environment. These books gave him, he later remarked, "a global framework for things he had observed as a young naturalist." His undergraduate work on an insect survey in the Arctic inspired his initial interest in the relationship between human culture and the environment. Ehrlich then went to the University of Kansas, where he met Anne Fitzhugh Howland, whom he married in 1954, and with whom he co-authored many books. As an undergraduate, Anne had also read Osborn's book, which confirmed her long-held fascination with nature. DDT was in wide use near the university, something the couple experienced firsthand one night when, while watching a movie at a drive-in theater, they were surrounded by a cloud of indiscriminate spraying. Paul Ehrlich earned his Ph.D. in 1957 with studies of the processes of natural selection that enabled insects to develop resistance to DDT. In 1959 he took a job at Stanford, where he moved up through the ranks, becoming a professor of biological sciences in

1966. By 1968, when he burst onto the national scene as the author of *The Population Bomb*, Ehrlich had published more than seventy scientific articles and reviews. He specialized in the study of the structure and evolution of the butterfly population (specifically the checkerspot butterfly) as a key to investigating larger questions about population biology and ecology. In 1961, he and his wife authored *How to Know the Butterflies*, a practical handbook for a lay audience. A year later, the publication of *Silent Spring* and the heated discussions that ensued intensified his interest in the impact of pesticides and eroded his faith that science and technology could solve all problems.[57]

From early on, Ehrlich's scientific research raised issues that connected science with public policy. His study of butterflies revealed the effects of economic development, population movements, technological change, and human error on nature. In 1964, Ehrlich applied the skepticism about taxonomy and the reification of categories that he had earlier developed for the world of biology to the concept of race. Standing in opposition to the racist theories of Carleton S. Coon and of his Stanford colleague William Shockley, Ehrlich revealed how problematic was the concept of race, subject as it was to all sorts of cultural, political, genetic, and environmental considerations. "Discussions of the biological origins and characteristics of subjectively determined race," he remarked, pointing to Coon's work, "are useful only for strengthening culturally determined prejudices against groups which have reality only in a social, rather than a biological, sense." Consequently, just as the "exchange of genetic material" between animal species was part of the evolutionary process, so too was "interbreeding" or "hybridization" between people from different "races." Indeed, Ehrlich continued, as he drew on work by zoologists, there was reason to believe that offspring of parents from two distinct population groups "would be, on the average, more fit in the sense of the population geneticist than the offspring of individuals from the same population."[58]

Yet in the end, the most consequential connection between science and politics that Ehrlich drew focused not on race but on population and environmentalism. His fieldwork in the hills above the Stanford campus, and more generally his observation of the booming California economy's impact on the environment, sensitized him to the delicate balance between humans and nature. As a researcher who traveled the world studying butterflies, Ehrlich understood the delicate interconnection of ecological systems. In the 1960s he increasingly sensed an emerging crisis as growth in population, affluence, and technology threatened the natural world. Many people in wealthy nations seemed to think that they were immune from the limitations the laws of nature imposed on human beings. Eventually, ecologists such as Ehrlich insisted, the human desire to dominate nature would backfire.[59]

In 1967, with Peter H. Raven, Ehrlich published in *Scientific American* a seminal article that helped launch the field of coevolution, the study of the evolutionary dynamics that occur when organisms such as predators and prey or hosts and parasites interact. They pictured a Darwinian struggle, emphasizing "the perennial onslaught of animals on plants." In order to protect themselves, plants developed "chemical weapons" such as insecticides, a process that Ehrlich and Raven found preferable to the "chemical warfare" humans had unleashed on the natural world. They emphasized how such interactions influenced the evolution of species, a process they labeled "communal evolution," or coevolution, and which they credited with producing diversity in the natural world. At the height of the civil rights movement in the early 1960s, Ehrlich had suggested that African Americans and whites could live intimately and peacefully together. Now, writing with Raven at the height of the war in Vietnam, Ehrlich both emphasized the ferocity of contact between plants and animals and suggested that both had devised ways of living together that were a marked improvement over the deadly interventions of humans. "By learning from the plants and sharpening their natural weapons," Ehrlich and Raven concluded, "we should be able to find effective ways of poisoning our insect competitors without poisoning ourselves." Whatever complicated message this might have carried for America's war in Vietnam, the ecological lesson was clear. Left to their own devices, nature's inhabitants learned to live with one another, antagonistically but cooperatively and effectively. Human intervention had to take advantage of the properties nature provided.[60]

While this article was in press, Ehrlich had an opportunity to consider further the lessons his research had taught him. On a sabbatical in 1966–67, as they traveled around the world, Paul and Anne Ehrlich sharpened their understanding of threats to the global environment. In search of a "tropical paradise of birds and butterflies," they found in the Solomon Islands "one large coconut plantation, each tree with a metal rat guard and all the vegetation between the trees cut close to the ground." What had happened in the New Jersey suburb of Ehrlich's childhood was visible elsewhere: economic development caused ecological change that was destroying the once unspoiled habitats of butterflies. When they returned to Stanford in 1967, the Ehrlichs "focused with increasing intensity on the population-resource-environment situation." What grew out of these concerns was a determination to write a book a broad public could understand, a decision also shaped by Ehrlich's awareness of famine in India throughout 1966. With the publication of *The Population Bomb*, Ehrlich executed a number of shifts: from focused, scientific work addressed to a specialized audience to writings for a wide audience that connected issues of population, resources, and the environment; and from research scientist and professor to public intellectual and environmental activist.[61]

The book appeared in May 1968, in the middle of a tumultuous year in the United States and around the world, when a series of events was preparing the ground for a dramatic and frightening vision of the nation's future. In January the Tet offensive in Vietnam made America's war more costly and victory less likely. In March, Senator Eugene McCarthy's strong showing in the New Hampshire primary resulted in President Johnson's announcement that he would not run for reelection. In April, an assassin killed Martin Luther King Jr. In the same month, student protests erupted on the Columbia University campus. In May, workers and students flooded the streets of Paris, an event that seemed to augur a revolution in the making. In June, Robert F. Kennedy was assassinated, and the Poor People's March took place in the nation's capital. In August, Soviet troops put down a popular uprising in Prague, and violence erupted on the streets of Chicago outside the convention of the Democratic Party.

With *The Population Bomb*, written in only three weeks so that it could appear before the presidential election, Ehrlich captured the urgency of the moment. The book warned of an impending catastrophe that would occur as the diminishing production of food came up against a dramatically increasing world population. Not all scientists agreed with Ehrlich that changes in agriculture, represented by the green revolution of plant scientist Norman Borlaug, would at best only forestall the crisis temporarily. Nor did everyone in the environmental movement share his neo-Malthusian catastrophism, which identified population growth as the most important if not the single cause of the environmental crisis; others gave more weight to excessive affluence in the developed world than to exploding population in less developed countries. By the early 1970s, Ehrlich and his colleagues were offering a formula that presented population, technology, and affluence as interacting variables. Even though, for Ehrlich, population rather than affluence was the culprit, he articulated a series of arguments that had wide currency: the fragility of the environment, the problem of exploiting natural resources, and the dangerous consequences of a spiraling standard of living. Moreover, he did so with exceptionally accessible, clear, lively, and dramatic prose.[62]

Ehrlich painted a terrifying picture of a world about to be devastated by overpopulation. His use of the word "bomb" in the book's title evoked for his readers a disaster on the scale of a nuclear explosion. Indeed, after the signing of the Nuclear Test Ban Treaty in 1963, attention increasingly shifted from nuclear to environmental threats. Thus, in some ways the emergence onto the national stage of Ehrlich and, more broadly, of environmentalism as an issue signaled a shift from physicists to biologists as the leading scientists concerned with public policy, and from nuclear to environmental issues as posing the most serious threat.[63]

Ehrlich opened his book with the story of the incident a few years previously that had transformed his intellectual comprehension of the issues to an emotional one. While in Delhi, he, his wife, and their daughter were riding in a flea-infested, barely functional taxi, passing through

a crowded slum area. The temperature was well over 100, and the air was a haze of dust and smoke. The streets seemed alive with people. People eating, people washing, people sleeping. People visiting, arguing, and screaming. People thrusting their hands through the taxi window, begging. People defecating and urinating. People clinging to buses. People herding animals. People, people, people, people. As we moved slowly through the mob, hand horn squawking, the dust, noise, heat, and cooking fires gave the scene a hellish aspect. Would we ever get to our hotel? All three of us were, frankly, frightened. It seemed that anything could happen—but, of course, nothing did. Old India hands will laugh at our reaction. We were just some overprivileged tourists, unaccustomed to the sights and sounds of India. Perhaps, but since that night I've known the *feel* of overpopulation.

With that scene fixed in the reader's mind, Ehrlich went on to offer an apocalyptic vision of famine, starvation, war, and death. "The battle to feed all of humanity is over," he announced in the book's first sentence. "In the 1970s," he continued, "the world will undergo famines—hundreds of millions of people are going to starve to death in spite of any crash programs embarked upon now." Lethal viruses might kill as many as 500 million people. The richer nations would become richer, the poorer ones poorer and more heavily populated. For Ehrlich, the world food crisis of 1966, when a rise in the numbers of people came up against a stagnant food supply, provided a warning of things to come. Perhaps the poor would no longer individually stick their begging hands through taxi windows but would collectively threaten world peace and American affluence.[64]

Unlike many environmentalists, Ehrlich did not follow Carson in evoking the beauty and transcendence of the natural world. Indeed, he admitted that he had decided not to write about "the pleasantness, beauty, indeed glory of many natural areas" because such a rhetorical strategy did not seem to work. When other conservationists adopted this tactic, he believed, they were helping to confirm the commitments of the already converted but were not persuading the skeptics. Ehrlich critiqued American affluence but linked the nation's wealth to global and environmental concerns. Echoing what Galbraith said in *The Affluent Society* but giving it a more environmental cast, Ehrlich reminded his readers how difficult it was to enjoy leisure time when vacation spots were crowded, how frustrating it was to fish in polluted rivers, and how fruitless it was to drive a luxury car through smog on a crowded highway. He noted that "gross national product" was an apt name, referring as the first word did to the "glut, waste, pollution, and ugliness of America today." Americans, he went on, were the "robber barons of all time. We have decided that we are the chosen people to steal all we can get of our planet's gradually stored and limited resources." The bill for such profligacy was starting to come due. Ehrlich argued that although the population crisis was most clearly visible in the less developed world, it was apparent in the United States as well. "We hear constantly," he noted, "of the headaches caused by growing population: not just garbage in our environment, but overcrowded highways, burgeoning slums, deteriorating school systems, rising crime rates, riots, and other related problems." The "enraged 'have-nots'" were losing their patience.[65]

Yet despite the strong threats of danger, Ehrlich also reassured Americans. After all, he saw population growth (and especially that of the developing world) rather than American affluence as the culprit. At one point, having listed sacrifices Americans would have to make, he went on to discuss the advantages of a way of life dictated by the fight against population explosion and environmental deterioration. Americans would live healthier, quieter, more crime free, and cleaner lives. They would have to work less and could enjoy a slower pace of life. "We may have more fishing, more relaxing, more time to watch TV, more time to drink beer (served in bottles that *must* be returned)," he wrote in a way that reassured his readers—especially those who drank beer and watched TV. Indeed, if there was a vision of a better life embedded in the book, it focused on a less crowded rather than a less affluent world. There are several possible explanations for Ehrlich's threatening an impending catastrophe at one moment and at the next promising a better world where American affluence still reigned. Perhaps he was ambivalent about the benefits of a rising standard of living. It is also possible that he decided that shock, pessimism, and the portrayal of a dismal future would immobilize Americans rather than energize them into action.[66]

If Ehrlich was sometimes cautiously optimistic about America's future, when it came to discussing the situation abroad, especially in the less developed nations, he was relentlessly pessimistic. Like Martin Luther King Jr., Ehrlich linked American affluence with the poverty of less developed countries; even more so than King, he insisted that the citizens of the United States had to realize that they existed within a global context. Ecology, disease, nuclear bombs, and humanitarian concerns were just some of the forces that bound the nation to the world. Yet for him, the simultaneous existence of American affluence and world poverty was the contradiction that provided the bonds of a common fate. "Nothing could be more misleading to our children," Ehrlich noted, "than our present affluent society. . . . As the most powerful nation in the world today, *and its largest consumer*, the United States cannot stand isolated." Although he identified the increase in population as the main problem, he also acknowledged the disproportionate impact of America's relatively small but hugely affluent society. Thus he lamented that less than 6 percent of the world's population "requires more than all the rest to maintain its inflated position." He was keenly aware of the way American affluence—symbolized by automobiles, tractors, and television sets—encouraged the rising expectations of people in poorer nations. As American affluence increased and the situation in Africa, Asia, and Latin America grew increasingly desperate, the urgent questions would become: "Will they starve gracefully, without rocking the boat? Or will they attempt to overwhelm us in order to get what they consider to be their fair share?"[67]

The population bomb also threatened environmental degradation. Population pressures would upset the delicate and complex ecological balance. To increase food production and thus stave off famine, governments and farmers had to clear forests and rely on dangerous pesticides, in both cases transforming complex and sustainable ecosystems into simple and unstable ones. But, in an oblique reference to Nader's *Unsafe at Any Speed*, Ehrlich wrote, "pesticide deaths are much less dramatic than head-on collisions." (Indeed, in some ways Ehrlich was questioning Nader's emphasis on the automobile as the chief cause of pollution.) Once upset by growing numbers of people, an endangered ecological system left the world more vulnerable to disease and produced adverse climate changes such as the greenhouse effect. Ehrlich also speculated that a polluted environment had serious psychological effects, with "riots, rising crime rates, disaffection of youth, and increased drug usage" following in the wake of a deteriorating natural world.[68]

Turning to solutions for the dire situation he described, Ehrlich asserted that "population control is the only answer." Decreasing the death rate through modern medicine and increasing the food supply were "palliatives" that might work in the short term but in the long run often did more harm than good by upsetting ecosystems. He called on the United States to take the lead in reducing population growth to zero or below, "by compulsion if voluntary methods fail." Although he flirted with introducing a "temporary sterilant to the water supply or staple food," in the end he proposed relying on a system of financial rewards and penalties. Ehrlich called for abortions sanctioned by doctors at a time before *Roe v. Wade*, when that option was just beginning to emerge in California. He also advocated the establishment of a federal Department of Population and Environment which would provide sex and environmental education, develop financial penalties against polluters, and support development of nontoxic insect controls.[69]

Yet as important as the American example was, Ehrlich realized that the real crisis was in developing nations. To protect the environment by limiting world population, he proposed that developed nations devise an international agency that would institute a system of triage, dividing nations into three groups and providing aid accordingly: those that could make it on their own, those it was possible to help toward self-sufficiency, and those, such as India, in such dire straits that it would be necessary to deny aid. Among the tactics he sanctioned were television campaigns developed on Madison Avenue that would "use the prospect of increased affluence as a major incentive for gaining cooperation" in programs of population control and agricultural development. Ehrlich realized the practical and political difficulties his proposals would face at home and abroad. By and large, he remained pessimistic about the prospect of solving the environmental and population threats facing the world.[70]

The solutions he proposed revealed the sense of urgency he felt, yet equally significant was the extensive advice he offered his readers. So many books of social criticism in the postwar period were long on analysis but remarkably short on both solutions and practical advice. Nader was the first of the authors under consideration here to move from a book to a sustained institutional effort. With *The Population Bomb*, Ehrlich broke new ground by devoting a substantial portion of the book to a combination of policy recommendations and advice. After having outlined solutions that might defuse the population bomb, he offered a long section, beginning with a chapter titled "What Can You Do?" in which he provided specific suggestions on what arguments to include in letters to politicians and editors as well as to opinion makers in the Roman Catholic Church, the media, and the business community. He elaborated points that his readers could use to overcome the resistance and objections of friends and associates. He offered suggestions as to how to organize grassroots action, including consumer boycotts of corporations that damaged the environment or opposed population control.[71]

Yet there was a disconnection between the seriousness of the situation he described and the far-reaching nature of his policy recommendations, on the one hand, and the relative timidity of the activism he endorsed, on the other. In a short section titled "Organizing Action Groups," in addition to calling for boycotts and suggesting that children bring IUDs to "show and tell" at their schools, Ehrlich recommended holding a weekly "letter-writing party," speaking to PTAs, and going on TV and radio talk shows. He expressed guarded optimism about the prospect of persuading the Catholic Church to agree to support population control involving not just private family planning but government programs. At a time when the civil rights, antiwar, and feminist movements were using approaches to grassroots activism and public protests that were inventive and radical, Ehrlich seemed excessively cautious. Perhaps the cycles of violence and repression so evident on the streets of America in 1968 led him to separate environmental activism from tactics that relied on working outside the system. Whatever the reason, there remained a gap between his pessimistic analysis and his faith in working within the system.[72]

This was quickly to change. Soon after publication of his book, Ehrlich would sanction a more insurgent politics, a trajectory similar to that of Friedan, Harrington, and Nader. In the early 1970s, he spoke of generating "a lot of civil disobedience, similar to what we saw in the early days of civil rights: demonstrations, picketing, sit-ins." Soon, he predicted, we will "begin to see boycotting of the automobile industry, the big oil companies, the utilities."[73]

The publication of *The Population Bomb* in 1968 transformed Ehrlich's career. Although the book received remarkably few reviews in the national media, it eventually sold over 3 million copies, rose to second place on the *New York Times* list of paperback best-sellers, and remained on the list for twenty-eight weeks. Kirkpatrick Sale called it "the most popular environmental book ever published." Although Ehrlich continued to publish the results of his scientific research, he now sought additional venues for his ideas. Whereas he had once written almost entirely for publications such as *Lepidopterists' News, Science,* and *Evolution,* in the late 1960s and early 1970s, his articles on issues of population and ecology also appeared in the *New York Times, National Wildlife, Saturday Review, Field and Stream,* and *McCalls.* Ehrlich turned to activism, too. In 1969 he became a founder and first president of Zero Population Growth (ZPG), which by early 1970 had 102 chapters in thirty states. He also lent his support to the legendary environmentalist David Brower, the founder of Friends of the Earth (FOE), who had just lost his job at the Sierra Club. On Earth Day, Ehrlich addressed ten thousand students at Iowa State.

By the early 1970s, Ehrlich was in the midst of a whirlwind of activity. Every week he received over three dozen requests to speak and traveled eighty thousand miles annually, giving as many talks as he could, many of them on college campuses. Articulate, witty, and forceful, Ehrlich made more than two dozen appearances on *The Tonight Show* with Johnny Carson and testified before congressional committees. In the decades after the publication of *The Population Bomb,* he remained focused on population and environmental issues. He continued a vigorous career that combined activism, scientific research, and publication of books and articles in both scientific and popular venues. His efforts brought him not only a wide audience but honors as well: an endowed chair at Stanford, an Emmy nomination, awards from the

United Nations, the MacArthur Foundation, and the Royal Swedish Academy of Sciences to name a few.[74] If Nader institutionalized his efforts through a complex organizational structure, Ehrlich, not unlike other activists of the 1970s, worked from his university and professional bases and relied as well on newly created activist organizations.

Ralph Nader, Martin Luther King Jr., and Paul Ehrlich helped unite moralist critiques with activism. Michael Harrington, Paul Goodman, Rachel Carson, and Oscar Lewis had written influential books, but the three subjects of this chapter demonstrated what it meant to link the written word with consumer activism and to do so in a sustained way that relied on institutionalizing adversarial impulses. Consumer protests had grown in force and visibility. These three writers and the movements they inspired helped delegitimize the cold war consensus by challenging the connection between materialism and pleasure emphasized by social scientists, market researchers, and businessmen. Consumer activists of the 1960s showed how ordinary citizens could develop a politics of purchasing—by not buying grapes produced on nonunion farms, by refusing to shop where African Americans could not work, by selecting safer automobiles, or by recycling glass, paper, and metals. Nader, King, and Ehrlich, however, also demonstrated how to build a lasting movement through institutions such as the Southern Christian Leadership Conference, Public Interest Research Groups, Zero Population Growth, and Friends of the Earth. King and Ehrlich offered global analyses that transformed the national focus of most writers on affluence into international visions and explored the connections between America's wealth and the poverty of much of the rest of the world. Together these contributions—developing and then institutionalizing a politics of affluence, as well as placing America's wealth in global perspective—laid the basis for protests against the excesses of globalization that would emerge in the new century. The trajectory of this period, in the three short but tension-packed years from Nader's *Unsafe at Any Speed* in 1965 to *The Population Bomb* in 1968, demonstrates the changing relationships between books and social movements.

The words of Nader, King, and Ehrlich also reveal just how critical affluence had become to key American writers of the late 1960s. They all drew on (and politicized) the new moralism as they chastised middle-class Americans for their excessive consumption. They assumed that the excess of commercial goods purchased by prosperous Americans was a problem. For King and Ehrlich, this consumption contrasted with the misery of America's and the world's poor, respectively. As a result of these books and related protests, the landscape for discussions of affluence was transformed by the early 1970s. The belief in an equitable and beneficent standard of living, a central component of the paeans to America's democratic capitalism in the 1950s, hardly disappeared; but by the early 1970s, words and events had knocked that belief off its pedestal. Americans were less confident that the benefits of affluence were as widespread as they had thought or even that the consumer culture was beneficent. Alternative values were now available, whether those of Christian self-restraint, youthful self-expression, greater balance between private pursuits and public welfare, consumer protection, or environmentalism. Yet whatever reservations had developed by 1968 paled in comparison with what the energy crisis of the 1970s would bring. Attention shifted from the specter of too much affluence to the specter of too little, as leading intellectuals, and even the nation's president, worried about excess.

7

The Energy Crisis and the Quest to Contain Consumption

Daniel Bell, Christopher Lasch, and Robert Bellah

In 1974, when Paul and Anne Ehrlich announced "the end of affluence" in a book of that title, they were not alone. The consumer protests beginning in the mid-1960s typically were based on the assumption that there was enough affluence to go around, but by the 1970s, many observers feared that this was no longer so. Writers, offering their own version of the new moralism, remained concerned that abundance was producing social corruption and excessive self-regard. Watergate, the war in Vietnam, soaring inflation, and rising energy prices turned 1960s optimism into 1970s pessimism and restored among millions of Americans a sense of limits to what they could expect as consumers. Deindustrialization, which saw the exportation of hundreds of thousands of high-paying jobs abroad (especially in the auto and steel industries), signified a series of important shifts—from Rust Belt to Sun Belt, from manufacturing to service sector, and from union to non-union jobs. Rising housing costs and decreasing rates of home ownership, declines in productivity, and shortages of key goods and services made the lives of millions of Americans more economically straitened. During the decade, as the historian Bruce J. Schulman has noted, Americans increased their personal debt and changed from being savers to spenders and investors. Stagflation, the simultaneous rise of prices and unemployment, seemed impervious to policy remedies. Prosperity and carelessness had increased the domestic use of oil from 5.8 billion barrels in 1949 to more than 16.4 billion in 1971. By the 1970s, this had given foreign oil producers unprecedented control of America's future. Inflation, sparked in part by rising oil prices, rose to 11 percent in 1974 and unemployment to 8.3 percent the following year. After both figures subsided they rose again: inflation to 13.4 percent in 1979 and unemployment as high as 7.8 percent in 1980. The rate of joblessness for African American and Hispanic workers was often at twice those figures. By 1980, the dollar was worth 40 percent of what it had been in 1967. Yet the numbers tell a complicated and contradictory story. Though by the end of the decade real GNP and the number of people employed were higher than in 1970, most Americans experienced the decade as one of economic pain. In 1973 the median income of American families reached a peak that it did not attain again for at least a decade and a half, and the vast majority of the nation's families experienced diminishing real incomes.[1]

Those who shaped American public opinion responded by reflecting on some of the key issues raised by affluence. With the energy crisis Ernest Dichter reaffirmed his commitment to an anti-puritanical vision. Yet George Katona grew pessimistic as he began to worry about the environmental and cultural consequences of America's embrace of a materialistic way of life. In his widely read essay "The Me Decade" (1976), Tom Wolfe charted contemporary paths toward self-discovery and self-transformation. In *Two Cheers for Capitalism* (1978), Irving Kristol asked whether affluence might undermine the nation's stability by intensifying yearnings that were left unsatisfied. Those who glorified unfettered markets, such as Milton Friedman, began to shape public opinion and public policy in the 1970s, though their impact would become dramatically more apparent in the 1980s. Some observers seemed to welcome the energy crisis, much as Lewis Mumford had looked to World War II as a catalyst to cleanse society of materialism and selfishness. Under the 1979 headline "Why a Depression Might Be Good for Us All," the Dartmouth College political scientist Roger D. Masters asked, "At what point does the cost of continued economic wealth exceed the benefits? Wouldn't a major depression," he wondered, "teach us the vital lesson that human life is more than physical comfort and a cost-of-living increase?" Masters was not alone. In 1980, John Tirman, another political scientist, welcomed austerity because continually increasing consumption distracted people from spiritual goals, degraded the environment, undermined the stability of communities and families, and threatened the values of simplicity and caring. "What America *really* needs is more shortages," wrote the *New York Times* editor and columnist James Reston when President Richard M. Nixon in 1973 called for conservation in response to a dramatic rise in oil prices—and in the power of the Organization of Petroleum Exporting Countries (OPEC). "We need to cut down, slow up, stay at home, run around the block, eat vegetable soup, call up old friends and read a book once in a while."[2]

Politicians and social scientists tried to devise policies to restore the work ethic, encourage savings, and lessen what they saw as unproductive consumption. Social scientists, worried that self-indulgence would undermine the fabric of American society, expressed concern about the dangers of profligate spending, both of the middle class and of those below. Some observers detected a shift among Americans toward nonmaterial pleasures. In *New Rules: Searching for Self-Fulfillment in a World Turned Upside Down* (1981), the pollster Daniel Yankelovich described an emerging sense among Americans that additional material goods were not making them feel better; rather, they sought deeper satisfactions in meaningful work, human relationships, leisure, community, and autonomy. Social scientists who carried out empirical studies that examined whether affluence made people happier offered sobering conclusions. In a 1974 article titled "Does Money Buy Happiness?" the distinguished demographer Robert Easterlin remarked, "To the outside observer, economic growth appears to be producing an ever more affluent society, but to those involved in the process, affluence will always remain a distant, urgently sought, but never attained goal." After 1959, reported the eminent sociologist Morris Janowitz, increasing levels of income did not produce a greater amount of personal satisfaction. In 1973, E. F. Schumacher declared that "small is beautiful" while *The Whole Earth Catalogue* (1968) offered practical advice on how to live more simply.[3]

Newspapers and magazines focused on the struggle of average American families to make ends meet. In March 1980 the *Los Angeles Times* featured a story about the Miller family of Temple City, California, under the headline "Family Prunes Luxuries: On $25,000 a Year, No More Malted Milks." A reporter for *Texas Monthly* told the story of the Mark Cunningham family of Plano, Texas, who sang "The $38,000 a Year, Wife and Two Kids, House and a Pool *Blues*." Howard J. Ruff's *How to Prosper in the Coming Bad Years*, which by early 1980 had sold 500,000 copies in hardcover and more than twice that figure in paper, warned that since the nation's wealth was an illusion, people should put their assets in gold, buy a year's supply of food, move to a small town, and wait for better days when the free market might return the nation to sanity and economic health.[4]

Three of the nation's leading intellectuals wrote widely read books in which they chastised Americans for their excessive participation in consumer culture. In *Culture of Narcissism: American Life in an Age of Diminishing Expectations* (1979), the historian Christopher Lasch argued that mass consumption had helped foster a new and dangerous self-indulgence. In *The Cultural Contradictions of Capitalism* (1976), the sociologist Daniel Bell described a society coming apart because of the decline of the work ethic and the rise of self-indulgence. He asserted that religion would promote self-restraint and called for a renewed sense of the public good. In *The Broken*

Covenant (1975), the sociologist Robert N. Bellah urged Americans to draw inspiration from national traditions, to turn away from excessive self-indulgence and instead embrace communal and ennobling virtues. Then in July 1979, an embattled President Jimmy Carter, who had read their works, spoke out, castigating his fellow citizens for their profligacy as consumers, an address that has become known as the "malaise" speech.[5] The interaction of Bell, Bellah, and Lasch, with the president underscored the complications that occur when intellectuals enter the inner sanctum of public policy debates. Their sophisticated jeremiads now found echoes in the words of a president whose religious beliefs and political difficulties led him to articulate his own version of a moralist position on affluence. Economic stringency had persuaded millions of Americans to take refuge in self-gratification, a proclivity both the president and the writers he consulted found problematic. The 1960s dealt what would appear in the ensuing decade to be a fatal blow to the cold war consensus; among the notions that took its place was a call for restrained consumption and for a restoration of a sense of public commitment.

Daniel Bell: *The Cultural Contradictions of Capitalism* (1976)

Daniel Bell, one of the most influential American sociologists of his generation, recommended in *The Cultural Contradictions of Capitalism* an appeal to the public good and religion to restrain excessive consumption. From the mid-1940s until at least the late 1970s, Bell was one of America's leading public intellectuals. Born in 1919, he grew up in New York on the Lower East Side in an impoverished Jewish immigrant household. Beginning at age thirteen, when he joined the Socialist Party's organization for young people, he lived in a world of fierce debates among communists, socialists, and anarchists, debates in which Bell from an early age took an anticommunist, right-wing socialist, and pro–labor union position. He attended City College of New York, where he honed his commitments to social democracy, graduating in 1938. He joined the staff of the *New Leader* and served as managing editor until he resigned in 1944. He then began a three-year stint on the faculty of the University of Chicago. In 1948 he began working for *Fortune* as labor editor, where he remained until 1958.[6]

Bell underwent a process of deradicalization in the late 1940s when he rethought his Marxist commitments. Despite leftist predictions, capitalism had not collapsed, fascism had not arrived in America, and Truman had consolidated the gains of the New Deal. The first sustained result of Bell's reconsideration of these issues was his 1952 *Background and Development of Marxian Socialism in the United States*, in which he charted the failure of left-wing radicalism to flourish in America. He had a knack for defining issues and then framing them in bold, fruitful, and controversial ways. *The New American Right* (1955), a collection of essays Bell edited, offered what at the time was the most influential analysis of McCarthyism. *The End of Ideology: On the Exhaustion of Political Ideas in the Fifties* (1960), provided the basis on which Columbia University granted him his doctorate and appointed him associate professor of sociology. In this landmark book, Bell argued that with the collapse of ideologies, by which he meant especially Marxism, there had emerged a more pragmatic consensus in which groups disagreed over a relatively narrow range of differences. In 1969 he moved on to a professorship at Harvard. Then, with *The Coming of Post-industrial Society: A Venture in Social Forecasting* (1973), he offered a provocative analysis of the shift from manufacturing to service industries, emphasizing the importance of technological elites and the turn to communalism in politics. From the late 1940s on, he remained, as he said of himself in 1978, "a socialist in economics, a liberal in politics, and a conservative in culture."[7]

His *Cultural Contradictions of Capitalism* had considerable resonance for those who were grappling with the consequences of the energy crisis. Bell offered a sweeping and complex analysis of an America which the excessive pursuit of affluence and self-gratification threatened to tear apart. Although he suggested solutions, it was hard not to read his book as pessimistic, almost apocalyptic. "The contradictions I see in contemporary capitalism," he declared in the opening paragraph, "derive from the unraveling of the threads which had once held the culture and the economy together, and from the influence of the hedonism which has become the prevailing value in our society." Once society had been an integral whole, he argued, with different realms operating in harmony; both industrialism and the larger culture depended on discipline and restraint. Now, America was coming apart: "The different realms respond to different norms, have different rhythms of change, and are regulated by different, even contrary, axial principles." Bell identified three such areas that, governed by opposing principles, were in a conflict so monumental that it threatened to undermine the health of Western society. The first was the "techno-economic," ruled by rationality, efficiency, and economizing. The second was the polity, in which expanding claims for social justice and equality had led to an ever-greater sense of entitlement among citizens. The third was the culture, in the sense of the search for meaning in expressive forms. What increasingly governed this sector was the "expression and remaking of the 'self' in order to achieve self-realization and self-fulfillment."[8]

In earlier ages these areas had operated in concert, but now they were in conflict. Since the 1870s, the cultural realm had grown increasingly powerful.

Its values had become so destructive that it threatened to undermine both the economy and the polity. By the 1920s, great forces had eroded the Protestant ethic of hard work and impelled the culture of pleasure to make claims in all realms of activity. Bell singled out the cult of artistic creativity, the emphasis on spontaneity and the new, changes in technology, the demise of the small town, the growth of advertising, and the rise in the standard of living. Pursuit of increasing prosperity drove the society, with envy and appearances in the saddle. Although Bell certainly realized the importance of long-range forces, he singled out the 1960s as the time when a culture of self-fulfillment threatened to triumph over all. "The rise of a hip-drug-rock culture on the popular level," in which "impulse and pleasure alone" dominated, would undermine "the social structure itself by striking at the motivational and psychic-reward system which has sustained it."[9]

Rejecting a Marxist interpretation of history that saw the economic base as the cause of changes in the political and cultural superstructure, Bell believed that "culture has become supreme." It had achieved such preeminence for several reasons. The commitment to the new and innovative, unchecked in the cultural realm because of the triumph of the avant-garde, made culture "the most dynamic component of our civilization." Society legitimated this position for expressive forms, sanctioning a "ceaseless search for a new sensibility." Although there was nothing to slow the adoption of the new and sensational in the culture, forces existed to check innovation elsewhere, such as resources in the economy and its institutions, as well as competing veto factions in politics.[10]

Thus, self-fulfillment and the chase after a higher standard of living had obliterated competing goals in the cultural realm. Religious virtues had lost their hold, and "pop hedonism" had triumphed, replacing guilt with anxiety. The United States, once held together by a covenant or social compact, had become a nation of self-seeking individuals who sought pleasure, not God. The pursuit of pleasure, based in part on consumption, not only suffused the culture but threatened the economy as well. Capitalism no longer had a "moral or transcendent ethic." Rather, by abandoning "a moral system of reward rooted in the Protestant sanctification of work," capitalism had "substituted a hedonism which promises moral ease and luxury." The result was a growing disjuncture between the requirements of an economy based on rationality and hard work and a culture committed to pleasure and play. Capitalism's dependency on the new, on instant gratification, and on a celebration of plenitude had had devastating consequences for both the work ethic and economic rationality.[11]

The triumph of gratification also ate away at the polity. In a world where scarcity and inequality reigned, it was possible to restrain demands that the state serve individual needs. But several ominous changes had occurred. More and more, the state had to fulfill not just individual ends but collective ones. Especially dangerous were the unrestrained claims that groups made on the public sector. As an example, Bell pointed to African Americans' demands for "rights as a 'property' of their color" and, especially through affirmative action, the shift "from a claim of equality of opportunity to equality of results." More generally, with "the ideological rationale of the impulse quest as a mode of conduct" driving people, the lack of restraint in the political realm became corrosive. "When everyone in society joins in the demand for more," he argued, "expecting this as a matter of right," limited resources led to an overloading of the political system with rapidly increasing claims of entitlement. Liberalism, with its "basic permissiveness" and its commitment to growth, was incapable of defining the boundaries of its largesse. By the 1960s, he argued, the public sector had irreversibly committed itself "to redress the impact of all economic and social inequalities." The result was what Bell called "the revolution of rising entitlements," not just among the poor and minorities but among all social groups who called on the government to meet not only their needs but also their wants. The nation had to face the question of how to restrain rising political demands for public provision of well-being, for such claims would overload an already strained public sector and, if unmet, would cause "increased political instability and discontent."[12]

For Bell, these tensions formed the cultural contradictions of capitalism. The conflicts between an economy based on rationality and efficiency, a polity based on equality and justice, and a culture based on pleasure had brought the nation to a breaking point. "This cultural contradiction," Bell claimed, "is, in the longer run, the most fateful division in the society." In a modern nation such as the United States, the demand for public goods and services conflicted with the requirement that an economic system be efficient. An expressive culture that emphasized irrationality threatened the rationality of the economy. Calls for social justice conflicted with the need to restrain inflation and enhance economic growth. Individualism expressed through fulfilling public and private needs undermined a polity committed to communal goals which restraint made possible.[13]

Bell offered two solutions to the dire situation he diagnosed. To begin with, he called for a return to religion. An atheist since age thirteen who identified himself as a Jew, he did not fully articulate how religion could serve as a counter to culture's excesses, and he avoided any discussion of the nature of this religion. Indeed, the roles he wanted religion to play were often more philosophical and social than spiritual. With secular meanings proved illusory, modernism and cultural radicalism exhausted, and bourgeois values devastated, what was useful to him about religion, as it was to Alexis de

Tocqueville, albeit in a different way, was that it set limits and imposed, in Bell's words, "moral norms on culture." Religion could restore "the continuity of generations, returning us to the existential predicaments which are the ground of humility and care for others." Religion also undergirded "a tragic sense of life," a powerful counter to the quest for self-fulfillment.[14]

If Bell's discussion of religion as a solution to the cultural contradictions of capitalism was sketchy, his treatment of the restoration of a commitment to a public good that transcended individual desires was focused and extensive. What Americans needed, he remarked, was "the spontaneous willingness to make sacrifices for some public good, and a political philosophy that justified the normative rules of priorities and allocations in the society." He called for a "public household" that was market oriented but did not abandon larger social goals. It would rely on "the principle of relevant differences in deciding the justice of various claims." The sense of common good would help reconcile political liberalism with demands for communal goals. In short, given the "recurrent restraint of 'scarcity,'" society had to come to "a consensual agreement on the normative issues of distributive justice." What was required was a sense of civil responsibility that would prompt people to "forgo the temptation of private enrichment at the expense of the public weal." The creation of a sense of public good would rest on the rejection of "bourgeois hedonism, with its utilitarian emphasis on economic appetite," and the restoration of "political liberalism, with its concern for individual differences and liberty."[15]

Bell's understanding of the world around him was powerful if problematic. From the perspective of more than a quarter of a century later, it is hard to accept that the culture of hedonism had triumphed so totally, that the pressures for entitlements were irresistible, or that the three realms were all that disjunctive. With drafts of chapters published as early as 1961, the book took its inspiration from Bell's reaction to the social movements of the 1960s even as it provided a guide for those perplexed by the 1970s. Thus, like many Jewish intellectuals shaped by radicalism in the late 1930s and early 1940s, Bell was responding to what he saw as the excesses of the 1960s—not only the hedonism, the experimentation with drugs and sex, the violence in cities and on university campuses, but also the demands of insurgent social groups. In comparison, he made few references to the key events of the 1970s: none to Watergate or explicitly to the energy crisis, and relatively few to Vietnam and the environment. Instead Bell focused on the cultural excesses of the previous decade even though he admitted that they were "largely spent." He lavished attention on the power of culture even as he acknowledged that "questions of culture have now receded," replaced by preoccupation "with the more nagging and threatening questions of shortages, scarcities, inflation, and structural imbalances of income and wealth within and between nations." Yet if the emotional center of Bell's effort was his grappling with the 1960s, the book had considerable explanatory power for the 1970s. The emphasis on entitlements, a return to religion, and the restoration of public good resonated with neoconservatism, a term coined by Michael Harrington.[16]

The Cultural Contradictions of Capitalism was a deeply pessimistic book. Bell pictured a nation torn asunder by conflicting principles, fights over scarce resources, the necessity for trade-offs, and an overloaded polity. Yet for him the real crisis was deeper than the particulars of any decade. In a profound sense, the cultural crisis was one "which beset bourgeois societies and which, in the longer run, devitalize a country, confuse the motivations of individuals, instill a sense of *carpe diem*, and undercut the civic will." What Americans had to confront, he asserted, was that with old faiths destroyed and new ones not yet established, nihilism was perhaps all that remained. Bell's pessimism rested on a sense of disorder and spiritual bankruptcy that stemmed from the triumph of an ethic of self-fulfillment. Affluence and the excessively expressive culture it underwrote had triumphed. The spiritual crisis that originated in an affluent society could be met only by a renewed sense of the public good and by a return to religion. With *The Culture of Narcissism*, published three years after *The Cultural Contradictions of Capitalism*, Christopher Lasch articulated many of these same themes in a book that reached a wider audience than had Bell's.[17]

Christopher Lasch: *The Culture of Narcissism* (1979)

Christopher Lasch (1932–1994) grew up in Omaha and in a Chicago suburb. His father was an editorial writer for the *Omaha World Herald* and then for the *Chicago Sun-Times*, and his mother, who held a Ph.D. in philosophy from Bryn Mawr, was a social worker, teacher, and volunteer. Lasch inherited from his parents a midwestern progressivism and what he later called a "militant" secularism. He graduated summa cum laude from Harvard in 1954 and earned his Ph.D. from Columbia in 1961, where he met and later married the daughter of the noted historian and public intellectual Henry Steele Commager. After teaching at Williams College, Roosevelt University, the University of Iowa, and Northwestern University, Lasch joined the faculty of the University of Rochester in 1970.[18]

Over the course of his life, Lasch made a series of ideological transitions that fundamentally shaped his response to affluence. From the late 1940s through the mid-1960s, he remained unequivocally on the left. In the 1940s and 1950s, he supported disengaging from the cold war with the USSR and worried about threats to civil liberties and the growth of "the militarization of American life." In the late 1950s and early 1960s, Lasch deepened his commitment to a radical analysis and politics. He appreciated President Eisenhower's 1960 warning about the hold of a military-industrial complex and rejected President Kennedy's embrace of cold war liberal realism. His critique of liberalism and the belief in progress found expression in his first book, *American Liberals and the Russian Revolution* (1962). In the early 1960s, his reading (including John Kenneth Galbraith's *Affluent Society* and Paul Goodman's *Growing Up Absurd*) and disillusionment with American politics, international relations especially, drove him further to the left. His disaffection became apparent in *The New Radicalism in America, 1889–1963: The Intellectual as a Social Type* (1965), in which he argued for an engaged detachment. With the Cuban missile crisis in 1962 and the escalation of the war in Vietnam, he aligned himself with the New Left and the burgeoning student movement as he protested American foreign policy and the complicity of the university in the military-industrial complex.[19]

By the late 1960s, however, he was growing increasingly disillusioned with what he later called the "pseudo-radicalism" that "only the children of privilege . . . could indulge themselves in," a stance prefigured in his earlier writings. More engaged in a generational battle than in the racial issues the civil rights movement highlighted, he opposed in particular the way increasingly radicalized students "indiscriminately condemned all institutions," including universities, and "equated 'liberation' with anarchic personal freedom." His response to the upheavals of the late 1960s found expression in *The Agony of the American Left* (1969), in which he criticized American radicals from the 1890s to the 1960s for their romanticism and alienation, their increasingly sloppy theory, and their willed irrelevance to the lives of people who might provide a mass base necessary for a social movement. He feared that the New Left was repeating the mistakes of its historical predecessors. Lasch considered himself a socialist scholar and immersed himself in Marxist literature, especially the reformulated Marxism of E. P. Thompson and Raymond Williams and the mixture of Sigmund Freud and Karl Marx offered by members of the Frankfurt school. This led him to engage the critique of mass culture articulated by both émigré and native-born intellectuals.[20]

By the mid-1970s, Lasch had begun to develop his own wide-ranging critique of American culture, a central component of which was his analysis of the corrosive power of consumer culture. Driven by corporate capitalism, he argued, the growth of materialism undermined the authenticity of human experience and fostered instead a devastating assault on restraint in the name of the pursuit of empty pleasure. He spelled out his position in a series of influential and provocative books from 1977 until his death in 1994, including *Culture of Narcissism*. In 1991 he described how in the 1970s his commitments as a husband and father of four had shaped his interest in issues of family life, character, and personality, the challenges to the authority of institutions and to the promise of sustaining public and private lives. Faced with a series of international crises and threats to the quality of public and private life, with his family and friends he hoped to recreate what he called "the intensity of common purpose, which could no longer be found in politics or the workplace." For him, "to see the modern world from the point of view of a parent is to see it in the worst possible light." His work as a historian and cultural critic grew from sources that were not only personal but also political and intellectual, as became abundantly clear in the books he wrote: *Haven in a Heartless World: The Family Besieged* (1977), *The Culture of Narcissism* (1979), *The Minimal Self: Psychic Survival in Troubled Times* (1984), *The True and Only Heaven: Progress and Its Critics* (1991), and the posthumously published *Revolt of the Elites and the Betrayal of Democracy* (1995).[21]

By the 1970s, Lasch had developed a tragic vision of American life in which his analysis of affluence and consumer culture played a central role. He warned both liberals and radicals that they had too much faith in progress, too little awareness of history, and too much distance from the people whose lives they were trying to improve. To Lasch, liberals were mistakenly optimistic in their belief that, along with freedom and democracy, history brought moral and material progress that allowed among other things, an increasing satisfaction of wants and desires through consumer culture. In contrast, he believed that progress involved increased control over all aspects of modern life—by corporations, by a centralized government that drew much of its inspiration from liberalism, and by the helping professions. Rather than liberating people, the progress that liberal individualists and corporate capitalists alike proposed had trapped them, stripping people of sources of genuine satisfaction. In the realm of production, routinized work had become alienating and separated from family life. Reformers, the state, and the professions had invaded the family, in the process undermining its authority and the realm of private life. Feminists had fully contributed to the undermining of the family and the fostering of a false sense of liberation. Elites, especially those on the left, had isolated themselves from the people they claimed to be helping. Consumer culture, the compensation offered by capitalists and liberals who believed in liberation offered in place of meaningful work and family life, further eroded psychological integrity. This left individuals with a sense of empty yearning that was impossible to fulfill. The search for self-fulfillment through consumption and therapy had turned America into a hedonist society. All these forces undermined real work, an authentic sense of self, and a morally grounded faith.[22]

In *The Culture of Narcissism*, the book central to understanding the mood of the late 1970s and Carter's speech specifically, Lasch was in the process of spelling out his larger vision. It had its origins in his earlier books, but its complete outlines (especially on the issue of remedies) would not become fully apparent until the 1990s. Although his words sounded like those of "a fire-breathing figure," noted his friend Jean Bethke Elshtain, in person he was a man of "rectitude and modesty." Frank Kermode, writing in the *New York Times Book Review*, was not alone in reading Lasch's book as "a civilized hellfire sermon, with little promise of salvation." Indeed, at the outset Lasch stated what he found so prominent in contemporary America: "the culture of competitive individualism, which in its decadence has carried the logic of individualism to the extreme of a war of all against all, the pursuit of happiness to the dead end of a narcissistic preoccupation with the self."[23]

In describing the culture of narcissism, Lasch relied on a growing body of psychiatric literature. In a leap that was as critical to his argument as it was problematic, he transformed narcissism from a disorder affecting individuals to a social illness. "On the principle that pathology represents a heightened version of normality," Lasch argued, "the 'pathological narcissism' found in character disorders . . . should tell us something about narcissism as a social phenomenon." Every generation develops its own characteristic form of mental illness, he declared, and for contemporary Americans it was narcissism, whose traits included "dependency on vicarious warmth provided by others combined with a fear of dependence, a sense of inner emptiness, boundless repressed rage, and unsatisfied oral cravings." True for people from all of American society, not just the middle class, this pathology went far beyond mere selfishness. When he used the phrase "age of diminishing expectations" in the subtitle of the book, Lasch was underscoring the connection between culture, personality, and economic conditions. In a nation ravaged by the erosion of savings by inflation, people no longer hoped to prosper and instead were struggling to survive.[24]

For Lasch, narcissism appeared in every corner of the culture. With tragic consequences, the liberal welfare state, media, corporations, and experts had transformed the society and in the process all but destroyed genuine forms of work, love, and community. Indeed, the book derived its power in good measure from his ability to reveal how the culture of narcissism was turning sports into spectacle, using celebrities to create a cult of personality, undermining genuine political engagement, and promoting a banal "pseudo-self-awareness" in therapies that were becoming a new religion. "The ideology of personal growth, superficially optimistic, radiates a profound despair and resignation," he lamented at a time when a wildly popular book urged readers to say, "I'm OK, You're OK." He called this "the faith of those without faith." In a society suffused by narcissism, people were cut off from their past and felt no commitment to the future. In his dystopian view, the past was a better time when the work ethic reigned and guilt still had power. In an especially controversial section, Lasch identified feminism as one of the forces, along with the intervention of experts and the state, that undermined the patriarchal family.[25]

Consumer culture and affluence were among the many causes of the rise of narcissism to such a powerful position. The "cult of consumption" suffused modern American society. American capitalism subordinated "possession itself to appearance and measures exchange value as a commodity's capacity to confer prestige—the illusion of prosperity and well-being." Elites in management and the professions no longer identified with hard work but with "an ethic of leisure, hedonism, and self-fulfillment." The ability to reproduce culture by mechanical means was eroding people's grasp on reality. The "self" itself had become a saleable good, as if the individual's "own personality were a commodity with an assignable market value." Advertising, by fostering an unquenchable appetite for goods and experiences, left consumers "perpetually unsatisfied, restless, anxious, bored." It held out the possibility that buying more would provide "the answer to the age-old discontents of loneliness, sickness, weariness, lack of sexual satisfaction; at the same time it creates new forms of discontent peculiar to the modern age," promising as it did self-fulfillment and a sense of completeness. The "propaganda of consumption" offered purchasable goods and experience as substitutes for political action, turned politics into spectacle, made alienation a commodity, and institutionalized envy. It fostered in women and young people a false sense of emancipation, freeing them "from patriarchal authority . . . only to subject them to the new paternalism of the advertising industry, the industrial corporation, and the state."[26]

The Culture of Narcissism was stronger on analysis than it was on solutions. Certainly the thrust of what he was saying was that Americans should give up infantile fantasies and take pleasure instead in genuine work, love, and community. He neither played up nor spelled out what he meant when he called for a "socialist revolution." Lasch framed the book with a vague call for a better future that relied on a combination of radical social change and conservative values. At the beginning of the book, Lasch noted that he had found evidence "of a general political revolt" stirring "in small towns and crowded urban neighborhoods, even in suburbs" where "men and women have initiated modest experiments in cooperation, designed to defend their rights against the corporations and the state." And he concluded that "the will to build a better society . . . survives, along with traditions of localism, self-help, and community action that only need the vision of a new society, a decent society, to give them new vigor." He staked his hopes on the connection between morality and work which he found surviving in people who did not take the promise of American life for granted.[27]

The Culture of Narcissism became a national best-seller and generated heated debate in print and at conferences. The review by Henry Allen in the *Washington Post* is especially revealing of the dangers Lasch faced. "How we've craved The Word," Allen wrote, apparently unaware that he was turning Lasch into a celebrity and the book into a commodity, both of which tendencies Lasch had exposed as problematic. "How we've ached for someone to define it all," he continued, "to wrap up the 1970s like a Christmas present." Allen hailed *The Culture of Narcissism* as "the big intellectual book of the season, the one for everyone to feel guilty about not reading," unintentionally underscoring what Lasch had to say about the vitiation of guilt in contemporary society. Lasch surely resented Allen's suggestion that some of what he wrote was "rooted in Lasch's personal experience, a sad heart at the supermarket." Nor could he have been pleased with Allen's picture of him as a historian who saw no necessity to use facts to bolster his case.[28]

When Lasch responded to his critics, he made clear how strongly he opposed the reading of his book as a jeremiad. In private correspondence, he lamented that people had misunderstood his book, especially in reading it as full of despair. "It appears to some readers as a 'pessimistic' book," he wrote a correspondent, "only in the current climate of escapism, and also perhaps because it does not propose 'alternatives,' 'solutions.'" His book, he asserted at a conference, was "a contribution to social theory and social criticism, not to the literature of moral indignation." On this occasion he stated a number of points more clearly and unambiguously than he had in the book itself. He claimed that he had directed his attack "not against selfishness or the pursuit of gain but against capitalism itself." He dissociated his work "in the strongest possible way, from . . . those pseudo-critical confections, neither honest journalism nor honest sociology, which the publishing industry likes to pass off as profound social commentary." He felt an urgency about this issue since his own publisher, in promoting the paperback version of his book, had placed it in the tradition of pop sociology with Alvin Toffler's *Future Shock* (1970) and Gail Sheehy's *Passages* (1976). He did not want to return to the past, he insisted. He wished to combine conservative values with radical analysis. Lasch reiterated, more strongly than he had in the book, his belief that socialism was the solution to society's problems. "Only a new movement for radical reform," he argued, "can provide a democratic focus for popular discontent." The left, he said, had made fundamental mistakes. He attacked the "aging revolutionaries" who, by adopting the strategies of liberation and values of self-indulgence, reflected "the culture of consumerism more than they challenge it." By promoting the hedonistic values of a cultural revolution, the left not only "played into the hands of the corporations" but also "turned its back on its proper constituency," the Middle Americans "who cling to family life, religion, the work ethic, and other ostensibly outmoded values and institutions as the only source of stability in an otherwise precarious existence." More clearly than he had in his book, he elaborated the consequences of living in an age of "diminishing expectations." Energy shortages, escalating prices and unemployment, and the end of Western colonialism were undermining "the economic foundation of hedonistic self-expression." The end of a period of unrestrained economic growth, plus the cultural crises of authority and values, would result in a series of Hobbesian battles that would "become increasingly desperate and bitter."[29]

In *The True and Only Heaven: Progress and Its Critics* (1991), Lasch extended these arguments, in the process making even clearer the direction in which he had been heading with *The Culture of Narcissism*. Now he found his heroes in people who opposed the liberal faith in optimism, progress, and liberation. He appreciated the moral realism of the lower middle class, which served for him as a counter to the corrosive belief in progress that experts and capitalism offered. He celebrated the prophetic tradition of figures such as Martin Luther King Jr. and Reinhold Niebuhr. He located a heritage of moral criticism that opposed unrestrained, compulsive consumption. Together, these and other social and intellectual traditions provided the basis for what he called a "populism" that emphasized the benefits of virtue rather than self-interest, satisfying work in place of empty consumption, a sense of human limitations instead of a belief in limitless self-fulfillment, particularism not universalism, and memory instead of nostalgia. These traditions provided the inspiration for his sense of limits to human achievement and economic development. They enabled him to replace unlimited optimism with bounded hope and a sense of the tragic. Lasch honored authentic selfhood, genuine civic participation, the producer ethic best achieved on a small scale, and resistance to the hope of a limitless consumer cornucopia. Lasch belongs on the left, as usually defined, because of his critique of larger-scale capitalist organizations, of the market as a mechanism for achieving justice, and of the consumer culture that results from corporate capitalism. Because he seemed more like a conservative than a friendly critic of the left from within, however, he has earned the admiration of the right. He criticized feminists, advocating patriarchy and the bourgeois family in place of women's liberation. He conveyed a sense of the tragic. He warned about the invasiveness of the welfare system and the elitism of experts and intellectuals. He celebrated work, moral responsibility, and self-restraint. And he made clear his admiration for the lower middle class.[30]

Robert Bellah: *The Broken Covenant* (1975)

Born in 1927 in a small town in Oklahoma where his father was editor and publisher of the local paper, Robert Bellah was descended on both sides of his family from Protestants who had lived in America for many generations. After his father died when Bellah was two, he moved to Los Angeles with his mother. From her he absorbed "fragments of a once coherent, Southern Protestant culture." In Los Angeles he went to a Presbyterian Sunday school that was, he later remarked, "conservative without being fundamentalist." He lived in a household where reading was important and in a heterogeneous neighborhood that included many Jews whom he counted among his friends. He grew up shaped by "fairly conventional Protestant and patriotic" beliefs, leavened by an education informed by the democratic ideals of John Dewey. Developing an increasingly liberal perspective during his high school years, he came to question the religious and political pieties he had once taken for granted. By his senior year of high school, he had begun to read Marxist literature.[31]

With this tension between conventionality and rebellion as a background, Bellah became radicalized at Harvard, which he entered after serving in the army from 1945 to 1946. In 1948 he married his high school sweetheart, who was Jewish. As an undergraduate he deepened his familiarity with Marxism, which became for him "a transposition of his Protestantism: idealistic, moral, puritanical," which enabled him to "escape from the constrictions of provincial American culture." He read Marx, increasingly questioned the rosy picture of American society with which he had grown up, and assumed a leadership position in the undergraduate unit of the Communist Party. In 1949, the party, in one of its hard-line moments, he later remarked, "engaged in a real intra-party witch-hunt" of which Bellah was a victim. Coming on the heels of the failed 1948 presidential campaign of Henry Wallace, this confronted Bellah with what he later called the "broken idol" of his radicalism. He later claimed that the Soviet Union had never really interested him. His academic pursuits led him to search instead among Native Americans and the Japanese for "a degree of cultural authenticity" and cultural integrity which he found missing in America.[32]

As a graduate student at Harvard from 1949 to 1955, when he studied both Asian languages and sociology, Bellah reformulated his political ideology. Though he never fully abandoned his radicalism, a number of influences caused Bellah to recast his politics: these included the final years of Stalin's rule, the sociology of Talcott Parsons, and the Christian existentialism of Paul Tillich. At the same time, during the McCarthy years he was subjected to threats to his academic freedom. In 1954, when Bellah was still a graduate student, McGeorge Bundy, then the dean of the Faculty of Arts and Sciences and later a chief architect of the Vietnam War, warned Bellah that unless he was completely candid about his past and present political belief and affiliations and those of his associates, he would lose his fellowship and his academic career would suffer. A week later the FBI picked Bellah up for questioning; he agreed to talk about himself but not others. In the spring of 1955, as Bellah was completing his thesis, Bundy offered a teaching appointment but again warned Bellah that his refusal to answer any question put to him in an authorized investigation would place his job in jeopardy. Refusing to accept the position on such terms, Bellah turned down the offer and went to Canada, where from 1955 to 1957 he held a position as a research associate at McGill University. When the hold of McCarthyism waned and Harvard changed its policy, Bellah returned in 1957. Ten years later he accepted a position in the sociology department at Berkeley, where he remained for the rest of his career.[33]

In Bellah's first book, *Tokugawa Religion: The Values of Pre-industrial Japan* (1957), he applied Max Weber's examination of the relationship between religious values and industrialization to premodern Japan. At a time when Americans were celebrating affluence, he chose to consider "the relation of religion to that ethic of inner-worldly asceticism which is so powerful in Japan" and which was present, he wrote, in communism as well. He noted that in Japan, "the obligation to hard, selfless labor and to the restraint of one's own desires for consumption" was closely connected to "the obligations to sacred and semisacred superiors which are so stressed in Japanese religion" and to "that state of selfless identification with ultimate nature." Thus the case of premodern Japan confirmed what Weber had asserted for premodern Europe. In Japan, the religious-based ethic of "diligence and frugality" not only helped purify "the self of evil desires and impulses" but also fostered the "economic rationalization" so necessary for industrialization.[34]

In the late 1950s and 1960s, Bellah remained politically engaged. He supported the civil rights movement and opposed American involvement in Vietnam. The events he witnessed from the mid-1950s on influenced him in profound ways. They shaped and reshaped the tensions he felt between pessimism and optimism, as well as between progressive American ideals and harsh, tragic realities. They reinforced his sense of connection to the great traditions in America's past even as they impelled him to search that past (and non-Western traditions) for strands he might use in an oppositional way. His engagement with Marxism and then later with existential Christianity undergirded his search for a wholeness from which to understand the world, albeit, as he remarked as he contemplated his lapse from orthodox Marxism, a wholeness that sought to reclaim "the self-critical, self-revising, non-totalistic aspects of tradition."[35]

Never abandoning the cross-cultural perspectives that had shaped him, by the mid-1960s he turned his attention to the study of his own nation. The 1960s both reinvigorated his oppositional stance and impelled him to search in the counterculture and new political movements on the left for adversarial forces that spoke to him of a sense of connection with American traditions. In a series of writings in the 1970s, he spelled out complicated arguments in which religion, socialism, and citizenship served as counters to the excesses of Americans, including self-interest and affluence. His views emerged most fully in a work he labeled a "jeremiad," *The Broken Covenant: American Civil Religion in Time of Trial,* delivered as a series of lectures in 1971 and published in 1975. In *Beyond Belief: The New Religious Consciousness* (1976), Bellah and his colleagues reported on their studies of political and religious movements in the Bay Area in the early 1970s. In separate articles, he filled out his argument in a variety of contexts. He was writing as the crises of Watergate and Vietnam were coming to a head from the perspective of Berkeley, where new experimental politics and religion first flowered, then were threatened by both internal disintegration and external repression. By the mid-1970s, Bellah reported in *Broken Covenant,* he had come to accept the tension between America's highest aspirations and the "cruel and bitter realities" of contemporary society. He embarked on a search for sources of religious and moral strength in the American tradition and in contemporary American life—sources he thought might provide salvation for the nation.[36]

Bellah's critique of American society in the 1970s rested on his sense that the nation had strayed from its historic moral and religious paths which had once provided the basis for resistance to excessive materialism and individualism. For him, America's deeply embedded and powerful, biblically based civil religion was a source of restraint on excessive self-interest, which he saw in the pursuit of material well-being, among other areas. Drawing on his view of America in the eighteenth century, he expressed appreciation for a society governed by republican virtue, which would lead "to a public spiritedness, a willingness of the citizen to sacrifice his own interests for the common good."[37]

In modern times, forces came together to undermine these moral and religious traditions. Republican virtue and liberal individualism, community and individualism, morality and economics, politics and religion, once bound closely together, were now increasingly torn apart. Over time, utilitarian individualism had corrupted biblical religion in such a way that American religion now fostered self-interest rather than morality or community. "A technical-rational model of politics" and an embrace of utilitarianism, underwritten by the triumph of the market and industrial capitalism, fostered a focus on means, not ends. A commitment to freedom, which had originally been intimately connected to virtue, over the course of American history had become equivalent to the "freedom to pursue self-interest." With the sense of self, interest, and virtue disconnected from a larger moral, religious, and communal vision came the demise of a set of common understandings and obligations to anything or anyone beyond the self. The triumph of liberal individualism had resulted in corruption and dependence, which he defined as "that pursuit of material things that diverts us from concern for public good, or what we would today call 'consumerism.'"[38]

Bellah was deeply pessimistic, finding around him more evidence of decline than of revival. "The specter of complete collapse looms on the horizon," he wrote, referring to defeats abroad as well as to social, economic, and environmental problems at home. He saw America in the 1970s facing a severe trial that would test "whether we can control the very economic and technical forces, which are our greatest achievement, before they destroy us." The narrow definition of virtue and success had, he believed, taken a heavy toll on women, the young, and especially on African Americans. Like Bell, Bellah believed that capitalism made accumulation a goal rather than a means. "The established structures of economic and political power seem perversely set on maximizing wealth and power," he wrote, at a tremendous cost to social and environmental justice.[39]

Bellah had difficulty locating sources of resistance to the demise of morally and religiously based restraints and to the triumph of a narrow definition of freedom. A practicing Episcopalian, he had little hope that mainline Christian churches, already facing declining membership and resources, could provide focal points of revival. As religious authority in the United States shifted away from denominations that historically expressed communal responsibility, "privatistic and self-centered" groups took hold. Although he cautioned his readers that fundamentalists were not "backwater yokels," he nonetheless saw little promise in evangelical or fundamentalist Protestantism. He thought it possible that authoritarianism would come to America through "right-wing Protestant fundamentalism" and rejected as utopian the possibility that a reinvigorated fundamentalism might "provide the mass base for a successful effort to establish the revolutionary alternative" that would include a critique of affluence.[40]

Nor could he find much reason for hope in American politics. "Purely technical and administrative solutions have again and again broken down," he wrote, cut off as they were both from the beneficiaries of social programs and from a sense of the larger goals they might fulfill. In Vietnam, Bellah believed, "our very intoxication with our own power" had led the nation "into untenable situations where the cost of 'victory' became so great that it was no longer tolerable." Although he acknowledged the rising crime rate, he found more serious "the corrosion of morality at the highest reaches of government and business." The perfidy and evil of Richard M. Nixon struck him especially hard. American presidents, he believed, doubtless with both Nixon and Lyndon Johnson in mind, had betrayed the national covenant. Nixon's pursuit of the war in Vietnam, his use of state power to hound radicals, and the corruption of the political system so evident in Watergate threatened to bring despotism to America. Moreover, the 1976 presidential campaign, in which the pious Jimmy Carter defeated a stolid Gerald Ford, promised little in the way of a fruitful marriage of politics and religion. Although Bellah found some evidence in the campaign of a yearning for the restoration of a lost tradition, all the nation had got was "vague and listless allusions to a largely misunderstood and forgotten past, and an attitude toward the present" that hardly probed "beneath the thinnest of surfaces."[41]

To reverse the appalling situation, Bellah called for "a new imaginative, religious, moral, and social context for science and technology" that would "make it possible to weather the storms that seem to be closing in on us in the late 20th century." Following Tocqueville, he saw religion as a force that would counter excessive commercialism and pursuit of self-interest. Bellah called for a restoration of a sense "of the covenant and virtue." With American lives "largely ruled by an insistent commercial culture that is a parody of any tradition," the nation needed a reaffirmation of "the outward or external covenant and that includes the civil religion in its most classical form" that was found in the Declaration of Independence, the Bill of Rights, and the Fourteenth Amendment to the Constitution.[42]

Bellah located the best hope for such revivals of religion and values in the political and cultural movements of the 1960s and their remnants, or successor movements, in the 1970s. He outlined his views in *Broken Covenant*, and in *The New Religious Consciousness* he relied on empirical studies of religious and political movements in the Bay Area to clarify them. He looked at the groups that emerged from the counterculture and the New Left for evidence of the revival of historically grounded visions that contained "an apocalyptic or millennial note," characteristics that, given his sense of American history and of Asian religions, he viewed favorably. He applauded their critique of a nation "infatuated with materialism" and of "liberal utilitarian culture." Their millennial vision, their moral critique of American society, and their role as a saving remnant evoked for him the American traditions he so admired but found missing throughout much of the nineteenth and twentieth centuries. Even though he praised these movements, he hardly issued a sweeping endorsement of them. He was well aware of their excesses and dangers. He feared that if driven by "cynicism and moral anarchism," these movements could lead to "authoritarianism if not fascism." Moreover, he feared that the watered-down version of political and cultural movements simply served to "reinforce the narrow individualism and concern with self-interest that is the underside of the old American tradition, but now with few ethical restraints." He saw these experiments as providing the first steps toward a "national movement" that would meld a vision that was at once socialist, moral, religious, and political.[43]

Although he found much to admire in the political radicalism of students in the late 1960s, of more importance to him was evidence of the "religious dimension of the cultural transformation of young people" who participated in the counterculture. He expressed a sympathetic understanding of those who had questioned "whether we could not, without losing the many good things in our society, have a freer impulse life, a richer imaginative consciousness, be less alienated from our bodies, be capable of more profound intimacy with a few and more community with many others." Bellah found in the counterculture the clearest challenge to utilitarian individualism, as tens of thousands of young people used music, drugs, and sexual experimentation to "question whether the quality of life was a simple function of wealth and power, or whether the endless accumulation of wealth and power was not destroying the quality and meaning of life, ecologically and sociologically." These young people drew on Asian religious and spiritual traditions which, more than a biblical tradition eviscerated by liberal individualism, provided a counter to the pursuit of affluence, status, and careerism. Yet in the end, despite his appreciation for the counterculture and his hope for the revival of older American traditions, Bellah found unlikely the possibility that the successors to the counterculture—American followers of Asian religions and practitioners of the human potential movement—were paving the way for a revolutionary situation that would return America to a simpler, less materialistic way of life.[44]

Bellah dedicated *Broken Covenant* to the memory of his Harvard teacher F. O. Matthiessen, who, he said, had "embodied the tragic dimension of American culture in his own life." The dedication evokes complicated issues. Matthiessen, one of the most influential American literary scholars, had taught Bellah when he was an undergraduate at Harvard. A homosexual, a Christian, and a socialist, he fought for a wide variety of causes, including academic freedom at Harvard and the election of Henry Wallace in 1948. He was subject to continuing bouts of depression and became despondent after the 1945 death of his lover. The Soviet suppression of Czechoslovakian democracy (which had led to the possibly suicidal death by defenestration of

his acquaintance Jan Masaryk) and the criticism of him as a Stalinist intensified his pessimism. On March 31, 1950, he took his own life by jumping out
the window of a Boston hotel. In *Broken Covenant*, Bellah remarked that
Matthiessen knew "through objective observation and personal tragedy that
this society is a cruel and bitter one, very far, in fact, from its own highest
aspirations."[45]

Both of these remarks about tragedy appeared in the book's preface, dated
June 1974, almost three years after Bellah delivered them as lectures. He
faced tragedy himself in the years between lectures and publication, and his
sense of personal tragedy surely deepened his pessimism about America,
which derived in larger measure from the contrast between his hopes for his
country and the social and political realities so prevalent in the 1970s. As in
the writings of Bell and Lasch as well, Bellah's pessimism had both political
origins and cultural resonance, which would become amplified when President Carter spoke to the nation on July 15, 1979.[46]

Daniel Bell, Christopher Lasch, and Robert Bellah authored powerful and
deeply pessimistic critiques of 1970s America as a consumer culture, a nation
threatened by excessive self-expression as well as by the demise of religious
traditions and a sense of public good. Although their analyses, politics, and
solutions differed in important ways (for example, Lasch, unlike Bell and
Bellah, did not see religion as a bulwark against consumerism), they shared a
number of commitments. What one observer said of Lasch applies to Bell
and Bellah as well: they combined "cultural conservatism with a politics of
the left." They all believed that America's pursuit of endless (and mindless)
affluence and self-gratification posed serious threats to personal and national
well-being. They were all working to shape a social vision, formed in the
1940s and dominant until the late 1960s, which seemed to have outlasted its
usefulness. As intellectuals, they wanted their ideas to have an impact and
make a difference. In 1979 their moment came. Jimmy Carter, who shared
their moralistic attitudes toward consumer culture, invited all three of them
to talk with him about their writings. At the time, Carter was contemplating
the consequences of the energy crisis for his presidency and for the nation.[47]

8

Three Intellectuals and a President
Jimmy Carter, "Energy and the Crisis of Confidence"

On July 15, 1979, President Jimmy Carter delivered an address titled "Energy and the Crisis of Confidence" to an audience of 65 million Americans. Commonly known as the "malaise" speech, although he did not use the word, this address was one of the most memorable and controversial ones by an American president in the second half of the twentieth century. Evoking a nation plunged into crisis by the excesses of affluence, Carter suggested a comprehensive energy policy. A wide range of factors shaped the speech, from the demands of international and domestic politics to the conflicting advice of those to whom he listened. As the historian Leo Ribuffo has made abundantly clear, the president's Christian faith also informed his response to both affluence and energy policy. A Baptist and born-again evangelical, Carter was deeply concerned with issues such as the sin of pride, the limits on human power, and the role of morality in personal life and public policy. He worried about maintaining the line between his private faith and his public pronouncements. He struggled to achieve humility and opposed display and artifice. Here he drew on traditions that went back to the Protestant Reformation and continued to characterize those American Protestant groups that remained true to their humble origins. The president's cultivation of "a plain style," Ribuffo has noted, "reflected his private battle against pride" which in turn affected both his demeanor and his politics. During his presidential campaign, he insisted on carrying his own garment bag. After taking the oath of office, he walked down Pennsylvania Avenue from the Capitol to the White House. He canceled special limousine services for leading staff members. He eliminated fancy tablecloths and seating in order of rank at the

White House mess. Early in his presidency, he sold off the presidential yacht *Sequoia*, convinced that to the greatest extent possible, a president paid by the taxpayers should not live with the trappings of wealth.[1]

When he delivered the speech, Carter and his presidency were in trouble, despite the recent achievement of the Camp David accords, in which he persuaded Israeli prime minister Menachem Begin and Egyptian president Anwar Sadat to sign a historic Middle East peace agreement. The president faced Republican opposition, a divided Democratic Party (with those to Carter's left led by Senator Edward Kennedy), warring factions within his own administration, and congressional deadlock. For most of the 1970s, Watergate, the inglorious end of the war in Vietnam, and an economy caught in stagflation (a combination of rising prices, high unemployment, and slow economic growth) had undermined national confidence. Although the problems Carter faced were in many ways intractable, to some extent he was his own worst political enemy. He lacked the skills necessary to deal with a fractured Congress. Inflexible and isolated, he was more given to grand schemes and moralistic pronouncements than to coordinated efforts to develop policy or skillful political maneuvering.

Nowhere was this clearer than in his continual attempts to promote a comprehensive energy policy, a quest beset by political and economic challenges that would have been difficult to resolve under the best of circumstances. Until the late 1940s, the United States had been an exporter of energy. In the ensuing decades American energy use grew at a fast pace, a result of prosperity and cheap energy costs. Consequently, the nation became more dependent on OPEC. By 1977, the United States was importing almost 50 percent of its oil, up from 35 percent in 1973. The July 15 speech was Carter's fifth on energy policy.

A number of factors undermined his policy initiatives, which focused on increasing domestic production and decreasing consumption in order to lessen reliance on imported oil. Complex government regulation of energy prices and pressure from environmentalists hampered efforts to increase domestic production, while ingrained habits of consumers, developed over decades of abundant energy supplies, hampered plans to promote conservation. OPEC acted as a powerful quasi-monopoly, since its ability to raise prices and control production was difficult if not impossible to challenge. Conservative politicians and energy businesses often had the upper hand in dealing with already straitened consumers. The signs of trouble for Carter and the nation were abundant. In the spring and summer of 1979, inflation was running at a rate of over 12 percent, with gasoline prices having increased 55 percent in the first half of the year. In mid-1979, a poll reported that almost two thirds of Americans felt that the nation was in very serious trouble. In

June, Carter's approval ratings slipped to the mid-20s, as low as Nixon's during the Watergate crisis. Revolution in Iran cut off a key source of petroleum, and OPEC raised oil prices yet again. High prices, combined with gas shortages, long lines at gas stations, and sporadic violence over supplies, hardly enhanced the popularity of an already beleaguered president. By summer an energy crisis equal in severity to that of 1973 engulfed the nation. A week before the speech, 90 percent of the gas stations in the New York City metropolitan area were closed. In response to all these challenges, Carter worked on developing an energy policy and an explanation of the predicament in which the nation found itself.[2]

Patrick Caddell and the Crisis of Confidence

Although Carter relied on a number of advisers, his pollster and "intellectual gadfly" Patrick Caddell served as the conduit for and synthesizer of ideas developed by intellectuals, including Daniel Bell, Robert Bellah, and Christopher Lasch. Caddell, then in his late twenties, was a maverick who had entered national politics as an undergraduate at Harvard, when he served as the chief pollster for George McGovern's presidential campaign in 1972 in Massachusetts. The only non-Georgian in Carter's inner circle, and a Roman Catholic, Caddell commanded Carter's attention because he had a reputation as a brilliant pollster and an innovative conceptualizer. They also shared a sense that profound moral and spiritual issues lay at the heart of the crisis Carter and the nation faced.[3]

On April 23, 1978, in response to First Lady Rosalynn Carter's suggestion, Caddell wrote a seventy-five-page memo to the president titled "Of Crisis and Opportunity," but known among White House staffers as "Apocalypse Now." Looking forward bleakly to the 1980 election, Caddell ranged widely as he warned Carter of the crisis he faced and the opportunity it afforded him for leadership that could turn him into a president of the stature of Abraham Lincoln or Franklin Roosevelt. Caddell's central message was that Americans felt a "malaise" which signaled the depth of the nation's crisis, one unique in U.S. history. "Psychological more than material," he advised the president, it was "a crisis of confidence marked by a dwindling faith in the future," which had especially affected the "better educated, wealthier and younger." Caddell laid out the origins of the crisis—the assassination of beloved leaders, Watergate, Vietnam, stagflation, skyrocketing energy prices. The result was growing disaffection from politics and government and the plummeting standing of the president in the polls. In Caddell's memo Ronald Reagan was nowhere in sight; on the horizon was a more immediate threat to Carter—the candidacy of Ted Kennedy.[4]

In a paragraph headed "The 'Me' Generation," Caddell briefly summarized Christopher Lasch's *Culture of Narcissism*. Referring to Tom Wolfe's characterization of a generation, Caddell wrote that "it has become a cliché, as the country has turned increasingly inward. Personal gratification has replaced national involvement everywhere. Christopher Lasch has written a depressing, important best seller 'Narcissism in America'—the title," which Caddell had got wrong, "tells much." Caddell then went on to highlight other symptoms. "Spending as if there is no tomorrow," Americans lived for the present, taking on increasing debt, which had "replaced the stable rock of steady, prudent future planning." Productivity and a lack of commitment to the work ethic had declined dangerously. Greed and "selfishness seems to predominate everywhere" instead of "sacrifice," philanthropy, and a sense of national purpose. In his analysis of the challenge of affluence, Caddell mentioned James MacGregor Burns's *Leadership* (1979), including the political scientist's discussion of Abraham Maslow's treatment of a hierarchy of needs. Once their lower needs were satisfied, Caddell noted, Americans would turn to "affection and belongingness." He quoted an editor of *U.S. News and World Report* who had written of the "ennui of affluence," and also cited a 1930 essay by John Maynard Keynes in which the distinguished English economist had emphasized that in the long run the challenge of affluence called for a "return to some of the most sure and certain principles of religion and traditional virtue," including "that avarice is a vice, . . . the love of money is detestable, that those walk most truly in the paths of virtue and sane wisdom who take least thought for the morrow."[5]

After summarizing what he had read, Caddell concluded that the "structure of crisis" was a consequence of America's emerging in the 1960s as "the first true leisure society." As Keynes had predicted, this produced a crisis in which the nation had to ask itself "what is the nature, purpose, structure, and function of a post-survival society?" The country's leaders had to "define or transmit those higher unrealized needs" that Maslow had identified. Unfortunately, Caddell argued, the political system "failed to address" those needs. "Rather, politics," Caddell wrote, echoing Lasch, "has taken on the nature of a spectator sport," with the personalities of politicians looming larger in the decision of voters. "Single issue constituencies," Caddell noted, recalling Bell's emphasis on the general good, undermined the promise of "rough consensus democracy." The mass media, television especially, lowered the quality of political debate. With politics failing, in the end this "spiritual crisis" would "lead the society to turn inward, the spiritual bonds will weaken, and invisibly, the country will become intangibly but inexorably only a shadow of its former self."[6]

Caddell called on Carter to seize the opportunity to become a different kind of leader. He recommended that the president restore a sense of public good by strengthening traditional values rather than by campaigning for specific policies and programs. Among these virtues he included personal responsibility, "excellence in work, . . . spiritual and moral value regeneration." What was needed was a covenant, Caddell asserted, perhaps echoing Robert Bellah, which would restore the country's sense of purpose and national greatness.[7]

A Dinner at the White House

In the following months, Caddell and the president began what Caddell called "a shared reading program" that included the works of Bell, Lasch, and Bellah. Caddell was instrumental in arranging a May 30, 1979, dinner. The president met with a group of people for an extended discussion, including Bell and Lasch, as well as Caddell and Rosalynn Carter, Common Cause founder John Gardner, Jesse Jackson, *Washington Post* writer Haynes Johnson, Bill Moyers, *Washington Monthly* editor Charles Peters, and White House press secretary Jody Powell.[8]

The best available record of the dinner appears in a witty and thoughtful fifty-eight-page memoir that Bell composed in the summer of 1979. Relying on notes he had jotted down when he returned to his hotel room, Bell carefully reconstructed the conversation and the social dynamics of the evening. He remarked that while they were eating the second course, the president turned to Bell, who was sitting to his immediate left, and began an intense conversation that lasted about twenty minutes. "I've read your recent book on *The Cultural Contradictions of Capitalism*," Carter remarked, "and a number of things you say interest me enormously. Do you believe," the president asked, "that there will be a return to religion?" Bell answered that as people searched for a larger meaning to their lives, organized religion no longer served as a fully satisfactory anchor. Perhaps, Bell speculated, this was a historic moment when people were looking for a different way of understanding life. When the president asked what this might involve, Bell responded by discussing the quest for the kind of religious experience that connects people to the past. Carter then took Bell aback by saying, "I read in your book that you call yourself a socialist in economics, a liberal in politics, and a conservative in culture. Would you explain this to me?" Bell answered by emphasizing how critical to people's self-respect and social decency was a reasonable standard of living, the provision of which was the basic responsibility of the community. He contrasted this with wants that are psychological in nature, which those on the left wished to satisfy in ways that would either level society or narrow differences. The president was most interested in the distinction between needs and wants and in whether Bell saw provision of health care as a basic need. Bell acknowledged that he did.[9]

After dinner, the group began what turned out to be a three-hour discussion. The president opened the conversation by saying that though he believed he was doing a good job, he wanted to hear his guests' opinions about what he perceived as changing American values and a crisis of confidence. Carter asked Caddell to talk about how polling data revealed that Americans had lost confidence in the government and in the nation's future. There ensued a somewhat rambling discussion with a few notable highlights. At one point Carter turned to Lasch, acknowledged that he had read *The Culture of Narcissism*, and expressed interest in hearing what Lasch had to say. Just as Lasch began his response, the president was briefly called away for a phone call and the group adjourned to a sitting room. The president's remark to Lasch was not pursued. When the conversation resumed, Bell responded to a question posed by Rosalynn Carter about how to restore values. He expressed skepticism that this was something a government could do. Rather, he asserted, values emerge from experience and develop over successive generations.[10]

When the conversation again flagged, Caddell tried to get it back on track by using Bell's notion of a general public interest to remind those assembled of the larger issues at stake. He linked the books by Bell and Lasch, wondering how it might be possible to restore trust among people in an age of narcissism. It was at that moment that Bell realized why Caddell had urged the president to read their books and invite them to the White House. If the president believed that he had been effective in doing his job, then, Bell surmised, he needed an explanation for why there was a crisis of confidence and why, in turn, his popularity and influence were at a low ebb. The answer was now clear to Bell. With *The Culture of Narcissism* and *The Cultural Contradictions of Capitalism*, Lasch and Bell had provided Caddell and in turn the president with ammunition to prove that Carter was doing as effective a job as he could. The fault lay with the American people and the values they embraced. The president's task was not to change how he governed but to transform what the American people valued and how they behaved.[11]

After the discussion had ended and the guests had departed, Carter wrote down what he wanted to remember of the evening. He listed all those who had attended and, after the names of Bell and Lasch, noted the titles of their books. Then he focused on capturing the gist of what Bell had said, the only person whose ideas he recorded. He summarized Bell's discussion of the three realms and their conflicting principles which constituted the cultural contradictions of capitalism. He noted what he recalled as Bell's argument that the "limits of [the] mundane" made people turn to religion and reiterated Bell's emphasis on "self-gratification" and the decline of "traditional values." He mentioned Bell's focus on the conflict between an "era of limits" and increasing "demands." In a world filled with crises in culture and politics and decreases in productivity and the work ethic, the president asked, "Can families be strengthened?" and wondered how it was possible to "mix [the] tangible" with the "intangible." Finally, he jotted down the words "Presidential leadership," followed by "Can America be rejuvenated?" In retrospect Bell found the evening frustrating; the conversation was full of generalities, and he was unsure how the Carters had appraised the gathering. It was nevertheless remarkable for a president to understand and try to come to terms with the core ideas of a leading intellectual. The May 30 dinner, and his reading of the works of some of those in attendance, helped convince Carter, a historian has commented, "that something was truly amiss in the nation's psyche."[12]

Soon after the evening at the White House, Lasch wrote Jody Powell a long letter (the initial *C* in the upper-right-hand corner indicates that the president also read it), in which Lasch insisted that it was impossible to consider "the moral crisis of the country" without paying attention to "the crisis of our political institutions and to the growing part played in the political process by the mass media." Lasch recalled that the discussion in the White House had begun with a consideration of polls that revealed "a profound reversal of values: decline of the work ethic, rising hedonism, lack of faith in the future, a desire to enjoy life in the present, political indifference and cynicism." He reminded his White House readers, as he had readers of his book, that the crises of the 1970s had their origins in the 1920s. It was at that point, he remarked, that American industry robbed workers of their skills, used marketing to foster hedonism, and then "held out the compensatory utopia of consumption to people who could no longer take pride and pleasure in their work." Lasch noted that although the quest for immediate gratification seemed to have triumphed, in fact people involved in "working-class and rural cultures" had "never been wholly sold on the delights of consumerism, partly because" of the hold of "countervailing influences— religion, family, a sense of continuity." Moreover, the condition of "unequal access to the consumer paradise" caused by rising prices and stalled economic growth was becoming so striking that increasing numbers would "question its reality and perhaps its validity as an ideal of the good life."[13]

Consequently, Lasch noted, just when "narcissistic gratification appears to have vanquished all competing systems of values, and is breathlessly celebrated by cultural trend-setters as the wave of the future," the economic conditions that made such celebrations possible were disappearing. He predicted that in the long run, the resulting pessimism would "probably repoliticize the electorate, sharpen class feeling, and lead to bitter conflicts over the distribution of wealth." Except for a decreasing number of privileged people who could pursue "narcissistic self-gratification," Americans thus faced a narrowing range of choices as consumers and the necessity to make considerable sacrifices. In such a situation, the nation encountered two dramatically different political alternatives. On the one hand, an elite might exhort "others to prodigies of austerity while itself living high on the hog, and imposing authoritarian discipline to silence those who call attention to the discrepancy between rhetoric and results." On the other hand, the option Lasch preferred was that "the necessary sacrifices will be shared equally by all." The central message of his letter involved a call on Carter to foster "genuinely popular movements" that would support egalitarian sacrifice in an age of diminished possibility. For Lasch, a thoroughgoing commitment to "social democracy" would also bring about an end to the treatment of politics as just another item in the consumer culture. Such a politics, he noted, would not unify the nation in the short term. "A new consensus will emerge, in all likelihood," he remarked in closing, "only after a period of upheaval and conflict—a painful prospect, but no worse, certainly, than a gradual slide into some form of authoritarianism."[14]

Meanwhile and not without irony for a critic of celebrity, Lasch's *Culture of Narcissism* was attracting a great deal of attention. It earned him an interview with a reporter from *People Magazine*, published on July 9, 1979. In typical *People* fashion, accompanying the article was a picture of Lasch with his wife, children, and pets. "The Lasches," the caption read, "relax with books and chess at their upstate New York home." In the interview, Lasch reiterated the central points of his book. Among the issues he focused on was what he saw as the narcissistic obsession with consumption. He pointed to the quest for "immediate gratification" achieved through the purchase of goods and experiences, the preference for leisure over work and spending over saving. The 1960s, especially the counterculture, Lasch said, had taught Americans about human potential, which narcissists now sought to achieve through consumption. "By his very nature," he remarked, "the narcissist has an insatiable craving for consumption. Without inner resources, he takes on the characteristics of the things he buys. In a real sense, the narcissist *is* what he buys." During the week the article appeared, according to a reporter at *Newsweek*, Carter "decried" *People*'s "pop-culture ethos," with its stories confirming "his sense of a nation whose familial values are in trouble and whose morals are in 'decline.'" In its own way, however, the *People* story reaffirmed family values. The article featured a picture of the Lasch family, in the backyard of their suburban Rochester home, relaxing with their dog, cat, books, and chess set. "Maybe I have a stable life and family," Lasch commented in the interview, "because we live here in the provinces."[15]

In private, Lasch explored the contradictions of his celebrity status. He acknowledged the problems inherent in his commitment to a one-career marriage, especially at a time of rampant inflation and, in his own case, a relatively low salary—a difficulty belatedly remedied when he received an offer from Northwestern University. Lasch was well aware that a vigorous schedule of writing and lecturing which enhanced his income also conflicted with his core values. Above all, he intensely disliked celebrity status and all its trappings. After the *People* interview, he wrote Robert Silvers, editor of the *New York Review of Books*, that the story confirmed "everything I've always known about the mechanics of celebrity-manufacture. . . . A somewhat naïve wish to assist the book's sales left me with little time for anything else and little privacy either. From now on I plan to go into hiding. A pox on promoters!"[16]

Conflicting Advice for a President

The article in *People* appeared in the midst of the most critical period of crisis over Carter's energy policy. On July 1, when Carter returned from a trip to Vienna (where he signed the SALT II treaty with the Soviet Union) and the Far East, the energy crisis and his own political troubles had become so severe that they commanded his immediate and sustained attention. Several days earlier Stuart Eizenstat, his domestic policy adviser, had warned him of a worsening situation. Referring to the domestic consequences of the energy crisis, he remarked that "nothing else has so frustrated, confused, angered the American people—or so targeted their distress at you personally." On July 3, Carter went to Camp David with his wife, carrying with him a new memo by Caddell. After reading it and a draft of a speech on energy he was scheduled to deliver July 5, Carter without explanation canceled the talk, something presidents rarely if ever do. He made this decision at the urging of Caddell, who, aside from Rosalynn Carter, was the only adviser who wanted the president to take this dramatic course of action.[17]

Advising Carter in a 107-page memo, Caddell called on the president to make a "breakthrough" by combining a dramatic speech with bold action. Caddell's reading had convinced him that material success had eroded the nation's sense of purpose. He referred to a number of writers, including Alexis de Tocqueville, for his idea that religion provided a counter to the dangers of affluence and Abraham Maslow for his notion of higher needs. From Lasch, Bell, and Bellah, political writer Elizabeth Drew commented in the *New Yorker*, Caddell "drew confirmation of the theory that as people give up on the future they put more emphasis on immediate gratification, and that the pursuit of immediate gratification weakens values needed for the future—

hard work, savings." Caddell focused especially on the consequences of the coming of age of the baby boom generation and the experience of the 1960s which resulted in a rejection of "religion and other older values." In the memo, he called on the president to hold a fireside chat, followed by an address to Congress. Caddell evoked Sidney Lumet's 1976 movie *Network*, in which a TV newscaster inspires frustrated citizens to shout, "'We're mad as hell and we're not going to take it any more!'" He called on Carter to make OPEC "a common enemy, but in action as well as rhetoric." Dramatic actions, he argued, would refocus the presidency and put Carter in a stronger position for the 1980 campaign. Arguing that "ONLY A RADICAL APPROACH WILL RALLY THE COUNTRY," Caddell called on the president not only to address policy issues but also to use them as "THE DRIVING ENGINE OF VALUE RESTORATION, NATIONAL UNITY, AND NATIONAL PURPOSE." Americans, he believed, were "more willing to sacrifice more and suffer more if they perceive a purpose, an enemy, and an end goal to that pain."[18]

Caddell proposed a broad range of programs. In a section on government policies toward oil companies, he wrote, "Energy provides the vehicle for confrontation of national interest over special interest" and urged that "we must be unsparing in hammering that point." He also called for curtailed consumption, an area, he noted, "where we can prove our resolve, unite our country, relearn values like sacrifice, unity, and send crucial signals to the world." The central problem Caddell identified, according to Drew, was a "malaise" that had emerged because the United States "was a goal-oriented society without goals." In a handwritten letter to Caddell, Carter called his analysis of the July discussions "a masterpiece."[19]

Carter remained at Camp David for a period of what turned out to be a week and a half, most of it taken up with a domestic summit. When it came time to turn the discussions into a speech, from within his administration Carter received conflicting recommendations which Eizenstat characterized as involving "the most acrimonious debate" during Carter's four years in office. The main disagreement surrounded the issue of whether the president should follow Caddell's suggestions that he scold citizens, call on them to restrain their consumption, and locate the larger spiritual and moral issues in Americans' selfishness and malaise. Eizenstat and Vice President Walter Mondale saw the difficulty the president and the nation faced as having to do primarily with the practical, albeit formidable issues of inflation, energy, and jobs. They felt it was wrong to criticize Americans for being selfish, as Carter interpreted Lasch, filtered through Caddell, as saying. Rather, the vice president believed that Americans, angry at government for failing to solve the nation's problems, were struggling with objectively difficult conditions brought on by inflation, threats to job security, and exploding energy costs.

The president should provide strong leadership in solving what Mondale considered the real problems rather than deliver a castigating sermon. The battle was more than one between those who took a broader view, like Caddell, and those with more mundane political interests. After all, Mondale and his allies, including inflation czar Alfred Kahn, had themselves relied on the arguments of intellectuals such as Theodore Lowi and Robert Dahl, who believed that interest group politics had fractured the sense of national purpose and as a result had paralyzed the political system.[20]

Greg Schneiders, who worked for Gerald Rafshoon on White House communications, opposed Caddell's approach, but from a different perspective. In a July 10 memo, he argued that Americans "don't want to hear Jimmy Carter *talk* about our problems and they certainly don't want to hear him whine about them." Were Carter to follow Caddell's advice, he would simply deliver "an interesting academic treatise" which might offer "some interesting and unconventional concepts." To the contrary, he warned the president to avoid "self-deprecating" comments about himself and "negative" remarks about the nation. People needed solutions to a crisis, not words about "the crisis of confidence in the country." Citizens "want to perceive [Carter] beginning to *solve* the problems, *inspire* confidence by his action, and lead." Rafshoon echoed Schneiders's suggestions and added his own biting critique of Caddell's approach. He called the pollster's initial draft of the speech "apocalyptic," and feared that delivering it might well be "counterproductive" and might even prove a "disaster."[21]

Meanwhile, Caddell continued to call on the president to pronounce that the nation was in a spiritual and psychological crisis. In a July 12, 1979, memo to Carter, Caddell summarized polling data that "signaled a rapid disintegration of optimism and efficacy in the country." This underscored the "increasing malaise" affecting the nation and the presidency. To bolster his case for a wide-ranging speech, Caddell reminded the president of the arguments writers had offered in their "INTELLECTUAL EXPLORATION." Lasch's book, he noted, examined how "people who lose sense of future turn inward for fulfillment which leads to vacuum and greater unhappiness," as well as a "loss of sense of meaning of life for future." In a newspaper article, Caddell told the president, Robert Bellah had "explored the loss of 'covenant' in the society" and "insisted that public confidence and commitment to the common good will destroy the conditions of freedom in society and precipitate the coming of tyranny." Daniel Bell, Caddell asserted, "combine[d] much of Lasch and Bellah." He summarized *The Cultural Contradictions of Capitalism*, emphasizing how "'modernism' and loss of faith," "much like narcissism," were "undermining the society." Caddell spoke of the battle between "civitas" and the increasing sense of entitlement. "Economic growth as secular religion," combined with inflation and slower increases in the GNP, "leads to change in character of society making restraint, discipline and common interest almost impossible." As a result, "values are weakened."[22]

Over 130 people—representing the worlds of politics, labor, business, religion, and ideas—were invited by Carter to a summit meeting at Camp David. At this summit, Hamilton Jordan handed out copies of Lasch's *Culture of Narcissism* in the hope that the guests might understand what was on the president's mind. As Bellah flew east from the Bay Area to attend the meeting, he jotted down what he wanted to say. He noted the opposing aspects of Carter's outlook—how his individual morality, derived from a Baptist tradition which allotted little responsibility to the public realm, conflicted with his technocratic mentality. He worried that "Hobbesian struggles" might emerge if the nation continued to face battles over shrinking resources. He had doubts that a "culture of narcissism" was gripping America, for he was seeing in California opposing traditions of public concern. If there was a danger in the "collapse of the covenant," there was nonetheless in the middle class "a reservoir or moral concern + civil virtue." He wanted Carter to reinvigorate the nation's sense of its public commitments, and to do so by relying on moral and religious traditions rather than technocratic imperatives. Reassert the "covenant basis of contract," he would urge the president, and exercise "a moral leadership capable of articulating latent moral conscience in the country." Defend "the most vulnerable part of the population," and develop "a non-paranoid international context." Yet in the end, Bellah wondered if "the real question is are we already too corrupt to maintain free institutions."[23]

On the evening of July 10, Bellah and nine others met with the president at Camp David for three hours. Bellah was the only academic; the other guests were what he called "religious functionaries," clergymen and officials of national religious organizations. "Bob," Carter asked him at one point, "what should I say? How much can the American people take?" Bellah responded, in what he later recalled as a "fairly impassioned statement asking' for almost a Jeremiah," by urging Carter not to tell the people what they wanted to hear—that it was all OPEC's fault and the energy crisis could be solved by technology. Instead, he urged Carter to be "a teaching President," one who tells the people "hard truths" and "who points out what it means to maintain our tradition in a given historic period." Bellah found allies at the meeting among the religious leaders, who "attacked the free enterprise system" and were "quite critical of our basic institutions." He reported that all the guests told the president, "Look, don't just invoke spiritual values and sacrifice if you're not going to say anything about the structural conditions that force people to be more selfish than they might want to be, like building the whole economy on the profit motive." Bellah came away from the meeting elated, feeling that he had possibly had some impact and that the president was willing to address national issues in a critical manner.[24]

While preparing his speech, according to Powell, Carter read, among other works, the books by Lasch and Bell as well as Bellah's newspaper article "Human Conditions for a Good Society," to which Caddell had called his attention. Here Bellah offered a condensed version of what he had written in *Broken Covenant*. He contrasted the biblical tradition, which emphasized a covenant that transcended self-interest and involved concern for others, with industrial capitalism, which rested on "the growth of a consumer economy and the stimulus through advertising of an insatiable desire for material things." He attacked luxury as "that pursuit of material things that diverts us from concern for the public good, that leads us to exclusive concern for our own good, or what we would today call consumerism." He lambasted the tax revolt that had started in California in the 1970s for using "the language of middle-class asceticism" to obscure "middle-class hedonism," which in turn made private consumption more important than the provision of public amenities. His own preference was for a "decentralization and democratization of economic institutions" which would undergird a revitalized and morally based public life. For him, such a prospect rested on a "spiritual awakening," necessary in an age of increasing "scarcity and simplicity," which would revitalize a covenant among Americans. Looking around him, Bellah found cause for hope on the local level, in churches and voluntary associations, and in the prospect that a leader like Martin Luther King Jr. might come on the scene and help foster among Americans the belief that "only sacrifice, love and concern for the common good will see us through the crises that lie ahead."[25]

When Carter actually sat down to write what he might say to the nation, he drew on what he had heard from a number of people, including the Berkeley sociologist. "Bob Bellah," the president wrote in notes as he prepared the speech, "said use the word 'covenant.'" What immediately follows this explicit reference are thoughts that may well have drawn on what Bellah told him. "We're on earth to share," the president wrote, "not grasp & waste. No material shortage can touch the important things like God's love for us or our love for one another. We're still a blessed nation—don't turn to anger. Fibre of our nation not damaged or even threatened. Need to revive our joy in producing, sharing, giving. Staying home may remind us of family blessings. Let ethics, morality guide technology." Elsewhere, in noting down what he wanted to include in the speech, Carter doubtless drew on Bellah's advice when he wrote, "Let us covenant together. We are on earth to share, not to grab and waste," words he did not include in the speech.[26]

The President Addresses a Nation

On July 15, President Carter delivered his address from the White House. His long stay at Camp David had created drama and mystery, heightening a sense of the importance of the speech. The problem the nation faced, Carter asserted, was "deeper than gasoline lines or energy shortages, deeper even than inflation or recession." After confessing his own failures as a leader and giving examples of the advice he received during his retreat at Camp David, he focused on the "crisis of confidence" that led Americans to doubt the meaning of their own lives, the future, and the nation's purpose, and as a consequence threatened to destroy "the social and the political fabric of America." And "just as we are losing our confidence in the future," Carter remarked (perhaps echoing Lasch, who had written that Americans were being increasingly cut off from their history) "we are also beginning to close the door on our past." Echoing Caddell's recent memo, Carter located this crisis in many sources, but especially in the tumultuous events of the previous two decades which had set America on a pessimistic course. The results were evident. Americans had lost faith in their government and in their leaders' ability to govern. Politicians felt a greater obligation to special interests than to a common purpose. People had lost respect for key social and political institutions. Productivity, savings, and the willingness to sacrifice had decreased. To solve both the energy crisis and the crisis of confidence, Carter held out the hope of getting the nation on the "path of common purpose and the restoration of American values." Carter called energy policy the "battlefield" on which the nation "could seize control again of our common destiny." After suggesting policy initiatives, he reiterated his claim that solving the energy crisis would "rekindle our sense of unity, our confidence in the future, and give our Nation and all of us individually a new sense of purpose."[27]

Carter's speech operated on a number of levels. It joined the disparate advice his aides had given him, combining Caddell's emphasis on a spiritual crisis with Eizenstat and Mondale's emphasis on policy changes. Confessing that he had failed the nation, Carter linked the people's loss of confidence in him with the nation's loss of faith in its institutions and its future. The president made energy policy the test of the nation's ability to solve its moral and spiritual problems. As a born-again Christian, he delivered a sermon that relied on a Christian drama of retreat (to Camp David), a confession of sinfulness (his letting the nation down, as well as the nation's journey into profligacy), a decision to commit himself and the nation to a battle against sin and for national recovery, and a claim of rebirth for himself and for America. As one scholar has shown, Carter, having discovered that Americans had fallen victim to self-indulgence, promised a new faith born of cleansing and rededication—one that operated simultaneously on the political, religious, and personal levels.[28]

Carter's speech was surely the most sustained attack any American president had ever made on consumer culture. As Ribuffo has argued, it "came as close to a call for a day of fasting and humiliation as any other modern presidential speech." In one of Carter's most sweeping claims about the sources of what threatened America, he referred to the consequences of affluence, contrasting "a nation that was proud of hard work, strong families, close-knit communities, and our faith in God" with what he saw as its opposite. "Too many of us now tend to worship self-indulgence and consumption," he remarked. As a consequence, "human identity is no longer defined by what one does, but by what one owns." Ultimately, this culture of consumption left Americans empty. "Owning things and consuming things," he said, "does not satisfy our longing for meaning." Americans, he concluded, had learned "that piling up material goods cannot fill the emptiness of lives which have no confidence or purpose." This was strong medicine. Americans expect optimism from their presidents, not chastisement. Although many Americans shared Carter's vision of a more moral consumption, many others wanted to resume pursuit of the good life, not be warned of its immorality. They wanted an acknowledgment of a crisis without having to make substantial changes in their way of life.[29]

The Intellectuals' Response

To what extent Carter drew on what Bell, Bellah, and Lasch had said and written, filtered through Caddell, or more directly through Carter's readings, is open to question. As Bell learned from John Gardner as they drove back to Bell's hotel after their evening at the White House, Carter heard but did not necessarily listen. The president was attentive to what others said, but he took from conversations, such as the ones he had with Bell, Bellah, and Lasch, only what he wanted to hear. Carter might well have given the same speech even if he had not absorbed the ideas of three of the nation's leading intellectuals (although he may have derived the title of the speech from Lasch's book, which speaks of a "crisis of confidence"). In some ways Bell was right: Carter's reading provided him a kind of intellectual cover and justification for his own political instincts, personal convictions, and ideological commitments, offering ways of articulating his moralism without compromising his perspective as an engineer. But in a basic sense, Carter's ideas on the crisis came from both deeper and broader sources than any one person's writings—deeper in that he drew on his heritage from his parents and his grounding in evangelical

Christianity, broader in that these ideas about the costs of excessive consumption were being commonly expressed in the 1970s.[30]

Yet the relationships between the writings of Bell, Bellah, and Lasch, Caddell's memos, and Carter's speech were complex and important. The flow of words and ideas points in a number of directions. It reminds us of the difficulty intellectuals have in communicating their ideas with any complexity to political figures and to the general public. It underscores how difficult it is to trace ideas from their origins in many sources to their end point in a single speech. It reveals the complicated interplay between intellectuals, the temper of the time, and political discourse. Yet Carter's engagement with these three thinkers provides evidence of a president's serious encounter with ideas and stands as a remarkable instance of the contribution of intellectuals to the national discussion. The reaction to Carter's speech was similarly complex, with politicians and the press divided in their response. After the speech, Carter's job approval rating shot up by 11 percent, though only to a lowly 37 percent. What is of particular interest here is how some observers understood the speech as a jeremiad against affluence. Carter had scolded the nation, noted the *Los Angeles Times*, like a "pastor with a profligate flock."[31]

Whatever short-term gain the speech provided, very quickly Carter was back at ground zero—low approval ratings, bad publicity, and political controversy. Two days after the speech, he began a major reorganization of his cabinet. In the resulting controversy, he lost the momentum the address to the nation had given him. Soon after the speech, Carter appointed Paul Volcker head of the Federal Reserve Board, which began the painful process of reducing the rate of inflation. In the short term, however, even higher prices and rates of inflation engulfed the end of the Carter presidency. Senator Edward Kennedy launched a challenge to Carter's renomination, the USSR invaded Afghanistan, and Iran took Americans hostage. By the summer of 1980, Carter had secured the Democratic nomination but faced a formidable Republican opponent, California governor Ronald Reagan. Speaking on election eve, Reagan denounced those who said "that a great national malaise is upon us." The cold war consensus did not die so easily. Throughout the 1980s and 1990s, Republicans continued to get tremendous mileage from reminding the voters of the "malaise" they had experienced under Democratic leadership. [32]

The response to Carter's speech by Bell, Bellah, and Lasch is also noteworthy. At the end of August 1979, Bell wrote to Caddell objecting to the notion, emphasized by Elizabeth Drew in her *New Yorker* article, that there was necessarily a tension between Caddell's emphasis on the moral dimensions of the crisis and Mondale's on the presumably more real issues of inflation and energy shortages. Bell thought it was a mistake to say, as Caddell or Carter might be understood as having alleged, that people's anxieties about rising prices and depleted savings were somehow not "real." Yet Bell also took issue with those who, like Mondale, would minimize the underlying cultural and social trends that underwrote an increasing emphasis on self-regard. The task before the president, Bell argued, was to find some way to link the two approaches in a convincing manner, making clear that Carter understood the seriousness of both sets of issues. Yet in the end, although Bell hoped that the president could find a way of successfully connecting policy and fundamental cultural change, he questioned the basic premise of such an approach and therefore of Carter's speech. It was all but impossible, he asserted, to use either a jeremiad or public policy to solve underlying cultural problems such as excessive hedonism.[33]

After watching the speech on television from his Berkeley home, Bellah reported that the president's talk had "terribly disappointed" him. He believed that Carter was an honest and decent person who did not know how to translate his private Baptist politics into policy. Carter, Bellah remarked, lacked "social vision," and instead relied on "technocrats" and "gimmicks" to guide him. He had hoped that Carter, facing a difficult political situation, "would turn his conscience into something more socially viable." What Carter had failed to do, he noted, was to translate "morality into a kind of politics that would be mobilizational in more than a superficial sense, because that would involve input and participation from people." Although Carter had referred to a spiritual crisis and criticized self-interest, Bellah found what he had to say superficial, unanalytic, lacking in coherence. Bellah wanted the president to explain that the combination of communitarian and individual-istic impulses that had served Americans so well in the past would no longer work. Facing a world of limits and tough decisions, Americans had to hear from the president that "we're not going to be able to afford the totally unlimited self-indulgence and the kind of economic system that feeds that self-indulgence any longer." Not unlike Lasch, Bellah saw two choices: an authoritarian government "that tells us what we can consume" or "a reorgan-ization of our society along volunteeristic lines in accordance with our long tradition of democratic processes." For Bellah, the latter involved mobilizing people politically and a willingness to "arouse lots of hostility and hatred." Instead, Bellah concluded, Carter had told Americans that though they might have to make small sacrifices, "you can have everything. You can have it all."[34]

Shortly after the speech, Lasch, like Bell, wrote Caddell a long letter. He noted that, though tempted to respond in public in order to "forestall charges from the Left that I've been seduced and coopted by too close proximity to power," he refused to comment to the press because "the real danger of cooptation, these days, comes from the media, which absorb and homogenize all points and turn them to the purpose of political entertainment." He told the president's pollster that he found the speech "courageous, powerful, and often moving—better in some ways than the policies it announced." Praising the talk as a "sermon" that had "great analytical depth and political force," he applauded the president's attempt "to connect moral and cultural issues on the one hand with economic issues on the other." He then told Caddell that the president's most urgent task was to "confront more openly . . . the social divisions" in the nation and "to address more directly the groups that have a real stake in change," the poor and working class, not those who were "wholly paralyzed" by the culture of narcissism, most notably "the managerial and professional elite." Consequently, he insisted, the president had to make clear "that sacrifices are going to be apportioned to the capacity to bear them, in accordance with elementary principles of justice." In November 1979, he wrote friends in jest that he was "completely disgusted with Carter for reject-ing my proposal for a crash program of igloo construction" to save energy and strengthen families. "To say that I'm bitter about Carter," he remarked with more seriousness, "would be an understatement." When Lasch wrote Caddell a second letter in February 1980, he complained that "my letters of last summer" had "obviously made no impression on the White House." Although Powell had acknowledged receipt of his earlier letter (but had not commented on its content), Lasch noted that Caddell had not even written to say that he had received it.[35]

In a November 8, 1979, letter to Bell, Lasch told the Harvard sociologist that "cynicism about politics and politicians shouldn't be set down to 'narcis-sistic' self-absorption." In addition, "It was pointless to ask for individual sacrifices from ordinary people when it was obvious that the big corporations were making money hand over fist." For Lasch, "the central question for American politics was whether the sacrifices imposed by the energy crisis" and a stagnant economy "would be equitably distributed and decided on in a democratic fashion or imposed on an unwilling electorate by an authoritarian central government." Lasch added that in a conversation he had with Powell and Caddell after the meeting with the president ended, neither of them had seemed "eager to discuss issues of this sort—to put it mildly—or to consider" a politics that "might invite the suspicion of 'left-wing demagoguery,'" a term Powell had used to describe Kennedy's positions. Like Bellah, Lasch felt that Kennedy was the one politician on the national scene who might provide the kind of leadership necessary to bring America through the crisis successfully.[36]

For Lasch, the meeting with Carter was especially troublesome, given his feelings about the role of the intellectual. In *The New Radicalism* (1965) and throughout his career, Lasch wondered how intellectuals might remain si-multaneously responsible, detached, engaged, and effective. As the historian

Robert Westbrook has written, "For Lasch the most troubling feature of this effort of the new radicals to overcome their social and cultural isolation was the loss of the detachment it entailed, a detachment he regarded as essential to the vocation of the intellectual." During the evening in the White House, Lasch had remained largely quiet. Bell attributed his silence to what he assumed was Lasch's uncertainty about his role as a critic of the nation who believed theoretically in speaking truth to power but now found himself in the very presence of power itself. Bell found Bill Moyers and Caddell more skillful than anyone else present at playing out "courtier politics." As one critic perceptively noted, "Lasch, who has been so attentive throughout his career to the peculiar dilemmas of intellectuals in America," with the media and presidential response to *Culture of Narcissism* had "provided a classic example of those dilemmas." In an interview shortly before he died, Lasch acknowledged that at the White House he had spoken very little, "being so overawed by this distinguished company, and feeling a little uncomfortable too because of having written so much about the perils of intellectuals as advisers to people in power. I wasn't sure," he admitted, "whether I should even be there in the first place."[37]

In his letter to Bell, Lasch confessed that, "disregarding all the things" he had said over a long period of time "about the folly of intellectuals' setting themselves up as advisers to men of power," he had sent a second memo to the White House after mid-July, "overpraising the speech." Lasch differed from Bell on two points. First, he thought that Carter was "on the right track in attempting, however clumsily, to link moral and cultural issues to economic ones." Second, he reiterated his call for "a decisive turn to the left." Lasch ruefully concluded his comments on his role as adviser to the president by remarking that he had "received no acknowledgement at all" of his "last communication." Bell replied that he had no problem with intellectuals who became advisers to powerful people, provided they were not intoxicated by it. Countering Lasch's notion of the intellectual as a detached critic, Bell remarked that in order to be an effective critic, one had to have political experience. If serious people declined to offer advice, then the task would fall to less intelligent people or more often to those who, failing to get tenure at the best institutions, joined the federal bureaucracy instead.[38]

Getting what was perhaps the last word, in *The Minimal Self: Psychic Survival in Troubled Times* (1984), Lasch discussed Carter's speech. The president, he wrote, "attributed the national 'malaise' to the spirit of self-seeking and the pursuit of 'things.'" This, "the conventional critique of narcissism" typical of both liberals and neoconservatives, "equates narcissism with selfishness and treats consumerism as a kind of moral lapse that can be corrected by exhortations about the value of hard work and family life. It deplores the breakdown of the work ethic and the popularization of a 'fun morality' that has allegedly crippled productivity, undermined American enterprise, and thus weakened" the nation's ability to compete in world markets. The problem with Carter's analysis, Lasch said, lay in "the failure to distinguish a moralistic indictment of 'consumerism' . . . from an analysis that understands mass consumption as part of a larger pattern of dependence, disorientation, and loss of control." Treating Carter like a social theorist, Lasch said that the president failed to connect the degradation of consumption and that of work, which together resulted in the promotion of "dependence, passivity, and a spectatorial state of mind."[39]

The writings of Bell, Bellah, and Lasch, in addition to their resonance in the presidency of Jimmy Carter, both shaped and captured a common response to the crises of the 1970s. By 1979, millions of Americans had grown deeply pessimistic about their ability to buy the goods and services they wanted, and about the nation's future. On the eve of World War II, Lewis Mumford had expressed the hope that wartime stringencies would force Americans to limit their consumption and thereby make the nation more moral. Now, forty years later, Bell, Bellah, Lasch, and Carter, to some degree or another embracing modern moralism, believed that the energy crisis might make Americans less narcissistic and self-indulgent, traits they connected with the excesses of affluence. The historic moment reveals the complications that result when intellectuals become involved with public policy generally and with a president specifically. The engagements of these writers with politics and their embrace of chastened consumption took place in a nation dramatically different from the one Mumford described as his fellow citizens were beginning to recover from the depression. The rhetoric of these 1970s critics of consumer culture was more insistent, their accusations more damning, precisely because choosing to buy a more fuel efficient car or turn down the thermostat is very different from not having enough money for public transportation or to buy coal. Moreover, Bell, Bellah, Lasch, and Carter issued their warnings on the eve of what would be the greatest expansion of affluence in American history.

Epilogue
The Response to Affluence at the End of the Century

On July 15, 1979, President Jimmy Carter delivered his "malaise" speech. Opposing him for the presidency the following year was Ronald Reagan. On the eve of his election in 1980, Reagan countered Carter's vision. At the time inflation was running at an annual rate of 13.5 percent, interest rates had reached 18 percent, and unemployment stood at over 7 percent. The Iranians were still holding fifty-two Americans hostage for what would turn out to be 444 days. Asking whether the nation had a future in which it could realize its ideals, Reagan, in a nationally televised address, remarked, "There are some who answer 'no'; that our energy is spent, our days of greatness at an end, that a great national malaise is upon us." He refuted those who said, "We must cut our expectations, conserve and withdraw, that we must tell our children . . . not to dream as we once dreamed." Instead, he offered a vision of an America triumphant—its economy strengthened by limiting government and by unleashing free enterprise, its international standing restored by a resurgence of military power that would defeat the Soviet Union.[1]

Underscoring the connection between the national mood, affluence at home, and strength abroad, Reagan declared that he found "no national malaise" in the land. But he warned that "any nation that sees softness in our prosperity" would be making a mistake, for if America's peace and security were threatened, "we will put aside in a moment the fruits of our prosperity." Rejecting the notion that Americans had to accept a lower standard of living, Reagan remarked that Carter "mistook the malaise among his own advisers, and in the Washington liberal establishment in general, for a malady affecting the nation as a whole." More than twenty years later, on the occasion of

Reagan's ninetieth birthday, a conservative commentator once again invoked the same theme. In 2001, Malcolm T. Owens recalled that "in 1980 the United States was in trouble. Malaise was in the air." He then went on to praise Reagan for unleashing the economy and undermining the USSR.[2]

In his inaugural address, Reagan was able to announce the release of the hostages in Iran. The contrasts between Carter's inauguration in 1977 and Reagan's four years later could not have been greater. After his inauguration Carter had walked down Pennsylvania Avenue from the Capitol to the White House. Reagan was driven in a limousine. A *Time* reporter called Reagan's "the biggest, most lavish, most expensive presidential welcome ever," with a price tag almost two and a half times what his predecessor's had cost. Nancy Reagan, who had declared a preference for "simpler clothes," was dressed in a $25,000 outfit for her husband's inaugural ball. In 1981, she spent $200,000 on new china for the White House. In the introduction to a book titled *Reagan's Ruling Class*, Ralph Nader quoted a reporter who characterized the inaugural celebrations as a "bacchanalia of the haves." "It made me sick— the rack of dresses and the fur coats," remarked Democratic columnist Maryon Allen, "the lineup of private jets and jeweled boots, the absolutely appalling overconsumerism, the insane jubilation." Even Republicans objected. Barry Goldwater, the party's standard bearer in 1964, called the festivities "ostentatious." A Republican civic leader from Houston told a reporter, "The thing that offended me most was the great extravagance at a time when we're supposed to be cutting the budget and showing restraint on all unnecessary frills."[3]

The Reagan years ushered in an economic boom that lasted for the remainder of the century. To be sure, there were significant threats that made the ride less than smooth. A serious recession came early in Reagan's presidency, and another during that of George H. W. Bush in 1990–91 helped elect William Jefferson Clinton to office in 1992. In the spring of 2000, the air started to go out of the stock market bubble. Moreover, the economic development of the final twenty years of the century, including the globalization that had transformed the international economy, created both winners and losers. Salaries of executives in large corporations soared, as did the income of celebrities in entertainment and sports, to say nothing of the dot-com millionaires who participated in the feast as long as it lasted. In contrast, millions of people led lives of grinding poverty. African Americans and Latinos in center cities and Native Americans on reservations struggled to make do in very different worlds. Single mothers experienced the feminization of poverty. The very word "homeless" reminded Americans that some were not just ill housed but housed not at all. Between the two extremes of rich and poor, many millions struggled to make ends meet. Hundreds of thousands of blue-collar workers experienced firsthand the interconnected processes of deindustrialization and deunionization. They and others managed by holding down multiple jobs or assuming increasing levels of debt while incomes remained stagnant.

From 1980 to 2000, the record of change was significant but mixed. The GNP increased, in real dollars, by about 55 percent. The stock market boomed, with the Dow Jones Industrial Average ballooning from 824.57 at the beginning of 1980 to 11,357.51 twenty years later. Yet during the period in question, the distribution of income in the United States grew substantially less equal. According to the Congressional Budget Office, by century's end the top 1 percent of the population, the richest 2.7 million, had as many after-tax dollars to spend as did the poorest 100 million. Moreover, that ratio had more than doubled since the first year of Carter's presidency, when the income of the wealthiest 1 percent equaled that of the poorest 49 million Americans. Indeed, the figures across the board showed the result of two decades of public policy decisions, stock market gains, transfer of jobs abroad, and the persistence of poverty (see table 4). Thus, despite a considerable rise in the GNP, the share of income and of income gains had gone disproportionately to those at the top. In many parts of the nation, the economic situation of the rich had improved markedly but the poor were worse off, while a significant percentage of those in between had seen their condition deteriorate slightly. [4]

The U.S. Census of 2000 highlighted other changes. "Census Data Show a Sharp Increase in Living Standard," announced a lead article in the *New York Times* during the summer of 2001. In excess of 90 percent of the nation's households had at least one car, truck, or van, with 18 percent owning three or more vehicles. Twenty-five percent of houses had at least seven rooms, and almost 20 percent of new residences covered more than 3,000 square feet. Yet

Table 4. Income distribution, 1977–1999

Household Groups	Average After-Tax Income (est.)		Change
	1977	*1999*	
1/5 with lowest income	$10,000	$8,800	12.0% decrease
Next lowest 1/5	$22,100	$20,000	9.5% decrease
Middle 1/5	$32,400	$31,400	3.1% decrease
Next highest 1/5	$42,600	$45,100	5.9% increase
Highest 1/5	$74,000	$102,300	38.2% increase
1% with highest income	$234,700	$515,600	119.7% increase

SOURCE: David Cay Johnston, "Gap Between Rich and Poor Found Substantially Wider," *NYT*, Sept. 5, 2000, A16.

the data also revealed the ambiguities of affluence and the persistence of poverty. "If people's homes are bigger," the reporter noted, "so are their mortgages, and if they own more cars, they also commute more hours to work." Tens of millions of Americans were taking on consumer card debt, at high interest rates and often as a significant proportion of their assets or even income, in order to sustain the standard of living they and marketers deemed essential. About 530,000 homes had no plumbing, and 3.2 million were without telephone service, both figures representing sharp decreases since 1940. Nevertheless, almost 13 percent of the nation lived in poverty, with children under eighteen suffering that fate disproportionately.[5]

Other data help capture the transformation of the landscape of affluence. The Internet and the World Wide Web, unavailable to the general public in 1990, a decade later connected more than 50 percent of American homes to a plethora of options unimaginable in 1945. By the end of the century, 99 percent of the nation's homes had radios, an average of 5.6 per home. If Americans in 1945 had no television sets and in 1955 had sets that broadcast in black and white on only a handful of channels, by 2000, 98.3 percent of households had television sets, with an average of 2.4 per home. About 85 percent of homes had a VCR, a device whose use the federal census did not even track in 1980. More than two out of every three homes had cable, a figure that had grown from 6.7 percent in 1970. The Jeep, which in 1945 was a stripped-down army vehicle that carried soldiers over mountains and through jungles, by 2000 had become an air-conditioned SUV carrying passengers over the rugged terrain of interstate highways and suburban streets. Upscale homes featured kitchens as performance spaces, three-car garages, dramatic atrium entryways, and separate bathrooms for him and her. A traveler visiting the United States from the world J. C. Furnas portrayed on the eve of World War II in *How America Lives* would find much that was unfamiliar, even startling: DVD, cell phones, jet travel, central air-conditioning, crack cocaine, AIDS, Prozac, soy milk, suburban shopping malls, and plastic—credit cards, automobile bumpers, Tupperware. Yet, despite all these changes, or perhaps because of them, survey data revealed that since the early 1970s, higher incomes had made people in the middle class and above less happy rather than more.[6]

How America Lives Revisited

Nothing like *How America Lives* was available to capture household patterns of spending so vividly and comprehensively for the century's end. Replacing Furnas's journalistic evocation of a nation of diverse consumers joined across class lines by democratic neighborliness was a sense of groups living in separate niches joined more through the mostly invisible ties of a market economy than by participation in anything resembling common choices as consumers. An assemblage of particular portraits goes a long way toward capturing patterns of consumer culture in the United States near century's end. In *Nickel and Dimed: On (Not) Getting By in America* (2001), Barbara Ehrenreich reported on her two-year effort to discover how service workers struggled to subsist on jobs that paid near the minimum wage. Her firsthand experience as a cleaning woman and a Wal-Mart salesperson, among other jobs, revealed the pain and exhaustion suffered by such workers, mostly single women, many of them deprived of the safety net of welfare programs the federal government no longer provided. She found that an hourly wage of six or seven dollars made unattainable a decent standard of living, including safe, stable housing. A year earlier three sociologists—Teresa A. Sullivan, Elizabeth Warren, and Jay Lawrence Westbrook—in *The Fragile Middle Class: Americans in Debt* (2000) had charted how Americans farther up the social scale relied on debt to achieve a middle-class way of life. At a time of extraordinary prosperity, they revealed "the fault lines that underlie the apparent economic stability of the American middle class." Among the forces threatening such Americans, they noted, were rising housing costs, expensive and often elusive health care, the marketing of goods, services, and consumer debt, the fear of downward mobility, the loosening of legal and social restrictions on divorce, and a whole range of temptations fostered by expanding notions of an acceptable standard of living.[7]

At the same time, evidence emerged that the wealthy were also struggling, but with the anxieties of affluence rather than the problem of finding adequate housing and health care. Just as the dot-com bubble was bursting, *Weekly Standard* editor David Brooks examined the lifestyles of the newly wealthy, whose jobs made it possible to be creative and, apparently by coincidence, financially successful. In *Bobos in Paradise: The New Upper Class and How They Got There* (2000), he examined how these "Bobos" combined bourgeois and bohemian lifestyles, making it difficult to "tell an espresso-sipping artist from a cappuccino-gulping banker." Purchasing peasant-inspired furniture, eating expensive organic foods and drinking gourmet coffees, pursuing pleasures that were at once lustful and high-minded, "Bobos" struggled to allay the anxieties of affluence by creating "a way of living that lets you be an affluent success and at the same time a free-spirit rebel." Above even these bourgeois-bohemians were billionaires and their families. The budgets of the very rich usually escape the gaze of journalists and sociologists, but on occasion divorce or child custody hearings expose their spending patterns to public scrutiny. One such instance occurred in 2002 when thirty-six-year old Lisa Bonder Kerkorian went to court to increase the $75,000 monthly child support payments from her eighty-four-year old ex-husband, the media billionaire Kirk Kerkorian. Of the $320,000 per month she was requesting to bring up their young daughter, $14,000 was budgeted for parties and play dates, $5,900 for meals eaten out and $4,300 for those consumed at home, $144,000 for transportation on private jets, and $436 for care of her daughter's pets. Neither Lisa Kerkorian nor the *New York Times* article in which the case was reported questioned what it meant for a single woman to live so extravagantly dependent on the court-enforced largesse of the man who had fathered her child. Rather, what drove her life and the reporter's coverage of it was conspicuous consumption: the pursuit of Burberry prams costing $4,240 and Loro Piana cashmere socks for $325 from Neiman Marcus in Beverly Hills.[8]

These sources only begin to suggest how earning and spending had changed since Furnas offered his profiles in 1941. A series of popular books published at century's end more fully capture the range of affluence and writers' responses to it. In the last two decades of the twentieth century, a torrent of books, Web sites, and television shows suggested the variety of ways in which people were wrestling with the consequences of affluence. An exploration of some of the more significant ones reveals persistent themes that emerged from these seemingly unending considerations. Combining inspiration and practical advice, some writers emphasized that the rich were no different from ordinary Americans, thus making it possible for millions to imagine how they too might escape the conditions that made life in the middle class so fragile. Others drew on a very different American tradition as they sang of the joys of simple living. Some observers offered one variant or another of a critique of affluence that, relying on a moral vision, called for a retreat from the world of excessive engagement with modern consumer culture. Finally, some critics rejected the moralism that had so dominated discussions of affluence in the twentieth century and offered ways of thinking in post-moralist terms.

How the Rich Are Just Like You and Me

A prominent theme, and one that followed familiar American patterns, evoked the democracy of riches. One variant was the message that the rich are no different from you and me. This emerged clearly in Thomas J. Stanley and William D. Danko's 1996 book *The Millionaire Next Door: The Surprising Secrets of America's Wealthy*, which sold more than 2 million copies and remained on the *New York Times* best-seller list for more than three years. The authors, who began their careers as professors of marketing and did research on the wealthy for financial service corporations, emphasized how ordinary were the lives of many of the nation's rich and from this concluded that wealth was within the reach of millions of others. The authors distinguished between income and wealth, disdaining those who pursued a "high-consumption life style" and instead celebrating frugal people who consumed sensibly, saved, and invested. "Wealth," they wrote, "is more often the result of a lifestyle of hard work, perseverance, planning, and, most of all, self-discipline." They explored the lives of people worth at least $1 million, most of whom had made their money in mundane jobs as farmers and paving contractors. Stanley and Danko filled the book with inspirational case studies and practical advice on spending and saving. The publisher marketed the book as a self-help guide. To the question on the back cover, "Can I ever become one of them?" came the reply, "Get the advice in this book." A quote from *Forbes* hammered home the political lesson: "Nearly anyone with a steady job can amass a tidy fortune."[9]

Stanley and Danko offered a masculine view of the road to wealth, in which men work hard in the gritty world while women, keeping their shopping to a minimum, stay at home, where they carefully control the household budget. In contrast, Suze Orman offered a feminized alternative. With *The 9 Steps to Financial Freedom*, Orman transformed herself from a stockbroker and financial planner into a wildly successful author whose best-selling books helped launch her as media star and celebrity. She wrote in a decidedly therapeutic tone, joining the spiritual and psychological with practical advice on wills, investments, retirement, and insurance. Unlike Stanley and Danko, Orman was vague in her assumptions about wealth. Although most of her examples concerned people in the middle class or slightly above, her advice could apply to those in a much wider range of situations. Like her male counterparts, she also relied on case studies. Hers, however, dealt more in feelings than theirs, operating as they did in the confessional mode and even including stories of her own emotional journey on the road from rags to riches. She urged her mostly female readers to overcome their fears and anxieties about money. Find the inner strength to act courageously, she told them, and use "the power of positive thinking" to create an "empowering message for yourself and instill it into your powerful mind to replace the fear you're leaving behind." Characteristically, unlike Stanley and Danko, Orman paid little attention to work and focused instead on managing money. Yet throughout she connected the spiritual and financial. She linked financial responsibility to love of family and self-respect, the energy a person devotes to money to the gifts it gives in return. "To get in touch with that voice from the core of our being," she wrote, acknowledging that this was God's voice, "is not only a step toward financial freedom. It's also a step toward spiritual serenity." Drawing on Eastern religions, she wrote that "we experience prosperity, true financial freedom, when our actions with respect to money are dharmic, or righteous actions—that is actions of generosity, actions of offering." The book ends with a reminder that "true financial freedom lies in defining ourselves by who and what we are, not by what we do or do not have," by self-worth rather than net worth. Whatever spiritual goals Orman herself achieved, she was able to attain material ones as well. As a *New York Times* reporter noted in early 2002, Orman had "franchised herself into desk calendars, spirituality cards, and videotapes," written a column for *Self* magazine, and made TV appearances from Oprah to CNBC.[10]

Critiques of Contemporary Consumer Culture

The strongest and in many ways the most compelling reactions to affluence toward the end of the century were the impassioned, morally charged critiques of consumer culture that appeared in a wide variety of media. The voluntary simplicity movement attracted hundreds of thousands of dedicated followers who downsized their lifestyles in order to lead more uncluttered and purposeful lives. Web sites took advantage of modern media to sing the praises of simple living. The Center for a New American Dream's <www.newdream.org>, the Simple Living Network's <www.simpleliving.net>, the New Road Map Foundation's <www.newroadmap.org>, <www.adbusters.org>, and <www.rprogress.org> offered practical suggestions on how to counter excess commercialism. Millions of people found in Eastern religions an alternative to the interminable chase after vacuous material satisfactions. Documentaries such as Jean Kilbourne's series *Killing Us Softly: Advertising's Image of Women* vividly portrayed the media exploitation of women. In late 1997 and 1998, PBS aired two programs, "Affluenza" and "Escape from Affluenza," which intentionally used the illness metaphor to describe a society sick with the excesses of affluence. With *Simple Abundance: A Daybook of Comfort and Joy*, Sarah Ban Breathnach offered a daily diary designed to inspire women to exchange spiritual plenty for its material counterpart by infusing daily activities such as shopping and cooking with sacred meaning.[11]

Activism against commercialism found expression in many venues and forms. So-called culture jammers took dramatic stances against hype, commercialism, and commodity fetishism. Animal rights and environmental activists campaigned against the way human beings exploited nature. The "buy local" movement, by focusing on non-chain stores and nearby farms, put one version of moral spending into practice. Evangelical Christians campaigned against media giants such as Disney for their use of violence and their undermining of conventional values. In the late 1990s, students on university campuses and protesters in the streets outside the meetings of the World Trade Organization campaigned vigorously against the excesses of globalization, in the process emphasizing the link between consumption of sneakers and T-shirts in the First World and exploitive labor conditions in the Third.

What suffused many of these books, Web sites, television programs, and movements was a sense that affluence was a disease that had to be cured. The producer of "Affluenza" recalled the moment when he hit upon the title of the TV show. The word, he noted, "suggested a disease resulting from over-consumption," one with "symptoms of a virus" which had reached epidemic proportions but could be cured. Indeed, behavioral scientists, pharmaceutical manufacturers, and therapists were working to develop a science of "onio-mania," compulsive shopping, or more humorously "aspendicitis," using measures such as the Addictive Buying Indicator and the Compulsive Buying Scale.[12]

The most powerful critiques of consumer culture emerged in a series of serious yet accessible books published between 1999 and 2001. In *Bowling Alone: The Collapse and Revival of American Community*, the political scientist Robert D. Putnam offered an immensely influential analysis of the decline of "social capital" since the late 1960s which had resulted in people bowling (or praying, working, volunteering, politicking) alone rather than in groups. The causes were many, but prominent among them was the way new media, particularly for members of a younger generation, had privatized people's lives, eroding social networks and reciprocity. With *Luxury Fever: Why Money Fails to Satisfy in an Era of Excess*, the economist Robert H. Frank echoed both Thorstein Veblen and John Kenneth Galbraith as he explored how the "virus" of extravagant spending infected the society. In *Do Americans Shop Too Much?*—a book endorsed by Ehrenreich and Galbraith and with a foreword by Ralph Nader—Juliet Schor answered the question in the affirmative. The current "shopping mania," she argued, "provokes considerable dis-ease." She described a "new consumerism," driven by the fact that the workplace and the mass media had replaced the neighborhood as the source of people's sense of what the good life involved. The trickle-down power of upscale dreams strained budgets and threatened family life, caused people to work longer, made authentic leisure harder to achieve, and undermined commitments to public well-being. In his best-selling *Fast Food Nation: The Dark Side of the All-American Dream*, the journalist Eric Schlosser analyzed the adverse impact of the consumption of fast foods on working conditions, health, farming, demography, and the environment. These authors went beyond analysis and description to offer policy recommendations. They put forth progressive versions of a politics of consumption that, sensitive to issues of equity and the environment, would restore balance to the nation's engagement with affluence and to the relationship between the local environment and the worlds beyond. Although Frank and especially Schor were at times moralistic in deploying the social disease model, more typically these books emerged from the passions of committed social democrats worried at century's end about the costs of excess. Together these books offered powerful condemnations less of the personal anxieties of affluence than of its social costs. The dust jacket copy of Putnam's book applies just as well to the others: "like defining works of the past that have endured," such as David Riesman's *Lonely Crowd*, Betty Friedan's *Feminine Mystique*, and Rachel Carson's *Silent Spring*, it "identified a central crisis at the heart of our society."[13]

Post-moralist Celebrations of Affluence

Responding to Schor, among others, the English professor and cultural critic James B. Twitchell remarked that whenever the "consumption police" mentioned luxury, the only alternative was to "grab your credit cards and head for the hills." Emphasizing that we buy meanings, not goods, Twitchell argued that the problem was "not that we are too materialistic, but that we are not materialistic enough." He asserted that what America needed was "not a politics of consumption," and certainly not one that called for the taxing of spending, "so much as a religion of consumption." In *Lead Us into Temptation: The Triumph of American Materialism* (1999), Twitchell combined a disdain for cultural elitism with an extraordinary grasp of the processes that drive consumer culture in a richly suggestive treatment of American affluence. He criticized tenured radicals turned cultural critics—a cross between "the village idiot and the schoolmarm"—who blamed corporations for turning innocent citizens into greedy consumers. Not unlike Ernest Dichter, Twitchell saw the pursuit of materialism as natural and rational, something that drew on our love of goods to fill genuine needs in a thoroughly democratic manner. He acknowledged that Americans, living in the midst of "mallcondo commercialism," relied on advertising and fashion because they lacked "that inner sense of value" that religion once provided. Yet he understood consumption as a process through which people generated meaning. In his final chapter, "The Liberating Role of Consumption," Twitchell both pulled back from and advanced his argument. He echoed the new moralism in saying, "It is more likely that the globalization of capitalism will result in the banalities of an ever-increasing, worldwide consumerist culture." Yet he also emphasized, in an expression of post-moralism, the "liberating and democratic" possibilities of consumption, especially for a new generation.[14]

Just as Twitchell offered a populist but culturally conservative version of post-moralism, Jesse Lemisch offered an equally populist but politically radical one. Lemisch, a red diaper baby, had impeccable New Left credentials: his scholarly research on shipboard workers as heralds of the American Revolution in the eighteenth century had made him one of the pioneers in the new social history of the 1960s. Lemisch supported Ralph Nader's presidential candidacy in 2000. Yet it was the commitment of Nader and the Greens to the new moralism that encouraged Lemisch to articulate his own version of post-moralism. Writing in the radical journal *New Politics* in the summer of 2001, Lemisch criticized Nader and the Greens for "abstemiously" turning "their backs on people's reasonable and deeply human longings for abundance, joy, cornucopia, variety and mobility, substituting instead a puritanical asceticism that romanticized hardship, scarcity, localism, and underdevelopment." Calling into question the tendency of Nader and many environmentalists to be parsimonious and to celebrate family farms, Lemisch wondered "what, after all, is the matter with food in abundance, and wonderful material goods?" If Twitchell lambasted cultural studies for its embrace of the Frankfurt school, Lemisch embraced the Frankfurt school's vision of the utopian possibilities of popular forms of expression. Those who rested their politics on "backwardness, Spartan living, and underdevelopment," he asserted, condemned "as intrinsically bad things whose badness is rooted only in their place in the existing capitalist market structure." Rather, he hoped for the utopian cornucopia of abundance that he believed possible under socialism.[15]

The work of Twitchell and Lemisch built on the development of a post-moralist position on affluence that emerged in the 1970s, with Mary Douglas and Baron Isherwood's *World of Goods* (1979) as the founding document. The origins of this approach lay in a number of often disparate and conflicting sources: among them members of the Birmingham school of sociology such as John Fiske and Dick Hebdige, communications scholars such as William Leiss, economists such as Albert O. Hirschman, the French sociologist Pierre Bourdieu, cultural anthropologists (perhaps even Oscar Lewis) who emphasized how ordinary people constructed meaning, those who reformulated or rejected the teachings of the Frankfurt school, and feminists who appreciated popular expressions of women's sexuality, fashion, and agency. Post-moralists came in a variety of political stripes. In some versions, like that offered by Francis Fukuyama and Dinesh D'Souza, post-moralism took on a conservative cast. In others the approach was populist and decidedly more left-leaning.

Generally speaking, post-moralists rejected the puritanical strain among American cultural critics who chastised people, especially members of the middle class, for their excessive materialism. They sought to move beyond the jeremiad, emphasizing not cleansing but acceptance and even celebration. Rejecting a top-down approach that emphasized unitary understandings of the meaning of goods, they uncovered the multiple interpretations people infused into objects and experiences. They understood people's longings for affluence as inevitable and genuine. They developed ways of sanctioning the hold of consumer desires—ways that were moral without being moralistic. From various political perspectives, they explored the utopian and liberatory possibilities of consumer culture. In short, their responses to affluence were appreciative yet analytic.[16]

Affluence and Nationhood in Response to 9/11

On the eve of World War II, the editor of the *Ladies' Home Journal* tried to rally a nation by linking democracy, comfort, nationhood, and neighborliness across class lines. At the same time, Lewis Mumford linked patriotism, democracy, and a chastened consumption. During the energy crisis of the 1970s, President Jimmy Carter, bolstered by the writings of Daniel Bell, Robert Bellah, and Christopher Lasch, called on citizen-consumers to repent of their self-indulgent, materialistic ways and restore to the nation a commitment to public order and delimited affluence. In the first year after the tragic events of September 11, 2001, the response was very different. Now the moralists with regard to consumer culture were the Islamic fundamentalists whose reaction to American affluence and consumer culture was as troubled as their actions were reprehensible. In the United States, the president, though on occasion half-heartedly issuing a call to national service, was ideologically incapable of urging Americans to sacrifice. This time the politics of the situation were such that there was no sustained call, involving either sacrifice or alternative technologies, for a dramatic, focused effort to free the nation from the grip of Middle Eastern oil. Initially there was some nervousness among corporations, high-end consumers, and especially advertising agencies and media companies about how Americans would receive evocations of luxury, self-expression, and indulgence. That did not last long. An external threat of unimaginable dimensions, the possibility of a recession, massive corporate scandals and bankruptcies, and a declining stock market prompted Americans to perceive consumption as a critical factor in the nation's health, and even its survival. We have to spend our way out of this danger, millions of Americans believed, so that the enemies who had attacked us would not have won. The consumer was in the saddle. Unlike in the situation the nation faced during World War II or the energy crisis, this time there seemed no turning back from a full embrace of affluence and a commercialized consumer culture. A January 2002 cartoon said it all: on the sweatshirt of a woman pushing a shopping cart appeared the words, "Ask Not What You Can Do For Your Country, SHOP."[17]

Notes

Abbreviations

AC-UM	Angus Campbell Papers, Bentley Historical Library, University of Michigan, Ann Arbor
AER	*American Economic Review*
AH	*Agricultural History*
AHR	*American Historical Review*
AJS	*American Journal of Sociology*
ANB	*American National Biography*
Annals	*Annals of the American Academy of Political and Social Science*
APSR	*American Political Science Review*
AQ	*American Quarterly*
AS	*American Studies*
ASR	*American Sociological Review*
BB-WHS	Bruce Barton Papers, Wisconsin Historical Society, Madison
BF-SLRI	Betty Friedan Papers, Schlesinger Library, Radcliffe Institute, Harvard University
BHG	*Better Homes and Gardens*
CF	*Canadian Forum*
CH	*Chicago History*
CL-UR	Christopher Lasch Papers, Department of Rare Books and Special Collections, University of Rochester Library, University of Rochester
CPL	Jimmy Carter Presidential Library, Atlanta

257

CVW-YU	C. Vann Woodward Papers, Yale University Archives, Sterling Memorial Library
CWH	*Civil War History*
DAB	*Dictionary of American Biography*
DBP	Daniel Bell Papers, Daniel Bell's residence, Cambridge, Mass.
DDV	*Der Deutsche Volkswirt*
DP-SU	David M. Potter Papers, Department of Special Collections, Stanford University
DSC-UC	Department of Special Collections, Regenstein Library, University of Chicago
EDP	Ernest Dichter Papers, originally seen in Dichter residence in Peekskill, N.Y., now located at Die Fachbibliothek am Institut für Publizistik-und Kommunikationswissenschaft, University of Vienna
FO-UM	Financial Operations Papers, Bentley Historical Library, University of Michigan
FRB	*Federal Reserve Bulletin*
GHQ	*Georgia Historical Quarterly*
GK-UM	George Katona Papers, Bentley Historical Library, University of Michigan
GS-B	Gustav Stolper Papers, Bundesarchiv, Berlin
HBR	*Harvard Business Review*
HHW-PU	H. H. Wilson Papers, Public Policy Papers, Department of Rare Books and Special Collections, Princeton University Library
HPE	*History of Political Economy*
IHN	*Intellectual History Newsletter*
JAH	*Journal of American History*
JFH	*Journal of Family History*
JPE	*Journal of Political Economy*
JScH	*Journal of Social History*
JSH	*Journal of Southern History*
JVM-HP	James V. McConnell Papers, History of Psychology Archives, University of Akron
LAT	*Los Angeles Times*
LHJ	*Ladies' Home Journal*
MH	*Maryland Historian*
MVHR	*Mississippi Valley Historical Review*
NEQ	*New England Quarterly*
NR	*New Republic*
NW	*Newsweek*
NY	*New Yorker*
NYRB	*New York Review of Books*

NYT	*New York Times*
NYTBR	*New York Times Book Review*
NYTM	*New York Times Magazine*
OHC-CU	Oral History Collection, Oral History Research Office, Butler Library, Columbia University
PM	*People Magazine*
POQ	*Public Opinion Quarterly*
PPPS	Vance Packard Papers, Rare Books and Special Collections, Pennsylvania State University Libraries, University Park
PSQ	*Presidential Studies Quarterly*
PSR	*Political Science Review*
RAH	*Reviews in American History*
RC-YU	Rachel Carson Papers, Yale Collection of American Literature, Beinecke Rare Book and Manuscript Library, Yale University
RES	*Review of Economics and Statistics*
RHR	*Radical History Review*
RL-UM	Rensis Likert Papers, Bentley Historical Library, University of Michigan
SCAN	*Smith College Associated News*
SEP	*Saturday Evening Post*
SG	*Survey Graphic*
SI	*Sports Illustrated*
SR	*Saturday Review*
SRL	*Saturday Review of Literature*, which changed its name to *Saturday Review* with the January 19, 1952, issue
UA-PU	University Archives, Mudd Library, Princeton University
USNWR	*U.S. News and World Report*
VPR-UM	Vice President for Research, Bentley Historical Library, University of Michigan
WBMC-JCL	White Burkett Miller Center of Public Affairs, University of Virginia, Jimmy Carter Library, Atlanta
WSJ	*Wall Street Journal*
YR	*Yale Review*

Introduction

1. For recent works on the history of consumer culture, see Kathleen G. Donohue, *Freedom from Want: American Liberalism and the Idea of the Consumer* (Baltimore: Johns Hopkins University Press, 2003), and Lizabeth Cohen, *A Consumers' Republic: The Politics of Mass Consumption in Postwar America* (New York: Knopf, 2003). For previously published portions of these projects, see Kathleen G. Donohue, "What Gender Is the Consumer? The Role of Gender Connotations in Defining the Political," *Journal of American Studies* 33 (Apr. 1999): 19–44; and "From Cooperative Commonwealth to Cooperative Democracy: The American

Cooperative Ideal, 1880–1940," in *Consumers against Capitalism? Consumer Cooperation in Europe, North America, and Japan, 1840–1990,* ed. Ellen Furlough and Carl Strikwerda (London: Rowman and Littlefield, 1999), 115–34; and Lizabeth Cohen, "A Middle-Class Utopia? The Suburban Home in the 1950s," in *Making Choices: A New Perspective on the History of Domestic Life in Illinois,* ed. Janice Tauer Wass (Springfield: Illinois State Museum, 1995), 59–67; "A Consumer's Republic: The Politics of Consumption in Postwar America: An Interview with Lizabeth Cohen," conducted by Lisa Kannenberg and Lisa Phillips, *Journal of the Rutgers University Libraries* 57 (1995): 6–23; "From Town Center to Shopping Center: The Reconfiguration of Community Marketplaces in Postwar America," *AHR* 101 (Oct. 1996): 1050–81; and "Citizens and Consumers in the Century of Mass Consumption," in *Perspectives on Modern America: Making Sense of the Twentieth Century,* ed. Harvard Sitkoff (New York: Oxford University Press, 2001), 145–61. In recent years a number of thoughtful books have worked to recast the history of consumer culture: see, for example, Andrew Hurley, *Diners, Bowling Alleys, and Trailer Parks: Chasing the American Dream in Postwar Consumer Culture* (New York: Basic Books, 2001); Michael Kammen, *American Culture, American Tastes: Social Change and the 20th Century* (New York: Knopf, 1999); Ted Ownby, *American Dreams in Mississippi: Consumers, Poverty, and Culture, 1830–1998* (Chapel Hill: University of North Carolina Press, 1995); Kathy Peiss, *Hope in a Jar: The Making of America's Beauty Culture* (New York: Metropolitan Books, 1998); Robert J. Samuelson, *The Good Life and Its Discontents: The American Dream in the Age of Entitlement, 1945–1995* (New York: Random House, 1995). In addition, three edited books capture the current state of the field: Lawrence B. Glickman, ed., *Consumer Society in American History: A Reader* (Ithaca: Cornell University Press, 1999); Jennifer Scanlon, ed., *The Gender and Consumer Culture Reader* (New York: New York University Press, 2002); and Juliet B. Schor and Douglas B. Holt, ed., *The Consumer Society Reader* (New York: New Press, 2000). Robert M. Collins, *More: The Politics of Economic Growth in Postwar America* (New York: Oxford University Press, 2000), an exploration of the public policy of affluence, focuses on issues parallel to this study.

2. My discussion of changing varieties of moralism draws on Daniel Horowitz, *The Morality of Spending: Attitudes toward the Consumer Society in America, 1875–1940* (Baltimore: Johns Hopkins University Press, 1985), esp. xvii–xix.

3. For an important analysis of the psychological turn in American thought in the years this book examines, see Ellen Herman, *The Romance of American Psychology: Political Culture in the Age of Experts* (Berkeley: University of California Press, 1995).

4. Among the major interpretations of American intellectual life in the postwar world are Paul R. Gorman, *Left Intellectuals and Popular Culture in Twentieth-Century America* (Chapel Hill: University of North Carolina Press, 1996); Alexander Bloom, *Prodigal Sons: The New York Intellectuals and Their World* (New York: Oxford University Press, 1986); Richard H. Pells, *The Liberal Mind in a Conservative Age: American Intellectuals in the 1940s and 1950s* (New York: Harper and Row, 1985); and Alan H. Wald, *The New York Intellectuals: The Rise and Decline of the Anti-Stalinist Left from the 1930s to the 1980s* (Chapel Hill: University of North Carolina Press, 1987).

5. Martin Jay, *The Dialectical Imagination: A History of the Frankfurt School and the Institute of Social Research, 1923–1950* (Boston: Little, Brown, 1973), esp. 173–218; quotes 216. See also Vanessa R. Schwartz, "Walter Benjamin for Historians," *AHR* 106 (Dec. 2001): 1721–42.

6. For the key documents, see William H. Whyte, *The Organization Man* (New York: Simon and Schuster, 1956), and David Riesman, *The Lonely Crowd: A Study of the Changing American Character* (New Haven: Yale University Press, 1950). An invaluable tool for tracking the popularity of books is Keith L. Justice, *Bestseller Index: All Books, by Author, on the Lists of*

"Publishers Weekly" and the "New York Times" through 1990 (Jefferson, N.C.: McFarland, 1998).

1. Chastened Consumption

1. Thaddeus Russell, *Out of the Jungle: Jimmy Hoffa and the Remaking of the American Working Class* (New York: Knopf, 2001), 207–8; Amy Bentley, *Eating for Victory: Food Rationing and the Politics of Domesticity* (Urbana: University of Illinois Press, 1998), 3–5, quote 3; Jean-Christophe Agnew, "Coming Up for Air: Consumer Culture in Historical Perspective," *IHN* 12 (1990): 14. This discussion also relies on Mark Weiner, "Consumer Culture and Participatory Democracy: The Study of Coca-Cola during World War II," *Food and Foodways* 6 (1996): 111–12; Robert B. Westbrook, "Fighting for the American Family: Private Interests and Political Obligation in World War II," in *The Power of Culture: Critical Essays in American History*, ed. Richard Wrightman Fox and T. J. Jackson Lears (Chicago: University of Chicago Press, 1993), 195–221; Robert B. Westbrook, "'I Want a Girl, Just Like the Girl that Married Harry James': American Women and the Problem of Political Obligation in World War II," *AQ* 42 (Dec. 1990): 587–614; Mark H. Leff, "The Politics of Sacrifice on the American Home Front in World War II," *JAH* 77 (Mar. 1991): 1296–1318.

2. For the way Americans before 1940 wrestled with the questions raised by consumer culture, see Daniel Horowitz, *The Morality of Spending: Attitudes toward the Consumer Society in America, 1875–1940* (Baltimore: Johns Hopkins University Press, 1985).

3. Robert S. Lynd and Helen M. Lynd, *Middletown: A Study in American Culture* (New York: Harcourt, Brace and World, 1929).

4. Robert S. Lynd, "Living in the Present," *Parents' Magazine* 9 (June 1934): 23 and 74. On Lynd's view of consumer culture, see Horowitz, *Morality of Spending*, 134, 135, 148–52, 158, and 164; Richard Wrightman Fox, "Epitaph for Middletown: Robert S. Lynd and the Analysis of Consumer Culture," in *The Culture of Consumption: Critical Essays in American History, 1880–1980*, ed. Richard Wrightman Fox and T. J. Jackson Lears (New York: Pantheon Books, 1983), 103–41.

5. Sheila Kishler Bennett and Glen H. Elder Jr., "Women's Work in the Family Economy: A Study of Depression Hardship in Women's Lives," *JFH* 4 (summer 1979): 153–54.

6. Alan Brinkley, *The End of Reform: New Deal Liberalism in Recession and War* (New York: Knopf, 1995), 66–72, 116–17, and 231–33. For a discussion of American life on the eve of World War II, see Ross Gregory, *America, 1941: A Nation at the Crossroads* (New York: Free Press, 1989). On the importance of wartime propaganda, see Alan M. Winkler, *The Politics of Propaganda: The Office of War Information, 1942–1945* (New Haven: Yale University Press, 1978). Among the most recent of the many books on America during the war are John W. Jeffries, *Wartime America: The World War II Home Front* (Chicago: Ivan R. Dee, 1996), and as a useful counter to the theme of the war's beneficent results, Michael C. C. Adams, *The Best War Ever: America and World War II* (Baltimore: Johns Hopkins University Press, 1994). For an important collection of essays, see Lewis A. Ehrenberg and Susan E. Hirsch, eds., *The War in American Culture: Society and Consciousness during World War II* (Chicago: University of Chicago Press, 1996).

7. Joseph Chamberlain Furnas produced a three-volume social history of the United States, which appeared in 1969, 1974, and 1978; see "J. C. Furnas, Wry Historian of American Life, Dies at 95," *NYT*, June 12, 2001, C19. For his account, see J. C. Furnas, *My Life in Writing: Memoirs of a Maverick* (New York: William Morrow, 1989), 236–37. For more scientific studies of wartime household budgets, see, for example, University of California,

Heller Committee for Research in Social Economics, *Quantity and Cost Budget for Dependent Families or Children* (Berkeley: University of California Press, 1943); U.S. Office of Price Administration, Division of Research, Consumer Income and Demand Branch, *Estimates of the Distribution of Consumer Income in the United States* (Washington, D.C.: Government Printing Office, 1942).

8. J. C. Furnas and the Staff of *Ladies' Home Journal, How America Lives* (New York: Henry Holt, 1941), 82–83; unidentified African American woman paraphrased 278. The sample included an unemployed union member and a college-educated engineer who worked at a General Electric factory (49–61 and 101–6). On the magazine in an earlier period, see Jennifer Scanlon, *Inarticulate Longings: The "Ladies' Home Journal," Gender, and the Promises of Consumer Culture* (New York: Routledge, 1995).

9. On the study's method and resources, see Furnas, *How America Lives*, 6–9. For some background information on the series and its role in reviving *Ladies' Home Journal*, see Bruce Gould and Beatrice Blackmar Gould, *American Story* (New York: Harper and Row, 1968), 202–6.

10. Mary Carson Cookman, "The Families and the Idea," in Furnas, *How America Lives*, 13. The translation into today's dollars, here and throughout the book, relies on the Consumer Price Index–Urban figures for urban consumers. For a perceptive review, see William Allen White, review of *How America Lives*, *SRL*, Mar. 15, 1941, 14. For a discussion of the series, see Nancy A. Walker, *Shaping Our Mothers' World: American Women's Magazines* (Jackson: University Press of Mississippi, 2000), 117–24.

11. Furnas, *How America Lives*, 223–24, 226, 230, and 236.

12. Ibid., 234 and 239.

13. Ibid., 223–24 and 229. For another example of the way the report minimized extravagance, see 141. For a discussion of the notion of comfort in the eighteenth century, see two works by John E. Crowley: "The Sensibility of Comfort," *AHR* 104 (June 1999): 749–82, and *The Invention of Comfort: Sensibilities and Design in Early Modern Britain and Early America* (Baltimore: Johns Hopkins University Press, 2001).

14. Furnas, *How America Lives*, 207, 213, and 214.

15. Ibid., 207, 215, 216, and 218.

16. Ibid., 212, 216, and 217–19.

17. Ibid., 35 and a picture caption between 40 and 41.

18. Ibid., 37, 38, and 44.

19. Ibid., 36, 42, and 43.

20. Ibid., 37–39, 42, and 45.

21. Gregory, *America, 1941*, 73–74, discusses household incomes in the early 1940s, noting that in 1941, $1,500 was close to the median cash income, with 25 percent of families having total (cash and goods) incomes below $1,000.

22. Furnas, *How America Lives*, 83.

23. Ibid., 82, 86, 87, 93, 94, and 95.

24. Ibid., 82, 87, and 96.

25. Ibid., 127, 128, 129, 130, and 132.

26. Ibid., 129–31.

27. Ibid., 174; on the relation between consumption, self-respect, and middle-class life, see 1 and 154.

28. Ibid., 162 and 141; Cookman, "Families and the Idea," 21.

29. J. C. Furnas, "How America Lives," in Furnas, *How America Lives*, 26; see also 42. For a similar statement, this one concerning a family in even less fortunate circumstances, see 157.

30. Furnas, *My Life in Writing*, 255; Furnas, "How America Lives," 26–27 and 30–31.

31. Furnas, "How America Lives," 29; Furnas, *How America Lives*, 275, 171, and 173. On self-denying wives, see Grace L. Pennock, "America's Housekeeping," in Furnas, *How America Lives*, 279–90, and on the hiding of achievements, 205 and 235.

32. Robert Lekachman, *The Ages of Keynes* (New York: Random House, 1966), 151.

33. Robert J. Havighurst and H. Gerthon Morgan, *The Social History of a War-Boom Community* (New York: Longmans, Green, 1951), 110 and 123.

34. University of California, Heller Committee for Research in Social Economics, *War-time Budgets for Three Income Levels* (Berkeley: University of California Press, 1944), 6, 14–15, 44, and 67–70; Havighurst and Morgan, *War-Boom Community*, 124–28 and 248; University of California, Heller Committee for Research in Social Economics, *Quantity and Cost Budgets for Three Income Levels* (Berkeley: University of California Press, 1942), 14; Heller Committee, *Wartime Budgets for Three Income Levels* (Berkeley: University of California Press; 1943), 6; University of California, Heller Committee for Research in Social Economics, *Wartime Budget for Three Income Levels* (Berkeley: University of California Press, 1945), 4; Richard R. Lingeman, *Don't You Know There's a War On? The American Home Front, 1941–1945* (New York: G. P. Putnam's Sons, 1970), 272; Geoffrey Perrett, *Days of Sadness, Years of Triumph: The American People, 1939–1945* (New York: Coward, McCann, and Geohegan, 1973), 129.

35. *Wartime Health and Education*, Hearings before a Subcommittee on Education and Labor, U.S. Senate (Washington, D.C.: Government Printing Office, 1945), 3: x–xi, quoted in Richard Pollenberg, *War and Society: The United States, 1941–1945* (Philadelphia: J. B. Lippincott, 1972), 88; Havighurst and Morgan, *War-Boom Community*, 126. Other information comes from Perrett, *Days of Sadness*, 354. Jeffries, *Wartime America*, 61–66, offers a carefully balanced analysis of the war as a leveling experience.

36. Bentley, *Eating for Victory*, 1; Harvey Green, *The Uncertainty of Everyday Life, 1915–1945* (New York: HarperCollins, 1992), 149; William L. O'Neill, *A Democracy at War: America's Fight at Home and Abroad in World War II* (New York: Free Press, 1993), 247–66. On the OPA, see Meg Jacobs, "'How About Some Meat?' The Office of Price Administration, Consumption Politics, and State-Building from the Bottom-Up, 1941–1946," *JAH* 84 (Dec. 1997): 910–41. On the politics of consumption in the 1930s, see Meg Jacobs, "'Democracy's Third Estate': New Deal Politics and the Construction of a 'Consuming Public,'" *International Labor and Working-Class History* 55 (spring 1999): 27–51.

37. Lawrence R. Samuel, *Pledging Allegiance: American Identity and the Bond Drive of World War II* (Washington, D.C.: Smithsonian Institution Press, 1997), xiv, 19, and 50.

38. For arguments along these lines, see Herbert Agar et al., *The City of Man: A Declaration on World Democracy* (New York: Viking, 1940), 17–18, 33, and 86; Archibald MacLeish, "The American Cause," *SG* 30 (Jan. 1941): 21–23; Stephen J. Sniegoski, "Unified Democracy: An Aspect of American World War II Interventionist Thought, 1939–1941," *MH* 9 (1978): 33–48. For biographical information I am relying on Donald L. Miller, *Lewis Mumford: A Life* (New York: Weidenfeld and Nicholson, 1989), esp. 389–451. For a useful summary of the major themes in Mumford's work, see Frank G. Novak Jr., "Lewis Mumford as a Critic of American Culture" (Ph.D. diss., University of Tennessee, 1975), esp. 180–85. On Mumford's cultural criticism through the 1930s, see Casey Nelson Blake, *Beloved Community: The Cultural Criticism of Randolph Bourne, Van Wyck Brooks, and Lewis Mumford* (Chapel Hill: University of North Carolina Press, 1990). For a discussion of Mumford's writings on simplicity, see David E. Shi, *The Simple Life: Plain Living and High Thinking in American Culture* (New York: Oxford University Press, 1985), 230–31 and 243–46.

39. Lewis Mumford, "What I Believe," *Forum* 84 (Nov. 1930): 265–66; Miller, *Mumford*, 326–29, summarizes this book.

40. For an example of his critique of liberalism, see Lewis Mumford, "The Corruption of Liberalism," *NR*, Apr. 29, 1940, 568–73.

41. Lewis Mumford, "The Social Responsibilities of Teachers" (1939), in *Values for Survival: Essays, Addresses, and Letters on Politics and Education* (New York: Harcourt, Brace, 1946), 139–40 and 143. For the controversy that Mumford's arguments provoked, see William L. O'Neill, *A Better World: The Great Schism: Stalinism and the American Intellectuals* (New York: Simon and Schuster, 1982), 32–38.

42. Lewis Mumford, *Faith for Living* (New York: Harcourt, Brace, 1940), 212, 283–84, 318, and 331. On his writing of the book, see Miller, *Mumford*, 404. For an earlier interventionist book that only briefly mentions the issue of a standard of living, see Lewis Mumford, *Men Must Act* (New York: Harcourt, Brace, 1939), 26–27. In his memoir, Arthur M. Schlesinger Jr. recalls that this book provoked him to object "to the moralistic hectoring of elders like Lewis Mumford, who saw college students as spoiled by luxury"; Arthur M. Schlesinger Jr., *A Life in the Twentieth Century: Innocent Beginnings, 1917–1950* (Boston: Houghton Mifflin, 2000), 245.

43. Mumford, *Faith for Living*, 217, 282, and 286.

44. Ibid., 312, 313, 315–17, and 319.

45. Lewis Mumford, "A Long-Term View of the War," *Progressive Education* 19 (Nov. 1942): 358–60.

46. Lewis Mumford, *The Condition of Man* (New York: Harcourt, Brace, 1944), 408 and 421. On Mumford's concerns about the adverse effects of his moralism, see Miller, *Mumford*, 413. For a review, see Daniel Bell in *Atlantic Monthly* 174 (July 1944): 131.

47. Mumford, *Condition of Man*, 407–8 and 414.

48. Ibid., 413–14 and 421–23.

49. Ibid., 415. See Lewis Mumford, *The Conduct of Life* (New York: Harcourt, Brace, 1951), 270–90, for a later example of his insistence on simplification of life, social renewal, and public participation.

50. Reinhold Niebuhr, *The Children of Light and the Children of Darkness: A Vindication of Democracy and a Critique of Its Traditional Defense* (New York: Charles Scribner's Sons, 1944), 23; Philip Wylie, *Generation of Vipers* (New York: Rinehart, 1942), 222–23. On Niebuhr's life in this period, see Richard Wrightman Fox, *Reinhold Niebuhr: A Biography* (New York: Pantheon, 1985), esp. 166–223.

51. Bruce Barton, "Another View of the Post-War World" [late Sept. 1943], 2, 4, and 6, box 70, BA 64, BB-WHS, 2, 4, and 6. To date this document, I am relying on Bruce Barton to DeWitt Wallace, Sept. 30, 1943, BB-WSHS, BA 63, box 70. I am grateful to the late Roland Marchand for bringing this document to my attention. On Barton, see T. J. Jackson Lears, "From Salvation to Self-Realization: Advertising and the Therapeutic Roots of the Consumer Culture, 1880–1930," in Fox and Lears, *Culture of Consumption*, 29–38.

52. The quotes are from Caroline F. Ware, *The Consumer Goes to War: A Guide to Victory on the Home Front* (New York: Funk and Wagnalls, 1942), 2 and 3; see also 1–4, 79, 84–85, and 155.

53. Lewis Mumford, Dec. 1, 1940, radio speech, in Mumford, *Values for Survival*, 57–58; Geddes Mumford to his parents, early 1944, quoted vii; Geddes Mumford to his parents, July 16, 1944, quoted in Lewis Mumford, *Green Memories: The Story of Geddes Mumford* (New York: Harcourt, Brace, 1947), 318; Geddes Mumford to his parents, Aug. 27, 1944, quoted 327; Miller, *Mumford*, 424. For the impact of the son's death on the father, see Miller,

Mumford, 424–27 and 435–45; Mumford, *Green Memories*; Lewis Mumford to Frederic J. Osborne, Dec. 13, 1944, in *Letters of Lewis Mumford and Frederic J. Osborne: A Transatlantic Dialogue, 1938–70*, ed. Michael R. Hughes (Bath: Adams and Dart, 1971), 69. For Mumford's continuing engagement with issues raised by his son's death, see Lewis Mumford, *My Works and Days: A Personal Chronicle* (New York: Harcourt Brace Jovanovich, 1978), 400–412.

54. Robert K. Merton, *Mass Persuasion: The Social Psychology of a War Bond Drive* (New York: Harper and Brothers, 1946), 55; Lingeman, *Don't You Know*, 271–72 and 283.

55. John Morton Blum, *V Was for Victory: Politics and American Culture during World War II* (New York: Harcourt Brace Jovanovich, 1976), 92–105 and 115–16; Lekachman, *Keynes*, 163.

56. Leff, "Politics of Sacrifice," 1297; John Kenneth Galbraith, *A Life in Our Times* (Boston: Houghton Mifflin, 1980), 172, quoted in Bentley, *Eating for Victory*, 3; Westbrook, "Fighting for the American Family," 213; advertisement for Nash Kelvinator in *SEP*, Apr. 17, 1943, inside front cover and facing page; Frank W. Fox, *Madison Avenue Goes to War* (Provo: Brigham Young University Press, 1975), 87, quoting a Norge advertisement in *BHG* (March 1945): 65. See Samuel, *Pledging Allegiance*, 207–9 and 217–18, on the campaign to turn wartime savings into postwar spending. On how Americans envisioned a postwar cornucopia, see Blum, *V Was for Victory*, 100–104; Fox, *Madison Avenue*, 85–89; Leff, "Politics of Sacrifice," 1313. For Caroline Ware's evocation of a postwar consumer society, see her *Consumer Goes to War*, 143 and 224–62.

57. Mumford, "Long-Term View," 358, 359, and 360.

2. Celebratory Émigrés

1. The quote is from Anthony Heilbut, *Exiled in Paradise: German Refugee Artists and Intellectuals in America from the 1930s to the Present* (New York: Viking, 1983), 119–20. Like another émigré, Albert O. Hirschman, Dichter and Katona believed that the passion for market consumption strengthened the social order; see Albert O. Hirschman, *The Passions and the Interests: Political Arguments for Capitalism before Its Triumph* (Princeton: Princeton University Press, 1977), 20–42.

2. Godfrey Hodgson, *America in Our Time* (New York: Random House, 1976), 67–98, discusses the ideology of the ruling consensus. Elizabeth A. Fones-Wolf, *Selling Free Enterprise: The Business Assault on Labor and Liberalism, 1945–60* (Urbana: University of Illinois Press, 1994), explores the contested meanings of the American way of life in the postwar period. For a briefer version of this chapter, see Daniel Horowitz, "The Émigré as Celebrant of American Consumer Culture: George Katona and Ernest Dichter," in *Getting and Spending: European and American Consumer Societies in the Twentieth Century*, ed. Susan Strasser, Charles McGovern, and Matthias Judt (Cambridge: Cambridge University Press, 1998), 149–66. In *The Business Response to Keynes, 1929–1964* (New York: Columbia University Press, 1981), Robert M. Collins explores the views of corporate leaders which in many ways parallel those of Dichter and Katona.

3. For full coverage of the first thirty years of the postwar period, see James T. Patterson, *Grand Expectations: The United States, 1945–1974* (New York: Oxford University Press, 1996), esp. 61–81 and 311–74.

4. Meg Jacobs, "'How About Some Meat?': The Office of Price Administration, Consumption Politics, and State-Building from the Bottom Up, 1941–1946," *JAH* 84 (Dec. 1997): 910–41, and "'Democracy's Third Estate': New Deal Politics and the Construction of

a 'Consuming Public,'" *International Labor and Working-Class History* 55 (spring 1999): 27–51.

5. Among the best sources of biographical information are "Ernest Dichter," in *Contemporary Authors*, New Revision Series 44 (Detroit: Gale Research Co., 1994), 108–9; "Ernest Dichter," in *Who's Who in America*, 44th ed. (Wilmette, Ill.: Macmillan, 1986), 707; "Ernest Dichter, 84, a Consultant on Consumer Motivation, Is Dead," *NYT*, Nov. 21, 1991, 12; Ernest Dichter, interview with Daniel Horowitz, Apr. 8, 1986, Peekskill, N.Y.; Bill Miksch, "Inside Dr. Dichter," *Sponsor*, Aug. 3, 1957, 33–36, and 57–59; "Ernest Dichter of Croton: 'A Doctor for Ailing Products,'" *Printers' Ink*, June 26, 1959, 76; Ernest Dichter, *Getting Motivated by Ernest Dichter: The Secret behind Individual Motivations by the Man Who Was Not Afraid to Ask "Why"* (New York: Pergamon Press, 1979). *Getting Motivated*, Dichter's autobiography, on which I have frequently relied for biographical information, is somewhat disorganized, vague as to details and chronology, and full of boastful and unqualified claims. Dichter's papers, which consist mainly of the reports he wrote for corporations and advertising agencies, are in the University of Vienna's Fachbibliothek am Institut für Publizistik-und Kommunikationswissenschaft; I saw them at the Dichter residence in Peekskill, N.Y., while he was still living. There is virtually nothing written on Dichter. One exception is Barbara B. Stern, "Literary Criticism and the History of Marketing Thought: A New Perspective on 'Reading' Marketing Theory," *Journal of the Academy of Marketing Science* 18 (fall 1990): 329–36. For a narrowly focused but nonetheless useful introduction to ideas about market research, see Robert Bartels, *The History of Marketing Thought*, 2d ed. (Columbus: Grid, 1976). Jagdish N. Sheth, David M. Gardner, and Dennis E. Garrett, *Marketing Theory: Evolution and Evaluation* (New York: John Wiley & Sons, 1988), is a more recent and more theoretically oriented treatment of American marketing thought in the twentieth century. Richard S. Tedlow, *New and Improved: The Story of Mass Marketing in America* (New York: Basic Books, 1990), which does not mention Dichter, is organized around a series of case histories. Walter A. Friedman, "The Peddler's Progress: Salesmanship, Science, and Magic, 1880–1940" (Ph.D. diss., Columbia University, 1996), recaptures the earlier history of marketing, including the reliance on psychology. On the emergence of mass marketing, see also Susan Strasser, *Satisfaction Guaranteed: The Making of the American Mass Market* (New York: Pantheon Books, 1989).

6. On his studies with Charlotte M. Bühler and other information in this discussion, see Dichter, Horowitz interview. He also studied with Karl Bühler. On the Bühlers, see Eileen A. Gavin, "Charlotte M. Bühler (1893–1974)," in *Women in Psychology: A Bio-Bibliographic Sourcebook*, ed. Agnes N. O'Connell and Nancy Felipe Russo (New York: Greenwood Press, 1989), 49–56; "Charlotte M. Bühler" and "Karl Bühler," in Leonard Zusne, *Biographical Dictionary of Psychology* (Westport, Conn.: Greenwood Press, 1984), 64–66; Charlotte Bühler, *From Birth to Maturity: An Outline of the Psychological Development of the Child* (London: Routledge and Kegan Paul, 1935). For additional information on his education, see Dichter, *Getting Motivated*, 43–44; Ernest Dichter, interview with Rena Bartos, "Ernest Dichter: Motive Interpreter," *Journal of Advertising Research* 17 (1977): 3. Dichter considered Moritz Schlick the teacher who most impelled him to ask questions that went beneath the surface. A founder of modern analytic philosophy, Schlick instructed Dichter in courses on logic and epistemology: Dichter, *Getting Motivated*, 70 and 178. For information on Schlick, see Béla Juhos, "Moritz Schlick," in *The Encyclopedia of Philosophy*, ed. Paul Edwards (New York: Macmillan, 1967), 7:319–24. His mentors also included Wilhelm Stekel and August Aichhorn. On Stekel, see "Wilhelm Stekel," in Zusne, *Biographical Dictionary of Psychology*, 407–8; Henri F. Ellenberger, *The Discovery of the Unconscious: The History and Evolution of Dynamic Psychiatry* (New York: Basic Books, 1970), 454, 456, 584–85, and 596–99; Reuben Fine, *A*

History of Psychoanalysis (New York: Columbia University Press, 1979), 73 and 87. On Aichhorn, see Ellenberger, *Discovery of the Unconscious*, 619, 831–32, and 847; Fine, *History of Psychoanalysis*, 107 and 409.

For Dichter's connection to Lazarsfeld, see Miksch, "Inside Dr. Dichter," 36. On these aspects of Lazarsfeld's work, see Lewis Coser, *Refugee Scholars in America: Their Impact and Their Experiences* (New Haven: Yale University Press, 1984), 112; Paul F. Lazarsfeld, "Public Attitudes toward Economic Problems," *Market Research* 5 (Aug. 1936): 13–15. On the fascists' investigation and detention of Dichter, see Dichter, *Getting Motivated*, 16–19. Lazarsfeld said of his research center that the government considered its "activities and personnel subversive, probably with reason"; Paul F. Lazarsfeld, "An Episode in the History of Social Research: A Memoir," in *The Intellectual Migration: Europe and America, 1930–1960*, ed. Donald Fleming and Bernard Bailyn (Cambridge: Harvard University Press, 1969), 295.

7. Dichter, *Getting Motivated*, 24, 29, and 41–42, quotes 24 and 41–42. Dichter's claim to have invented motivational research (MR), and to have done so on the spot, should be taken with a grain of salt. Dichter is hardly the only claimant to the position of founder or preeminent leader in MR; also on such a list would be Pierre Martineau of the *Chicago Tribune*, Burleigh Gardner of Social Research, Inc., and Louis Cheskin of Color Research Institute of America. On Martineau, see Dennis G. Martin, *Origins of Motivation Research: The Advertising Legacy of Pierre Martineau* (Washington, D.C.: American Advertising Federation, 1991). Louis Cheskin, contesting Dichter's claim to have founded MR, asserted that he first used the approach in 1935; see Vance Packard, *The Hidden Persuaders* (New York: David McKay, 1957), 25–26.

8. Dichter, *Getting Motivated*, 35; advertisement for Ivory soap, *SEP*, Mar. 14, 1942, 44. Although he did not always acknowledge the influence of his fellow Austrian, it is not hard to trace Lazarfeld's impact—both his pathbreaking work in market research and his development of a research institute. In the end, Dichter neglected his mentor's emphasis on the quantitative approach and gave everything a Freudian twist. The organization of Lazarsfeld's applied contract work under the auspices of an interdisciplinary research center in Vienna and later in the United States served as a model for Dichter after 1946, as he built on and corrupted what Lazarsfeld later described as his career as a "managerial scholar"; see Lazarsfeld, "Memoir," 272, 279, 281–86, 295–98, 312, and 319, quote 286. In his autobiography, Dichter minimizes Lazarsfeld's importance, something he on occasion acknowledged elsewhere. For Lazarsfeld's early contributions to marketing research, see his chapters in Arthur William Kornhauser, *The Techniques of Market Research from the Standpoint of a Psychologist* (New York: American Management Association, 1935); Lazarsfeld's contributions to Committee on Marketing Research Technique, American Marketing Association, *The Technique of Marketing Research* (New York: McGraw-Hill, 1937); Lazarsfeld, "Memoir," 297. As early as 1934, Lazarsfeld published a paper in the United States that could have laid the ground for some of Dichter's approach, especially the focus on motivation and interpretation, the centrality of subjective data gathered from interviews, and the importance of studying the process of decision making for purchases; see Paul Lazarsfeld, "The Psychological Aspect of Market Research," *HBR* 13 (Oct. 1934): 54–71. For a very useful discussion of Lazarsfeld's work, see Jean Converse, *Survey Research in the United States: Roots and Emergence, 1890–1960* (Berkeley: University of California Press, 1987), esp. 131–44, 149–52, and 257–72. See also Heilbut, *Exiled in Paradise*, 94–100. On how Lazarsfeld figured out how to persuade corporations and advertising agencies that they could benefit from sophisticated methods of market research, see Lazarsfeld, "Psychological Aspect," 71; Arthur W. Kornhauser and Paul F. Lazarsfeld, *The Techniques of Market Research from the Standpoint of a Psychologist* (New York: American Management Association, 1935);

American Marketing Association, *Technique of Marketing Research*. For Theodor W. Adorno's criticism of Lazarsfeld's commitment to carry out scientific research for the benefit of capitalism, see Heilbut, *Exiled in Paradise*, 94–99.

9. The quotes are from "Psychoanalysis in Advertising," *Time*, Mar. 25, 1940, 46–47; Dichter, *Getting Motivated*, 14 (see also 35–42); "Ernest Dichter of Croton," 80; Miksch, "Inside Dr. Dichter," 36. An examination of the relevant data does not support Dichter's claim that automobile manufacturers had not previously advertised in women's magazines: see, for example, advertisements in *LHJ* 55 (Feb. 1938): 40, and 55 (Jan. 1938): 48. On his, and Lazarsfeld's work for CBS, see "Report on Listener Reactions: Based on Lazarsfeld-Stanton Program analyzer," prepared by CBS research department, Program Analysis Division, Apr. 1945, EDP; Ernest Dichter, "Psychodramatic Research Project on Commodities as Intersocial Media," *Sociometry*, 7 (1944): 432; Ernest Dichter, "On the Psychology of Radio Commercials," in *Radio Research, 1942–1943*, ed. Paul F. Lazarsfeld and Frank N. Stanton (New York: Duell, Sloane and Pearce, 1944), 461–81; for information on Lazarsfeld, see James Gilbert, *A Cycle of Outrage: America's Reaction to the Juvenile Delinquent in the 1950s* (New York: Oxford University Press, 1986), 114–16.

10. On Dichter's work in this period, see Dichter, *Getting Motivated*, 60–66, 68, and 74; "Ernest Dichter of Croton" 80; Martin Mayer, *Madison Avenue, U.S.A.* (New York: Harper and Brothers, 1958), 233–42; Perrin Stryker, "'Motivation Research,'" *Fortune* 53 (June 1956): 144–47, 222, 225, 226, 228, 230, and 232; Miksch, "Inside Dr. Dichter," 33–35 and 58; "The Talk of the Town: Meaningful Patterns" *NY*, Jan. 3, 1959, 17–19; Robert H. Boyle, "Not-So-Mad-Doctor and His Living Lab," *SI*, July 24, 1961, 50–56; "Encounter: Ernest Dichter," *Austriakultur*, Mar.–Apr. 1993, 6. For the early development of MR, see Packard, *Hidden*, 25–32 and 268–71; "Inside the Consumer: The New Debate: Does He Know His Own Mind?" *NW*, Oct. 10, 1955, 89–93. On Dichter's method, see Ernest Dichter, "Toward an Understanding of Human Behavior," in *Motivation and Market Behavior*, ed. Robert Ferber and Hugh G. Wales (Homewood, Ill.: Richard D. Unwin, 1958), 21–31; Ernest Dichter, *The Strategy of Desire* (Garden City, N.Y.: Doubleday, 1960), 61–84 and 283–88; [Ernest Dichter], "The Psychology of Bread: A Psychological Study of the Appeals and Motives at Work in Bread Advertising and Merchandising," memorandum prepared by Research Department at J. Stirling Getchell, Inc., [1940], EDP; Ernest Dichter, "Psychology in Market Research," *HBR* 25 (summer 1947): 432–43.

For portraits of Dichter, see unidentified observer, quoted in Boyle, "Not-So-Mad-Doctor," 50; Miksch, "Inside Dr. Dichter," 33–35 and 58; "The Talk of the Town," 17–19; "Encounter: Ernest Dichter," 6. Throughout the twentieth century, but especially since the 1920s, market researchers and public relations experts had emphasized the importance of the nonrational in human behavior. For example, in "Henry Charles Link," *DAB*, supplement 5 (New York: Charles Scribner's Sons, 1977): 433–34, Richard Tedlow notes the use of psychological approaches in advertising during the 1920s. For additional evidence along these lines, see Edward L. Bernays, *Biography of an Idea: Memoirs of Public Relations Counsel Edward L. Bernays* (New York: Simon and Schuster, 1965). For assessments of Dichter's work, and MR more generally, see William Leiss, Stephen Kline, and Sut Jhally, *Social Communication in Advertising: Persons, Products, and Images of Well-Being*, 2d rev. and enlarged ed. (Scarborough, Ont.: Nelson Canada, 1990), 143–44; Stephen Fox, *Mirror Makers: A History of American Advertising and Its Creators* (New York: William Morrow, 1984), 183–87. For a later appraisal, see Horace S. Schwerin and Henry S. Newell, *Persuasion in Marketing: The Dynamics of Marketing's Great Untapped Resource* (New York: John Wiley & Sons, 1981), 104–5. For some of the debate, see Stanley C. Hollander to Daniel Horowitz, June 23, 1994, original in author's possession;

Alfred Politz, quoted in Stryker, "'Motivation Research'" 222; Dichter, "Psychology in Market Research," 443; N. D. Rothwell, "Motivational Research Revisited," *Journal of Marketing* 20 (Oct. 1955): 150–54; Fox, *Mirror Makers*, 184–86 and 194; James V. McConnell, "A Report on Two Lectures on Motivation Research Given by Dr. Dichter—October 20–21," 3, 4, 15, and 16, box M974, JVM-HP; date is probably early 1950s. On the Americanization of Freud, see Nathan G. Hale, *The Rise and Crisis of Psychoanalysis in the United States: Freud and the Americans, 1917–1985* (New York: Oxford University Press, 1995).

11. Ernest Dichter, *Psychology of Everyday Living* (New York: Barnes and Noble, 1947), 142–45. For how his early work reveals that he easily shifted between selling goods and promoting therapeutic self-understanding, see [Ernest Dichter] "The Car—'Seven League Boots,'" ca. 1942, EDP. For other examples of the therapeutic role, [Ernest Dichter], "The Psychology of Car Buying: A Psychological Study Undertaken to Answer Two Vital Questions about Car Buying," prepared by the Research Department, J. Stirling Getchell, January 1940, 6A, EDP.

12. Dichter, *Everyday Living*, 233–35, 238, and 239. As early as 1946, reacting to what he understood as the sickness that produced Nazism and also fearing threats to American democracy, Dichter portrayed himself as a healer offering mass therapy to a sick nation; see Ernest Dichter, "Radio and Television Audience Research," 380, ca. 1945, copy in author's possession. Dichter also tried to assuage Americans' fear of the atomic bomb. He had, as a reporter remarked in 1946, "a great need to sound out people's fears and misconceptions on the subject and then set them straight"; Saul Pett, "Radio Ringside," press release from International News Service, June 6, [1946], EDP.

13. On the response to McCarthyism, see Dichter, Horowitz interview; for the lesson learned from the Nazis, see Dichter, *Getting Motivated*, 103 and 154. For a discussion of the political uses of psychology in the postwar period, see Ellen Herman, *The Romance of American Psychology: Political Culture in the Age of Experts* (Berkeley: University of California Press, 1995).

14. Betty Friedan, *The Feminine Mystique* (New York: W. W. Norton, 1963), 208. Throughout the 1950s and 1960s, Hedy Dichter played a critical, supporting role in her husband's life. She gave up her career in music and served instead as the more active parent and as her husband's traveling companion, sounding board, treasurer, property manager, and interior decorator; see "Encounter: Ernest Dichter," 6; Miksch, "Inside Dr. Dichter," 36 and 57.

15. [Dichter], "Psychology of Car Buying," 82; [Ernest Dichter], "The Psychology of Household Tavern Products," report prepared by the Research Department of J. Stirling Getchell, Inc., Aug. 1940, 9 and 11, EDP.

16. Ernest Dichter, "Electrical Appliances in the Postwar World: A Psychological Study of Women's Attitudes," report for Crowell Collier Publishing Corp. [1945], 1–10 and 16, EDP; "Today's Woman as a Consumer," *Motivations* 1 (Sept. 1956): 1–3. For some changes he made in his estimates and descriptions by 1947, see Dichter, *Everyday Living*, 152–57.

17. "Typology: The Classification of Consumers by Psychological Types as a Tool for Advertising and Merchandising," *Motivations* 3 (Sept. 1958): 31–33. In this case and others, what appeared unsigned in *Motivations* was "Prepared by the staff of the Institute for Motivational Research under the creative direction of Dr. Ernest Dichter"; see *Motivations* 3 (Sept. 1958): 1.

18. Dichter, "Electrical Appliances," 10; Ernest Dichter, quoted in Friedan, *Feminine Mystique*, 210.

19. Dichter, *Everyday Living*, 18, 227, and 230–31; Ernest Dichter, *Handbook of Consumer*

Motivations; The Psychology of the World of Objects (New York: McGraw-Hill 1964), 126–27. For later examples, see "The Psychology of House Cleaning Products," *Motivations* 2 (May 1957): 10–13. For the study for which Dichter became most famous, on General Mills' development of Bisquick as a product through which women could express their creativity, see "Inside the Consumer," 92. For Dichter's discussions of women's sexuality and consumer culture, see Dichter, *Everyday Living*, 143; Ernest Dichter, "A Psychological View of Advertising Effectiveness," *Journal of Marketing* 14 (July 1949): 63; "The Five New Meanings of Beauty," *Motivations* 1 (May 1956): 9–11; Dichter, *Handbook*, 156. For Dichter's work on the Barbie doll, see M. G. Lord, *Forever Barbie: The Unauthorized Biography of a Real Doll* (New York: William Morrow, 1994), 40–41, including quote from Ernest Dichter, ed., "A Motivational Research Study in the Field of Toys for Mattel Toys, Inc.," unpublished study prepared by the Institute for Motivational Research, June 1959, 5. For an example of how Dichter tried to leash explosive female sexuality to consumer culture, see "Put the Libido Back into Advertising," *Motivations* 2 (July 1957): 13–14.

20. Vance Packard, in transcript for NBC radio program, "Conversation," May 6, 1957, 13, PPPS; Dichter, Horowitz interview. On the impact of Packard's work, see Dichter, *Getting Motivated*, 82–85 and 105. For information on his operation, see "Ernest Dichter of Croton," 80; Miksch, "Inside Dr. Dichter," 35; Boyle, "Not-So-Mad-Doctor," 50; "Inside the Consumer," 89–93. At some point, probably around 1970, Dichter discarded what would have been an unparalleled trove of historical material: thousands of hours of tape-recorded interviews with consumers about their feelings toward goods and services. As it is, what remains in the institute's published and unpublished reports are some quotes from the interviews and the much more extensive interpretations by Dichter and his colleagues.

21. The quotes are from Dichter, *Strategy*, 192, 204, and 169; see also 206, 207, and 209.

22. Ibid., 59, 170, 217, 21, 171–72, and 93; see also 128.

23. [Ernest Dichter], "The Psychology of Breakfast Cereals," memorandum prepared by Research Department at J. Stirling Getchell, Inc. [1939 or 1940], 4–5, EDP; Dichter, quoted in James J. Nagel, "Social Scientists Hit on Aloofness," *NYT*, Mar. 19, 1953, 45; Dichter, *Strategy*, 112, 253, 255, and 273.

24. Dichter, quoted in Carl Spielvogel, "Advertising: Recession?" *NYT*, Mar. 19, 1958, C 43; Dichter, *Strategy*, 263 and 17.

25. Dichter, *Strategy*, 179, 180, 88, and 110; Ernest Dichter, "Discovering the 'Inner Jones,'" *HBR* 43 (May 1965): 7. Dichter also argued for more attention to market segmentation; see "Does Your Prestige Stop Sales?" *Motivations* 1 (Feb. 1957), 1–2.

26. Peter Bart, "Advertising: 'M.R.' Use Is Dwindling," *NYT*, Dec. 18, 1962, 11; Eric Clark, *The Want Makers. The World of Advertising: How They Make You Buy* (New York: Viking Penguin, 1989), 78–79; Stern, "Literary Criticism," 331; Peter Bart, "Advertising: A Talk with a Motivation Man," *NYT*, Nov. 5, 1963, 49; Dichter, *Getting Motivated*, 4 and 118–19. For a survey of efforts to market to the African American community, see Robert E. Weems Jr., *Desegregating the Dollar: African American Consumerism in the Twentieth Century* (New York: New York University Press, 1998). On Dichter's reluctance to use African American models, see Bart, "Talk With," 49.

27. Randall Rothenberg, "Capitalist Eye On the Soviet Consumer," *NYT*, Feb. 15, 1989, D 19. See also Dichter, *Getting Motivated*, 139–41; Philip H. Dougherty, "Advertising: Finding Statistics," *NYT*, Jan. 17, 1973, 58; "Dichter Leaves Institute, but Takes Jargon with Him," *Advertising Age*, Jan. 29, 1973, 60; Pace, "Dichter," 12. Late in his life, Dichter taught courses at a number of universities; see "Dichter," in *Contemporary Authors*, 108–9. For a late example of his continuing advocacy of MR, see Ernest Dichter, "Testing Nonverbal Commu-

nications," in *Nonverbal Communication in Advertising*, ed. Sidney Hecker and David W. Stewart (Lexington, Mass.: D. C. Heath, 1989), 29–42.

28. Ernest Dichter, "Energy Crisis—Boom or Doom," unpublished speech, 13, ca. 1974, EDP; for Dichter's epitaph, see Dichter, *Getting Motivated*, 65. Dichter's "Why Not?" may have been a play on, and an optimistic inversion of, Paul Lazarsfeld, "The Art of Asking WHY in Market Research," *National Marketing Review* 1 (1935): 32–43. In *The Conquest of Cool: Business Culture, Counterculture, and the Rise of Hip Consumerism* (Chicago: University of Chicago Press, 1997), Thomas Frank demonstrates that people involved in advertising were precursors of 1960s counterculture; for his discussion of Dichter's suggestion that advertisers learn from psychedelics how to do their jobs more effectively, see 113–14.

29. On this battle between business and labor over inflation, see Meg Jacobs, "Inflation: 'The Permanent Dilemma' of the American Middle Classes," in *Social Contracts under Stress: The Middle Classes of America, Europe, and Japan at the Turn of the Century*, ed. Olivier Zunz, Leonard Schoppa, and Nobuhiro Hiwatari (New York: Russell Sage Press, 2002), 130–53. For Peter Drucker, another émigré intellectual, the corporate manager served the role that the consumer had for Katona, as the balance wheel of a capitalist system.

30. Toni Stolper, *Ein Leben in Brennpunkten Unserer Zeit: Wien, Berlin, New York; Gustav Stolper, 1888–1947* (Tübingen: Rainer Wunderlich Verlag, 1960), 198–99. For background information on Katona's generation of émigrés from Hungary to Germany and Austria, see Lee Congdon, *Exile and Social Thought: Hungarian Intellectuals in Germany and Austria, 1919–1933* (Princeton: Princeton University Press, 1991); Lee Congdon, *Seeing Red: Hungarian Intellectuals in Exile and the Challenge of Communism* (DeKalb: Northern Illinois University Press, 2001). The Bentley Historical Library at the University of Michigan has two boxes of Katona's papers, mostly copies of published materials. Among the collections that contain material, albeit shed relatively little light on the relationship between Katona, his mentors, and his colleagues, are the Toni Stolper Collection at the Leo Baeck Institute in New York; the Gustav Stolper Papers at the Bundesarchiv in Berlin; the Papers of Max Wertheimer at the New York Public Library; material in the possession of Michael Wertheimer of Boulder, Colorado; and several collections in the Archives of the History of American Psychology at the University of Akron.

The best introduction to Katona's life and work, on which I have drawn at a number of points and which contains a bibliography of Katona's writings, is Richard Curtin, "Curtin on Katona," in *Contemporary Economists in Perspective*, ed. Henry W. Spiegel and Warren J. Samuels (Greenwich, Conn.: JAI Press, 1984): 2:495–522. For additional information, see Daniel Horowitz, "George Katona," in *ANB* (New York: Oxford University Press, 1999), 12: 394–95; obituary for George Katona, *NYT*, June 19, 1981, B6; George Katona, *Psychological Economics* (New York: Elsevier, 1975), viii–ix; and Burkhard Strumpel, James N. Morgan, and Ernest Zahn, ed., *Human Behavior in Economic Affairs: Essays in Honor of George Katona* (San Francisco: Jossey-Bass, 1972). On turn-of-the-century Budapest, see John Lukacs, *Budapest 1900: A Historical Portrait of a City and Its Culture* (London: Weidenfeld and Nicholson, 1988).

31. For his writings during this period, see Georg Katona, "Konsumfinanzierung: Die Amerikanische und die deutsche Praxis," *DDV*, Nov. 19, 1926, 241; Georg Katona, "Das 'Verkaufen.' Ein Grund-problem der amerikanischen Wirtschaft," *DDV*, Oct. 29, 1926, 149–51. For his optimism following the stock market crash in 1929, see Georg Katona, "Der New Yorker Börsenkrach," *DDV*, Nov. 1, 1929, 139–42. In contrast, in 1971, Katona noted that on October 29, 1929, he had written "a lead editorial predicting that prosperity had ended and a depression was coming"; George Katona, "Reminiscences," in Strumpel, Morgan, and Zahn, eds., *Human Behavior*, 12. For other writings in this period, see Georg Katona, "Die

Wirtschaftskrise in Amerika," *DDV*, Apr. 15, 1932, 948–53; "Amerikas Krisenbakämpfung: Leistungen und Plane," *DDV*, June 6, 1932, 1216; "Konjunkturoptimismus in Amerika," *DDV*, Aug. 12, 1932, 1511–13; and "Die amerikanische Bankenkrise," *DDV*, Mar. 3, 1933, 695–98. Designed to provide readers with the background information necessary to make investment decisions, much of what Katona wrote on economics in Berlin involved detailed technical discussions of the financial situation of business and government in Germany and the United States.

On the connections between Katona and Stolper, see Günter Schmölders, "George Katona und die Große Depression: Das Berliner Umfeld," in *Ehrenpromotion von Prof. Dr. George Katona, Ann Arbor, Michigan am 15. Jun 1981* (Berlin: Presse-und Informationsstelle der Freïen Universitat, [1982]), 32. The correspondence between Stolper and Katona in these years describes their departure, the formation of their business arrangements, and Stolper's termination of their relationship because illness prevented Katona from returning to work: see, for example, George Katona to Gustav Stolper, July 30, 1933; Stolper to Katona, Aug. 28, 1933; contract between Stolper and Katona, Sept. 27, 1933; and Stolper to Katona, July 12, 1936, GS-B. For his acknowledgment of Stolper's influence, see Katona, *Psychological Economics*, ix. Although scholars have fully recognized the impact of Gestalt psychology on Katona's work, they have ignored or left unexplored the influence of Stolper's economics; see Coser, *Refugee Scholars*, 180; Curtin, "Curtin on Katona," 500. Katona continually recognized the influence of both mentors; see, for example, George Katona, "Interdisciplinary Research," in *Ehrenpromotion*, 39–40. Nonetheless, he often spoke of Wertheimer affectionately and of Stolper in a matter-of-fact manner; Peter Katona, telephone interview with Daniel Horowitz, Sept. 30, 1986. For differential reference to his two mentors, see Katona, *Psychological Economics*, ix, and Katona, "Reminiscences," 12–13. Fritz Ringer, *The Decline of the German Mandarins: The German Academic Community, 1890–1933* (Cambridge: Harvard University Press, 1969), 9, 61–63, and 202–3, sheds light on a number of factors in Stolper's orientation. On Stolper's views soon after his arrival, see Gustav Stolper, "Politics Versus Economics," *Foreign Affairs* 12 (Apr. 1934): 357–76; Gustav Stolper, "Your United States," *SG* 24 (Feb. 1935): 60–62; Gustav Stolper, "Your United States: Inflation," *SG* 24 (Apr. 1935): 200; Gustav Stolper, "Your United States: The Budget," *SG* 24 (Mar. 1935): 117–18. For his later position, see Gustav Stolper, *This Age of Fable: The Political and Economic World We Live In* (New York: Reynal and Hitchcock, 1942); Gustav Stolper, *German Economy 1870–1940: Issues and Trends* (New York: Reynal and Hitchcock, 1940); Gustav Stolper, "A Partnership for Disaster," *Nation's Business* 31 (May 1943): 32. On Stolper's politics, see Stolper, *Ein Leben*. For a discussion of the DDP and of Stolper's place in it, see Bruce B. Frye, *Liberal Democrats in the Weimar Republic: The History of the German Democratic Party and the German State Party* (Carbondale: Southern Illinois University Press, 1985), 1–5, 59–60, 87–88, 100, 106, 109–11, 117, 160–64, 168–74, and 192. On the contributions of émigrés to one field, see Earlene Craver, "The Emigration of the Austrian Economists," *HPE* 18 (spring 1986): 1–32; Coser, *Refugee Scholars*, 137–44. Questions of expectations and optimism were major issues in business cycle theory in 1930s; see, for example, Gottfried von Haberler, *Prosperity and Depression: A Theoretical Analysis of Cyclical Movements* (1937), rev. ed. (Geneva: League of Nations, 1938). For an instance of inflation and statism as major concerns for émigrés, see Friedrich A. Hayek, *The Road to Serfdom* (Chicago: University of Chicago Press, 1944).

32. George Katona, *Organizing and Memorizing: Studies in the Psychology of Learning and Teaching* (New York: Columbia University Press, 1940). For contrasting reviews of the book, see Arthur W. Melton, *American Journal of Psychology* 54 (July 1941): 455–57, and Donald K. Adams, *Character and Personality* 10 (Dec. 1941): 163–64. On his debt to Wertheimer, see

Katona, *Psychological Economics*, ix. On Wertheimer and Gestalt psychology, see Solomon E. Asch, "Gestalt Theory," in *International Encyclopaedia of the Social Sciences* (New York: Macmillan, 1968): 6:158–75; Michael Wertheimer, "Max Wertheimer, Gestalt Prophet," *Gestalt Theory* 2 (1980): 3–17; Abraham S. Luchins, "Max Wertheimer," in *International Encyclopedia of the Social Sciences*, 16:522–26; Abraham S. Luchins and Edith H. Luchins, eds., *Wertheimer's Seminars Revisited: Problem Solving and Thinking* (Albany: Faculty-Student Association of SUNY-Albany, 1970); Max Wertheimer, foreword to George Katona, *Organizing and Memorizing*, vi; Max Wertheimer, *Productive Thinking* (New York: Harper and Brothers, 1945), 64–65 and 189–90. Jean M. Mandler and George Mandler, "The Diaspora of Experimental Psychology: The Gestaltists and Others," in Fleming and Bailyn, *Intellectual Migration*, 371–419; and Michael M. Sokal, "The Gestalt Psychologists in Behaviorist America," *AHR* 89 (Dec. 1984): 1240–63, discuss the migration of Gestalt psychologists to the United States. For Wertheimer's comments on the relevance of Gestalt to the fight against Hitler, see Max Wertheimer, "On the Concept of Democracy," in *Political and Economic Democracy*, ed. Max Ascoli and Fritz Lehmann (New York: W. W. Norton, 1937), 283. On the relationship between Wertheimer's politics and psychology, see Peter M. Rutkoff and William B. Scott, *New School: A History of the New School for Social Research* (New York: Free Press, 1986), 123–27. For an earlier and more experimentally based attempt to explore the relationship between events in Germany and contemporary psychology, see Kurt Lewin, Ronald Lippitt, and Ralph K. White, "Patterns of Aggressive Behavior in Experimentally Created 'Social Climates,'" *Journal of Social Psychology* 10 (1939): 271–99. Of lesser but substantial importance to Katona was the work of Kurt Lewin. On the scholarship of this important émigré psychologist, see Kurt Lewin, *A Dynamic Theory of Personality: Selected Papers* (New York: McGraw-Hill, 1935), 250–54; Alfred J. Marrow, *The Practical Theorist: The Life and Work of Kurt Lewin* (New York: Basic Books, 1969), 244–59, summarizes Lewin's Berlin experiments.

George Katona, *War without Inflation: The Psychological Approach to Problems of War Economy* (New York: Columbia University Press, 1942), 14, 18–19, 20, 23, 57–58, 61, 81, 147, 204. Of all of the books Katona wrote, *War without Inflation* was reviewed most extensively and favorably; see, for example, Sylvia F. Porter, *SRL*, Dec. 26, 1942, 19; James A. Ross Jr., *Annals* 227 (May 1943): 172–73. In George Katona, "Psychological Analysis of Business Decisions and Expectations," *AER* 36 (March 1946): 44–62, he refers to his early work on this subject.

For understanding the debates at the New School, I have drawn on Rutkoff and Scott, *New School*, esp. 107–13 and 127. Of considerable influence on Katona's thinking were the following discussions of class relations and mass society: Hans Speier, "The Salaried Employee in Modern Society," *Social Research* 1 (Feb. 1934): 111–33; Mark Mitnitzky, "Economic Effects of Changes in Consumers' Demand," *Social Research* 1 (May 1934): 199–218; Arthur Feiler, "The Consumer in Economic Policy: German Experience with Consumer Representation," *Social Research* 1 (Aug. 1934): 287–300; Emil Lederer, *State of the Masses: The Threat of the Classless Society* (New York: W. W. Norton, 1940). During the 1920s, Marschak had participated in this debate but by the 1930s his scholarship focused primarily on econometric dimensions of consumption: compare Jacob Marschak, "Der Neue Mittelstand," *Grundriss der Nationaloekonomik* 9 (1926): 120–24, with his later works such as "Consumption (Problems of Measurement)," in *Encyclopedia of the Social Sciences* (New York: Macmillan, 1931): 4:295–301; "Individual and National Income and Consumption" and "Sources for Demand Analysis: Market, Budget, and Income Data," in Cowles Commission for Research in Economics, *Report of Fifth Annual Research Conference in Economics and Statistics Held at Colorado Springs, July 3 to 28, 1939* ([Chicago]: University of Chicago, 1939), 68–70 and 72–75; and "Family Budgets and the So-Called Multiplier," *Canadian Journal of Economics and Political Science* 5 (Aug. 1939): 358–62. See also Emil Lederer and Jacob Marschak, *The New Middle Class* (1926), trans. S. Ellison (New York: Works Progress Administration, 1937); Emil Lederer, *The Problem of the Modern Salaried Employee: Its Theoretical and Statistical Basis* (1912), trans. E. E. Warburg (New York: Works Progress Administration, 1937). For evidence that Katona participated "often" in seminar discussions on topics such as the emergence of the Nazis, class relations in Germany, and the role of the media, see Abraham S. Luchins to author, Feb. 17, 1987, author's possession.

For other work in this period, see George Katona, *Price Control and Business: Field Studies among Producers and Distributors of Consumer Goods in the Chicago Area, 1942–44* (Bloomington, Ind.: Principia Press, 1945). From 1942 to 1944 Katona lived in Chicago, where he was director of research for the Committee on Price Control and Rationing. The project was organized jointly by the Cowles Commission for Research in Economics at the University of Chicago and the Conference on Price Research of the National Bureau of Economic Research. Jacob Marschak arranged for Katona to work on this project. A Menshevik who had fled to Germany from Russia in 1919, Marschak had known Katona in Germany and at the New School. For background on Marschak and the Cowles Commission, see Clifford Hildreth, *The Cowles Commission in Chicago, 1939–1955* (Berlin: Springer-Verlag, 1986), esp. 1–4 and 133. No reviews of *Price Control* appeared in major papers or journals. Katona surely knew of Lazarsfeld. In the 1930s Lazarsfeld worked with Rensis Likert, then an assistant professor of psychology at New York University, on new techniques of market research, including unstructured interviews; see Lazarsfeld, "Memoir," 296–97. It was Likert who invited Katona to join the staff of the USDA and then went with him to Ann Arbor, where he headed the SRC. One of the few items in Katona's papers from the 1940s is a memorandum from Lazarsfeld that touched on the use of surveys which combined economics and psychology and were pertinent to government policy; see Paul Lazarsfeld, "A New Problem Memorandum," May 25, 1942, GK-UM.

33. Katona, *War without Inflation*, 186–88 and 196; Katona, *Price Control*, 223; George Katona, "The Role of the Frame of Reference in War and Post-war Economy," *AJS* 49 (Jan. 1944): 340 and 346–47.

34. On the early surveys and then the move to Ann Arbor, see Rensis Likert, "Courageous Pioneer: Creating a New Field of Knowledge," in Strumpel, Morgan, and Zahn, *Human Behavior*, 4–6. See Lawrence Samuel, *Pledging Allegiance: American Identity and the Bond Drive of World War II* (Washington, D.C.: Smithsonian Institution, 1997), 54, on Likert's role in bond drives. The USDA had carried out a study of why people bought war bonds and how they spent the proceeds when they cashed them in. For the wartime studies, see Division of Program Surveys, "Memorandum on Studies for the Treasury Department" [probably 1943], 1, GK-UM. For information on the origin of the SRC in wartime Washington work, see interview of Rensis Likert, RL-UM. On the transition from Washington to Ann Arbor, see "Curtin on Katona," 502. In 1949 the university established the Institute of Social Research as an umbrella unit over the SRC: see University of Michigan, Survey Research Center, *Second Annual Report of the Survey Research Center* (Ann Arbor: Institute for Social Research, 1949), announcement before 1; James N. Morgan, "A Quarter Century of Behavioral Research in Economics, Persistent Programs and Diversions," in Strumpel, Morgan, and Zahn, *Human Behavior*, 15. For changing patterns of support, see George Katona et al., *1961 Survey of Consumer Finances* (Ann Arbor: Institute for Social Research, 1962), vi. On the history of the ISR and the survey's role within it, see Converse, *Survey Research*, esp. 340–82. Over time, Katona's project diminished as a proportion of the ISR's total effort but nonetheless grew in

size; for earlier figures, see SRC, "Summary of Operations, 1946–47," in University of Michigan, Accounting Department, "Statements of Institute for Social Research," vol. 1, FO-UM; for later figures, see ISR, "Informal Meeting with President Fleming and the University Executive Officers, Nov. 3, 1972," VPR-UM. At the outset, the SCF accounted for over 40 percent of the ISR's costs, but by 1972 it commanded only 13.5 percent. The ISR revenues grew from slightly under $250,000 in its first year to almost $7 million by 1972: ISR, "Informal Meeting." The number of full-time employees increased from 14 at the beginning to almost 350 by 1970: "Comments on 1969–70 Financial Operations of the Institute for Social Research," table VI, VPR-UM. At the outset the federal government supplied almost 98.8 percent of the ISR's funding, a figure that dropped to 28.1 percent in the mid-1950s and then rose to 54.5 percent by 1972; ISR, "Informal Meeting." According to the same document, funds from foundations peaked at 42.5 percent in 1954–55 and then fell to 9.9 percent by 1971–72; university support increased, reaching a high of 16.6 percent in 1962–63 and settling at 13.3 percent in 1971–72; and other sources, mostly corporate, reached a high point of 40.1 percent in 1955–56 and ended up at 22.3 percent in 1971–72. On the field of psychological economics, see Peter E. Earl, *The Economic Imagination: Towards a Behavioural Analysis of Choice* (Armonk, N.Y.: M. E. Sharpe, 1983).

35. In making these comments on Katona as a person, I have relied on Peter Katona, interview.

36. "Curtin on Katona," 505–7, summarizes some of the controversies surrounding Katona's work. For praise of *War without Inflation*, including that from a friend, see Carl Landauer, *AER* 33 (Mar. 43): 161–62; and William Fellner, *JPE* 51 (Aug. 1943): 370–71. For a favorable review of *Psychological Analysis of Economic Behavior*, see Walter A. Weisskopf, *JPE* 60 (Apr. 1952): 165–66. In contrast, Katona's later books received unfavorable or silent treatment from economic journals: *Mass Consumption Society* went unnoticed in the principal periodicals in economics, and *Powerful Consumer* received unfavorable reviews; see Margaret G. Reid, *AER* 51 (Mar. 1961): 163–64; and F. Thomas Juster, *JPE* 69 (Oct. 1961): 503–4. In "On the Predictive Value of Consumer Intentions and Attitudes," *RES* 41 (Feb. 1959): 1–11, James Tobin discussed the doubts that economists, including himself, had about the predictive values of attitudinal data but also recognized Katona's "imaginative and pioneering work" (11). For a discussion of the debates surrounding the reliability of the survey and Katona's work, see Harold T. Shapiro, "The Index of Consumer Sentiment and Economic Forecasting: a Reappraisal," in Strumpel, Morgan, and Zahn, *Human Behavior*, 373–96. On recent skepticism about the explanatory power of consumer confidence surveys, see Louis Uchitelle, "Consumer Confidence Index Goes from an Aha to a Hmm," *NYT*, June 8, 2002, A1 and 19.

The Katona papers contain clippings from newspapers, the business press, government documents, and financial services that shed light on the SCF's influence. For other sources on the debate over the impact of Katona's contribution, see Charles Dollard, interview of 1966, 204, OHC-CU; Neil H. Jacoby, interview of 1970, 91–92, OHC-CU; Philip Revzin, "Consumer-Sentiment Surveys Proliferate, but Many Concerns Use Them Cautiously," *WSJ*, Jan. 8, 1977, 26; Dan Dorfman, "Will the Real Consumer Please Stand Up?" *New York Magazine*, Nov. 1, 1976, 10–11; American Psychological Association, "Distinguished Professional Contribution Award for 1977: George Katona," *American Psychologist* 33 (Jan. 1978): 69–72; Robert D. Hershey Jr., "Viewing the Economy with Consumer Eyes," *NYT*, Apr. 4, 1990, D1 and 6; Sylvia Nasar, "Confidence Index Shows Brighter Consumer Outlook," *NYT*, Mar. 21, 1992, 37 and 39; Judith H. Dobrzynski, obituary for Fabian Linden, *NYT*, Dec. 20, 1995, B15; Dorfman, "Real Consumer," 11–12.

37. On émigrés, the social sciences, and research institutes, see Lazarsfeld, "Memoir," 283,

286, and 302–3. For a discussion of the questions raised by a social research institute, see Paul Lazarsfeld, "The Sociology of Empirical Social Research," *ASR* 27 (Dec. 1962): 763–67. On a later but somewhat different revival of behavioral economics, this one more grounded than Katona's work in economics, see Louis Uchitelle, "Following the Money, but Also the Mind," *NYT*, Feb. 11, 2001, sec. 3, 1 and 11.

38. "Surveys of Liquid Asset Holdings," *FRB* 31 (Sept. 1945): 865; Lewis Mandell et al., *Surveys of Consumers, 1971–72* (Ann Arbor: Institute for Social Research, 1973), 303–26.

39. George Katona, "Financial Surveys among Consumers," *Human Relations* 2 (Jan. 1949): 6. Morgan, "A Quarter Century," 17–18, briefly discusses changes in funding. The best summaries of Katona's contributions are "Curtin on Katona," 495–518, and the essays in Strumpel, Morgan, and Zahn, *Human Behavior*. For Katona's formulation of the Index of Consumer Sentiment in 1952, see George Katona and Eva Mueller, *Consumer Expectations, 1953–1956* (Ann Arbor: Survey Research Center, n.d.), 91–105. On advances in methods, see Converse, *Survey Research*, 368; Angus Campbell and George Katona, "A National Survey of Wartime Savings," *POQ* 10 (fall 1946): 375–76. On the increasing scale of the project, Richard T. Curtin, "Indicators of Consumer Behavior: The University of Michigan Survey of Consumers," *POQ* 46 (fall 1982): 341. Katona directed the SCF, which was the principal activity of the Economic Behavior Program of the SRC, itself a part of the Institute for Social Research of the University of Michigan. For the organizational structure, see ISR booklet, probably 1967, in AC-UM.

40. "Surveys of Liquid Asset Holdings," 869–70.

41. "A National Survey of Liquid Assets," 847; Katona, "Financial Surveys among Consumers," 3 and 8–11. On the alarm and persistent optimism, see "A National Survey of Liquid Assets" *FRB* 32 (June 1946): 578, and (Aug. 1946): 846 and 854; "Survey of Consumer Finances," *FRB* 33 (June 1947): 649 and 656.

42. George Katona, *The Powerful Consumer: Psychological Studies of the American Economy* (New York: McGraw-Hill, 1960), 33–50 and 215–19.

43. Katona gave glimpses of this overall interpretation in his 1946 and 1947 surveys, spelled them out somewhat more fully in Katona, "Financial Surveys among Consumers," 3–11, and offered the first complete statement in George Katona, *Psychological Analysis of Economic Behavior* (New York: McGraw-Hill, 1951). His three general books on America as an affluent society neither received reviews outside the academic community nor attracted a significant readership. *Book Review Digest* lists no non-academic review of *Powerful Consumer* and only one, in *Christian Science Monitor*, for *Mass Consumption Society*. Those who earned their living from marketing naturally found his approach useful. In light of his argument that the consumer was a hero, it was ironic but hardly surprising that the business press welcomed Katona's work. In 1965, *Forbes* regretted that the "barely readable" style of *Mass Consumption Society* would prevent it from becoming as widely read as Galbraith's *Affluent Society*. "Katona's book," the magazine writer commented, "is a solid defense of our free enterprise system and its fruits." In 1975 a reviewer in *Business Week* asserted that *Psychological Economics* should be "required reading for corporate executives, economics professors, government economists, Wall Street analysts, all marketing, communications, and advertising executives, and everyone else who is interested in a richer understanding of the consumer sector"; see Reavis Cox, review of *Psychological Economics*, *Journal of Marketing Research* 13 (Aug. 1976): 320–21; "Katona vs. Galbraith," *Forbes*, Dec. 1, 1965, 52; Morris Cohen, "Should Economics Get on the Couch?" *Business Week*, Aug. 1, 1975, 6 and 9; "Power of the Consumer," *WSJ*, Feb. 4, 1964.

44. George Katona, *The Mass Consumption Society* (New York: McGraw-Hill, 1964), 9–14.

45. Katona, *Powerful Consumer*, 238, and *Mass Consumption Society*, 58. See also George Katona, "A Study of Purchase Decisions," in *Consumer Behavior*, ed. Lincoln H. Clark (New York: New York University Press, 1955): 1:31–32; George Katona, "Rational Behavior and Economic Behavior," *Psychological Review* 60 (1953): 309. In his arguments about the importance of consumer attitudes, Katona took exception to central elements of more orthodox economics. He believed that most economists had paid insufficient attention to the consumer, to psychological factors, and to deductive methods. Katona agreed with the emphasis John Maynard Keynes had placed on expectations but argued that Keynes, in his analysis of the forces driving a national economy, had neglected the role of the consumer. Moreover, Katona believed that a wide range of economists, including Keynesians and monetarists, had underplayed the importance of psychological attitudes. See Katona, *War without Inflation*, 204–5; George Katona and Rensis Likert, "Relationship between Consumer Expenditures and Savings: The Contribution of Survey Research," *RES* 28 (Nov. 1946): 197–99; Katona, *Psychological Analysis*, 133–37, 140–42, and 146.

46. George Katona, "Economic Psychology," *Scientific American* 191 (Oct. 1954): 32 and 35; George Katona, "Attitude Change: Instability of Response and Acquisition of Experience," *Psychological Monographs: General and Applied*, no. 463 (1958): 29 and 32–35. For later restatements of these themes, see Katona, *Powerful Consumer*, 238–42, and Katona, *Mass Consumption Society*, 25 and 129.

47. Katona, *Mass Consumption Society*, 53 and 64–67. For his defense of the American way of life in a popular forum, see George Katona, "America's Prosperity Is Freedom's Best Hope," *This Week Magazine*, June 30, 1963, 7 and 14–15.

48. George Katona, *The People versus the United States: An Education Resource Unit* (Washington, D.C.: Government Printing Office, 1952), 1–2; Katona, *Powerful Consumer*, 28 and 208; Katona, *Psychological Analysis of Economic Behavior*, 260; George Katona, "Psychology and Consumer Economics," *Journal of Consumer Research* 1 (1974): 2.

49. George Katona, "The Predictive Value of Data on Consumer Attitudes," in *Consumer Behavior*, ed. Lincoln H. Clark (New York: New York University Press, 1955): 2:72; Katona, *Mass Consumption Society*, 4 and 6. See also Katona, *Psychological Analysis*, 52 and 121; George Katona, "The Psychology of the Recession," *American Psychologist* 14 (1959): 137; Katona, *Mass Consumption Society*, 30, 114, and 131; and Katona, *Powerful Consumer*, 130–31 and 137.

50. Katona, *Mass Consumption Society*, 6 and 67–68; Katona, *Powerful Consumer*, 137, 173, and 191; George Katona, Burkhard Strumpel, and Ernest Zahn, *Aspirations and Affluence: Comparative Studies in the United States and Western Europe* (New York: McGraw-Hill, 1971), 171.

51. Katona, *Mass Consumption Society*, 66. See also George Katona et al., *1966 Survey of Consumer Finances* (Ann Arbor: Institute for Social Research, 1967), 268; George Katona, *1967 Survey of Consumer Finances* (Ann Arbor: Institute for Social Research, 1968), 7. The word "poverty" did not appear in the index of Katona's 1960 book *The Powerful Consumer* but did have such a place four years later in *The Mass Consumption Society*. For a later example of Katona's analysis of the causes and consequences of poverty, see Katona, Burkhard, and Zahn, *Aspirations and Affluence*, 22 and 197–99.

52. "A National Survey of Liquid Assets," 579; George Katona et al., *1970 Survey of Consumer Finances* (Ann Arbor: Institute for Social Research, 1971), 269.

53. Katona et al., *1970 Survey*, 253 and 273–77.

54. For a summary of his later views of business behavior, see Katona, *Psychological Economics*, 287–333. During World War II, Katona moved beyond the fervid anti-statism Stolper

expressed in the 1940s; see Katona, *War without Inflation*, 101 and 149; Katona, "Psychological Analysis of Business Decisions and Expectations," 62; and Katona, *Psychological Analysis*, 286, 295, and 297.

55. Katona, *Mass Consumption Society*, 318 and 308. See also Katona, *Psychological Economics*, 361. Surprisingly, Katona never explored the connection between the German inflation of 1922–23 and the rise of Nazism. Although he did not refer to the discussions of the 1920s and 1930s about the relationship between class, standard of living, and totalitarianism, his answer was clear. In his review of *Organizing and Memorizing*, Katona's friend Carl Landauer encouraged him to join the debate more explicitly by taking "issue with those philosophers and 'practical' men who consider the masses essentially irrational"; Landauer, review, 161.

56. Katona, "Interdisciplinary Research," 42–44 and 47. His wife predeceased him by a few years.

57. Katona, "Reminiscences," 11–12. On the bitterness other émigrés felt, see Heilbut, *Exiled in Paradise*, viii.

58. For the emphasis on "the powerful anti-capitalist sentiments of the German-Jewish social science community" in Europe, see Irving Louis Horowitz, "Between the Charybdis of Capitalism and the Scylla of Communism: The Emigration of German Social Scientists, 1933–1945," *Social Science History* 11 (summer 1987): 119. Lewis A. Coser, *Refugee Scholars*, 3–15, offers the best analysis of the factors underlying the success or failure of émigrés. See also Heilbut, *Exiled in Paradise*; Peter Gay, "Weimar Culture: The Outsider as Insider," in Fleming and Bailyn, *Intellectual Migration*, 36. Laura Fermi, *Illustrious Immigrants: The Intellectual Migration from Europe, 1930–41* (Chicago: University of Chicago Press, 1968), 37, 47–48, and 112, mentions Katona in passing and discusses the migration from Hungary, the situation of Jews in Hungary, and the outbreak of anti-Semitism there in 1920. Coser, *Refugee Scholars*, 5–10, notes the positive correlation between refugee success in America and the degree of assimilation. Coser also provides an extended exploration of the role of refugees as outsiders. For a discussion of the applicability of the concept of marginality to a situation like the one Katona faced, see Converse, *Survey Research*, 257–59. Donald P. Kent, *The Refugee Intellectual: The Americanization of the Immigrants of 1933–1941* (New York: Columbia University Press, 1953), 193, 212, and 217–18, and H. Stuart Hughes, "Social Theory in a New Context," in *The Muses Flee Hitler: Cultural Transfer and Adaptation, 1930–1945*, ed. Jarrell C. Jackman and Carla M. Borden (Washington, D.C.: Smithsonian Institution Press, 1983), 111–20, focus on other aspects of the émigré experience which help explain Katona and Dichter.

3. A Southerner in Exile, the Cold War, and Social Order

1. For information of Potter's life, I have relied on Don E. Fehrenbacher, Howard R. Lamar, and Otis A. Pease, "David M. Potter: A Memorial Resolution," *JAH* 58 (Sept. 1971): 307–10; Don E. Fehrenbacher, "David M. Potter," in "Biographical Supplement," *International Encyclopedia of the Social Sciences* (New York: Free Press, 1979), 18:645–47; Don E. Fehrenbacher, "David Morris Potter," in *Encyclopedia of American Biography*, ed. John A. Garraty (New York: Harper and Row, 1974), 873–74; C. Vann Woodward, "David Morris Potter," in C. Vann Woodward, *The Future of the Past* (New York: Oxford University Press, 1989), 353–58 (originally published as C. Vann Woodward, "David M. Potter [1910–1971]," in *Year Book of the American Philosophical Society* [1971]: 139–43); Howard Temperley, "David M. Potter," in *Clio's Favorites: Leading Historians of the United States, 1945–2000*, ed. Robert A. Rutland (Columbia: University of Missouri Press, 2000), 138–55. Much less useful is Denis

Brogan, "David M. Potter," in *Pastmasters: Some Essays on American Historians*, ed. Marcus Cunliffe and Robin W. Winks (New York: Harper and Row, 1969), 316–44. I have also relied on Howard R. Lamar, interview with Daniel Horowitz, Apr. 14, 1986, San Marino, Calif.; Cushing Strout, interview with Daniel Horowitz, Apr. 2, 1985, Research Triangle Park, N.C.; Don E. Fehrenbacher, interview with Daniel Horowitz, Apr. 14, 1986, San Marino, Calif. For a bibliography of his works, see George Harmon Knoles, comp., "Bibliography of the Published Work of David M. Potter," in David M. Potter, *Freedom and Its Limitations in American Life*, ed. Don E. Fehrenbacher (Stanford: Stanford University Press, 1976), 65–89.

2. Potter was certainly not a southern reactionary, a racist, or even a southern conservative, as those terms are generally understood. In the 1940s he opposed racial segregation and never defended a white master class as necessary to keep African Americans in their place. He never looked back wistfully to the antebellum South, the Confederacy, or the "Lost Cause" as the lodestars of his sense of a beneficent social order. No diehard southern conservative would have spent his adulthood in Yankee institutions. Especially useful on southern intellectual history are Daniel J. Singal, *The War Within: From Victorian to Modernist Thought in the South, 1919–1945* (Chapel Hill: University of North Carolina Press, 1982); Michael O'Brien, *Rethinking the South: Essays in Intellectual History* (Baltimore: Johns Hopkins University Press, 1988), 157–78; Michael O'Brien, *The Idea of the American South, 1920–1941* (Baltimore: Johns Hopkins University Press, 1979); and Paul V. Murphy, *The Rebuke of History: The Southern Agrarians and American Conservative Thought* (Chapel Hill: University of North Carolina Press, 2001). Among the other discussions of southern intellectual life, including regional ideologies, are Fred Hobson, *Tell about the South: The Southern Rage to Explain* (Baton Rouge: Louisiana State University Press, 1985); Eugene D. Genovese, *The Southern Tradition: The Achievement and Limitations of an American Conservatism* (Cambridge: Harvard University Press, 1994), and *The Slaveholders' Dilemma: Freedom and Progress in Southern Conservative Thought, 1820–1860* (Columbia: University of South Carolina Press, 1992); David Brion Davis, "Southern Comfort," *NYRB*, Oct. 5, 1995, 43–46; Richard H. King, *A Southern Renaissance: The Cultural Awakening in the American South, 1930–1955* (New York: Oxford University Press, 1980); Michael O'Brien, "Conservative Thought in the Old South: A Review Article," *Comparative Studies in Society and History* 34 (July 1992): 566–76.

3. David M. Potter, handwritten notes for talk that begins, "The U.S. today is the defender of the conservative position" [mid- to late 1950s], box 16, DMP-SU. I rely on internal evidence to determine when Potter wrote this document, especially evidence that he had been reading Arthur M. Schlesinger Jr., *Age of Jackson* (Boston: Houghton Mifflin, 1945); Louis Hartz, *The Liberal Tradition in America: An Interpretation of American Political Thought since the Revolution* (New York: Harcourt Brace, 1955); and Richard Hofstadter, *Social Darwinism in American Thought, 1860–1915* (Philadelphia: University of Pennsylvania Press, 1945). For Potter's own and later acknowledgment of himself as a conservative, see David M. Potter to Eugene D. Genovese, Nov. 26, 1966, "Genovese Paper" folder, box 18, DMP-SU.

4. Paul Pickrel to Rupert Wilkinson, Jan. 17, 1988, copy in author's possession; David M. Potter, high school commencement address, 1928, "Papers" folder, box 7, DMP-SU; David M. Potter, "C. Vann Woodward," in Cunliffe and Winks, *Pastmasters*, 376; Temperley, "Potter," 139. Potter and Woodward sat next to each other in a U.S. history class, and Woodward visited Potter's home in Atlanta; C. Vann Woodward, *Thinking Back: The Perils of Writing History* (Baton Rouge: Louisiana State University Press, 1986), 94. For his description of Atlanta in these years, see David M. Potter, "C. Vann Woodward," in Cunliffe and Winks, *Pastmasters*, 375. For Woodward's intellectual world in the 1930s, see Woodward, *Thinking Back*, 9–27.

5. Lamar, interview.

6. Fehrenbacher, Lamar, and Pease, "Potter," 308; David M. Potter to C. Vann Woodward, June 19, 1965, box 11, "P" file, CVW-YU; Fehrenbacher, interview; David M. Potter, *The South and the Sectional Conflict* (Baton Rouge: Louisiana State University Press, 1968), v–vi; Potter, "C. Vann Woodward," 375–76; David Potter, quoted in Woodward, *Thinking Back*, 15. See also Lamar, interview; Pickrel to Wilkinson.

7. Potter, "C. Van Woodward," 398; David M. Potter, "David M. Potter: Interpreting American History," in John A. Garraty, ed., *Interpreting American History: Conversations with Historians* (New York: Macmillan, 1970), 2:319. For his posthumous book, see David M. Potter, *The Impending Crisis, 1848–1861*, completed and edited by Don E. Fehrenbacher (New York: Harper and Row, 1976). Potter was responsible for almost all of what appeared in the book up to the middle of 520; Fehrenbacher wrote everything that followed; see Don E. Fehrenbacher to Charles Royster, Dec. 14, 1985, copy in author's possession. Potter shared this "blundering generation" hypothesis with most historians of his generation regardless of where they had grown up; for his views, see, for example, David M. Potter, *Lincoln and His Party in the Secession Crisis* (New Haven: Yale University Press, 1942), 19 and 374–75. As an illustration of the way he muted his politics, it would be hard to tell from his published writings how he felt about Franklin D. Roosevelt and the New Deal.

8. Potter, *Sectional Conflict*, vi.

9. Lamar, interview, discussed Potter's moves within the New Haven area. For the intensity of Potter's feelings about moving, see David M. Potter to Paul Pickrel, Aug. 12, 1966, box 1, DMP-SU. To date his father's death in the late 1930s, see his mother's letter dated "Thursday night," 1939, box 2, DMP-SU. For other biographical information, see "David Morris Potter," in *Contemporary Authors*, vol. 108 (Detroit: Gale Research Co., 1983), 374–75; Dorothy Norman to David M. Potter, Apr. 11, 1951, box 4, DMP-SU; David M. Potter, draft of letter to "Willie," May 2, 1951, box 4, DMP-SU; Pickrel to Wilkinson; Lamar, interview; Fehrenbacher, interview; Gerald [Capers] to David M. Potter, Jan. 12, 1953, box 4, DMP-SU; James Harvey Young, "Defining America: David Potter's *People of Plenty*," *Timeline: A Publication of the Ohio Historical Society* 13 (1996): 19.

10. Lamar, interview; Fehrenbacher, "Potter," in *Encyclopedia of American Biography*, 874. Another Stanford colleague, Carl Degler, echoed this evaluation. "Ideologically and politically," he wrote in 1971, "Potter was conservative. . . . As a confirmed opponent of optimism he did not expect much improvement from any change, though he recognized that change was inevitable." Focusing on Potter's "ability to discover paradox and irony in history," Degler ascribed it to an eagerness to "eye things [that] were rarely what they seemed to others"; Carl N. Degler, obituary for David M. Potter, *AHR* 76 (Oct. 1971): 1273–74. For the edited books on two crises in U.S. history, see David M. Potter and Thomas G. Manning, eds., *Nationalism and Sectionalism in America, 1775–1877: Select Problems in Historical Interpretation* (New York: Henry Holt, 1949), and *Government and the American Economy, 1870–Present: Select Problems in Historical Interpretation* (New York: Henry Holt, 1950). For other appraisals of the problems of leadership, see David M. Potter, "Notes for remarks on FD Roosevelt before History Journal Club" [mid- to late 1930s], box 16, DMP-SU; David M. Potter, "Horace Greeley and Peaceable Secession," *JSH* 7 (May 1941): 145–59. During the depression, although he made clear his preference for Darwinian survival of the fittest, he also wrote of bolstering the economy by stimulating consumption, making the distribution of wealth more democratic, and strengthening the power of labor in its battle with capital. For one of Potter's favorable appraisals of the New Deal, see David M. Potter, "Interpreting the New Deal," typewritten essay [1963], "Talk on New Deal" folder, box 28, DMP-SU. For Potter's skepti-

cism about American communists in the 1930s, see Potter, "C. Vann Woodward," 377. On his doubt that liberals and leftists were morally superior and free of irrationality, see David M. Potter, review of *The Radical Right*, ed. Daniel Bell, *New Leader*, June 24, 1963, 27.

11. David M. Potter, introduction to *Trail to California: The Overland Journal of Vincent Geiger and Wakeman Bryarly*, ed. David M. Potter (New Haven: Yale University Press, 1945), 1–73, quotes 49. See also David M. Potter, review of Daniel Bell, *End of Ideology*, *NR*, May 23, 1960, 17–18.

12. Twelve Southerners, "Introduction: A Statement of Principles," in *I'll Take My Stand: The South and the Agrarian Tradition* (New York: Harper and Brothers, 1930), xxiv and xxvii–xxviii; for a review of the book by Potter's mentor, see Ulrich B. Phillips, review of *I'll Take My Stand*, *YR* 20 (spring 1931): 611–13. For other discussions of the book, see Grace Elizabeth Hale, *Making Whiteness: The Culture of Segregation in the South, 1890–1940* (New York: Pantheon Books, 1998), 138–46, 200, and 257, and Murphy, *Rebuke of History*. On some recent scholarship on the Southern Renaissance, see O'Brien, *Rethinking the South*, 157–78. For changing perspectives on notions about the South, see O'Brien, *The Idea of the American South*. In David M. Potter, "The Enigma of the South" (1961), in Potter, *South and the Sectional Conflict*, 10 and 12, he invoked Phillips to make clear that he dissented from the authors of *I'll Take My Stand*, who emphasized agrarianism as what made the South distinctive.

13. David M. Potter, "Future of the Negro in the United States," *The Listener*, July 15, 1948, 85–86 and 97. For a discussion of southern white liberals in this period, see Morton Sosna, *In Search of the Southern South: Southern Liberals and the Race Issue* (New York: Columbia University Press, 1977), esp. 140–71. On the response of intellectuals to civil rights, see Carol Polsgrove, *Divided Minds: Intellectuals and the Civil Rights Movement* (New York: W. W. Norton, 2001).

14. Potter, "Future of the Negro," 85, 86, and 97. For a statement of Potter's cold war anticommunism, see David M. Potter, "The Marshall Plan and American Foreign Policy," *Current Affairs*, Feb. 21, 1948, 6 and 10–15. On the connection between the cold war and civil rights, see Mary L. Dudziak, *Cold War Civil Rights: Race and the Image of American Democracy* (Princeton: Princeton University Press, 2000).

15. Temperley, "Potter," 152; Potter, "Future of the Negro," 85, 86, and 97.

16. David M. Potter, "The Work of Ulrich B. Phillips: A Comment," *AH* 41 (Oct. 1967): 360–62. For Potter's relationship with his mentor, see David M. Potter, "The Rise of the Plantation System in Georgia," *GHQ* 16 (June 1932): 117 and 135; "A Bibliography of the Printed Writings of Ulrich Bonnell Phillips," *GHQ* 18 (Sept. 1934): 270–82; and "Introduction," 1960 typescript copy for Academic Reprint Series, Arizona University Press, box 17, DMP-SU. For the paper to which he was responding, see Eugene D. Genovese, "Race and Class in Southern History: An Appraisal of the Work of Ulrich Bonnell Phillips," *AH* 41 (Oct. 1967): 345–58. For an exchange of letters in connection with the work out of which this article arose, see C. Vann Woodward to David M. Potter, Nov. 29, 1966; Potter to Genovese, Nov. 26, 1966; Genovese to Potter, Jan. 4, 1965; Genovese to Potter, Dec. 6, 1966, "Genovese Paper" folder, box 18, DMP-SU.

For the writings of Phillips, see Ulrich B. Phillips, "The Central Theme of Southern History," *AHR* 34 (Oct. 1928): 31; Ulrich B. Phillips, *American Negro Slavery: A Survey of the Supply, Employment, and Control of Negro Labor as Determined by the Plantation Regime* (1918) (reprint, Baton Rouge: Louisiana State University Press, 1966), 296; Ulrich B. Phillips, *Life and Labor in the Old South* (Boston: Little, Brown, 1929), 196. On Phillips, see Merton L. Dillon, *Ulrich Bonnell Phillips: Historian of the Old South* (Baton Rouge: Louisiana State

University Press, 1985); John Herbert Roper, *U. B. Phillips: A Southern Mind* (Macon, Ga.: Mercer University Press, 1984), 1, 4, 106, 107, 110, 113, 127, 132, and 157; Singal, *War Within*, 37–57; John David Smith, introduction to *Ulrich Bonnell Phillips: A Southern Historian and His Critics*, ed. John David Smith and John C. Inscoe (Athens: University of Georgia Press, 1993), esp. 8–9.

17. On his respect for Cash's work, see Pickrel to Wilkinson.

18. David M. Potter, note card with quote from *I'll Take My Stand*, xxvii–xxviii, "Walgreen Notes" folder, box 17, DMP-SU. On the origins of *People of Plenty*, see Fehrenbacher, "David M. Potter," in *International Encyclopedia*, 646; Pickrel to Wilkinson; Potter, "Potter: Interpreting American History," 2:316; Temperley, "Potter," 149.

19. It is also possible that Potter was responding to George W. Pierson, "The Moving American," *YR* 44 (autumn 1954): 99–112, a much more one-dimensional and celebratory treatment of mobility by a Yale colleague; on the connection to Pierson's work, see Pickrel to Wilkinson.

20. Charles R. Walgreen to Robert M. Hutchins, Apr. 10, 1935, reproduced in Robert M. Hutchins, *President's Report to the University of Chicago Board of Trustees, 1934–35*, 1–2, DSC-UC; conversation reported by Charles R. Walgreen before a committee of the Illinois legislature, in Robert Coven, "Red Maroons: Academic Freedom and Student Radicalism at the University of Chicago," unpublished 1991 paper, 1, fn. 3, copy in author's possession. On the context of the relationship between Walgreen and the university, see Robert Coven, "Red Maroons," *CH* 21 (spring/summer 1992): 20–37. On the Walgreen fund, see "Walgreen Gives $500,000 for Institute at Chicago University, Which He Criticized," *NYT*, June 6, 1937, 19. On issues such as the possibility of social mobility and the power of class distinctions, the lectures were somewhat more critical of America than the book: see, for example, lecture 2, which became the basis for chap. 4; David M. Potter, "II. Abundance, Status and Mobility," box 4, folder 12, Walgreen Foundation records, DSC-UC. I am grateful to Robert Coven for researching the Walgreen material and comparing what he found with what appears in Potter's book. On the influence of anticommunism on Potter, see Pickrel to Wilkinson. For letters concerning William R. Coe's decision to fund American studies at Yale in order to fight communism and support free enterprise, see David M. Potter to Dr. Humphrey, Feb. 19, 1956, and David M. Potter to William R. Coe, Dec. 21, 1955, "W. R. Coe—American Studies" folder, box 8, DMP-SU.

21. Pickrel to Wilkinson. See David M. Potter, handwritten notes for talk at Northern California American Studies Association meeting, Mar. 25, 1966, San Francisco State College, in "Symposium on *People of Plenty* at S.F. 1966" folder, box 18, DMP-SU, for his retrospective view of his book. Here Potter acknowledged that he might have been "too uncommitted" and that he paid too little attention to poverty and to the South. For another retrospective discussion of the lack of attention to poverty in *People of Plenty*, see Potter, "Interpreting American History," 2:316.

22. David M. Potter, *People of Plenty: Economic Abundance and the American Character* (Chicago: University of Chicago Press, 1964), vii. The trade publication of the advertising industry printed Potter's chapter on advertising; see "Historian Calls Advertising the 'Institution of Abundance' in New Study of American Economy," *Advertising Age*, Oct. 4, 1954, 76–78, 80, and 82.

23. Potter, *People of Plenty*, 8 and 59.

24. Ibid., 88 and 89.

25. Ibid., 81, 83, 84, 88, and 89, quotes 84. For Potter's questioning of the Turner thesis, see 142–65.

26. Ibid., 113; see also 111, 112, 115, 117, 127, 134, and 139. On these themes in Potter's book, see Eric J. Sandeen, *Picturing an Exhibition: "The Family of Man" and 1950s America* (Albuquerque: University of New Mexico Press, 1995), 5–6.

27. Potter, *People of Plenty*, 175, 177, and 188; see also 172, 178, 182, and 184. Several years later, Potter worried that he was mistakenly associated with a positive view of advertising; see David M. Potter to the editor of *AHR*, early 1959, "Review of Status Politics" folder, box 18, DMP-SU.

28. Potter, *People of Plenty*, 194–98, 202, and 208.

29. Ibid., 200.

30. Ibid., 201, 202, and 206. For other statements of Potter's view of women, see David M. Potter, "American Leisure as an Economic Force," typescript of essay, 1955, box 17, DMP-SU (this essay later appeared in *Challenge: The Magazine of Economic Affairs* 4 [Dec. 1955]: 42–46), and "American Women and the American Character," presented as a lecture 1959; first published 1962 in David M. Potter, *History and American Society: Essays of David M. Potter*, ed. Don E. Fehrenbacher (New York: Oxford University Press, 1973), 278–303. For a feminist critique of Potter's views of women, see Linda Gordon et al., "Historical Phallacies: Sexism in American Historical Writing," in *Liberating Women's History: Theoretical and Critical Essays*, ed. Berenice A. Carroll (Urbana: University of Illinois Press, 1976), 55–74; reprinted, with revisions, from *Women's Studies* 1 (1972). In 1955, *Good Housekeeping* commissioned Potter to write a research paper on the role of women's magazines in educating women about new appliances; Tom Wolfe, then a graduate student at Yale in American studies, did the research. In the resulting essay, Potter began to work out his argument that generalizations about American history applied to men but not women; see David M. Potter, essay for *Good Housekeeping*, "Good Housekeeping" folder, box 17, DMP-SU. As far as I can determine, the paper never appeared in print.

31. Potter, *People of Plenty*, 204–6.

32. Ibid., 93, 96, and 98.

33. C. Vann Woodward, "The Search for Southern Identity" (1958), in *The Burden of Southern History* (Baton Rouge: Louisiana State University Press, 1960), 16–18.

34. Potter, *People of Plenty*, 101–3. Years later Potter made clear that, in speaking of a people of plenty, he had not meant "to express a smug feeling or a spirit of self-congratulation"; David M. Potter, "The Age of Abundance," 12, handwritten talk, 1963, "Broadcast at Texas" folder, box 19, DMP-SU.

35. Potter, *People of Plenty*, 103–4 and 115.

36. Ibid., 104–6 and 108; Richard Hofstadter, *The Age of Reform: From Bryan to F.D.R.* (New York: Knopf, 1955).

37. Potter, *People of Plenty*, 109–10.

38. Ibid., 76, 118, and 121; see also 92.

39. Ibid., 121 and 122.

40. Ibid., 98.

41. For discussions of the dangers of status anxieties, see the essays in Daniel Bell, ed., *The New American Right* (New York: Criterion Books, 1955).

42. Potter, *People of Plenty*, 17 and 29.

43. Ibid., 71. Focusing mainly on Potter's treatment of national character, no reviewer at the time captured the traditionalism of his values, although two of them (Archie Jones and Fred Shannon) believed that Potter had exaggerated in claiming how widely shared was American affluence; see Gerald Carson, *NYTBR*, Nov. 14, 1954, 41; Karl W. Deutsch, *YR* 44 (Dec. 1954): 292–95; George Caspar Homans, *NEQ* 27 (Dec. 1954): 553–54; Archie H. Jones, *AJS*

61 (Nov. 1955): 283; C. Wright Mills, *SR*, July 16, 1955, 19; H. C. Nixon, *APSR* 49 (June 1955): 547–49; Boyd C. Shafer, *AHR* 60 (Jan. 1955): 380–81; Fred A. Shannon, *MVHR* 41 (March 1955): 733–34; Alice Felt Tyler, *Annals* 298 (Mar. 1955): 194–95; Dennis H. Wrong, *CF* 35 (Apr. 1955): 21–22. David E. Stannard, "American Historians and the Idea of National Character: Some Problems and Prospects," *AQ* 23 (May 1971): 202–20, skillfully probes the problems with Potter's handling of issues of national character; in addition, see Rupert Wilkinson, *The Pursuit of American Character* (New York: Harper and Row, 1988), 21–24. Two more recent observers suggestively hint at but do not really develop the connections between Potter's southernness and his ideology; see Rupert Wilkinson, "Journeys to American Character: Margaret Mead, David Potter, and David Riesman," April 1989 manuscript in author's possession; Robert M. Collins, "David Potter's *People of Plenty* and the Recycling of Consensus History," *RAH* 16 (June 1988): 321–35. For a thoughtful essay on some aspects of Potter's outlook, see Robert W. Johannsen, "David M. Potter, Historian and Social Critic: A Review Essay," *CWH* 20 (Mar. 1974): 35–44. For a critique of Potter's definition of affluence, see Jackson Lears, "Reconsidering Abundance: A Plea for Ambiguity," in *Getting and Spending: European and American Consumer Societies in the Twentieth Century*, ed. Susan Strasser, Charles McGovern, and Matthias Judt (Cambridge: Cambridge University Press, 1998), 449–50, 454, and 456.

44. Martin Duberman, review of *The South and the Sectional Conflict*, *NYTBR*, Jan. 12, 1969, 14. For his later works and collections of his essays, see Potter, *South and the Sectional Conflict*; David M. Potter, *The South and the Concurrent Majority*, ed. Don E. Fehrenbacher and Carl N. Degler (Baton Rouge: Louisiana State University Press, 1972); Potter, *History and American Society*. For his discussion of the role of the historian as public intellectual, see Potter, *People of Plenty*, ix and xiii. For an advertising executive's criticism of Potter's writing as too specialized, see Carson, review, 41.

45. Potter, "Enigma of the South," 16. For other examples of his definition of a southern way of life, see, David M. Potter, "The Historian's Use of Nationalism and Vice Versa" (1963), in Potter, *History and American Society*, 94; David M. Potter, review of C. Vann Woodward, *The Burden of Southern History*, *YR* 50 (Dec. 1960): 292–93. For more evidence on the themes discussed in this section, see the following works by David M. Potter: headnote (1968) to "On Understanding the South" (1964), in *South and Sectional Conflict*, 17–33; "American Individualism in the Twentieth Century" (1963), in Fehrenbacher, *History and American Society*, 273–74; "John Brown and the Paradox of Leadership among Negroes," in *South and the Sectional Conflict*, 202; "Address at the Annual Commissioning . . . June 13, 1970," typescript of speech, "ROTC–My Address" folder, box 18, DMP-SU; "Talk to Law School group, 1960," handwritten lecture notes, 5, 13, and 18, box 28, DMP-SU; "A Minority within a Minority," *YR* 46 (winter 1956): 265; letter to Charles Blitzer, Jan. 12, 1964, box 5, DMP-SU; paper delivered at symposium at Smith College, "The Culture of Suburbia," Apr. 16, 1959, box 28, DMP-SU; "Lecture at Greensboro" folder, box 28, DMP-SU; handwritten and typewritten talk that begins, "In the year . . . ," 1960; "Rejection of the Prevailing American Society" (1969), in *History and American Society*, 352, 354, 355, and 388; "Commentary: Theory versus Practice in American Values and Performance," in *The American Style: Essays in Value and Performance*, ed. Elting E. Morison (New York: Harper and Row, 1958), 327–33; comments in Advertising Council, *The American Round Table: Discussions on People's Capitalism: An Evaluation of its Contribution to Our Well-Being . . .* (New York: Advertising Council, 1957), 10–12, 15–16, 18–19, 52–54, and 49; comments in Advertising Council, *The American Round Table: People's Capitalism, Part II . . .* (New York: Advertising Council, 1957), 3, 14–15, 17, 26, 28, 39–40, and 47; review of Bell, *End of Ideology*, 17–18; "Television, The Broad View: The Historical Perspective," in *The Meaning of Commercial Television*, ed. Stanley

T. Donner (Austin: University of Texas Press, 1967), 51–68; Potter, *Concurrent Majority*, 3 and 68; Potter, "Enigma of the South," 16; "Social Cohesion and the Crisis of the Law" (1970), in *History and American Society*, 407, 408, and 412–17. Robert H. Haddow has demonstrated that these forums on people's capitalism were part of a successful effort by the Advertising Council to legitimize its campaign, which President Dwight D. Eisenhower urged them to undertake, to promote the linkage between democracy and free enterprise; Robert H. Haddow, *Pavilions of Plenty: Exhibiting American Culture Abroad in the 1950s* (Washington, D.C.: Smithsonian Institution Press, 1997), 56–59. For evidence of how easy it was for contemporaries to misconstrue his position, see David M. Potter and Mr. Mullins, radio interview, May 22, 1955, box 16, DMP-SU.

46. David M. Potter, marginal notes in his copy of page proofs of *The Affluent Society*, 190 and 92A, box 38, DMP-SU; David M. Potter, review of John Kenneth Galbraith, *The Liberal Hour, SR*, Aug. 13, 1960, 36. See also David M. Potter, review of John Kenneth Galbraith, *The Affluent Society, SR*, June 7, 1958, 31–32.

47. Potter, "Culture of Suburbia," 1, 4, 6, and 8. This discussion also draws on David M. Potter, "In the Year," 21 and 25. In the last ten years of his life he worked on a history of alienation in America, publishing a little on that topic in 1963 and leaving behind some important fragments. David M. Potter, "The Roots of American Alienation" (1963), in *History and American Society*, 304–33.

48. David M. Potter, "Tasks of Research in American History" (delivered in 1963), in *History and American Society*, 30 and 32; Potter, "Roots of American Alienation," 310, 317, and 329; Potter, *Freedom and Its Limitations*. For another expression of his conservatism, in which he balanced pessimism and optimism, see David M. Potter, "Abundance and Adaptability in the American Character," spring 1966 talk, "Paper at Hayward" folder, box 28, DMP-SU.

49. Potter, "Rejection," 339–40.

50. For Tate's ideas, see King, *Southern Renaissance,* Singal, *War Within*, 56; Potter, *South and Sectional Conflict*, vi. Among the other sources on southern thought that have some relevance to understanding Potter are O'Brien, *Idea of the American South*, esp. xiv and 220–27; Potter, *South and the Sectional Conflict*, vi.

4. Critique from Within

1. This chapter hardly covers all the critiques of affluence in the period. For some others, see Ad Hoc Committee on the Triple Revolution, *The Triple Revolution* (Santa Barbara: Ad Hoc Committee on the Triple Revolution, 1964); the works of Thomas Merton and Dorothy Day; two classical texts of the Beat movement, Allen Ginsberg, *Howl, and Other Poems* (San Francisco: City Light Pocket Bookshop, 1956), and Jack Kerouac, *On The Road* (New York: Viking Press, 1957). Also important are life satisfaction studies which attempted to quantify the pleasure gained from more goods and services; for summaries of this field, see Angus Campbell, *The Sense of Well-Being in America: Recent Patterns and Trends* (New York: McGraw-Hill, 1981); Robert E. Lane, "Markets and the Satisfaction of Human Wants," *Journal of Economic Issues* 12 (Dec. 1978): 799–827.

The 1950s through the early 1960s was an especially fertile moment for these discussions. David Riesman, *The Lonely Crowd: A Study of the Changing American Character* (New Haven: Yale University Press, 1950), continued to inform writers well into the 1960s and even beyond. See also Daniel J. Boorstin, *The Image or What Happened to the American Dream* (New York: Atheneum, 1962). For the treatment of the United States as a leisure society, see Robert

Theobald, *The Challenge of Abundance* (New York: C. N. Potter, 1961); Norman Jacobs, ed., *Culture for Millions? Mass Media in Modern Society* (Princeton: Van Nostrand, 1959); and Max Kaplan, *Leisure in America: A Social Inquiry* (New York: Wiley, 1960). For the questioning of increased affluence during the presidential campaign of Adlai Stevenson in 1956 and among liberal economists at the same time, see Charles H. Hession, *John Kenneth Galbraith and His Critics* (New York: New American Library, 1972), 66–68. For the debate on "national purpose," including the meaning of abundance, during the presidency of Dwight D. Eisenhower, see Robert Griffith, "Dwight D. Eisenhower and the Corporate Commonwealth," *AHR* 87 (Feb. 1982): 87–122. If there was one moment that captured this identification of affluence with American democracy and free enterprise, it was the "kitchen debate" that took place in Moscow on July 24, 1959, between Vice President Richard M. Nixon and Soviet Premier Nikita Khrushchev; see Elaine T. May, *Homeward Bound: American Families in Cold War Era* (New York: Basic Books, 1988), 16–19.

2. Peggy Lamson, *Speaking of Galbraith: A Personal Portrait* (New York: Ticknor and Fields, 1991), 57. For discussion of the importance of the OPA, see Meg Jacobs, " 'How About Some Meat?' The Office of Price Administration, Consumption Politics, and State Building from the Bottom Up, 1941–1946," *JAH* 84 (Dec. 1997): 910–41. For biographical information, I am relying on Lamson and on John Kenneth Galbraith, *A Life in Our Times: Memoirs* (Boston: Houghton Mifflin, 1981). Richard Parker has a biography forthcoming from Farrar, Straus and Giroux.

3. John Kenneth Galbraith, "Introduction to the Second Edition," in *The Affluent Society* (Boston: Houghton Mifflin, 1969), xxviii. For his discussion of the writing, reception, and impact of *The Affluent Society*, see Galbraith, *Life in Our Times*, 335–54.

4. Galbraith, *Affluent Society*, 139–60 and 197–225. At several points in the book, Galbraith hinted at the precariousness of an economy built on compulsive consumption; see, for example, 278–79. For his view of the diminished power and prestige of the wealthy during the postwar years, see 88. For a critique of Galbraith's views of advertising, see Michael Schudson, "Criticizing the Critics of Advertising: Towards a Sociological View of Marketing," *Media, Culture, and Society* 3 (1981): 3–12.

5. Galbraith, *Affluent Society*, 97 and 325–27. For the changes Galbraith made in his discussion of poverty, without fully acknowledging the importance of the work of Michael Harrington, see Galbraith, *Affluent Society*, 2d ed., xxvi and 285–96. In the original edition, Galbraith titled one chapter "The New Position of Poverty" (322–33). In 1953 or 1954, Galbraith began on a book with the working title "Why People Are Poor," for which he drafted several chapters but put them aside to write *The Great Crash, 1929*, and later *Affluent Society*; see Lamson, *Galbraith*, 116 and 130–31; Galbraith, *Life in Our Times*, 305–8. In his introduction to the second edition, Galbraith responded to those who criticized him for his views of poverty; see Hession, *Galbraith*, 130–31. For a perceptive discussion of Galbraith's ideas and impact, see Felicia Ann Kornbluh, "A Right to Welfare? Poor Women, Professionals, and Poverty Programs, 1935–1975" (Ph.D. diss., Princeton University, 2000), 35–77. For contemporary criticism of Galbraith for minimizing the extent of poverty in the United States, see Hession, *Galbraith*, 129–34.

6. Galbraith, *Affluent Society*, 158, 140, 279–80, and 350. The idea of the "Dependence Effect" came under attack by orthodox economists even though it was a commonplace notion among social critics; for the controversy, see Hession, *Galbraith*, 98–106.

7. Galbraith, *Affluent Society*, 251, 266–67, and 161.

8. Ibid., 133 and 253.

9. Ibid., 293, 340, 311–12, and 315; see also 312. Kornbluh, "Right to Welfare?" 44–47,

explores the role of Galbraith's divorce of work from economic security in a postwar tradition of political economy that undergirded changes in welfare policy.

10. For Galbraith's weak response to objections that the sales tax was regressive, see *Affluent Society*, 316–17. For a recent appreciation and assessment of Galbraith's work, see Helen Sasson, ed., *Between Friends: Perspectives on John Kenneth Galbraith* (Boston: Houghton Mifflin, 1999), esp. the following essays: Robert B. Reich, "Galbraith in the New Gilded Age," 88–99; Robert Heilbroner, "Ken Galbraith as a Worldly Philosopher," 100–103; Stephen A. Marglin, "John Kenneth Galbraith and the Myths of Economics," 114–38. For another appreciative examination of Galbraith's contribution, see James Ronald Stanfield, *John Kenneth Galbraith* (New York: St. Martin's Press, 1996). For a discussion of the critiques of Galbraith, including those by conservatives, see James P. Young, *The Politics of Affluence: Ideology in the United States since World War II* (San Francisco: Chandler Publishing, 1968), 137–42. On Galbraith's role in the Kennedy administration, see Arthur M. Schlesinger Jr., *A Thousand Days: John F. Kennedy in the White House* (Boston: Houghton Mifflin, 1965), 628, 648–51, 1003–4, and 1010.

11. Loren J. Okroi, *Galbraith, Harrington, Heilbroner: Economics and Dissent in an Age of Optimism* (Princeton: Princeton University Press, 1988), 47; David M. Potter, review of Galbraith, *Affluent Society*, *SR*, June 7, 1958, 32. On the response to the book, including an examination of the reviews, see Lamson, *Galbraith*, 134–39, 142, 144–46; Hession, *Galbraith*, 88–134.

12. Arthur Schlesinger Jr., "The Future of Liberalism," *Reporter*, May 3, 1956, 9; Galbraith quoted in Stanfield, *Galbraith*, 53. On qualitative liberalism, see also Arthur Schlesinger Jr., "Where Does the Liberal Go From Here?" *NYTM*, Aug. 4, 1957, 7, 36, and 38. See also Galbraith, *Life in Our Times*, 450–53. For Galbraith's revision of his chapter on poverty in a later edition, see *Affluent Society* 2d ed., 285–96.

13. Edwin L. Dale Jr., "'Great Debate' in Capital: Is U.S. Misusing Wealth?" *NYT*, Feb. 7, 1960, 1; Edwin L. Dale Jr., "Big Debate: Public vs. Private Spending," *NYT*, Mar. 13, 1960, 4:5; John F. Kennedy, "The New Frontier," acceptance speech, Democratic National Convention, July 15, 1960, 7, printed copy in author's possession; "The Port Huron Statement," 1962, in James Miller, *"Democracy is in the Streets": From Port Huron to the Siege of Chicago* (New York: Simon and Schuster, 1987), 338. In 1969, Stephan Thernstrom criticized Galbraith for perpetuating 1950s notions of America as an affluent society; Stephan Thernstrom, "The Myth of American Affluence," *Commentary* 48 (Oct. 1969): 74–78.

14. For the full version of my discussion of Packard, and its documentation, see Daniel Horowitz, *Vance Packard and American Social Criticism* (Chapel Hill: University of North Carolina Press, 1994), and "Introduction: Social Criticism in an Age of Conformity and Anxiety," in *American Social Classes in the 1950s: Selections from Vance Packard's "The Status Seekers,"* ed. Daniel Horowitz (Boston: Bedford Books of St. Martin's Press, 1995), 1–27.

15. Vance Packard, *The Hidden Persuaders* (New York: David McKay, 1957), 3, 19, 21, 25, 171, and 227; also 4, 184–85, 201–2, 212–13, and 217.

16. Ibid., 57, 176, 228, 230, 257, 262, and 263.

17. Schudson, "Criticizing the Critics," 6; Raymond A. Bauer, "Limits of Persuasion," *HBR* 36 (Sept.–Oct. 1958): 107 and 110.

18. Vance Packard, *The Status Seekers* (New York: David McKay, 1959), 8 and 3; Editors of *Fortune*, *The Changing American Market* (Garden City, N.Y.: Hanover House, 1955), 14, 21, 57, 67, 79, 80, and 250.

19. Packard, *Status Seekers*, 61–74.

20. Ibid., 7, 9–10, and 307–8.

21. Ibid., 8–10, 26, 35, 98, 102, 116, 124–25, 276, and 328–29.

22. Ibid., 17–21, 90, 118, 195, and 304–5.

23. Ibid., 340, 346–47, and 351–52.

24. Editors of *Fortune, Changing American Market*, 250.

25. Vance Packard, *The Waste Makers* (New York: David McKay, 1960), v, 6, 7, 10, 16, 20–21, 163, 233, and 245.

26. Ibid., 7, 8, 17, and 25.

27. Ibid., 4–5, 160–67, and 233.

28. Ibid., 186–87 and 189.

29. Ibid., 159–60, 212, 215–31, and 236.

30. Ibid., 159–60, 296, and 299.

31. Ibid., 244–45, 252–53, 264, and 274.

32. Ibid., 200, 273, 284, 286, 287, 290, and 292.

33. Ibid., 16, 294, 296, and 309–11.

34. Ibid., 314, 318, 323, 325, and 326.

35. Ibid., 326–27, 183–84, 234, 244, 311, and 313.

36. Ibid., 184 and 307.

37. Leonard Sloane, "Consumers Spur Industry Response," *NYT*, Jan. 7, 1973, sec. 3, pt. 2, 49.

38. For the full story of Friedan's life, along with complete documentation, see Daniel Horowitz, *Betty Friedan and the Making of "The Feminine Mystique": The American Left, the Cold War, and Modern Feminism* (Amherst: University of Massachusetts Press, 1998). Although Potter's picture of women was in some ways more nuanced, he nonetheless joined Dichter and Katona in his portrait of the largely satisfied middle-class suburban housewife whose role as a consumer was central to her own well-being and that of the nation; see David M. Potter, "American Women and the American Character" (presented as a lecture 1959; first published 1962), in *History and American Society: Essays of David M. Potter*, ed. Don E. Fehrenbacher (New York: Oxford University Press, 1973), 278–303. For an essay that complicates the view of postwar suburbia, see Lizabeth Cohen, "A Middle-Class Utopia? The Suburban Home in the 1950s," in *Making Choices: A New Perspective on the History of Domestic Life in Illinois* (Springfield: Illinois State Museum, 1995), 59–67.

39. Friedan, *Feminine Mystique*, 282, 206–7, and 228.

40. Ibid., 211; Ernest Dichter, *The Naked Manager* (Toronto: Macmillan of Canada, 1974), 90 and 95; Ernest Dichter, quoted in Don Daniels column, *Wheeling (West Virginia) News Register*, Sept. 17, 1970, 25.

41. Friedan, *Feminine Mystique*, 337.

42. Ellen Herman, *The Romance of American Psychology: Political Culture in the Age of Experts* (Berkeley: University of California Press, 1995), 276–303, quote 277. On the use of psychology, see also Barbara Ehrenreich, *The Hearts of Men: American Dreams and the Flight from Commitment* (New York: Anchor Press, 1983), 88–98. For a later statement of the relationship between psychology and women's oppression, see Naomi Weisstein, " 'Kinde, Kuche, Kirche' As Scientific Law: Psychology Constructs the Female" (1968), in *Sisterhood Is Powerful: An Anthology of Writings from the Women's Liberation Movement*, ed. Robin Morgan (New York: Random House, 1970), 228–45.

43. For what male social critics wrote on women, see Packard, *Status Seekers*, 120, 122, 159–62, 170–73, and 259–60; Packard, *Hidden Persuaders*, 169–70; William H. Whyte Jr., *The Organization Man* (New York: Simon and Schuster, 1956), 267–404; Riesman, *Lonely Crowd*, 80, 81, 120, 149, 156, 163–64, 170, 203, 303, 312–13, 320, and 330–34.

44. C. Wright Mills, *The Power Elite* (New York: Oxford University Press, 1956). If some of the shortcomings of *The Feminine Mystique* came from Friedan's reworking of a familiar genre, others stemmed from the way the published version differed from early drafts. Had Friedan written the book she started out to write and was clearly capable of producing, she would have focused on the issues of power, racism, politics, and the systematic oppression of women which some astute critics have accused her of neglecting; see Horowitz, *Betty Friedan*, 196–223.

45. On her strategy, see Donald Meyer, "Betty Friedan," in *Portraits of American Women: From Settlement to the Present*, ed. G. J. Barker-Benfield and Catherine Clinton (New York: St. Martin's Press, 1991), 603 and 605.

46. *The Feminine Mystique* was her most influential but hardly her last statement on consumer culture; see Horowitz, *Betty Friedan*, 224–55, for her career after 1963.

47. Thernstrom, "Myth of American Affluence," 74 and 75.

5. From the Affluent Society to the Poverty of Affluence, 1960–1962

1. This chapter covers some but hardly all of the key books of the early 1960s. On the working-class and consumer culture, see David Caplovitz, *The Poor Pay More: Consumer Practices of Low-Income Families* (New York: Free Press of Glencoe, 1963); Bennett Berger, *Working-Class Suburb: A Study of Auto Workers in Suburbia* (Berkeley: University of California Press, 1960). For an influential critique of suburban life from an urbanist perspective, see Jane Jacobs, *The Death and Life of Great American Cities* (New York: Random House, 1961).

2. Albert O. Hirschman, *Shifting Involvements: Private Interest and Public Action* (Princeton: Princeton University Press, 1982), 62. Note how in *The Waste Makers* (New York: David McKay, 1960), Vance Packard focused less on the impact of affluence on the environment than on the nation's values. In the wide-ranging "A Right to Welfare? Poor Women, Professionals, and Poverty Programs, 1935–1975" (Ph.D. diss., Princeton University, 2000), Felicia Ann Kornbluh examines the implications of affluence for intellectual inquiry and social policy; see esp. 35–77 for a discussion that covers many of the writers considered in this book, including Galbraith, Lewis, and King.

3. John Kenneth Galbraith, review of *Growing Up Absurd*, *NYTBR*, Oct. 30, 1960, 10 and 12.

4. Alfred Kazin, "The Girl from the Village," *Atlantic Monthly* 227 (Feb. 1971): 62–63, quoted in Richard King, *The Party of Eros: Radical Social Thought and the Realm of Freedom* (Chapel Hill: University of North Carolina Press, 1972), 81; Kazin, who normally disliked Goodman intensely, was describing a fictional figure named Ricardo whom King identified as Goodman. Paul Goodman, *New Reformation: Notes of a Neolithic Conservative* (New York: Random House, 1970), 202. On his contribution to Gestalt, see Paul Goodman, F. S. Perls, and Ralph Hefferling, *Gestalt Therapy* (Chicago: University of Chicago Press, 1951). Taylor Stoehr, the leading scholar on Goodman, has edited a series of books of Goodman's writings, the most relevant of which is *Decentralizing Power: Paul Goodman's Social Criticism* (Montreal: Black Rose Books, 1994); Stoehr's introduction provides a cogent and sympathetic review of Goodman's life and ideas; for Goodman's publications, see "Selected Bibliography," xvi–xviii, which contains reference to bibliographies, memoirs, and critical assessments. For his reconsideration of Goodman's book, see Taylor Stoehr, "Growing Up Absurd—Again," *Dissent* 37 (fall 1990): 486–94. For Goodman's trenchant critique of the genre of social criticism offered by Packard and Friedan, see "Social Criticism," in *Decentralizing Power*, 1–10; Goodman wrote this piece in 1963, but it remained unpublished at the time of his death. Other than Stoehr's

work, among the best discussions of Goodman are King, *Party of Eros*, 78–115, and Kevin Mattson, *Intellectuals in Action: The Origins of the New Left and Radical Liberalism, 1945–1970* (University Park: Pennsylvania State University Press, 2002), 97–144. See also Theodore Roszak, *The Making of a Counter Culture: Reflections on the Technocratic Society and Its Youthful Opposition* (Garden City, N.Y.: Doubleday, 1969), 178–204; Kingsley Widmer, *Paul Goodman* (Boston: Twayne Publishers, 1980). For a chronology of Goodman's life, see Widmer, *Goodman*, 13–15. On Goodman's discussion of juvenile delinquency, see James Gilbert, *A Cycle of Outrage: America's Reaction to the Juvenile Delinquent in the 1950s* (New York: Oxford University Press, 1986), 200.

5. Taylor Stoehr, "The Goodman Brothers' *Communitas*," in *Percival Goodman: Architect-Planner-Teacher-Painter*, ed. Kimberly J. Elman and Angela Giral (New York: Columbia University Press, 2001), 39; Percival Goodman and Paul Goodman, *Communitas: Means of Livelihood and Ways of Life* (Chicago: University of Chicago Press, 1947), 83. King, *Party of Eros*, 86, notes that Goodman's 1945 articles in *politics*, written at a time when many predicted the return of a depression, assumed widespread affluence and therefore the necessity for left intellectuals to deal less with old economic questions and more with new, cultural ones concerning the quality of life in mass, affluent society.

6. Mattson, *Intellectuals in Action*, 113; Paul Goodman, *Growing Up Absurd: Problems of Youth in the Organized System* (New York: Random House, 1960), 17 and 25; see also 73 and 140. For treatments of the book, on which my discussion draws, see King, *Party of Eros*, 102–6; Widmer, *Goodman*, 65–70; Stoehr, "Growing Up Absurd—Again," 486–94. For the history of the book's publication, see, in addition to Stoehr and King, Norman Podhoretz, *Making It* (1967; reprint, New York: Bantam Books, 1969), 219–20.

7. Goodman, *Growing Up Absurd*, 31, 53, xv, 65, and 52.

8. Ibid., 12 and 216; King, *Party of Eros*, 103.

9. Goodman, *Growing Up Absurd*, 13, 160, and 194.

10. Ibid., 161–62, 57, 194–95, 167, and 170; see also 89 and 160.

11. King, *Party of Eros*, 79; see also Stoehr, introduction x. The sales figures come from Widmer, *Goodman*, 65. For a discussion of some of the reviews, see Stoehr, "Growing Up Absurd—Again," 488–90; on Goodman's long-term impact, see 490–94.

12. Roszak, *Making*, 184; Stoehr, introduction, vii. On Goodman's political engagement, see Mattson, *Intellectuals in Action*, 117 and 122–44. For the widening gap between Goodman and young people, see his *New Reformation*. In mentioning older men who interpreted the lives of younger ones, I am thinking of Herbert Marcuse, *Eros and Civilization: A Philosophical Inquiry into Freud* (Boston: Beacon Press, 1955); *One-Dimensional Man: Studies in the Ideology of Advanced Industrial Society* (Boston: Beacon Press, 1964); and *An Essay on Liberation* (Boston: Beacon Press, 1969), esp. 7–16 and 49–50; Norman O. Brown, *Life against Death: The Psychoanalytic Meaning of History* (New York: Random House, 1959); Roszak, *Making*; Charles Reich, *The Greening of America* (New York: Random House, 1970); and Philip Slater, *The Pursuit of Loneliness: American Culture at the Breaking Point* (Boston: Beacon Press, 1970), esp. 81–118. On Goodman's impact, see King, *Party of Eros*, 106–12; Stoehr, "Growing Up Absurd—Again," 494. On education, see the following books by Paul Goodman: *The Community of Scholars* (New York: Random House, 1962); *Compulsory Mis-education* (New York: Horizon Press, 1964); *"People or Personnel" and "Like a Conquered Province"* (New York: Random House, 1967), 75–122, 142, 146, 261, 269–70, and 279–96. For a critical assessment, see Christopher Lasch, review of *People or Personnel, Commentary* 40 (Nov. 1965): 116–20. Stanley Aronowitz, "When the New Left Was New," in *The 60s without Apology*, ed. Sohnya Sayres et al. (Minneapolis: University of Minnesota Press, 1984), 21, calls the SDS

"the first organized expression of the postscarcity generation's new nationalism." The relationship between the counterculture, its advocates, the business community, and actual experiences with consumption among the young in the 1960s is complicated. For a thoughtful discussion, see Thomas Frank, *The Conquest of Cool: Business Culture, Counterculture, and the Rise of Hip Consumerism* (Chicago: University of Chicago Press, 1997).

13. For information on Lewis's life, I am relying on Susan M. Rigdon, *The Culture Façade: Art, Science, and Politics in the World of Oscar Lewis* (Urbana: University of Illinois Press, 1988), 1–26; for a bibliography of his works, see 301–9. The historian Philip Foner lost his job at CCNY in 1941 during a purge of radicals.

14. Rigdon, *Culture Façade*, 24; see also 16. For the story of the quiet dismissal of an assistant professor of music at the University of Illinois in 1953, see Ellen W. Schrecker, *No Ivory Tower: McCarthyism and the Universities* (New York: Oxford University Press, 1986), 258. On the role of Ruth Maslow Lewis, see Rigdon, *Culture Façade*, 18.

15. Rigdon, *Culture Façade*, 27–47.

16. Oscar Lewis, *Five Families: Mexican Case Studies in the Culture of Poverty* (New York: Basic Books, 1959), 5 and 51. Rigdon, *Culture Façade*, 4 and 49, discuss shifts in his method. In the early 1950s, Lewis first turned his attention to the urban poor when he studied villagers who had moved from Tepoztlán to Mexico City. In the scholarship that resulted, he focused on the ability of the villagers to make this shift without the social disorganization he emphasized in his later work; Rigdon, *Culture Façade*, 48. On the tensions in his work, see Rigdon, *Culture Façade*, 5.

17. Daniel M. Friedenberg, review, *NR*, Nov. 13, 1961, 17.

18. Oscar Lewis, introduction to *Children of Sánchez* (1961; reprint, Harmondsworth: Penguin Books, 1964), xii. For letters from Lewis on his work in Mexico City, see Rigdon, *Culture Façade*, 219–44.

19. Lewis, *Children*, 271.

20. Ibid., 489, 502, and 507.

21. Ibid., xxiv and xxiii.

22. Ibid., xvii and xii. On Lewis's familiarity with popular books on U.S. culture, see xv. Ruth Maslow Lewis, e-mail to Daniel Horowitz, July 5, 2001, copy in author's possession, acknowledges that Oscar Lewis read the key books by Packard and Galbraith.

23. Oscar Lewis to Conrad Arensberg, Nov. 3, 1960, in Rigdon, *Culture Façade*, 225. The discussion of the tasks the concept accomplished relies on Rigdon, *Culture Façade*, 58. In *Five Families*, Lewis mentioned the term once (1) and devoted one paragraph to the subject (2), in which he did not discuss the culture of poverty as pathological. One of the families he focused on, he noted, exhibited "relatively little of the disorganization and breakdown which is so often associated with the urbanization process" (13–14). Another of his five families was nouveau riche, having made a successful transition from the tenements (16).

24. Lewis, *Children*, xxxi; for his not very systematic discussion of the culture of poverty, see xxiv–xxxi. Compare W. W. Rostow, *Stages of Economic Growth, a Non-Communist Manifesto* (Cambridge: Cambridge University Press, 1960). Rigdon, *Culture Façade*, x–xi and 51–63, writes perceptively about the problems Lewis had with the concept of the culture of poverty.

25. Elizabeth Hardwick, review, *NYTBR*, Aug. 27, 1961, 1; Edgar Z. Friedenberg, review, *Commentary* 33 (Jan. 1962): 79; review, *Time*, Sept. 1, 1961, 65–66; Daniel Friedenberg, review, 17; Mirra Komarovsky, review, *ASR*, 27 (June 1962): 432. Other reviews from which this discussion draws are Carleton Beals, *SRL*, Sept. 16, 1961, 27–28; Robert Hatch, *Nation*, Oct. 14, 1961, 250–51; R. H. S. Crossman, *New Statesman*, Apr. 20, 1962, 562–63. Although

included in the "—And Bear in Mind" list, the book did not appear on the *New York Times* best-seller list in September or October. Reviewers did discuss the concept, but it did not dominate the reviews: see Edgar Friedenberg, review, 82. No book by Oscar Lewis appeared on the national best-seller list.

26. Rigdon, *Culture Façade*, 88–98. According to Rigdon, Lewis was on "pins and needles" during the 1950s, fearing a possible investigation, but was never called before university or government officials; Susan Rigdon, telephone conversation, Feb. 17, 2001. According to Ruth Maslow Lewis, during the 1950s, although she and her husband did not know anyone at the University of Illinois who was under attack, they were struck by the suspicion and political silence among people they knew; Ruth Maslow Lewis, e-mail. Lewis returned to the culture of poverty thesis frequently. See, for example, his letters in Rigdon, *Culture Façade*, 219–300; Oscar Lewis, *La Vida: A Puerto Rican Family in the Culture of Poverty—San Juan and New York* (New York: Random House, 1966), xlii–lii; Oscar Lewis, "The Culture of Poverty," *Scientific American* 215 (Oct. 1966): 19–25. For an early critique of the concept, see Jack L. Roach and Orville R. Gursslin, "An Evaluation of the Concept 'Culture of Poverty,'" *Social Forces* 45 (Nov. 1966): 383–92. For later discussions, see James T. Patterson, *America's Struggle against Poverty, 1900–1980* (Cambridge: Harvard University Press, 1981), 115–25; Michael Katz, *The Undeserving Poor: From the War on Poverty to the War on Welfare* (New York: Pantheon Books, 1989), 16–23; Stephen Steinberg, *Ethnic Myth: Race, Ethnicity, and Class in America* (1982; reprint, Boston: Beacon Press, 1989), 106–27; Nicholas Lemann, *The Promised Land: The Great Black Migration and How It Changed America* (New York: Knopf, 1991), 150–51.

27. Rigdon, *Culture Façade*, 87. For a full discussion of the debates and Lewis's response, see Rigdon, *Culture Façade*, esp. 72–182; Maurice Isserman, *The Other American: The Life of Michael Harrington* (New York: Public Affairs, 2000), 180, 214–16, 399 fn. 16, 407 fn. 157. On his 1966 response, see Lewis, *La Vida*, xlii–lii.

28. On the last years of his career, see Rigdon, *Culture Façade*, 72–86 and 175; the sales figures rely on data from 73 and 84 fn. 2.

29. Review, *Time*, 66; Michael Harrington, review of Oscar Lewis, *The Children of Sánchez*, *Commonweal*, Nov. 17, 1961, 214; Isserman, *Other American*, 84. Some reviewers suggested the relevance of what Lewis described to North American society, but his book did not suggest to them that there might be poor people in the United States; see Edgar Friedenberg, review, 80. For one of Lewis's responses to Harrington's use of his term, see Lewis, *La Vida*, xlii. Lewis estimated that only one in five people in the United States living below the poverty line was enmeshed in the culture of poverty; Lewis, *La Vida*, li. For another review of Lewis by Harrington, see Harrington's review of *Pedro Martinez: A Mexican Peasant and His Family*, *NYTBR*, May 3, 1964, 3. For Harrington's thoughtful discussion of Lewis's position on the culture of poverty, see his review of Oscar Lewis, *La Vida*, *NYTBR*, Nov. 20, 1966, 1 and 92. For biographical information, I am relying on Isserman, *Other American*. Other discussions include Michael Harrington, *Fragments of the Century* (New York: Dutton, 1973); Loren J. Okroi, *Galbraith, Harrington, Heilbroner: Economics and Dissent in an Age of Optimism* (Princeton: Princeton University Press, 1988), 109–175. Harrington knew Goodman during these years; Harrington, *Fragments*, 69.

30. Isserman, *Other American*, 140.

31. Ibid., 175–82.

32. Michael Harrington, *The Other America: Poverty in the United States* (New York: Macmillan, 1962), 1 and 2. On the origins of the book, see Isserman, *Other American*, 175–

82. Like *Growing Up Absurd, The Other America* began as a series of articles in *Commentary,* a periodical Norman Podhoretz was beginning to transform.

33. Harrington, *Other America*, 9, 4, 14, 15, 16, 122, and 138. For evidence that Harrington first learned of the concept from reading Lewis, see Oscar Lewis to Lloyd Ohlin, Feb. 1, 1966, quoted in Rigdon, *Culture Façade*, 170 fn. 7. Lewis refers here and elsewhere to Harrington's encounter with *Five Families* in 1959, but I have not been able to locate the review he mentions. He may instead have been referring to Harrington's 1961 review; see Oscar Lewis to Richard Morse, Nov. 23, 1965, in Rigdon, *Culture Façade*, 244.

34. Harrington, *Other America*, 29, 31, 36, 82, 71, 63, and 75.

35. Ibid., 162, 172, and 167.

36. Ibid., 171, 172, 174, and 159.

37. Ibid., 15 and 18. This discussion also relies on ibid., 17. In discussing Harrington's strategies for enhancing the book's appeal, I draw substantially on Isserman, *Other American*, 196–98. On the way Harrington agonized over not acknowledging that he was a socialist, see Isserman, *Other American*, 19; Harrington, *Fragments*, 179. See also Christopher Lasch, review of *Socialism* by Michael Harrington, *NYRB*, July 20, 1972, 15–20.

38. This discussion relies heavily on Isserman, *Other American*, 197–99 and 206–20; see also Arthur M. Schlesinger Jr., *A Thousand Days: John F. Kennedy in the White House* (Boston: Houghton Mifflin, 1965), 1010.

39. Lyndon B. Johnson, quoted in Isserman, *Other American*, 209; Marion Magid, "The Man Who Discovered Poverty," *New York Herald Tribune Magazine*, Dec. 27, 1964, 11, quoted in Isserman, *Other American*, 207. On the familiarity within the White House with Harrington's book and Macdonald's essay, see Lemann, *Promised Land*, 130. For the essay itself, see Dwight Macdonald, "Our Invisible Poor," *NY*, Jan. 1, 1963, 82ff. According to Walter Heller, in the summer of 1963, Galbraith did not think it politically feasible to develop a poverty program; quoted in Lemann, *Promised Land*, 132. In addition, according to Heller's notes from a meeting with Kennedy a few days before his death, the president said, "I'm still very much in favor of doing something on the poverty theme if we can get a good program, but I also think it's important to make clear that we're doing something for the middle-class man in the suburbs"; notes of Walter Heller, Nov. 20, 1963, in Lemann, *Promised Land*, 134.

40. Isserman, *Other American*, 214; Harrington, *Other America*, 162. This discussion of the impact of the book relies heavily on Isserman, *Other American*, 198–220. On Harrington's agonizing over moving out of voluntary poverty (and attacks on him for doing so), see Harrington, *Fragments*, 180–83. Harrington noted that he "had always objected to those radicals who pictured the good society as a place of Spartan asceticism. The bourgeoisie had, it seemed to me, developed a number of valuable things—among them democratic liberties, good food, clean airy rooms with fresh sheets—that were not evil in the least, only maldistributed"; Harrington, *Fragments*, 180. On how conservatives used the notion of a culture of poverty in ways Harrington would oppose, see Isserman, *Other American*, 305–6 and 340–41.

41. "Required Reading," *Time*, June 8, 1998, 108.

42. Gerda Lerner to Betty Friedan, Feb. 6, 1963, box 20a, folder 715, BF-SLRI.

43. Linda Lear, *Rachel Carson: Witness for Nature* (New York: Henry Holt, 1997), is the authoritative biography. Mary McCay, *Rachel Carson* (New York: Twayne Publishers, 1993), is a briefer treatment, focusing mainly on Carson as a nature writer. Paul Brooks, *The House of Life: Rachel Carson at Work* (Boston: Houghton Mifflin, 1972), is a biography by her editor. Additional information is in Linda Lear, introduction to *Lost Woods: The Discovered Writing of Rachel Carson* (Boston: Beacon Press, 1998), ix–xiv. In telling the story of Carson's life, I have

drawn on all these sources. For other scholarship on Carson, see H. Patricia Hynes, "Ellen Swallow, Lois Gibbs, and Rachel Carson: Catalysts of the American Environmental Movement," *Women's Studies International Forum* 8 (1985): 291–98; Vera Norwood, "Heroines of Nature: Four Women Respond to the American Landscape," *Environmental Review* 8 (spring 1984): 34–56; Sara Anderson, "The View from Outside: A Study of the Work of Rachel Carson, Jane Jacobs, and Betty Friedan," *New England Journal of History* 52 (spring 1995): 40–53.

44. Rachel Carson, *Under the Sea-Wind* (New York: Simon and Schuster, 1941).

45. Rachel Carson, *The Edge of the Sea* (Boston: Houghton Mifflin, 1955). For an example of evil human intervention, see Rachel Carson, *The Sea Around Us* (1951; reprint, New York: New American Library, 1954), 77.

46. *Always, Rachel: The Letters of Rachel Carson and Dorothy Freeman, 1952–1964*, ed. Martha Freeman (Boston: Beacon Press, 1995), beautifully captures Carson's particularly intense relationship with another woman. On a significant women's protest in the early 1960s, see Amy Swerdlow, *Women Strike for Peace: Traditional Motherhood and Radical Politics in the 1960s* (Chicago: University of Chicago Press, 1993).

47. On Carson's work on *Silent Spring*, see Lear, *Carson*, 312–427; McCay, *Carson*, 64–70; Brooks, *House of Life*, 227–72. Carson, long interested in the relationship between the use of chemicals and cancer, completed the draft of a work on this subject before she discovered in 1960 that she had the disease; Lear, *Carson*, 365. Obviously there is a relationship, albeit one difficult to fathom, between knowledge of her own impending death, the urgency she felt, the treatment she decided upon, and her writing about the link between cancer and chemicals. For cartoons in response to *Silent Spring*, see Brooks, *House of Life*, between 238 and 239.

48. Rachel Carson, National Symphony Orchestra speech, Sept. 25, 1951, in Carson, *Lost Woods*, 89; Rachel Carson, remarks at the acceptance of the National Book Award for Nonfiction, Jan. 29, 1952, ibid., 91–92; Rachel Carson, "Mr. Day's Dismissal," letter to editor of *Washington Post*, Apr. 22, 1953, ibid., 100; Lear, *Carson*, 220. On her growing awareness of environmental dangers, see Rachel Carson, "Preface to the Second Edition of *The Sea Around Us*" (1961), in Carson, *Lost Woods*, 107–9. Paul Boyer, *By the Bomb's Early Light: American Thought and Culture at the Dawn of the Atomic Age* (New York: Pantheon Books, 1985), discussed the impact of the specter of atomic power on American culture. On Galbraith's influence, see Rachel Carson to Paul Brooks, Sept. 11, 1958, folder 1527, box 87, RC-YU.

49. Rachel Carson, speech given at the Theta Sigma Phi Matrix Table dinner, Apr. 21, 1954, Columbus, Ohio, in Carson, *Lost Woods*, 161–63.

50. Rachel Carson, *Silent Spring* (1962; reprint, Greenwich, Conn.: Fawcett Publications, 1964), 25 and 319.

51. Ibid., 16, 17, and 59.

52. Vera L. Norwood, "The Nature of Knowing: Rachel Carson and the American Environment," *Signs* 12 (summer 1982): 755; Carson, *Silent Spring*, 53, 16, 24, and 39. For an exploration of the feminist dimensions of Carson's writings, see also Carolyn Merchant, "Women and the Environmental Movement," *Environment* 23 (June 1981): 6–13 and 38–40; Christine Oravec, "Rachel Louise Carson (1907–1964), Author, Naturalist, Environmental Advocate," in *Women Public Speakers in the United States, 1925–1993: A Biocritical Source Book*, ed. Karlyn Kohrs Campbell (Westport, Conn.: Greenwood Press, 1993), 72, 74, and 78.

53. Carson, *Silent Spring*, vii, 14, 97, and 95; see also 217.

54. Ibid., 157, 16, and 18; on the impact of chemicals on heredity, see 18, 24, 25, 30, 168, 179, and 186.

55. Ibid., vii, 12, 28, 46, 63, 83, 85, 86, 87, 100, 130, 142, 144 and 166.

56. Ibid., 161 and 22; this discussion also draws on 157–67 and 229.

57. Ibid., 23, 161, 64, and 216.

58. Ibid., 31; Rachel Carson, "Tomorrow's Spring," speech delivered at the All-Women Conference sponsored by the National Council of Women of the United States at the Waldorf-Astoria, Oct. 11, 1962, folder 1885, box 101, RC-YU; Rachel Carson, speech, reprinted in "Garden Club Federation of Pennsylvania News Spring 1963," folder 1743, box 97, RC-YU. For her discussion of protests, see Carson, *Silent Spring*, 69, 87, 97, and 144. In one case, a man led these protests; see 144.

59. Carson, *Silent Spring*, 118, 157, 118–19, 244, and 261.

60. On the book's impact, see McCay, *Carson*, 63–83; Brooks, *House of Life*, 292–329; Lear, *Carson*, 417 and 429–73. For an example of her response to her critics before women's clubs, see Rachel Carson, speech given to the Women's National Press Club, Washington, D.C., Dec. 5, 1962, in Carson, *Lost Woods*, 202–10; Rachel Carson, speech given to the Garden Club of America, New York, Jan. 8, 1963, in Carson, *Lost Woods*, 212–22. On her fear of revelatory attacks, see Linda Lear, headnote to 1963 letter from Rachel Carson to Dr. George Crile Jr., in Carson, *Lost Woods*, 223–24. On making the private political more generally, see W. J. Rorabaugh, *Kennedy and the Promise of the Sixties* (Cambridge: Cambridge University Press, 2002). On the history of pesticides in the United States before Carson's book, see James Whorton, *Before "Silent Spring": Pesticides and Public Health in Pre-DDT America* (Princeton: Princeton University Press, 1974). For the controversy surrounding her book and the ensuing debates over the impact of pesticides, see Frank Graham Jr., *Since "Silent Spring"* (Boston: Houghton Mifflin, 1970). For more recent evidence of the impact of Carson's work, see John H. Cushman Jr., "After 'Silent Spring,' Industry Put Spin on All It Brewed," *NYT*, Mar. 26, 2001, A14; see also the 2001 PBS documentary "Trade Secrets," reviewed in Neil Genzlinger, "Rendering a Guilty Verdict on Corporate America," *NYT*, Mar. 26, 2001, B8.

61. Lear, headnote, 117; Rachel Carson, speech given to the Kaiser-Permanente Symposium "Man against Himself," Oct. 18, 1963, in Carson, *Lost Woods*, 231. For her opposition to the inhumane treatment of animals, see Rachel Carson, "To Understand Biology," from *Humane Biology Projects* (New York: Animal Welfare Institute, 1960), in Carson, *Lost Woods*, 192–96.

62. On the collapse of the liberal-labor alliance, see Meg Jacobs, "The Politics of Plenty in the Twentieth-Century United States," in *The Politics of Consumption: Material Culture and Citizenship in Europe and America*, ed. Martin Daunton and Matthew Hilton (Oxford: Berg, 2002), 223–39. In making the distinction between the 1960s and The Sixties, I have drawn on David A. Hollinger, *Science, Jews, and Secular Culture: Studies in Mid-Twentieth-Century American Intellectual History* (Princeton: Princeton University Press, 1996), 4–7.

6. Consumer Activism, 1965–1970

1. On the history of consumer protests, see Dana Frank, *Buy American: The Untold Story of Economic Nationalism* (Boston: Beacon Press, 1999); Annelise Oreleck, *"Common Sense & a Little Fire": Women and Working-Class Politics in the United States, 1900–1965* (Chapel Hill: University of North Carolina Press, 1995); and two works by Lawrence B. Glickman, *A Living Wage: American Workers and the Making of a Consumer Society* (Ithaca: Cornell University Press, 1997), and "The Strike in the Temple of Consumption: Consumer Activism and Twentieth-Century American Political Culture," *JAH* 88 (June 2001): 99–128. On the history

and structure of the post-1965 consumer movement, see Robert N. Mayer, *The Consumer Movement: Guardians of the Marketplace* (Boston: Twayne Publishers, 1989). For a more complete listing of scholarship on consumer protests, see Felicia Ann Kornbluh, "A Right to Welfare? Poor Women, Professionals, and Poverty Programs, 1935–1975" (Ph.D. diss., Princeton University, 2000), 387–90.

2. Kornbluh, "A Right to Welfare?" 386; for her full argument on these issues, see 7–8, 26, and 328–496. See also Felicia A. Kornbluh, "To Fulfill Their 'Rightly Needs': Consumerism and the National Welfare Rights Movement," *RHR* 69 (fall 1997): 76–113. On Chávez, see Richard Griswold del Castillo and Richard A. Garcia, *César Chávez: A Triumph of Spirit* (Norman: University of Oklahoma Press, 1995); Jacques Levy, *César Chavez: Autobiography of La Causa* (New York: W. W. Norton, 1975); Sam Kushner, *Long Road to Delano* (New York: International Publishers, 1975). In *Silent Spring* (Greenwich, Conn.: Fawcett Publications, 1962), 37, Rachel Carson had mentioned the deleterious effect the use of pesticides had on farm workers in California. Nader's early writing on farm workers is discussed later in this chapter.

3. Kathy McAfee and Myrna Wood, "Bread and Roses," excerpted from a June 1969 issue of *Leviathan* in *Feminism in Our Time: The Essential Writings, World War II to the Present*, ed. Miriam Schneir (New York: Vintage Books, 1994), 136; Amy Erdman Farrell, *Yours in Sisterhood: "Ms." Magazine and the Promise of Popular Feminism* (Chapel Hill: University of North Carolina Press, 1998), 5. On the protests at *Ladies' Home Journal*, see Ruth Rosen, *The World Split Open: How the Modern Women's Movement Changed America* (New York: Viking, 2000), 300; for Rosen's discussion of the way corporations co-opted feminism and promoted what she calls "consumer feminism," see 308–17.

4. See, by Herbert Marcuse, *Eros and Civilization: A Philosophical Inquiry into Freud* (Boston: Beacon Press, 1955); *One-Dimensional Man: Studies in the Ideology of Advanced Industrial Society* (Boston: Beacon Press, 1964); and *An Essay on Liberation* (Boston: Beacon Press, 1969), esp. 7–16 and 49–50; Norman O. Brown, *Life against Death: The Psychoanalytic Meaning of History* (New York: Random House, 1959); Theodore Roszak, *The Making of a Counter Culture: Reflections on the Technocratic Society and Its Youthful Opposition* (Garden City, N.Y.: Doubleday, 1969); Charles Reich, *The Greening of America* (New York: Random House, 1970); Philip Slater, *The Pursuit of Loneliness: American Culture at the Breaking Point* (Boston: Beacon Press, 1970). David E. Shi, *The Simple Life: Plain Living and High Thinking in American Culture* (New York: Oxford University Press, 1985), 251–61 explores experiments in simplicity.

5. For biographical information, I am relying on Charles McCarry, *Citizen Nader* (New York: Saturday Review Press, 1972), esp. xi–xiv and 3–79; Robert F. Buckhorn, *Nader: The People's Lawyer* (Englewood Cliffs, N.J.: Prentice-Hall, 1972); David Bollier, *Citizen Action and Other Big Ideas: A History of Ralph Nader and the Modern Consumer Movement* (Washington, D.C.: Center for Study of Responsive Law, 1991), esp. 1–4; Jay Acton and Alan LeMond, *Ralph Nader: A Man and a Movement* (New York: Warner, 1972); Kevin Graham, *Ralph Nader: Battling for Democracy* (Denver: Windom Publishing, 2000); "Ralph Nader: Activism in the Public Interest," <www.votenader.org/biography.html>. Among the other books I have consulted on Nader are Thomas Whiteside, *The Investigation of Ralph Nader: General Motors vs. One Determined Man* (New York: Arbor House, 1972); David Sanford, *Me & Ralph: Is Nader Unsafe for America?* (Washington, D.C.: New Republic Book Company, 1976); and Ralph de Toledano, *Hit & Run: The Rise—and Fall?—of Ralph Nader* (New Rochelle, N.Y.: Arlington House, 1975). For a history of the legal profession that sheds light on the world Nader faced and to some extent transformed, see Jerold S. Auerbach, *Unequal Justice: Lawyers and Social*

Change (New York: Oxford University Press, 1976). There is remarkably little scholarly work that places Nader in a historical context; for exceptions, see Harry H. Stein, "American Muckraking of Technology," *Journalism Quarterly* 67 (summer 1990): 401–9; Joel W. Eastman, *Styling vs. Safety: The American Automobile Industry and the Development of Automotive Safety, 1900–66* (Lanham, Md.: University Press of America 1984). "Quiet—smart—can be found either at home or at the restaurant—woman hater" were the words that appeared under Nader's picture in his high school yearbook; see *The Miracle*, 1951 yearbook of Gilbert High School, copy in author's possession.

6. Harper Hubert Wilson (H. H. Wilson), quoted in finding aid, 1, HHW-PU. His first book was *Congress: Corruption and Compromise* (New York: Rinehart, 1951), in which he explored how the reluctance of Congress to discipline its own members undermined public trust and democracy. Wilson eventually made suppression of civil liberties by anticommunists the main cause he pursued. See the following articles in *The Nation*: "Cynics and Feeble Good Men," Nov. 24, 1951, 438–41; "Academic Freedom and American Society," June 28, 1952, 658–62; "Why They Voted for McCarthy," Sept. 20, 1952, 225–27; "The Senate Sellout," Jan. 24, 1953, 64–66; "Monsters and Men," Apr. 25, 1953, 350; "Failure of the Citizen," Sept. 11, 1954, 215–16. On Wilson's course, see H. H. Wilson, "Introduction: Politics 203, 1954," folder 16, box 4, HHW-PU. For Wilson's use of Mills, see material for exams in Politics 203 in HHW-PU, folder 15, box 4, especially an undated (not long after 1950) "Suggested Exam." On the importance of Mills to Wilson, I am also relying on Otto Butz, telephone interview with author, Oct. 12, 2001. Butz, a preceptor in Wilson's course, later produced a book that contains self-portraits of Princeton undergraduates of Nader's generation: Otto Butz, comp. and ed., *The Unsilent Generation: An Anonymous Symposium in Which Eleven College Seniors Look at Themselves and Their World* (New York: Rinehart, 1958). For biographical information on Wilson, see finding aid to HHW-PU. Nader and Wilson remained in touch after Nader's graduation; see H. H. Wilson to Ralph Nader, Jan. 25, 1971, folder 4, box 4, HHW-PU.

7. Ralph Nader, "Lebanese Agriculture" (senior thesis, Princeton University, 1955, UA-OU). The best source on Nader's years at Princeton and Harvard is Jack Lee Goodman Jr., "An Uphill Battle: Ralph Nader's Struggle against the Corporate State, 1955–1976" (senior thesis, Princeton University, 1989, UA-PU); for Nader's work on Puerto Rico, see 32–33. Concerning his focus on Native Americans, see Graham, *Nader*, 43; I have not been able to locate Nader's article on this topic. On Nader at Princeton, I am also drawing on Gary Nash, interview with author, Oct. 11, 2001. Nader joined Prospect Club, the club of outsiders which accepted the rejects of more prestigious ones. As if to underscore his outsider status, Nader did not appear in the yearbook picture of the members of Prospect Club; see *Bric-A-Brac* (Princeton: Princeton University, 1955), 179.

8. See the following articles by Ralph Nader in the *Harvard Law Record*: "The Commonwealth Status of Puerto Rico," Dec. 13, 1956, 2–8; "Legislative Neglect Keeps Migrant Workers Mired in 'Asiatic-Type' Poverty," Apr. 10, 1958, 3 and 6; "Do Third Parties Have a Chance?" (co-authored with Theodore Jacobs), Oct. 9, 1958, 1 and 4. For reference to his presidency of the publication's board, see Ralph Nader, "An Answer to Administrative Abuse," *Harvard Law Record*, Dec. 20, 1962, 15. On the themes that suffuse his writings at Princeton and Harvard, see Goodman, "Uphill Battle," 34, 43, 50, and 51.

9. Ralph Nader, quoted in Buckhorn, *Nader*, 36.

10. Ralph Nader, "An Ombudsman for the U.S.?" *Christian Science Monitor*, Apr. 1, 1963; Nader, "An Answer," 13 and 15; Daniel Patrick Moynihan, "Epidemic on the Highways," *Reporter*, Apr. 30, 1959, 16–23.

11. Ralph Nader, "The American Automobile: Designed for Death?" *Harvard Law Record*, Dec. 11, 1958, 1–2; Ralph Nader, "The *Safe* Car You Can't Buy," *Nation*, May 11, 1959, 310–13, quotes 312. For a later article, see Ralph Nader, "Fashion or Safety," *Nation*, Oct. 12, 1963, 214–16. On a different subject, see Ralph Nader, "Blue-Law Blues," *Nation*, June 10, 1961, 499–500 and 508. For an article on Roscoe Pound, see Arthur Train Jr. and Ralph Nader, "Grand Old Man of the Law," *Reader's Digest* 79 (Feb. 1961): 163–66.

12. On the development of the book, see McCarry, *Citizen Nader*, 7–8. See also Lewis Mumford, review of *Unsafe at Any Speed*, *NYRB*, Apr. 28, 1966, 3–5.

13. Ralph Nader, *Unsafe at Any Speed: The Designed-in Dangers of the American Automobile* (New York: Grossman Publishers, 1965), vii and ix.

14. Ibid., x.

15. Ibid., 213.

16. Ibid., 36, xi, 3, and 236.

17. Ibid., 233; "J. C. Furnas, Wry Historian of American Life, Dies at 95," *NYT*, June 12, 2001, C19; Nader *Unsafe*, 234.

18. Nader, *Unsafe*, ix, 295, 338, 326, and 8.

19. Ibid., 332, 342, and 343.

20. McCarry, *Citizen Nader*, 13. James Ridgeway, "The Dick," *NR*, Mar. 12, 1966, 11–13.

21. "The Decade's Most Notable Books," *Time*, Dec. 26, 1969, 56. There were no books by women on the list, not even Friedan's *Feminine Mystique* or Carson's *Silent Spring*. *Unsafe at Any Speed* reached as high as number five on the best-seller list and remained there for several months.

22. Jessica Mitford, *The American Way of Death* (New York: Simon and Schuster, 1963). In addition to the work of James Ridgeway and Daniel Patrick Moynihan, see William Haddon Jr., Edward A. Suchman, and Donald Klein, *Accident Research* (New York: Harper and Row, 1964); Jeffrey O'Connell and Arthur Myers, *Safety Last: An Indictment of the Auto Industry* (New York: Random House, 1966). On the revival of consumer issues, see Michael Pertschuk, *Revolt against Regulation: The Rise and Pause of the Consumer Movement* (Berkeley: University of California Press, 1982), 5–45.

23. This discussion of Nader's impact draws on McCarry, *Citizen Nader*. Matthew T. Lee, "The Ford Pinto Case and the Development of Auto Safety Regulations, 1893–1978," *Business and Economic History* 27 (winter 1998): 390–401, provides an overview of federal auto regulation; see also Richard S. Tedlow and Reed E. Hundt, "Cars and Carnage: Safety and Hazard on the American Road," *Journal of Policy History* 4 (1992): 435–52.

24. Buckhorn, *Nader*, 36 and 245–58.

25. In drawing this picture, I am relying on McCarry, *Citizen Nader*, 6 and 106–25; Pertschuk, *Revolt against Regulation*, 31–33. For a clear delineation of Nader's organizations and useful discussion of his organizational style, see Susan Gross, "The Nader Network," *Business and Society Review* 13 (spring 1975): 5–15.

26. The historian Grace Hale has used the 1939 incident as part of her description of the process by which, from 1890 to 1940, whiteness and blackness suffused consumer culture. Southern whites used depictions of happy slaves on antebellum plantations and segregated public facilities to link whiteness and consumer culture. At the same time, new settings of consumption, such as railroads and eventually buses and local branches of national stores, opened up space where African Americans could protest their exclusion from sites of consumption. See Grace Elizabeth Hale, *Making Whiteness: The Culture of Segregation in the South, 1890–1940* (New York: Pantheon Books, 1998), 123 and 126; for information on the picture of King, see 279 and picture and caption facing 147. For a discussion of the depictions of

African Americans in advertising and the fight to change and increase their representation, see Marilyn Kern-Foxworth, *Aunt Jemima, Uncle Ben, and Rastus: Blacks in Advertising, Yesterday, Today, and Tomorrow* (Westport, Conn.: Greenwood Press, 1994).

27. David Levering Lewis, *King: A Biography*, 2d ed. (Urbana: University of Illinois Press, 1978), 9. For biographical information, I am relying on Lewis, *King;* Stephen Oates, *Let the Trumpet Sound: The Life of Martin Luther King Jr.* (New York: Harper and Row, 1982); David Garrow, *Bearing the Cross: Martin Luther King Jr. and the Southern Christian Leadership Conference* (New York: William Morrow, 1986). Of central importance to this or any study of King are *The Papers of Martin Luther King, Jr.*, ed. Clayborne Carson (Berkeley: University of California Press, 1992–). To date, four volumes have appeared, covering the years through 1958; see especially the introductions by Carson to vols. 1 (1992): 1–57; 2 (1994): 1–37; 3 (1997): 1–33; and 4 (2000): 1–38. See also *The Autobiography of Martin Luther King Jr.*, ed. Clayborne Carson (New York: Warner Books, 1998). On the development of King's views, see Thomas F. Jackson, "Recasting the Dream: Martin Luther King Jr., African American Political Thought, and the Third Reconstruction, 1955–1968" (Ph.D. diss., Stanford University, 1994); see also Thomas F. Jackson, "Dilemma and Dreams: Martin Luther King Jr. and Black America's War on Poverty, 1955–1995," forthcoming. On what he calls King's "asceticism," see Thaddeus Russell, "'A Process of Self-Purification': Citizenship and Desire in the Postwar Labor and Civil Rights Movements," 2, unpublished paper, April 2002, copy in author's possession. On King's rhetoric, see Keith D. Miller, *Voice of Deliverance: The Language of Martin Luther King Jr. and Its Sources* (New York: Free Press, 1992).

28. Robert E. Weems Jr., *Desegregating the Dollar: African American Consumerism in the Twentieth Century* (New York: New York University Press, 1998), 56; this book, esp. 56–79, is the best source on African Americans, consumption, and protest in the 1960s. See also Robin D. G. Kelley, *Race Rebels: Culture, Politics, and the Black Working Class* (New York: Free Press, 1994), esp. 55–75; Kathy M. Newman, "The Forgotten Fifteen Million: Black Radio, the 'Negro Market,' and the Civil Rights Movement," *RHR* 76 (winter 2000): 115–35. For protests in the 1930s, see Cheryl L. Greenberg, "'Or Does It Explode?' Black Harlem in the Great Depression* (New York: Oxford University Press, 1991), 114–39. There are many albeit largely scattered sources in which to examine the literature on the African American consumer market in addition to Weems, *Desegregating the Dollar*. Paul K. Edwards, *The Southern Urban Negro as a Consumer* (New York: Prentice-Hall, 1932), is an important pioneering study. *Ebony* magazine provides a window into upper-end consumption in the black community; see, for example, "Why Negroes Buy Cadillacs," *Ebony*, Sept. 1949, 34. Raymond A. Bauer and Scott Cunningham, *Studies in the Negro Market* (Cambridge: Marketing Science Institute, [1970]), includes a discussion (10–14) of the history of surveys of the African American market. Carl H. Nightingale, *On the Edge: A History of Poor Black Children and Their American Dreams* (New York: Basic Books, 1993), esp. 135–65 and the accompanying footnotes, explores the relationship between marketing strategies and social experience. M. M. Manring, *Slave in a Box: The Strange Career of Aunt Jemima* (Charlottesville: University Press of Virginia, 1998), explores an icon. Hale, *Making Whiteness*, 121–97, provides a penetrating analysis of the relationship between consumption and segregation. On the social dynamics of African American consumption practices, see Lizabeth Cohen, *Making a New Deal: Industrial Workers in Chicago, 1919–1939* (Cambridge: Cambridge University Press, 1990), 148–54. Harold Cruse, *The Crisis of the Negro Intellectual* (New York: William Morrow, 1967), 64–95 and 305–36, provides a framework for understanding the relationship between African American consumption and activism. At the Smithsonian Institution's National Museum of American History, Fath Davis Ruffins's ethnic imagery project provides invaluable images used in advertising.

29. Kern-Foxworth, *Aunt Jemima*, xix, 39–41, 175, and 85. On the position of African American nationalists, see Russell, "Citizenship and Desire," 19–20.

30. King, "Autobiography," 360; Carson, introduction, 1:31; Martin Luther King Jr., speaking in early 1952, quoted in Coretta Scott King, *My Life with Martin Luther King Jr.* (1969; reprint, New York: Avon Books, 1970), 71. In the 1950s, King delivered a sermon in which he told his congregation, "In the midst of all your material wealth, you are spiritually and morally poverty-stricken"; Martin Luther King Jr., *The Measure of a Man* (1959; reprint, Philadelphia: Pilgrim Press, 1968), 35–36.

31. Martin Luther King Jr., "An Autobiography of Religious Development" (1950), in *Papers*, 1:359; Martin Luther King Jr., *Stride toward Freedom: The Montgomery Story* (New York: Harper and Row, 1958), 94–95. This discussion also draws on Garrow, *Bearing the Cross*, 374; Jackson, "Recasting the Dream," 43.

32. Martin Luther King Jr., "Rediscovering Lost Values," sermon delivered at Second Baptist Church, Detroit, Feb. 28, 1954, in King, *Papers*, 2:252 and 254–55. In reporting on his 1959 trip to India, King noted, "In contrast to the poverty-stricken, there were Indians who were rich, had luxurious homes, landed estates, fine clothes, and showed evidence of over-eating. The bourgeoisie—white, black, or brown—behaves about the same the world over"; King, *Autobiography*, 125. King echoed these themes in an advice column he wrote in *Ebony* from September 1957 to December 1958; see Russell, "Citizenship and Desire," 16–19.

33. Martin Luther King Jr., "The Birth of a New Age," address delivered in Buffalo at the fiftieth anniversary of Alpha Phi Alpha, Aug. 11, 1956, in King, *Papers*, 3:345; Martin Luther King Jr., "Facing the Challenge of a New Age," speech delivered in Montgomery, Dec. 1956, in *Testament of Hope: The Essential Writings and Speeches of Martin Luther King Jr.*, ed. James Melvin Washington (San Francisco: Harper, 1991), 142–43. On the relationship between politics and materialism, see Russell, "Citizenship and Desire," 15.

34. Martin Luther King Jr., "Some Things We Must Do," address delivered at the Second Annual Institute on Nonviolence and Social Change at Holt Street Baptist Church, Dec. 5, 1957, *Papers*, 4:339–40. See also Martin Luther King Jr., "The Things That Are God's," sermon delivered on Oct. 27, 1957 at Dexter Avenue Baptist Church, *Papers*, 4:310.

35. Paul R. Mullins, *Race and Affluence: An Archaeology of African America and Consumer Culture* (New York: Kluwer Academic/Plenum Publishers, 1999), 100. Among other places to begin an examination of African American attitudes to and experience with consumption are E. Franklin Frazier, *Black Bourgeoisie* (Glencoe, Ill.: Free Press, 1957), 71–78, 83–85, 125–29, 174–88, 195–212, and 229–38; E. Franklin Frazier, "Durham: Capital of the Black Middle Class," in *The New Negro*, ed. Alain Locke (1925; reprint, New York: Atheneum Press, 1968), 339–40; Cornel West, *Race Matters* (1993; reprint, New York: Vintage Books, 1994), 55.

36. Jackson, "Recasting the Dream," 94; Tom Jackson, e-mail to author, Aug. 24, 2002.

37. For other statements on affluence, see, for example, Martin Luther King Jr., *Strength to Love* (copyright 1963; first published 1977; reprint, Philadelphia: Fortress Press, 1981), 67–75; on these sermons, see also Jackson, "Recasting the Dream," 188–94. On the process of writing and publishing *Where Do We Go from Here?* see Oates, *Trumpet Sound*, 422–27. Garrow, *Bearing the Cross*, 543–45, makes clear that others had a critical role in shaping the contents of the book; see also 567–68 for the book's reception. On resistance to King's message, see Russell, "Citizenship and Desire," 22–25. I am grateful to Russell for encouraging me to think about the way resistance in the African American community prompted King to shift his attention; Thaddeus Russell to author, e-mail, Apr. 18, 2002, copy in author's possession.

38. Martin Luther King Jr., *Where Do We Go from Here? Chaos or Community?* (Boston: Beacon Press, 1967), 12.

39. Ibid., 3, 4, 12, and 87.

40. Jackson, "Recasting the Dream," iv. On the issue of when and how King's radicalism developed, see also Gerald D. McKnight, *The Last Crusade: Martin Luther King Jr., the FBI, and the Poor People's Campaign* (Boulder, Colo.: Westview Press, 1998), 3–4 and Michael Eric Dyson, *I May Not Get There with You: The True Martin Luther King Jr.* (New York: Free Press, 2000), 83. Among the most important efforts to recover King's radicalism are Jackson, "Dilemma and Dreams"; Dyson, *I May Not Get There;* and McKnight, *Last Crusade.*

41. King, *Where,* 81 and 86.

42. Ibid., 111 and 85–86.

43. Ibid., 115–16 and 133. Jackson, "Recasting the Dream," 343, discusses King's 1966 view of the link between poverty and overconsumption. For King's call for a redefinition of the relationship between work and consumption, see Jackson, "Recasting the Dream," 343–44.

44. King, *Where,* 111–13; Nightingale, *On the Edge,* 135. On King's efforts in Chicago, see James R. Ralph Jr., *Northern Protest: Martin Luther King Jr., Chicago, and the Civil Rights Movement* (Cambridge: Harvard University Press, 1993).

45. King, *Where,* 43, 138, and 143; Reinhold Niebuhr, *Moral Man and Immoral Society: A Study in Ethics and Politics* (New York: Charles Scribner's Sons, 1932), 254. For this aspect of Operation Breadbasket, see Jackson, "Recasting the Dream," 172.

46. King, *Where,* 144. On Operation Breadbasket, see King, *Where,* 144–45; Oates, *Trumpet Sound,* 417 and 461; Lewis, *King,* 233, 355, and 366; Garrow, *Bearing the Cross,* passim Jackson, "Recasting the Dream," 476–78.

47. King, *Where,* 131; for the statement about imitating whites, see 123.

48. Ibid., 130, 133, 87, and 85. King was surely aware of the danger that corporations would try to co-opt the efforts of African Americans to improve their position. "The distinctive nature of the Negro revolution," wrote scholars involved in a study of the market for consumer goods among African Americans, "is that it is not a revolution to overthrow the established order so much as it is a revolution to achieve full membership in that order"; Raymond A. Bauer, Scott M. Cunningham, and Lawrence H. Wortzel, "The Marketing Dilemma of Negroes," *Journal of Marketing* 29 (July 1965): 1. Weems, *Desegregating,* 70–79, identifies the major beneficiaries of the black struggle as white businesses whose self-interest impelled them to try to capture markets.

49. King, *Where,* 171, 172, and 186; Martin Luther King Jr., "A Time to Break Silence," in *A More Perfect Union: Documents in U.S. History,* ed. Paul F. Boller Jr. and Ronald Story, 3d ed. (Boston: Houghton Mifflin, 1902), 2:222; this essay originally appeared in *Freedomways,* spring 1967, 103–17.

50. Lewis Mumford, *The Myth of the Machine: Technics and Human Development* (New York: Harcourt Brace Jovanovich, 1967), 3; the quotation from *The Condition of Man* appears on 3. Lewis Mumford, *The Myth of the Machine: The Pentagon of Power* (New York: Harcourt, Brace, Jovanovich, 1970), 328–39. Mumford opposed the war beginning in 1965 and fought with his publisher, who objected to his inclusion of any reference to the war in Vietnam in a book on ancient history; Donald L. Miller, *Lewis Mumford: A Life* (New York: Weidenfeld and Nicholson, 1989), 513 and 516. In the second volume, *The Myth of the Machine: The Pentagon of Power,* Mumford, with both nuclear war and the war in Vietnam on his mind, lamented the undemocratic way elites made decisions, something especially troubling when they also had control of vast technological powers; Miller, *Mumford,* 538–39.

51. The best treatments of postwar environmentalism, on which I have relied in these paragraphs, are Kirkpatrick Sale, *The Green Revolution: The American Environmental Movement, 1962–1992* (New York: Hill and Wang, 1993); and Hal K. Rothman, *The Greening of a Revolution? Environmentalism in the United States Since 1945* (Fort Worth: Harcourt Brace College Publishers, 1998).

52. Bill McKibbin, "David Brower, 1912–2000: Remembering the Twentieth Century's Greatest Environmentalist," *Rolling Stone*, Dec. 20, 2000– Jan. 4, 2001, <www.foe.org/news/ rollingstone.html>. Susan R. Schrepfer, "Nuclear Crucible: Diablo Canyon and the Transformation of the Sierra Club, 1965–1985," *California History* 71 (summer 1992): 212–37, explores debates in the Sierra Club over tactics and objectives. Donald Fleming, "Roots of the New Conservation Movement," *Perspectives in American History* 6 (1972): 40, includes Ehrlich when he speaks of "the new politico-scientists" who came "to perceive themselves as a kind of Fifth Estate of the realm, working in tandem with the Fourth Estate to keep the public and public officials informed and aroused about scientific issues with a social dimension." On Brower's life, see David R. Brower, *For Earth's Sake: The Life and Times of David Brower* (Salt Lake City: Peregrine Smith Books, 1990).

53. On Earth Day, see Hal Rothman, *Saving the Planet: The American Response to the Environment in the Twentieth Century* (Chicago: Ivan R. Dee, 2000), 146–48; on the new publications, see Shi, *Simple Life*, 269; on the concerns of radicals, see George Wiley, head of National Welfare Rights Organization, quoted in Barry Commoner, *The Closing Circle: Nature, Man, and Technology* (New York: Knopf, 1971), 7.

54. See, for example, in the earlier group, Garrett Hardin, *Nature and Man's Fate* (New York: Holt, Rinehart and Winston, 1959); Roderick Nash, *Wilderness and the American Mind* (New Haven: Yale University Press, 1967); Barry Commoner, *Science and Survival* (New York: Viking Press, 1966), and *Closing Circle*; Donella H. Meadows et al., *The Limits to Growth: A Report for the Club of Rome's Project on the Predicament of Mankind* (New York: Universe Books, 1972); E. F. Schumacher, *Small Is Beautiful: Economics as If People Mattered* (London: Briggs and Briggs, 1973). For later influential books, see Garrett Hardin, *Exploring New Ethics for Survival: The Voyage of the Spaceship "Beagle"* (New York: Viking Press, 1972); Annette Kolodny, *The Lay of the Land: Metaphor as Experience and History in American Life and Letters* (Chapel Hill: University of North Carolina Press, 1975); Jonathan Schell, *The Fate of the Earth* (New York: Knopf, 1982); Amory B. Lovins, *Soft Energy Paths: Toward a Durable Peace* (New York: Penguin, 1977); Bill McKibben, *The End of Nature* (New York: Random House, 1989); William Ophuls, *Ecology and the Politics of Security: A Prologue to a Political Theory of the Steady State* (San Francisco: W. H. Freeman, 1977); Carolyn Merchant, *The Death of Nature: Women, Ecology, and the Scientific Revolution* (San Francisco: Harper and Row, 1980). On Commoner, see Fleming, "New Conservation," 40–51 and 60–63.

55. Frances Moore Lappé, *Diet for a Small Planet* (New York: Ballantine Books, 1971), xi and xiv.

56. Paul R. Ehrlich, *A World of Wounds: Ecologists and the Human Dilemma* (Oldendorf/ Luhe, Germany: Ecology Institute, 1997), 2–3; see also Ehrlich, *World of Wounds*, 6. For biographical information, I am relying on Ehrlich, *World of Wounds*, 1–6; Paul R. Ehrlich and Anne H. Ehrlich, *Betrayal of Science and Reason: How Anti-environmental Rhetoric Threatens Our Future* (Washington, D.C.: Island Press, 1996), 3–9; "Paul R. Ehrlich," in *Contemporary Authors*, New Revision Series 28 (Detroit: Gale Research, 1990): 151–52; Donald W. Cox, *Pioneers of Ecology* (Maplewood, N.J.: Hammond, 1971), 84–89; Peter Raven, telephone interview, Aug. 23, 2001; *Paul Ehrlich and the Population Bomb*, documentary film (Princeton, N.J.: Films for the Humanities and Sciences, 1996); <www.stanford.edu/group/CCB/Staff/

paul.thm>; <www.pbs.org/kqed/population_bomb/theshow/bio.htm> and its companion site <www.population_bomb/theshow/ow.html>. There are scattered discussions of his life in Paul R. Ehrlich, *Human Natures: Genes, Cultures, and the Human Prospect* (Washington, D.C.: Island Press, 2000). The best source (albeit a tendentious one) on the ideas of the new environmentalists remains Fleming, "New Conservation," 7–91. Adam Rome, *The Bulldozer in the Countryside: Suburban Sprawl and The Rise of American Environmentalism* (New York: Cambridge University Press, 2001), 142, discusses Ehrlich's writings but does not connect them to his experience with suburban sprawl as a child in suburban New Jersey or an adult near San Francisco.

57. Ehrlich and Ehrlich, *Betrayal*, 3. See William Vogt, *Road to Survival* (New York: William Sloane Associates, 1948); Fairfield Osborn, *Our Plundered Planet* (Boston: Little, Brown, 1948). On Osborn, the son of the influential anti-immigrationist Henry Fairfield Osborn, see Elizabeth Noble Shor, "Fairfield Osborn," in *ANB* (New York: Oxford University Press, 1999), 16:783–84. For an example of the way he connected his research with larger issues, see Paul R. Ehrlich and Richard W. Holm, "Patterns and Populations," *Science*, Aug. 31, 1962, 652–57; Paul R. Ehrlich and Anne H. Ehrlich, *How to Know the Butterflies* (Dubuque, Iowa: Wm. C. Brown, 1961). In 1963 he co-authored a science textbook, Paul R. Ehrlich and Richard W. Holm, *The Process of Evolution* (New York: McGraw-Hill, 1963). In 1970 he made clear his esteem for Carson in his introduction to Rachel Carson, *Silent Spring* (Greenwich, Conn.: Fawcett Publications, 1970), xv–xxvii.

58. Paul S. Ehrlich and Richard W. Holm, "A Biological View of Race," in *The Concept of Race*, ed. Ashley Montagu (New York: Free Press, 1964), 175 and 176; Carleton S. Coon, *The Origin of Races* (New York: Knopf, 1962). See also Barry Commoner et al., "Science and the Race Problem: A Report of the AAAS Committee on Science in the Promotion of Human Welfare," *Science*, Nov. 1, 1963, 558–61.

59. On Ehrlich in particular, see Raven interview; on the nature of an ecological vision, see Stephen Bocking, *Ecologists and Environmental Politics: A History of Contemporary Ecology* (New Haven: Yale University Press, 1997), and Donald Worster, *Nature's Economy: A History of Ecological Ideas* (Cambridge: Cambridge University Press, 1977), 316–48.

60. Paul R. Ehrlich and Peter H. Raven, "Butterflies and Plants," *Scientific American* 216 (June 1967): 105 and 113.

61. Ehrlich and Ehrlich, *Betrayal*, 5 and 6. For evidence that he completed the writing in April 1968, see Paul Ehrlich, *The Population Bomb* (New York: Ballantine Books, 1968), 87.

62. For a critique of Ehrlich's position on the supply of food, see Rolland Dewing, "Food Production in the United States: The Myth and the Reality," *Indiana Social Studies Quarterly* 29 (spring 1976): 87–95. For the differences between Ehrlich and Commoner, see Commoner, *Closing*, 232–33; Fleming, "New Conservation," 60–61. For discussions of Ehrlich's ideas, see Bob Pepperman Taylor, *Our Limits Transgressed: Environmental Political Thought in America* (Lawrence: University Press of Kansas, 1992), 28–32; Fleming, "New Conservation," 52–57. On the formula, see Ehrlich, *Human Natures*, 289. The formula was $I = PAT$, meaning that the impact (I) of population on the environment equaled population size (P), multiplied by affluence (A), times the effects of technologies (T) that underwrote consumption.

63. See Ehrlich, quoted in Cox, *Pioneers*, 84. On the implications of this shift for Commoner's career, see Fleming, "New Conservation," 46.

64. Ehrlich, *Population Bomb*, 15–16 and 11; this discussion also relies on 71.

65. Ibid., 65, 149, 150, and 24–25; see also 151.

66. Ibid, 153; see also 168.

67. Ibid., 11 and 133; see also 22–23.

68. Ibid., 54 and 64.

69. Ibid., 11, 130, and 135. Ehrlich also critiqued the people of the U.S. and western Europe for wanting to dominate nature rather than living in harmony with it and tentatively offered the example of hippies as people who showed the way to an alternative style of life: ibid., 170 and 171.

70. Ibid., 163.

71. Ibid., 131–213.

72. Ibid., 182; see also 148.

73. Ehrlich, quoted in Cox, *Pioneers*, 89.

74. Sale, *Green Revolution*, 22. As executive director of the Sierra Club, Brower wrote the foreword to *The Population Bomb*. In 1969 the board of the Sierra Club fired Brower. "A last-minute resignation notwithstanding, 'ejected' was the word," wrote John McPhee in *Encounters with the Archdruid* (New York: Farrar, Straus, and Giroux, 1971), 211. *Book Review Digest* lists remarkably few reviews of books by Ehrlich, and those mostly for librarians. The sales figure comes from Cox, *Pioneers*, 86. For a critique of Ehrlich from a libertarian perspective, see Henry Hazlitt, "Poverty and Population," *Freeman* 21 (July 1971): 414–22. For an analysis of the language of environmentalists, including Ehrlich, and their opponents, see M. Jimmie Killingsworth and Jacqueline S. Palmer, "The Discourse of 'Environmentalist Hysteria,'" *Quarterly Journal of Speech* 81 (Feb. 1995): 1–19. For a full bibliography of Ehrlich's works, see <www.stanford.eu/group/CCB/Staff/Paulbiblio.htm>. In the few years following *The Population Bomb*, Ehrlich was incredibly prolific, and in a variety of genres. For ecological books for a general audience, see Paul R. Ehrlich and Richard L. Harriman, *How to Be a Survivor* (New York: Ballantine Books, 1971); Dennis C. Pirages and Paul R. Ehrlich, *Ark II: Social Response to Environmental Imperatives* (San Francisco: W. H. Freeman, 1974). For textbooks, see Paul R. Ehrlich and Anne H. Ehrlich, *Population Resources Environment* (San Francisco: W. H. Freeman, 1970); John P. Holdren and Paul R. Ehrlich, ed., *Global Ecology: Readings toward A Rational Strategy for Man* (New York: Harcourt Brace Jovanovich, 1971); Paul R. Ehrlich, Anne H. Ehrlich, and John P. Holdren, *Human Ecology* (San Francisco: W. H. Freeman, 1973).

7. The Energy Crisis and the Quest to Contain Consumption

1. Paul R. Ehrlich and Anne H. Ehrlich, *The End of Affluence: A Blueprint for Your Future* (New York: Ballantine Books, 1974). Kenneth E. Morris, *Jimmy Carter: American Moralist* (Athens: University of Georgia Press, 1996), 9–17, explores many of the dimensions of the decade's malaise. The best overview of the decade is Bruce J. Schulman, *The Seventies: The Great Shift in American Culture, Politics, and Society* (New York: Free Press, 2001); see 121–43 on shifts in the economy, including consumer behavior.

2. Roger D. Masters, "Why a Depression Might Be Good for Us All," *NYT*, Aug. 31, 1979, A23; James Reston, "Who Needs More Gas?" *NYT*, Nov. 11, 1973, E13. For a response to Reston, see John P. Sisk, "The Fear of Affluence," *Commentary* (June 1974): 61–67. See also John Tirman, "Austerity as a Guide," *NYT*, Nov. 9, 1980, E19. On Dichter and Katona, see Ernest Dichter, "Consumer Goods—Boom or Doom?" published talk, ca. 1974, source unknown, EDP; George Katona and Burkhard Strumpel, *A New Economic Era* (New York: Elsevier, 1978), 2, 6, and 115. See also Irving Kristol, *Two Cheers for Capitalism* (New York: Basic Books, 1978), 37; and Tom Wolfe, "The Me Decade and the Third Great Awakening" (1976), in *The Purple Decades* (New York: Farrar, Straus and Giroux, 1982), 265–93. Wolfe

ascribed the flourishing of belief in self-discovery to the postwar economic boom, not, as Lasch would, to the economic turmoil of the 1970s.

3. Robert A. Easterlin, "Does Money Buy Happiness?" *Public Interest* 30 (winter 1973): 10. This discussion also relies on Daniel Yankelovich, *New Rules: Searching for Self-Fulfillment in a World Turned Upside Down* (New York: Random House, 1981); Morris Janowitz, *The Last Half-Century: Societal Change and Politics in America* (Chicago: University of Chicago Press, 1978), 155; David E. Shi, *The Simple Life: Plain Living and High Thinking in American Culture* (New York: Oxford University Press, 1985), 266–72. In *Shifting Involvements: Private Interest and Public Action* (Princeton: Princeton University Press, 1982), Albert O. Hirschman historicized and reflected on the disappointments inherent in consumer culture.

4. Sue Avery, "Family Prunes Luxuries: On $25,000 a Year, No More Malted Milk," *LAT*, Mar. 2, 1980, sec. 12, 1; Howard J. Ruff, *How to Prosper in the Coming Bad Years* (New York: Times Books, 1979); Michael Ennis, "The $38,000 a Year, Wife and Two Kids, House and a Pool *Blues*," *Texas Monthly*, Sept. 1980, 134. For a thoughtful essay that explores the gloom of the period, see Jason Epstein, "Help!" *NYRB*, Feb. 21, 1980, 7–10. For studies of household patterns of living, see Editors of *Wall Street Journal*, *Americans and Their Pocketbooks: How Your Neighbors Earn and Spend Their Money* (New York: Dow Jones, 1964); David Caplovitz, *Making Ends Meet: How Families Cope with Inflation and Recession* (Beverly Hill: Sage Publications, 1979).

5. Among the many other important writings on these themes are Lester C. Thurow, *The Zero-Sum Society: Distribution and the Possibilities for Economic Change* (New York: Basic Books, 1980); Robert L. Heilbroner, *An Inquiry into the Human Prospect* (New York: W. W. Norton, 1974); George Gilder, *Wealth and Poverty* (New York: Basic Books, 1981); William Leiss, *Limits to Satisfaction: An Essay on the Problems of Needs and Commodities* (Toronto: Toronto University Press, 1976); Fred Hirsch, *Social Limits to Growth* (Cambridge: Harvard University Press, 1976); Maxine Schnall, *Limits: A Search for New Values* (New York: Clarkson N. Potter, 1981); Alan Wolfe, *America's Impasse: The Rise and Fall of the Politics of Growth* (New York: Pantheon Books, 1981); William Ophuls, *Ecology and the Politics of Scarcity: Prologue to a Political Theory of the Steady State* (San Francisco: W. H. Freeman, 1977).

6. For information on Bell's career and ideas, see Howard Brick, *Daniel Bell and the Decline of Intellectual Radicalism: Social Theory and Political Reconciliation in the 1940s* (Madison: University of Wisconsin Press, 1986); Nathan Liebowitz, *Daniel Bell and the Agony of Modern Liberalism* (Westport, Conn.: Greenwood Press, 1985); Malcolm Waters, *Daniel Bell* (London: Routledge, 1996). For an article published shortly before his visit to the Carter White House, see Ron Chernow, "The Cultural Contradictions of Daniel Bell," *Change* 11 (March 1979): 12–17.

7. Daniel Bell, "Foreword: 1978," to *The Cultural Contradictions of Capitalism*, 2d ed. (New York: Basic Books, 1978), xi. See also Daniel Bell, *The Background and Development of Marxian Socialism in the United States* (Princeton: Princeton University Press, 1967), originally published in Donald D. Egbert and Stow Persons, ed., *Socialism and American Life* (Princeton: Princeton University Press, 1952); Daniel Bell, ed., *The New American Right* (New York: Criterion Books, 1955); Daniel Bell, *The End of Ideology: On the Exhaustion of Political Ideas in the Fifties* (Glencoe, Ill.: Free Press, 1960); Daniel Bell, *The Coming of Post-industrial Society: A Venture in Social Forecasting* (New York: Basic Books, 1973). See Christopher Lasch, review of *The Coming of Post-industrial Society*, *NYRB*, Oct. 18, 1973, 63–66. For Bell's response, see letter to editor, *NYRB*, Jan. 24, 1974, 49–52. On the process of deradicalization, see Brick, *Daniel Bell*, 142–92.

8. Daniel Bell, *Cultural Contradictions of Capitalism* (New York: Basic Books, 1976), xi, 10, and 11–13.

9. Ibid., 51, 54, and 121–45. Bell seemed to waver between an explanation that cited culture as the locus of change and one that emphasized economic forces. Similarly, and not unrelated, he moved between seeing America as transformed well before the 1960s and arguing that this decade was determinative; see, e.g., 55.

10. Ibid., 33–34.

11. Ibid., 72, 71, and 84.

12. Ibid., 197, 22–23, 79, 226, 233, and 235.

13. Ibid., 84.

14. Ibid., 157 and 30. The key section for his discussion of religion is 146–71.

15. Ibid., 25, 26–27, 236, 255, 245, and 277.

16. Ibid., 81 and 23; this discussion also draws on 38, 51, and 186–91. For mentions of inflation, see, e.g., 27 and 238–43. For relatively rare references to the war in Vietnam, see 179, 182, and 217. Only at one point did he acknowledge the war as "the catalyst of social tensions," though he soon passed on to other issues (190–91). On neoconservatism, see Peter Steinfels, *The Neoconservatives: The Men Who Are Changing American Politics* (New York: Simon and Schuster, 1979). For the first use of the term, see Chernow, "Bell," 13. For information on when he published earlier versions of sections that appeared in the book, see Bell, *Cultural Contradictions*, xv–xvi.

17. Bell, *Cultural Contradictions*, 28–29. For a discussion of Bell's contributions, see a series of articles in *AQ* 34 (spring 1982): Lawrence Veysey, "A Postmortem on Daniel Bell's Postindustrialism," 49–69; Richard Wrightman Fox, "Breathless: The Cultural Consternation of Daniel Bell," 70–77; Richard Gilman, "The Perils of Postindustrialism" 77–82; Daniel Bell, "Mr. Veysey's Strabismus," 82–87.

18. Christopher Lasch, in Casey Blake and Christopher Phelps, "History as Social Criticism: Conversations with Christopher Lasch," *JAH* 80 (March 1994): 1313. For biographical information, I am relying on Christopher Lasch, *The True and Only Heaven: Progress and Its Critics* (New York: W. W. Norton, 1991), 25–39; Blake and Phelps, "History as Social Criticism," 1310–32; Richard W. Fox, "An Interview with Christopher Lasch," Sept. 25, 1993, *IHN* 16 (1994): 3–14; Jean Bethke Elshtain, "The Life and Work of Christopher Lasch: An American Story," *Salmagundi* 106–7 (spring–summer 1995): 146–61; Barbara Rowes, interview with Christopher Lasch, "Gratification Now Is the Slogan of the '70s, Laments a Historian," *People*, July 9, 1979, 34–36; information on book jackets. For his view of Mumford, see Christopher Lasch, "Lewis Mumford and the Myth of the Machine," *Salmagundi* 49 (summer 1980): 4–28.

19. Lasch, *True and Only Heaven*, 25; on his discussion of his shift from the left, see 26. For his other books, see Christopher Lasch, *The American Liberals and the Russian Revolution* (New York: Columbia University Press, 1962); Christopher Lasch, *The New Radicalism in America, 1889–1963: The Intellectual as a Social Type* (New York: Knopf, 1965). In this discussion of Lasch's changing politics, I am relying on, in addition to his books (especially Lasch, *True and Only Heaven*, 25–39), Blake and Phelps, "History as Social Criticism"; Steven Watts, review of four books by Lasch, "Sinners in the Hands of an Angry Critic: Christopher Lasch's Struggle with Progressive America," *AS* 33 (fall 1992): 113–20; Louis Menand, "Christopher Lasch's Quarrel with Liberalism," in *The Liberal Persuasion: Arthur Schlesinger Jr., and the Challenge of the American Past*, ed. John Patrick Diggins (Princeton: Princeton University Press, 1997), 233–50 (a different version appeared as Louis Menand, "Man of the People," *NYRB*, Apr. 11, 1991, 39–44).

20. Lasch, in Blake and Phelps, "History as Social Criticism," 1322; Lasch, *True and Only*

Heaven, 27; and see 27–30. For his other works on which this discussion draws, see Christopher Lasch, *The Agony of the American Left* (New York: Knopf, 1969), and *The World of Nations: Reflections on American History, Politics, and Culture* (New York: Knopf, 1973). In the latter, Lasch made clear that he rejected the idea, associated with Bell, that Americans were living in a postindustrial society "to which the older criticism of capitalism formulated by Marx and other nineteenth-century critics is now hopelessly irrelevant" (xi).

21. Lasch, *True and Only Heaven*, 32 and 33. His later books include Christopher Lasch, *Haven in a Heartless World: The Family Besieged* (New York: Basic Books, 1977); *The Culture of Narcissism: American Life in an Age of Diminishing Expectations* (New York: W. W. Norton, 1979); *The Minimal Self: Psychic Survival in Troubled Times* (New York: W. W. Norton, 1984); *Women and the Common Life: Love, Marriage, and Feminism*, ed. Elisabeth Lasch-Quinn (New York: W. W. Norton, 1997).

22. The summary of his tragic vision relies on Menand, "Christopher Lasch's Quarrel with Liberalism," 233–50.

23. Frank Kermode, review of *Culture of Narcissism*, *NYTBR*, Jan. 14, 1979, 1; Elshtain, "Lasch," 146–47; Lasch, *Culture of Narcissism*, xv. For Lasch's drawing on David Riesman, *The Lonely Crowd* (1950), as a model, see Blake and Phelps, "Lasch," 1313; Fox, "Lasch," 5 and 12.

24. Lasch, *Narcissism*, 38 and 33; on the pervasiveness of narcissism in all social groups, see 26. In *The Psychiatric Persuasion: Knowledge, Gender, and Power in Modern America* (Princeton: Princeton University Press, 1994), esp. 306–9, Lizabeth Lundbeck explores the tendency in psychiatric literature to conflate normality and pathology.

25. Lasch, *Narcissism*, 71 and 51; Thomas A. Harris, *I'm OK, You're OK: A Practical Guide to Transactional Analysis* (New York: Harper and Row, 1969). Among the other best-selling books that doubtless attracted Lasch's attention were Robert J. Ringer, *Looking Out for Number One* (Beverly Hills: Los Angeles Books, 1977); Harold H. Bloomfield, Michael P. Cain, and Dennis T. Jaffe, *TM: Discovering Inner Energy and Overcoming Stress* (New York: Delacorte Press, 1975); Wayne W. Dyer, *Your Erroneous Zones* (New York: Funk and Wagnalls, 1976).

26. Lasch, *Narcissism*, 32, 221, 63–64, 72, 73–74.

27. Ibid., 231, 206, xv, and xxx. In "Doomsayer of the Me Decade: Christopher Lasch," *Washington Post*, Jan. 24, 1979. Allen noted that Lasch "sees no solutions, not capitalism, not socialism. 'It's difficult to suggest a remedy that isn't worse than a disease.'"

28. Allen, "Doomsayer." *Culture of Narcissism* was on the *New York Times* best-seller list for twenty-three weeks and reached as high as number eleven.

29. Christopher Lasch to Paula Cronin, June 19, 1979, folder 3, box 5, CL-UR; Christopher Lasch, "Politics and Social Theory: A Reply to the Critics," *Salmagundi* 46 (fall 1979): 194, 196, 199, 200, and 201. On Lasch's response to the feminist reaction to the book, see correspondence with Stephanie Engel in folder 4, box 5, CL-UR. For his later views, see Christopher Lasch, "Afterword: The Culture of Narcissism Revisited," in *The Culture of Narcissism* (New York: W. W. Norton, 1991), 237–49, which originally appeared in *The World and I* (Feb. 1990). See Alvin Toffler, *Future Shock* (New York: Random House, 1970); Gail Sheehy, *Passages: Predictable Crises of Adult Life* (New York: Dutton, 1976). Among the many critiques of Lasch are Jesse F. Battan, "The 'New Narcissism' in Twentieth-Century America: The Shadow and Substance of Social Change," *JScH* 17 (winter 1983): 199–220; Peter Clecak, *America's Quest for the Ideal Self: Dissent and Fulfillment in the 60s and 70s* (New York: Oxford University Press, 1983), 246–60; Watts, "Sinners in the Hands of an Angry Critic," 119–20; Daniel Dervin, "Steve and Adam and Ted and Dr. Lasch: The New Culture and the Culture of Narcissism," *Journal of Psychohistory* 9 (winter 1982): 355–73; Fred Siegel, "The Agony of

Christopher Lasch," *RAH* 8 (Sept. 1980): 285–95; Michael Kammen, review of Lasch, *Culture of Narcissism*, *RAH* 7 (Dec. 1979): 452–58; Dennis H. Wrong, "Bourgeois Values, No Bourgeoisie? The Cultural Criticism of Christopher Lasch," *Dissent* 26 (summer 1979): 308–14; James Seaton, "Critique as Bestseller: *The Culture of Narcissism*," *Centennial Review* 25 (spring 1981): 169–84. For a feminist critique of Lasch, see Michèle Barrett and Mary McIntosh, "Narcissism and the Family: A Critique of Lasch," *New Left Review* 135 (Sept.–Oct. 1982): 35–48. For appreciative critiques of both Lasch and Bell from a conservative position, see Russell Nieli, "Social Conservatives of the Left: James Lincoln Collier, Christopher Lasch, and Daniel Bell," *PSR* 22 (1993): 198–292.

30. For a summary of attacks from the left and right, see Watts, "Sinners in the Hands of an Angry Critic," 117. Looking back on his interest in moralism and religion, Lasch found it difficult to "draw any direct connections" with his life experiences. "I certainly hadn't undergone some kind of religious conversion"; Lasch, Fox interview, 13.

31. See, by Robert N. Bellah, *The Broken Covenant: American Civil Religion in Time of Trial* (New York: Seabury Press, 1975), viii; introduction to *Broken Covenant*, 2d ed. (Chicago: University of Chicago Press, 1992), v and vii; *Beyond Belief: Essays on Religion in a Post-traditional World* (New York: Harper and Row, 1970), xii. For biographical information, see Bellah, *Broken Covenant*, viii and xv; *Beyond Belief*, xi–xvii; and introduction, vi–xiii.

32. Bellah, *Beyond Belief*, xiii; Robert N. Bellah, interview quoted in Ellen Schrecker, *No Ivory Tower: McCarthyism and the Universities* (New York: Oxford University Press, 1986), 59; Robert N. Bellah, letter to editor, *NYRB*, July 14, 1977, 38–39; Bellah, introduction, vii; Bellah, *Beyond Belief*, xiii.

33. Bellah, *Beyond Belief*, xiv–xv; Sigmund Diamond, *Compromised Campus: The Collaboration of Universities with the Intelligence Community, 1945–1955* (New York: Oxford University Press, 1992), 20–21; Bellah, letter to editor, *NYRB*, July 14, 1977, 38–39; McGeorge Bundy, letter to editor, *NYRB*, July 14, 1977, 39; Schrecker, *No Ivory Tower*, 59, 262–63, and 292. On Berkeley in the years around Bellah's arrival, see W. J. Rorabaugh, *Berkeley at War: The 1960s* (New York: Oxford University Press, 1989).

34. Robert N. Bellah, *Tokugawa Religion: The Values of Pre-industrial Japan* (Glencoe, Ill.: Free Press, 1957), 195–96. For his comments on the USSR, whose focus on attainment of goals came "perilously close to totalitarianism," see Bellah, *Tokugawa*, 193.

35. Bellah, *Beyond Belief*, xix. This discussion also draws on Bellah, introduction, ix; Bellah, *Beyond Belief*, xi–xxi.

36. Bellah, introduction, x; Bellah, *Broken Covenant*, viii. For the study of Bay Area religion, see Charles Y. Glock and Robert N. Bellah, eds., *The New Religious Consciousness* (Berkeley: University of California Press, 1976); Bellah co-authored the preface with Glock (xi–xvii) and authored two articles: "The New Consciousness and the Berkeley New Left," 77–92, and "New Religious Consciousness and the Crisis in Modernity," 333–52. For one of the journal articles in which he elaborated his argument, see Robert N. Bellah, "Religion and Legitimation in the American Republic," *Society* 15 (May–June 1978): 16–23. Bellah is best known for two contributions. First was his stimulus of and contribution to the debate on civil religion, which he sparked with his essay "Civil Religion in America," *Daedalus* 96 (winter 1967): 1–21, and reprinted in Bellah, *Beyond Belief*, 168–89. Second was his most influential book, which, because of its publication date, lies outside the scope of my analysis: Robert N. Bellah et al., *Habits of the Heart: Individualism and Commitment in American Life* (Berkeley: University of California Press, 1985). For other later writings, see Robert N. Bellah and Phillip E. Hammond, *Varieties of Civil Religion* (San Francisco: Harper and Row, 1980). For a bibliography of his publications to 1970, see *Beyond Belief*, 289–91.

37. Bellah, "Religion and Legitimation," 18. For an earlier discussion of the notion of civil religion, see Robert Bellah, "Civil Religion in America," in *Beyond Belief*, 168–86.

38. Bellah, *Broken Covenant*, xii; Bellah, "Religion and Legitimation," 22. This discussion also draws on Robert N. Bellah, "New Religious Consciousness and the Crisis of Modernity," in *New Religious Consciousness*, 336; Bellah, *Broken Covenant*, x.

39. Bellah, *Broken Covenant*, 149, 1, and 85; see also xi, xii, and 82.

40. Bellah, "Religion and Legitimation," 23; Bellah, "New Consciousness," 337, 351, and 352. On his hopes for American religion, see Bellah, *Broken Covenant*, xi; on his not finding a religious revival among fundamentalists or evangelicals promising, see 160.

41. Bellah, *Broken Covenant*, 152, 149, and xi; Bellah, "Religion and Legitimation," 22. For one ray of hope he saw in American politics, see his response to Congresswoman Barbara Jordan's speech at the 1986 Democratic Convention calling for a national community that was ethical and spiritual ("Religion and Legitimation," 20). For a statement of his opposition to the war in Vietnam, see Bellah, "Civil Religion," 185. On his reaction to Nixon, see Bellah, *Broken Covenant*, 142, and "Religion and Legitimation," 23.

42. Bellah, *Broken Covenant*, xiv, xv, and 151. His reference to Tocqueville is in "Religion and Legitimation," 21.

43. Bellah, *Broken Covenant*, 153–55, 157–58, and 137–38.

44. Robert N. Bellah and Charles Y. Glock, preface to *New Religious Consciousness*, xi–xvii; Bellah, *Broken Covenant*, 84; Bellah, "New Consciousness," 338. On his pessimism about successors to the counterculture, see "New Consciousness," 352; for his response to the impact of Asian religion on the United States, see 341. Bellah also acknowledged that "conspicuous consumption" had influenced the counterculture (34). Far more sympathetic to the student left of the 1960s than either Bell or Lasch, Bellah explored radicalism for evidence of the "political side of the new consciousness." Yet overall, he believed that political radicals had turned away from religion, thus cutting themselves off from "the indigenous American ethical and religious tradition of social concern"; Robert N. Bellah, "The New Consciousness and the Berkeley New Left," in *New Religious Consciousness*, 77–92, quote 77. "Perhaps the deepest reason for the collapse of the New Left," he wrote, "was the weakness verging on nonexistence of an old Left for it to be the new Left of" (83). For a comment that may well be a critique of Bell's *Coming of Post-industrial Society* (1973), see Bellah, "New Consciousness," 349.

45. Bellah, *Broken Covenant*, xv and viii. The preface is not noticeably more pessimistic than the published lectures, though it is not clear to what extent, if any, Bellah injected additional notes of pessimism and tragedy into the published version of his lectures; he mentions (vii) that he revised the lectures before publishing them in book form. For his discussion of the themes of loss in his life (father, religion, ideology, and nation), see Bellah, *Beyond Belief*, xx–xxi. For information on Matthiessen, I am relying on Frederick C. Stern, *F. O. Matthiessen: Christian Socialist as Critic* (Chapel Hill: University of North Carolina Press, 1981), 3–45; Kenneth S. Lynn, "Teaching: F. O. Matthiessen," *American Scholar* 46 (winter 1976–77): 86–93.

46. In 1999, Bellah's wife published a biography of their eldest daughter, Tammy, who committed suicide in 1973 at age nineteen; Melanie Bellah, *Tammy: A Biography of a Young Girl* (Berkeley: Aten Press, 1999).

47. Wrong, "Bourgeois Values," 313. For Lasch's prodding of Bellah on populism versus communitarianism, see Lasch, *Revolt of the Elites*, 101, 102, 108, 112, and 121.

8. Three Intellectuals and a President

1. Leo P. Ribuffo, "God and Jimmy Carter," in *Right, Left, Center: Essays in American History* (New Brunswick: Rutgers University Press, 1992), 228. Among the most helpful discussions of the speech are Leo Ribuffo, " 'Malaise' Revisited: Jimmy Carter and the Crisis of Confidence," in *The Liberal Persuasion: Arthur Schlesinger Jr. and the Challenge of the American Past*, ed. John Patrick Diggins (Princeton: Princeton University Press, 1997), 164–84, and J. William Holland, "The Great Gamble: Jimmy Carter and the 1979 Energy Crisis," *Prologue* 22 (spring 1990): 63–79. For a discussion of the energy crisis, simple living, and Carter's speech, see David E. Shi, *The Simple Life: Plain Living and High Thinking in American Culture* (New York: Oxford University Press, 1985), 266–72. For other commentaries, see Kenneth E. Morris, *Jimmy Carter: American Moralist* (Athens: University of Georgia Press, 1996), 1–19 and 251–62; Robert A. Strong, "Reclaiming Leadership: The Carter Administration and the Crisis of Confidence," *PSQ* 16 (fall 1986): 636–50; Dan F. Hahn, "Flailing the Profligate: Carter's Energy Sermon of 1979," *PSQ* 10 (fall 1980): 583–87; Elizabeth Drew, "A Reporter at Large: Phase—In Search of a Definition," *NY*, Aug. 27, 1979, 45–73 passim; Hedrick Smith, "Remaking of Carter's Presidency: Sixteen Days of Shifts and Reappraisals," *NYT*, July 22, 1979, 1 and 30; Hendrik Hertzberg, "Jimmy Carter, 1977–1981," in *Character above All: Ten Presidents from FDR to George Bush*, ed. Robert A. Wilson (New York: Simon and Schuster, 1995), 190–94; Scott Kramer, "Struggles of an Outsider: The 1979 Energy Crisis and President Carter's Call for Confidence" (senior thesis, Department of History, Princeton University, 1992), copy in CPL. In *Jimmy Carter*, Morris places the energy crisis, Carter's morality, the July 15, 1979, speech, and the malaise of the 1970s at the center of his analysis; see esp. 1–19 and 240–88.

For background information on the Carter presidency, I have drawn on Morris, *Jimmy Carter*; Burton I. Kaufman, *The Presidency of James Earl Carter Jr.* (Lawrence: University Press of Kansas, 1993), esp. 133–50; Peter G. Bourne, *Jimmy Carter: A Comprehensive Biography from Plains to Postpresidency* (New York: Scribner, 1997); Gary M. Fink and Hugh Davis Graham, eds., *The Carter Presidency: Policy Choices in the Post–New Deal Era* (Lawrence: University Press of Kansas, 1998), esp. John C. Barrow, "An Age of Limits: Jimmy Carter and the Quest for a National Energy Policy," 158–78; Ribuffo, "God and Jimmy Carter," 214–48; Betty Glad, *Jimmy Carter: In Search of the Great White House* (New York: W. W. Norton, 1980); James Fallows, "The Passionless Presidency," *Atlantic Monthly* 243 (May 1979): 33–48, and (June 1979): 75–81. On Carter's own discussion of the search for a national energy policy, see Jimmy Carter, *Keeping Faith: Memoirs of a President* (New York: Bantam Books, 1982), 91–124, with discussion of the events of July 1979 on 114–21. For another insider's perspective on the events of early July, see Rosalynn Carter, *First Lady from Plains* (Boston: Houghton Mifflin, 1984), 302–5.

2. The best source of information on energy use and policy is Martin V. Melosi, *Coping with Abundance: Energy and Environment in Industrial America* (New York: Knopf, 1985), esp. 277–94.

3. "Playboy Interview: Pat Caddell," *Playboy*, Feb. 27, 1980, 68; for biographical information on Caddell, see Peter R. Range's introduction to the interview, 63–64. Historians and others have differed about the impact of the ideas of Bell, Bellah, and Lasch on Carter. Kenneth E. Morris claims too much for the influence of Bellah, see Morris, *Jimmy Carter*, 4, 326 fn. 21; 323 fn. 7, and 324 fn. 8. In " 'Malaise' Revisited," 171–72, Ribuffo plays down the influence of the three on Carter's thinking and his speech. In addition to the evidence cited later in this discussion that Carter engaged their ideas, see Gordon Stewart, Speechwriters

Sessions, 75, WBMC-CPL; Holland, "Great Gamble," 65. For a picture of Caddell on the eve of Carter's election, see Michael Wheeler, *Lies, Damn Lies, and Statistics: The Manipulation of Public Opinion in America* (New York: Liveright, 1976), 59–66.

4. Patrick H. Caddell, "Of Crisis and Opportunity," 1 and 11, memo dated Apr. 23, 1979, Presidential Files: Jody Powell, folder "Memoranda: President Carter 1/10/79–4/23/79," box 40, CPL.

5. Caddell, "Of Crisis and Opportunity," 25, 26, 32–33; Marvin Stone, editorial comment, from *USNWR*, Feb. 5, 1979, quoted 27; John Maynard Keynes, quoted 35, from "Economic Possibilities for Our Grandchildren," in *The Collected Writings of John Maynard Keynes* (1931; reprint, London: Macmillan, 1972), 9:330–31. Among others Caddell cited were James Q. Wilson, "American Politics, Then and Now," on changes in political institutions.

6. Caddell, "Of Crisis and Opportunity," 36, 40, 49, 51, and 59.

7. Ibid., 66; the reference to a covenant appears on 70.

8. Caddell, "Playboy Interview," 79. The only published account of the evening I have been able to locate, aside from Drew's reporting, is in Theodore H. White, *America in Search of Itself: The Making of the President, 1956–1980* (New York: Harper and Row, 1982), 259–60, in which White apparently relies on what Bell wrote. In *Morale* (New York: W. W. Norton, 1978), John W. Gardner called for a renewal of American values but did not focus on issues of affluence.

9. Daniel Bell, "Dinner at the White House," Sept. 1, 1979, 22–25 and 27, Memoir: Dinner at the White House, Daniel Bell: Writings, September 1979, DBP. Lasch felt that Bell had failed to report his two admittedly minor contributions to the discussion: his emphasis on the reality behind people's loss of faith in government, which stemmed in good measure from Vietnam and Watergate, and the importance of the even distribution of sacrifices; Christopher Lasch to David Nahmias, Feb. 2, 1985, folder 6, box 5, CL-UR.

10. Bell, "Dinner," 29 and 33–34.

11. Ibid., 35–36.

12. Jimmy Carter, handwritten notes, May 30, 1979, Office of Staff Secretary, Handwriting File, 5/10/79 folder, box 133, CPL; Holland, "Great Gamble," 65–66. On Bell's assessment of the evening, see Bell, "Dinner," 41 and 44.

13. Christopher Lasch to Jody Powell, June 10, 1979, 1–3, President's Handwriting Files, 7/20/79 [1] folder, box 140, CPL. Ribuffo claims that the president underlined three phrases in Lasch's letter: "decline of the work ethic, . . . lack of faith in the future, a desire to enjoy life in the present"; Ribuffo, "'Malaise' Revisited," 172. An archivist at the Jimmy Carter Library, however, remarked to the author (Apr. 3, 2001) that the underlinings in question are different from those of the president. For his account and assessment of the evening, see Christopher Lasch to his parents, June 11, 1979, folder 8, box 5, CL-UR.

14. Lasch to Powell, June 10, 1979, 3–5, 8, 9, and 13.

15. Barbara Rowes, interview with Christopher Lasch, "Gratification Now Is the Slogan of the '70s, Laments a Historian," *PM*, July 9, 1979, 34–36; Lasch quoted 36; Peter Goldman, "To Lift a Nation's Spirit," *NW*, July 23, 1979, 22–23.

16. Lasch did not "like this celebrity status that I had inherited somehow" with *The Culture of Narcissism*; Richard W. Fox, "An Interview with Christopher Lasch," Sept. 25, 1993, *IHN* 16 (1994): 13. Christopher Lasch to Robert Silvers, May 21, 1979, folder 11, box 5, CL-UR. See also Christopher Lasch to Wini Breines, Aug. 4, 1949, folder 3, box 5; Christopher Lasch to Aunt Marian, Oct. 25, 1979, folder 12, box 5, CL-UR; and three letters from Lasch to his parents: Jan. 30, May 24, and June 18, 1979, folder 8, box 5, CL-UR.

17. Stuart Eizenstat, memo to President Jimmy Carter, July 28, 1979, Office of Staff Secretary, Handwriting File, "Trip to Japan and Korea, 6/22/79–7/1/79 [1]" folder, box 137, CPL. For Caddell's identity as the "ringleader" behind urging the president to cancel the speech, see Hamilton Jordan, memo to President Jimmy Carter, July 3, 1979, Chief of Staff—Jordan, "Speech, President's 7/15/79" folder, box 37, CPL.

18. Drew, "A Reporter at Large," 56; [Patrick H. Caddell], [breakthrough memo], 49–50, n.d. (probably late June or early July 1979), White House Central File, Utilities, "UT 5/19/79–1/20/81" folder, box UT-1, CPL. After searching for several days, I was unable to find a complete copy of the "breakthrough" memo in the Jimmy Carter Library. Caddell, in "Playboy Interview," 79, used the words "plan" and "blue book" to label the memo; Drew used the phrase "breakthrough" to characterize it, a word that appears frequently in the memo; Drew, "A Reporter at Large," 54. On Tocqueville's concerns about the way Americans, especially the middle class, indulged in creature comforts, and how religion might restrain that pursuit, see Alexis de Tocqueville, *Democracy in America*, ed. Phillips Bradley (New York: Vintage Books, 1954), 2:136–41 and 144–60.

19. [Caddell], [breakthrough memo], 49–51, 53, and 54; Jimmy Carter to Pat Caddell, July 16, 1979, Office of Staff Secretary, Presidential Handwriting File, 7/16/79 [2] folder, box 139, CPL.

20. Stuart Eizenstat, interview, Jan. 29–30, 1982, 80, box 1, WBMC-CPL. For more information on the disagreements, see Drew, "Reporter at Large," 59. On Mondale's position, see Steven M. Gillon, *The Democrats' Dilemma: Walter F. Mondale and the Liberal Legacy* (New York: Columbia University Press, 1992), 259–63. For material on the decision-making process, there are two sets of interviews in the Carter Library. One is a series of exit interviews done before and after the November 1980 election. The other, of much higher quality, was carried out in the early 1980s by political scientists and historians at the White Burkett Miller Center of Public Affairs at the University of Virginia. For exit interviews, see Stuart Eizenstat, interview, Jan. 1, 1981, 14–17, exit interviews, box 2, CPL; Gerald Rafshoon, interview, Sept. 12, 1979, exit interviews, box 6, CPL. For the Miller Center interviews, see Jimmy Carter, interview, 65–67, Nov. 29, 1982, Miller Center interviews, box 1, WBMC-CPL; Eizenstat, interview, Jan. 29–30, 1982, box 1, 79–85, WBMC-CPL; interviews of speechwriters, interviews, 59–86, Speechwriters Session, Dec. 3 and 4, 1981, box 1, WBMC-CPL; Hamilton Jordan, interview, 38–42, Nov. 6, 1981, box 1, WBMC-CPL; Jerry Rafshoon, interview, 30–35, Apr. 8, 1983, Miller Center interviews, box 3, WBMC-CPL. Pat Caddell's interview for the Miller Center is closed, but see Caddell, "Playboy Interview," 76–80.

21. Greg Schneiders, memo to Gerald Rafshoon, 1–2, July 10, 1979, Rafshoon collection, "Memoranda from Jerry Rafshoon—June, July, August 1979" folder, box 28, CPL; Jerry Rafshoon, memo to President Jimmy Carter, July 10, 1979, 1, Speechwriters, Chronological file, "7/15/79–Address to the Nation—Energy/Crisis of Confidence [1]" folder, box 50, CPL.

22. Patrick H. Caddell, "Memorandum to the President," July 12, 1979, 1 and 3–4, Office of Staff Secretary, Presidential Handwriting file, "Camp David 7/5/79–7/12/79 [6]" folder, box 138, CPL. In this memo Caddell was offering the president a strategy for briefing journalists on his upcoming speech.

23. Robert N. Bellah, handwritten notes, probably July 9, 1979, Robert N. Bellah Papers, residence of Robert N. Bellah, Berkeley. On the distribution of books, see Bell, "Dinner," 45.

24. Robert Bellah, interview, July 16, 1979, in John Raeside, "A Night at Camp David," *Express: The East Bay's Free Weekly*, July 27, 1979, 1, 3, and 4.

25. Robert Bellah, "Human Conditions for a Good Society," in "Ideals in Transition: Tomorrow's America," Centennial Edition of *St. Louis Post-Dispatch*, Mar. 25, 1979, 8–11,

quotes 9 and 11. For Carter's reading list, see Joseph [Jody] L. Powell Jr., letter to editor, *NYTM*, Aug. 19, 1979, 78. Among the works Carter "found relevant" were Tocqueville, *Democracy in America*, "particularly sections in which de Tocqueville warns of the problems of affluence"; Henry Ford 2nd, "Goals and Attitudes," in *St. Louis Post-Dispatch*; John Gardner, *Morale*; John Herbers, "Washington: An Insiders Game" in *NYTM*; John Maynard Keynes, "The Future," in *Essays in Persuasion*; Christopher Lasch, *The Culture of Narcissism*; Charles Peters, "A Platform for the 1980's," in *Washington Monthly*; Albert Sommers, "A Collision of Ethics and Economics," in *Across the Board*; James Q. Wilson, "American Politics: Then and Now," in *Commentary*. For additional confirmation of the impact of the readings, and Caddell's summaries of them, on Carter, see Holland, "Great Gamble," 65.

26. Jimmy Carter, handwritten notes for speech, unnumbered page, probably July 11, 1979, Office of Staff Secretary, Presidential Handwriting File, "President's Address to the Nation 7/15/79 [2]" folder, box 139, CPL. I arrive at these dates because the president was writing after his meeting with Bellah on July 10 but before his speechwriters came up with an almost final version on July 12, 1979.

27. Jimmy Carter, "Energy and National Goals," speech of July 15, 1979, in *Public Papers of the Presidents of the United States: Jimmy Carter, 1979* (Washington, D.C.: Government Printing Office, 1980), 2:1235–40. Ribuffo correctly calls the speech "Energy and the Crisis of Confidence." According to Ribuffo ("God and Jimmy Carter," 240), it was "largely drafted by Caddell." Hertzberg ("Carter," 192) says that the first part of the speech, in which Carter criticized himself, was "wholly conceived and written by Carter." My own guess is that Carter shaped the speech in fundamental ways but that others were responsible for different sections. There are many drafts of this speech, and it is not always easy to determine authorship; see, for example, the material in Office of Staff Secretary, Presidential Handwriting file, "President's Address to the Nation, 7/15/79" folder, box 139, CPL; Speechwriters Chronological File, "Address to the Nation—Energy/Crisis of Confidence" folder, box 50, CPL. Early drafts, influenced by and perhaps from the hand of Pat Caddell, made references to the "Me Generation" and linked that characterization to lack of concern for the poor and community life. Early drafts also spoke of the "moral capital of our religious traditions"; see, for example, untitled draft, July 11, 1979, 2 and 5, Speechwriters Chronological File, "Address to the Nation—Energy/Crisis of Confidence [1]" folder, box 50, CPL; "Draft #2," July 10, 1979, 5, Speechwriters Chronological File, "Address to the Nation—Energy/Crisis of Confidence [1]" folder, box 50, CPL.

28. Hahn, "Flailing the Profligate," 583–87, effectively argues for the parallels between Carter's speech and his commitments as an evangelical Christian.

29. Ribuffo, "God and Jimmy Carter," 240; Carter, "Energy," 1237. Most of this key paragraph did not appear in the draft of July 12, 1979, a draft that in other ways resembles the speech as delivered; Speechwriters, Chronological File, "7/15/79 Address to the Nation—Energy/Crisis of Confidence [2]" folder, box 50, CPL.

30. Christopher Lasch, *The Culture of Narcissism: American Life in an Age of Diminishing Expectations* (New York: W. W. Norton, 1979), xiii. On the deeper and broader sources, see Ribuffo, "God and Jimmy Carter," 223–24, 226, and 234.

31. *Los Angeles Time*, quoted in Ribuffo, "'Malaise' Revisited," 173. For other understandings of the religious dimensions of the speech, see Goldman, "To Lift," 20, 24, and 25. On the results of the speech, see Ribuffo, "'Malaise' Revisited," 173–74; Holland, "Great Gamble," 73; Hahn, "Flailing the Profligate," 583.

32. Ronald Reagan, "Vision for America," 6, television address, Nov. 3, 1980, news release of same date, Ronald Reagan Library, Simi Valley, Calif.

33. Daniel Bell to Patrick Caddell, Aug. 28, 1979, 2–3, "Dinner at White House: Jimmy Carter/Pat Caddell, June–August 1979," DBP. Bell returned to these issues a few weeks later, see cover letter to Bell, "Dinner"; Daniel Bell to Pearl, Sept. 1, 1979, Memoir: Dinner at the White House, Daniel Bell, Writings, September 1979, DBP.

34. Bellah, "A Night at Camp David," 1, 3, and 4.

35. Christopher Lasch to Pat [Caddell], July 18, 1979, folder 6, box 20, CL-UR; Christopher Lasch to Pat [Caddell], Feb. 9, 1980, folder 6, box, 20, CL-UR; Christopher Lasch to Louise and Bob Horowitz, Sept. 27, 1979, folder 6, box 5, CL-UR. For other reactions to Carter's speech, see Christopher Lasch to Ed [Gumbert], Sept. 27, 1979, folder 5, box 5, CL-UR; Christopher Lasch to Jonathan B. Nimer, Sept. 27, 1979, folder 9, box 5, CL-UR.

36. Christopher Lasch to Daniel Bell, Nov. 8, 1979, "Dinner at White House: Jimmy Carter/Pat Caddell, June–August 1979," DBP. For an even later recollection of the evening by Lasch, see Fox interview, 12. For Bellah on Kennedy, see Bellah, "A Night at Camp David," 4.

37. Robert Westbrook, "Christopher Lasch, the New Radicalism, and the Vocation of Intellectuals," *RAH* 23 (March 1995): 179; Bell, "Dinner," 30 and 50; James Seaton, "Critique as Bestseller: *The Culture of Narcissism*," *Centennial Review* 25 (spring 1981): 184; Lasch, Fox interview, 12. Lasch's demeanor, which some observers interpreted as a result of arrogance rather than of timidity, no doubt made him less comfortable in the White House than the more gregarious Bell, who was more of an outgoing participant-observer.

38. Lasch to Bell, Nov. 8, 1979; Daniel Bell to Christopher Lasch, Nov. 13, 1979; Daniel Bell: Personal, Dinner at the White House, Jimmy Carter/Pat Caddell, June–August 1979, DBP.

39. Christopher Lasch, *The Minimal Self: Psychic Survival in Troubled Times* (New York: W. W. Norton, 1984), 24 and 27–28. In this book, Lasch criticized Bell's argument in *Cultural Contradictions of Capitalism*; Bell, he wrote, equated consumerism with hedonism, whereas Lasch characterized it as a "state of uneasiness and chronic anxiety" (27–28 fn.); see also Christopher Lasch, *True and Only Heaven: Progress and Its Critics* (New York: W. W. Norton, 1991), 35.

Epilogue

1. Ronald Reagan, "A Vision for America," 6, television address delivered Nov. 3, 1980, copy of news release of same date, Ronald Reagan Library, Simi Valley, Calif., ellipses in original.

2. Ibid.; Ronald Reagan, foreword to James C. Roberts, *The Conservative Decade: Emerging Leaders of the 1980s* (Westport, Conn.: Arlington House, 1980), vii; Malcolm T. Owens, "Ronald Reagan, Hedgehog," Feb. 2001, editorial, <www.ashbrook.org/publicat/oped/owens/01/reagan.html>.

3. Walter Isaacson, "America's Incredible Day," *Time*, Feb. 2, 1981, 10; Nancy Reagan, quoted in Paul Gray, "A First Lady of Priorities and Proprieties," *Time*, Jan. 5, 1981, 25; "The World of Nancy Reagan," *NW*, Dec. 21, 1981, 22; Elizabeth Bumiller, quoted in Ralph Nader, introduction to Ronald Brownstein and Nina Easton, *Reagan's Ruling Class: Portraits of the President's Top 100 Officials* (Washington, D.C.: Presidential Accountability Group, 1982), vii; Maryon Allen, quoted in Laurence Leamer, *Make-Believe: The Story of Nancy and Ronald Reagan* (New York: Harper and Row, 1983), 3; Barry Goldwater and Marcia Carter, quoted in Isaacson, "Incredible Day," 11.

4. David Cay Johnston, "Gap Between Rich and Poor Found Substantially Wider," *NYT*,

Sept. 5, 2000, A16. On the middle class, see Janny Scott, "Boom of the 1990's Missed Many In Middle Class, Data Suggest," *NYT*, Aug. 31, 2001, A1 and 21.

5. Eric Schmitt, "Census Data Show a Sharp Increase in Living Standards," *NYT*, Aug. 17, 2001, A1 and 10.

6. On life satisfaction studies, see David Leonhardt, "If Richer Isn't Happier, What Is?" *NYT*, May 19, 2001, A15 and 17; Tim Kasser, *The High Price of Materialism* (Cambridge: MIT Press, 2002); Robert Lane, *The Loss of Happiness in Market Democracies* (New Haven: Yale University Press, 2000).

7. Barbara Ehrenreich, *Nickel and Dimed: On (Not) Getting By in America* (New York: Henry Holt, 2001); Teresa A. Sullivan, Elizabeth Warren, and Jay Lawrence Westbrook, *The Fragile Middle Class; Americans in Debt* (New Haven: Yale University Press, 2000), xiv. For some other pictures of the standard of living at the middle and lower rungs of the society, see, by Katherine S. Newman, *Falling from Grace: The Experience of Downward Mobility in the American Middle Class* (New York: Free Press, 1988), and *Declining Fortunes: The Withering of the American Dream* (New York: Basic Books, 1993).

8. David Brooks, *Bobos in Paradise: The New Upper Class and How They Got There* (New York: Simon and Schuster, 2000), 10 and 42; Alex Kuczyinski, "Can a Kid Squeeze By on $320,000 per month?" *NYT*, Jan. 20, 2002, sec. 9, 1 and 6.

9. Thomas J. Stanley and William D. Danko, *The Millionaire Next Door: The Surprising Secrets of America's Wealthy* (New York: Simon and Schuster, 1996), 13 and 2; promotional material and *Forbes* quote from back cover of paperback edition. For other books in this genre, see Ric Edelman, *Ordinary People, Extraordinary Wealth: The Eight Secrets of How 8,000 Ordinary Americans Became Successful Investors and How You Can Too* (New York: Harper-Collins, 1999); Bob Davis and David Wessel, *Prosperity: The Coming Twenty-Year Boom and What It Means to You* (New York: Random House, 1998).

10. Suze Orman, *The 9 Steps to Financial Freedom: Practical and Spiritual Steps So You Can Stop Worrying* (New York: Crown Publishers, 1997), 2, 29, 196, and 281. See also Suze Orman, *The Courage to be Rich: Creating a Life of Material and Spiritual Abundance* (New York: Penguin Putnam, 1999).

11. For an immensely useful guide to the range of positions on issues of consumer culture, see Juliet B. Schor and Douglas B. Holt, eds., *The Consumer Society Reader* (New York: New Press, 2000). For some of the other books I found useful for this discussion, see Sarah Ban Breathnach, *Simple Abundance: A Daybook of Comfort and Joy* (New York: Warner Books, 1995); John de Graff, David Wann, and Thomas H. Naylor, *Affluenza: The All-Consuming Epidemic* (San Francisco: Berrett-Koehler Publishers, 2001); Joe Dominguez and Vicki Robin, *Your Money or Your Life: Transforming Your Relationship with Money and Achieving Financial Independence* (New York: Viking Press, 1992); Jerome Segal, *Graceful Simplicity: Toward a Philosophy and Politics of Scaling Down and Enjoying More* (New York: Henry Holt, 1999); Kalle Lasn, *Culture Jam: The Uncooling of America* (New York: HarperCollins, 1999); and a series of books by Elaine St. James, including *Simplify Your Work Life: Ways to Change the Way You Work So You Have More Time to Play* (New York: Hyperion, 2001).

12. De Graff, Wann, and Naylor, *Affluenza*, xi; Jeff Stryker, "Oniomaniacs Come Out of the Closet," *NYT*, July 21, 2002, sec. 4, 2.

13. Robert D. Putnam, *Bowling Alone: The Collapse and Revival of American Community* (New York: Simon and Schuster, 2000), quote from inside back jacket; Robert H. Frank, *Luxury Fever: Why Money Fails to Satisfy in an Era of Excess* (New York: Free Press, 1999), 3; Juliet B. Schor, "The New Politics of Consumption," in *Do Americans Shop Too Much?* ed. Joshua Cohen and Joel Rogers (Boston: Beacon Press, 2000), 3–33, quotes 3 and

7; Eric Schlosser, *Fast Food Nation: The Dark Side of the All-American Meal* (Boston: Houghton Mifflin, 2001). See also Brian L. Goff, *Spoiled Rotten: Affluence, Anxiety, and Social Decay in America* (Boulder, Colo.: Westview Press, 1999); David G. Myers, *The American Paradox: Spiritual Hunger in an Age of Plenty* (New Haven: Yale University Press, 2000); Robert Manning, *Credit Card Nation: The Consequences of America's Addiction to Credit* (New York: Basic Books, 2000). Skillful journalistic reporting on consumer society became a powerful stream: see, for example, David Brancaccio, *Squandering Aimlessly: My Adventures in the American Marketplace* (New York: Simon and Schuster, 2000); Malcolm Gladwell, *The Tipping Point: How Little Things Can Make a Big Difference* (Boston: Little, Brown, 2000).

14. James B. Twitchell, "The Stone Age," in *Do Americans Shop Too Much?* 45 and 47–48; James B. Twitchell, *Lead Us into Temptation: The Triumph of American Materialism* (New York: Columbia University Press, 1999), 15, 18, 11, 271, and 286.

15. Jesse Lemisch, "Nader vs. the Big Rock Candy Mountain," *New Politics* 8, n.s. (summer 2001): 12–14 and 16.

16. For anthropologists, see Marshall Sahlins, *Culture and Practical Reason* (Chicago: University of Chicago Press, 1976); Mary Douglas and Baron Isherwood, *The World of Goods* (New York: Basic Books, 1971); and Daniel Miller, *A Theory of Shopping* (Ithaca: Cornell University Press, 1998). For Albert O. Hirschman, begin with *Exit, Voice, and Loyalty; Responses to Decline in Firms, Organizations, and States* (Cambridge: Harvard University Press, 1970). For feminist versions, see Elizabeth Wilson, *Adorned in Dreams: Fashion and Modernity* (Berkeley: University of California Press, 1987); Janice Radway, *Reading the Romance: Women, Patriarchy, and Popular Literature* (Chapel Hill: University of North Carolina Press, 1984); Amy Richards and Jennifer Baumgardner, *Manifesta: Young Women, Feminism, and the Future* (New York: Farrar, Straus, and Giroux, 2000). On the Birmingham school, see John Fiske, *Reading the Popular* (Boston: Unwin and Hyman, 1989), and Dick Hebdige, *Subculture: The Meaning of Style* (London: Routledge, 1979). In an editorial note, Schor and Holt (*Consumer Society Reader*, 287–88) provide a list of writers who offer a "reconsideration of consumption" that I call post-moralist; see also their introduction, xvii–xxix. Twitchell, *Lead Us into Temptation*, discusses many of the same strands in what he calls "the newer academic view"; quote 42 and the key footnote 43–44. For other expressions of post-moralism, see Dinesh D'Souza, *The Virtue of Prosperity: Finding Values in an Age of Techno-Affluence* (New York: Free Press, 2000); Gary Cross. *An All-Consuming Century: Why Commercialism Won in Modern America* (New York: Columbia University Press, 2000); Daniel Harris, *Cute, Quaint, Hungry, and Romantic: The Aesthetics of Consumerism* (New York: Basic Books, 2000); Michael Schudson, "Delectable Materialism: Were the Critics of Consumer Culture Wrong All Along?" *American Prospect* 5 (spring 1991): 26–35; Francis Fukuyama, *Trust: Social Virtues and the Creation of Prosperity* (New York: Free Press, 1999). The *Journal of Consumer Research*, which began publication in 1974, reflects new attitudes to its subject.

17. Ann Telnaes cartoon, *American Prospect*, Jan. 28, 2002, 3. See the following items in the *New York Times*: Daniel Altman, "Consumers Keeping the Faith Despite of Woes of Business," July 8, 2002, sec. 1, 2; David Brooks, "Love the Service Around Here," Nov. 25, 2001, sec. 6, 34; Stuart Elliott, "Bowing to Nation's Mood, Retailer Cancels Issue of Racy Catalogue," Oct. 17, 2001, C1; Bob Herbert, "Stepping Up to the Plate," July 8, 2002, A21; Lynn Hirschberg, "Luxury in Hard Times," Dec. 2, 2001, sec. 6, 68–75, 92, 100, and 124; Robert F. Kennedy Jr., "Better Gas Mileage, Greater Security," Nov. 24, 2001, A25; David Leonhardt, "Recovery and the Reluctant Consumer," Dec. 10, 2001, C1; Frank Rich, "The Day before Tuesday," Sept. 15, 2001, A23; Edward Rothstein, "Damning (Yet Desiring) Mickey and the Big Mac," Mar. 2, 2002, B9; Stephanie Strom, "In Tougher Times, It's a Life

of Affluence Minus Trimmings," Oct. 23, 2001, C1; Paco Underhill, "The Return of the Shopper," Nov. 24, 2001, A25. In addition, see Lila Abu-Lughod, "Movie Stars and Islamic Moralism in Egypt," in *The Gender and Sexuality Reader: Culture, History, Political Economy*, ed. Roger N. Lancaster and Micaela di Leonardo (New York: Routledge, 1997), 502–12; John M. Berry, "Survey Indicates Rising Confidence: Moods Shift as Attacks Recede in Time," *Washington Post*, Oct. 13, 2001, E1.

Acknowledgments

Writing about books, authors, and ideas has made me abundantly aware of how much I rely on the work, help, and encouragement of others. I have no illusions that this book will have an impact on national consciousness similar to that of the best-sellers whose histories I explore. Nor can I imagine that the response to this book will transform my life as earlier responses did those of the writers whose works are the focus of my scholarship. Nonetheless, like the subjects of my own effort, I have relied on the kindness and dedication of research assistants, librarians, strangers, colleagues, scholars, publishers, family, and friends.

Smith College has provided a supportive environment and tangible help conducive to bringing this project to fruition. The Committee on Faculty Compensation and Development has offered material assistance at every step. My colleagues in the American Studies Program, as well as its secretary, Barbara Day, have intensified my appreciation of what it takes to keep a program flourishing. Smith students have ably and imaginatively served as research assistants, among them Erin Blakemore, Rae Goldstein, Carrie Gray, Jessica Lampron, Rachel Ledford, Claire Null, and Gina Rourke. The staff of William Allen Neilson Library helped me locate and obtain what little material was not already available in its splendid collections. Librarians at the Sophia Smith Collection and the Smith College Archives made every effort to make their collections accessible to me. At several points since I started teaching at Smith College in 1989, I have been able to benefit from the college's exceptionally generous provisions for sabbaticals.

Farther afield has been the indispensable help of others who allowed my

319

work to go smoothly. Robert Coven of the University of Chicago explored the collection pertinent to David Potter's Walgreen lectures which led to his writing *The People of Plenty*. Early on, Dorothee Schneider translated and interpreted material on George Katona. When I started my work on this project, Christine Weideman's research at the University of Michigan on George Katona was useful, and then as I finished, she guided me through the C. Vann Woodward Papers at Yale University. John Dwyer and Cornelia Dwyer made my stays in Atlanta both pleasant and fruitful; Joan Heifetz Hollinger and David Hollinger did the same in both Ann Arbor and Berkeley. Historians at the University of Texas at Austin, the University of Virginia, and the Five College History reading group in the Pioneer Valley of Massachusetts listened attentively as I presented earlier versions of chapters and then responded with probing questions that enabled me to clarify what I was trying to say. During the long period when I have worked on this book, three institutions have awarded me fellowships. Early on, a year at the National Humanities Center provided an ideal environment to get the work under way. Much later, a Fellowship for College Teachers from the National Endowment for the Humanities gave me valuable time off. Then a year at the Schlesinger Library at what was then Radcliffe College enabled me to complete work on my book on Betty Friedan. Any historian seeking a publisher who makes book making a pleasure could do no better than to sign on with the University of Massachusetts Press. Once again, Clark Dougan, a historian in his own right, has been a superb listener, advice giver, and editor.

Librarians have continuously reminded me how essential they are to historical scholarship. Among those on whom I have relied are Bernard R. Crystal of the Rare Book and Manuscript Library, Columbia University; Ronald J. Grele of the Oral History Research Office at the same institution; David Linke of the archives at Princeton University; Linda J. Long of the Department of Special Collections, Stanford University; Krista L. Ovist at the Joseph Regenstein Library of the University of Chicago; John A. Popplestone of the Archives of the History of American Psychology, University of Akron; and Nancy M. Shawcross of the Van Pelt–Dietrich Library at the University of Pennsylvania. In addition, I am grateful to the librarians of Schlesinger Library at Radcliffe Institute, special collections at Pennsylvania State University, Harvard University, and the Jimmy Carter Presidential Library for easing access to their collections.

My citations only begin to recognize the scholars and interviewees on whose work and words I have drawn. Special thanks to a long but surely incomplete list of people who answered questions both big and small: Paul Alpers, Lizabeth Cohen, Robert Coven, Robert Collins, Gerald D. Feldman, Richard Wrightman Fox, Robert Haddow, Grace Hale, Stanley C. Hollander,

David Hollinger, Tom Jackson, Sidney J. Levy, Howard R. Lamar, Jesse Lemisch, Ruth Maslow Lewis, Roland Marchand, Kevin Mattson, Donald Miller, David Montejano, James N. Morgan, Richard Pells, Paul Pickrel, Gaines Post Jr., Alfonso Procaccini, Leo P. Ribuffo, David Riesman, Susan Rigdon, Dorothy Ross, Fath Davis Ruffins, Thaddeus Russell, Michael Schudson, Michael Sokal, Frank Stricker, Klemens von Klemperer, Robert Westbrook, Rupert Wilkinson, and Allan M. Winkler.

Readers have gone over earlier versions with care, warning me about pitfalls that I may nonetheless not always have avoided. Edmund S. Morgan, Dan Singal, and Michael O'Brien graciously responded to my chapter on Potter. Maurice Isserman and Taylor Stoehr gave exceptionally careful readings that drew on their own knowledge of Michael Harrington and Paul Goodman, respectively. Bruce J. Schulman, David Glassberg, and Robert Weir gave the section on intellectuals and the energy crisis thoughtful readings. Paul Gorman helped me place what I was trying to say in a broader perspective. Larry Glickman and Howard Brick, the readers for the University of Massachusetts Press, offered exactly the right combination of attention, encouragement, and suggestions for improvements. When I was completing work on the manuscript, Clark Dougan, Meg Jacobs, and Kevin Rozario helped me think through ways of turning disparate parts into a more integral whole. At every step along the very long road that brought this writing project to conclusion, my most faithful writing buddies—Bob Abzug, Lynn Dumenil, Helen Lefkowitz Horowitz, and Judy Smith—listened, read, warned, suggested, and encouraged.

Helen Horowitz has helped in ways that are at once too subtle, momentous, and immeasurable to capture adequately. In the dedication I only begin to express how our relationship, now beginning its fifth decade, matters. She helped me raise and then launch into the world two wonderful children— Ben Horowitz and Sarah Horowitz—who in their distinctive ways remind me what it means to take seriously the relationship between spending and morality. Friend, companion, fellow walker in cities, co-conspirator, cook, scholar, wife, and lover only begins to suggest the range of what Helen means to me. In the contexts that made this book possible, she gave my work multiple, careful, and richly suggestive readings which have immeasurably strengthened what I wished to say.

Index

DANIEL HOROWITZ was born in New Haven, Connecticut. He graduated from Yale, studied at Pembroke College, Cambridge, England, and received a Ph.D. from Harvard. He has received two fellowships from the National Endowment for the Humanities, one from the National Humanities Center, and an appointment as Honorary Visiting Fellow at the Schlesinger Library, Radcliffe College, Harvard University. Among his publications are *The Morality of Spending: Attitudes toward the Consumer Society in America, 1875–1940* (1985), selected by *Choice* as one of the outstanding academic books of 1985; *Vance Packard and American Social Criticism* (1994); and the award-winning *Betty Friedan and the Making of "The Feminine Mystique": The American Left, the Cold War, and Modern Feminism* (1998). Professor Horowitz has taught at Harvard, Wellesley College, Skidmore College, Carleton College, and the University of Michigan. He has spent most of his career at Scripps College in California, where he eventually was Nathaniel Wright Stephenson Professor of History and Biography, and at Smith College (1989 to the present), where he is Mary Huggins Gamble Professor of American Studies and directs the American studies program.

Professor Horowitz lives in Northampton and Cambridge, Massachusetts, with his wife, Helen Lefkowitz Horowitz. They are the parents of Sarah Horowitz and Benjamin Horowitz.